FACING
THE
BEAR

To Matt,

FACING THE BEAR
SCOTLAND AND THE COLD WAR

TREVOR ROYLE

BIRLINN

First published in 2019 by
Birlinn Ltd
West Newington House
10 Newington Road
Edinburgh
EH9 1QS

www.birlinn.co.uk

ISBN: 978 1 78027 526 0

British Library Cataloguing-in-Publication Data
A catalogue record for this book is available on request from the British Library

Typeset by Biblichor Ltd, Edinburgh
Printed and bound by Gutenberg Press, Malta

Contents

List of Plates

Picture Credits

List of Abbreviations

ABM	anti-ballistic missile
AGI	Auxiliary, General Intelligence (trawler)
AOSNI	Air Officer Scotland and Northern Ireland
ASUR	Anti Surface Unit Role
ASW	anti-submarine warfare
BEWC	British East–West Centre
CEW	Centrimetric Early Warning
CPGB	Communist Party of Great Britain
DAC	Direct Action Committee Against Nuclear War (AKA Emergency Committee for Direct Action Against Nuclear War)
DERA	Defence Evaluation and Research Agency
EVW	European Voluntary Workers
FCO	Foreign and Commonwealth Office
FOSNI	Flag Officer Scotland and Northern Ireland
GIUK	Greenland–Iceland–United Kingdom (gap)
GLCM	Ground Launched Cruise Missile
HF/DF	high frequency direction finder
HSF	Home Service Force
ICBM	intercontinental ballistic missile
INF	Intermediate-Range Nuclear Forces (treaty)
IRBM	intermediate-range ballistic missile
JIC	Joint Intelligence Committee
LSL	Landing Ship Logistic
MAC	Military Airlift Command
MIRV	multiple independently targetable re-entry vehicle
NCANWT	National Committee for the Abolition of Nuclear Weapons Tests
NOSS	Navy Ocean Surveillance Satellites

NUM	National Union of Mineworkers
PRA	Permanently Restricted Area
QRA	Quick Reaction Alert
RNTF	Royal Naval Torpedo Factory
SAC	Strategic Air Command
SALT	Strategic Arms Limitation Talks
SAM	surface-to-air missile
SAR	Search and Rescue
SNP	Scottish National Party
SSBN	Ship Submersible Ballistic Nuclear
SSN	Submarine Nuclear (attack or hunter-killer)
SSOD	Union of Soviet Societies for Friendship
START 1	Strategic Arms Reduction (treaty)
TRA	Temporary Restricted Area
UKASACS	United Kingdom Air Surveillance and Control System

Preface and Acknowledgements

IT WAS ON the road from Moscow to Zagorsk in November 1977 that I began to understand that the Cold War might be something of a fraud, a confrontation dreamed up by politicians, East and West, to scare us all senseless and to swell the pockets of arms manufacturers. I was part of a small group of writers visiting the Soviet Union at the invitation of the Soviet Writers' Union, the others being the poet Liz Lochhead and the novelist Allan Massie, and we were late for lunch. As our guide and translator became more agitated I suggested that we phone ahead from one of the towns which lined the road. It soon became clear that this would be impossible for all sorts of nonsensical technical reasons. The Russian capital is only 75 km from the town which houses the Trinity-Sergius Monastery we were due to visit, but a simple phone call was off limits. Coming on top of the scantily filled department stores in Moscow (even the world-famed GUM in Red Square was a disappointment) and the shabby restaurants reserved for nomenklatura who had access to the foreign-currency *Beryozka* shops, this seemed to be a different place from the Soviet Union which was leading the space race and whose nuclear missiles threatened the West on a daily basis. And it was indeed another world. For a group from Scotland, a country which was on the front line throughout the confrontation thanks to its geographical position and the presence of American and British nuclear weaponry, the road to Zagorsk was a real eye-opener.

Not that our hosts were inhospitable. On the contrary, they went out of their way – within reason – to make us feel welcome. After a few days in Moscow we took the overnight train to Leningrad, as it then was, before flying to Tbilisi in Georgia which offered a completely different experience. For a start Georgians considered themselves to be an independent people with their own language and culture, and the country was also home to Stalin's birthplace at Gori, which we duly visited. But

the highlight was our last night back in Moscow, when we were entertained to dinner at the British Embassy. Our host was the resident
minister, a brilliant if unorthodox diplomat, Robert Wade-Gery, whose
previous appointment had been Madrid and who likened the experience of transferring to Leonid Brezhnev's Moscow as 'like going into a
dark tunnel'. To our delight the other guests were the distinguished
poet Yevgeny Yevtushenko and his British-born partner and soon-to-be
wife, the translator Jan Butler; after dinner we all piled into an embassy
car to drive to Peredelkino, south-west of Moscow, to light candles at
the grave of Boris Pasternak. At the time the village with its church and
cemetery had not yet been designated a 'historical and cultural reserve'
and was supposedly off limits, but with Wade-Gery and Yevtushenko
at the helm there were no problems. Until I visited the Soviet Union the
true significance of Pasternak had escaped me. In the West we take so
many freedoms for granted that it is difficult to realise fully the courage
of Pasternak's rebellion against authority, the clearness of his voice in
speaking to the outside world at a time when his seminal novel *Dr
Zhivago* had been refused publication in the Soviet Union. He died in
May 1960 but it was to be another 28 years before *Dr Zhivago* saw the
light of day in Moscow; it had taken a man strong in spirit to risk its
publication in the West during the tortured days of the 1950s and then
to accept the Nobel Prize for Literature, which his son said had caused
Pasternak nothing but grief and harassment at the hands of the state.
More than any other factor, the Soviet treatment of Pasternak underscored the madness of the period and reinforced the importance of our
visit to Peredelkino, where my diary tells me 'we stood around the grave
talking without false seriousness and hugging each other for warmth
and in affection beneath the snow-filled sky'.

In most respects the Cold War was a pale imitation of a conflict,
being an ideological bipolar confrontation between the Soviet Union
and its Warsaw Pact allies and the United States of America (USA) and
its allies in the North Atlantic Treaty Organisation (NATO). It ran
roughly from the end of the Second World War until the events following the fall of the Berlin Wall in 1989 which led to the collapse of the
Communist system of government in eastern Europe two years later,
and during that time it consumed huge resources and created dangerous international tensions. Although it never quite descended into 'hot'
war with open hostilities – the Berlin airlift of 1948, the Cuban missile
crisis of 1962 and the Yom Kippur War in 1973 were exceptional

near-misses – much of the confrontation was dominated by intensive espionage and counter-espionage, 'proxy' wars in Africa and the Middle East, and by the Korean War (1950–3) and the Vietnam War (1955–75) in which both sides tested their weaponry and each other's resolve. The Cold War also sparked an expensive and dangerous arms race which hastened the development of weapons of mass destruction and introduced the fear of nuclear annihilation – the US had nuclear weapons in 1945 and the Soviet Union exploded its first atomic bomb in 1949, although the Soviets did not achieve parity in nuclear warheads and delivery systems until the 1970s.

For much of the period Scotland was on the front line, mainly due to its position on NATO's 'northern flank' – the waters of the north-east Atlantic and the Norwegian and Barents Seas with the vital Greenland-Iceland–UK (GIUK) gap through which Soviet nuclear-armed submarines and strategic bombers would have attacked in the event of an outbreak of hostilities. That made Scotland the first major obstacle: it would have been in those northern seas and over Scottish skies that the first battles would have been fought. That accounted for the build-up of sophisticated anti-submarine warfare facilities and air defences in Scotland and it was from the American and British bases on the Clyde that the strategic submarines would have launched the response by way of Polaris and Poseidon missiles, each one of them capable of destroying Hiroshima several times over. If Scotland had not existed NATO would have been hard pressed to invent a similar facility. It should also be remembered that Scots military personnel made a substantial contribution to NATO forces in West Germany and that Scottish soldiers, sailors and airmen saw active service in the Korean War, many of them being conscripts doing their National Service.

The presence of so much weaponry in Scotland, particularly of the nuclear variety, prompted protest and this had an effect on the body politic. When the US Navy sited Polaris-equipped submarines at Holy Loch near the Clyde following a US–UK deal in 1960 the area became a focal point for protestors under the banner of the Campaign for Nuclear Disarmament (CND) which had been founded two years earlier to mobilise opposition to the nuclear deterrent. The movement attracted pacifists, Christians, environmentalists, trade unionists and politicians and it became a vocal and highly visible component of the Scottish political scene, particularly on the left although the only party to espouse outright opposition to nuclear weapons was the Scottish

National Party (SNP). Throughout that time, it is safe to say that Scotland would have been a prime target for enemy planners and perhaps that helps to explain the personal concern of those who supported CND in Scotland. As more than one commentator has pointed out, the campaign against nuclear weapons is one of the longest-running single issues in Scottish politics and continued into the twenty-first century as a devolved Scotland maintained its opposition to the presence of nuclear-armed Trident submarines at the Royal Navy's base at Faslane on the Clyde.

For Scotland the end of the Cold War in the 1990s saw a vast reduction in military activity and associated UK defence expenditure. The US submarines left their forward operating base at Holy Loch in 1992, presumably never to return, and consecutive defence reviews changed forever Scotland's Cold War infrastructure. Two of the three RAF bases in Scotland, at Kinloss and Leuchars, were closed in 2012 and 2015 respectively and re-emerged as army barracks, leaving only RAF Lossiemouth with its Eurofighter Typhoons to continue the watch in northern skies. Previously secretive facilities such as the US Navy listening post at RAF Edzell were abandoned in 1997 or were turned over to automated operations, as happened at RAF Buchan in 2004, and the Army also contracted, with all the surviving line infantry regiments being amalgamated in 2006 in the multi-battalion Royal Regiment of Scotland. When the maritime headquarters at Pitreavie closed in 1996 and its command bunker was sealed it seemed as if the final vestige of Cold War history in Scotland had been eradicated, but it was not the final curtain for the nuclear presence. Far from it: the Royal Navy's black-hulled strategic submarines remained in Scottish waters and their Trident missiles continued to have a global reach. First developed as a submarine base during the Second World War, Faslane on the eastern shore of the Gare Loch became the RN Clyde Submarine Base (HMS *Neptune*) in 1967 and was home to the UK nuclear deterrent in the shape of four Resolution-class strategic submarines equipped with Polaris/Chevaline missiles. It also housed a squadron of hunter-killer submarines and other related units and was the centre for the Navy's submarine training programme. Together with the armaments depot at nearby Coulport on Loch Long, which housed and maintained the missiles and their warheads, it was the main facility for housing the UK's nuclear weapons.

The base not only survived the end of the Cold War but prospered. In the 1980s the government decided to replace Polaris with the new missile system known as Trident, also designed and built in the US, which would be bigger and more powerful than its predecessor. As such it needed a new delivery system and the decision was taken to construct four new Vanguard strategic submarines which would be based at an expanded and modernised Faslane. The first boat, HMS *Vanguard*, arrived in July 1992 and the last Polaris boat, HMS *Repulse*, left the base four years later to be decommissioned at Rosyth. That same year, 1996, Faslane became HM Naval Base Clyde and the centre of all maritime operations in Scotland under the command of a Commodore; it is also home to the Royal Navy's senior officer in Scotland, the Flag Officer Scotland and Northern Ireland (FOSNI) and is the equal of similar UK naval bases in Portsmouth and Plymouth. At the same time the Royal Dockyard at Rosyth was closed as a naval base and transferred to the private sector (Babcock Thorne) at a selling price of £20.5 million. Although the new naval base at Faslane was also home to the Navy's minor war vessels – patrol boats and mine counter measure vessels – the presence of the four Trident boats and the associated nuclear facilities at Coulport was an affront to those who oppose nuclear weapons, and the base remained a focus for demonstrations by protestors. The issue also provoked heated debates during the referendum campaign to vote on independence for Scotland in 2014. The SNP, the Scottish Socialist Party and the Scottish Green Party are all opposed to the development of nuclear weapons and their presence in Scotland and if there had been a majority 'yes' vote in the referendum on 18 September 2014, an independent Scotland would have demanded the removal of the Trident boats and their nuclear-armed missiles. In that case, although the Cold War had come to an end, its aftershock was still being felt in Scotland over a quarter of a century later.

In writing this book I owe several debts of gratitude. No book of this kind could have been written without access to the pioneering investigative work undertaken by Duncan Campbell and Malcolm Spaven in their excellent studies, respectively, *The Unsinkable Aircraft Carrier* and *Fortress Scotland*. I was also helped by the publication of the papers from the Scotland's Cold War conference held at Glasgow Caledonian University in January 2003 and expertly edited by Brian P. Jamieson, whose doctoral thesis on the introduction of the Trident system is now in the public domain at https://theses.gla.ac.uk/6551/. At a late stage in my research I was greatly helped by Ann Galliard of Sandbank near Dunoon, who provided much useful local knowledge about the period known as the 'American years' when the Holy Loch and its US strategic submarines put the Cowal peninsula firmly in the line of fire. On that score I must thank Arlene Messersmith for recording the memories of those who lived through the American deployment at Holy Loch and in similar fashion my thanks go to Iain Ballantyne and Jim Ring for their pioneering work in interviewing Britain's Cold War nuclear submariners and creating two fine naval histories which helped immeasurably in my researches. Not for the first time in my writing career I am indebted to my old friend Lieutenant-Colonel Willie Macnair, late Queen's Own Highlanders, who read the chapter on the espionage and counter-espionage war and made many helpful suggestions – although I must insist that any remaining errors are my responsibility alone.

I have a personal motivation for writing this book. During the latter stages of the Cold War I was invited to write on defence matters for the newspaper *Scotland on Sunday*, at that time edited by my old friend Andrew Jaspan, and he encouraged me to write a series of articles which examined Scotland's role in the UK defence structure. Without his support and encouragement this book would not have been written. I also commented extensively on the same subject for BBC Scotland and it would be remiss of me not to remember my main producers, Jack Regan and Geoff Cameron, both alas no longer with us but certainly not forgotten. This is my third book examining Scotland's role in the wars of the twentieth century, and they would never have been published but for the enthusiastic support of Hugh Andrew, the estimable publisher of Birlinn Books. He and his team made the task a pleasure and I am particularly grateful to Andrew Simmons and Helen Bleck for overseeing the production process with their usual aplomb and professionalism.

Trevor Royle
Edinburgh/Angus
January 2019

Prologue

Saxa Vord

HERE THE NEEDLE starts north.[1] Unst is the northernmost extremity in Scotland and the United Kingdom. Part of the Shetland Islands group, the island is only 12 miles long and 5 miles wide, it is home to around 700 people and lies just to the north of the adjoining islands of Yell and Fetlar. A remote and unforgiving place with low rocky shores and occasional sandy beaches, its northern coast is bisected by the inlet of Burra Firth, an austere yet wildly beautiful rock-strewn bay overlooked by high cliffs where the land gives way to the waters of the Norwegian Sea. At this point the seascape is dominated by the rocky protuberances of Out Stack and Muckle Flugga with its famous lighthouse (now no longer inhabited) but the land is overshadowed by a low-lying hill to the east. Known as Saxa Vord and named after a Norse giant called Saxi, it is instantly recognisable by virtue of the camouflaged 'golf ball' style radome and its associated buildings, standing sentinel on this far-flung frontier. To begin with the military presence in such a remote wilderness comes as a shock and the tarmacked road seems out of place as it meanders up the 950-foot slope, but this is where the country's frontline began during the years of the Cold War. Known to the military planners as Royal Air Force Station Saxa Vord, it opened in 1957 and was home to No. 91 Signal Unit, whose task was to monitor the skies to the north as part of the United Kingdom Air Surveillance and Control System (UKASACS). In short, this was the first line of defence against encroaching Soviet aircraft, a watching and listening post whose sole purpose was to make good the station's motto, *Praemoneo de Periculis* ('Forewarn of Danger'), mounted fittingly on a crest which represented an oncoming Viking longboat warship.

The site's value to the country's defences had become apparent during the Second World War, when it was developed by the Royal Navy in February 1940 as Admiralty Experimental Station No. 4, equipped with radar equipment to track German surface ships and submarines attempting to break out into the North Atlantic and to intercept hostile aircraft in the skies above. Although it ceased operations in July 1945 it was not the end of the story. In 1956 the site was redeveloped by the RAF as part of its Centrimetric Early Warning (CEW) system known as ROTOR 3 which provided low-level and surface cover to the north and west of the British Isles. Other CEW stations in Scotland were also opened at Aird Uig on the island of Lewis and Faraid Head in Sutherland, but Saxa Vord was the longstop. Over the years the site was developed and improved as radar systems became more sophisticated, and in 1962 the radome was constructed to give much-needed protection to the array of radar equipment – some idea of the problem had come three years earlier when the Type 80 equipment was blown away in a gale, and 30 years later the same station was in the grip of a wind recorded at 197 miles per hour, an unofficial British record for wind speed. Never populated by more than 200 service personnel, RAF Saxa Vord was one of the service's most remote and challenging postings, but judging from the recorded reminiscences few seem to have been unimpressed by the island's raw beauty and by the knowledge that it was a job worth doing.[2] The official line was that they were there to intercept potentially hostile aircraft entering UK airspace and the RAF made much of the fact that 'enemy' bombers were intercepted regularly and effectively by Quick Reaction Alert (QRA) fighters from stations such as Leuchars or further south from Lincolnshire. RAF figures claim that between 1957 and 1987 the station controlled 442 separate sorties, resulting in the interception of more than 800 Soviet bomber and reconnaissance aircraft, but the reality was that the majority of the intercepted Soviet aircraft were maritime patrol aircraft going about their legal business, usually in transit to exercises over the Atlantic. Later, as the Cold War became less tense, the station's work ran down, so much so that by 1982 it was reported that interceptions of hostile aircraft had been reduced to around one a week.[3]

Nevertheless, RAF Saxa Vord was an integral part of the country's defences in a period when Scotland was called upon to play a key role in NATO's forward maritime defence strategy aimed at containing a Soviet threat from its naval and air forces based in Murmansk and the Kola Peninsula. This was recognised in 1972, when a secret government report listing possible targets in the event of a nuclear war revealed that Saxa Vord would probably be hit by a three-megaton bomb.[4]

Perceived by some strategists as a well-equipped (though land-locked) aircraft carrier, Scotland had two roles: to guard the North Atlantic approaches in time of war and to provide the forward base for prosecuting any naval war which might have broken out in the Norwegian Sea as Soviet naval and air forces attempted to win control of the vital Iceland–Greenland gap. In the spring of 1989, just months before the collapse of the Warsaw Pact which presaged the end of the Cold War the following decade, Air Vice-Marshal David Brook, the senior RAF commander in Scotland, paraphrased the position when he said: 'Scotland is very much the forward base in the UK for maritime operations as we perceive them, with NATO's forward strategy of prosecuting any war which might occur in the Norwegian Sea.'[5]

To meet the challenge as Brook and his NATO colleagues saw it in the early 1990s, some 10 per cent of the UK's naval and air forces were deployed in Scotland. For the Royal Navy this meant 10,000 personnel and 52 warships, including four Type 42 destroyers, 35 minor war vessels (minehunters, minesweepers and Fisheries Protection Squadron patrol vessels), nine fleet and patrol submarines plus four Resolution-class strategic submarines equipped with Polaris nuclear missiles at Faslane on the Clyde, while the main RAF stations were at Leuchars in Fife (two squadrons of Tornado F3 air defence fighters), Lossiemouth in Moray (two squadrons of Tornado GR1 maritime strike aircraft) and Kinloss, also in Moray which housed the Nimrod MR2 maritime patrol aircraft. Both the senior naval and air force commanders shared headquarters at Pitreavie Castle near Dunfermline in Fife with a command bunker which would have become the UK's strategic nerve centre if Fleet Headquarters at Northwood outside London had been destroyed in the event of a major war. All this was in addition to a substantial US presence in Scotland, the most obvious being the ten strategic submarines equipped with Poseidon nuclear missiles which had been based at the Holy Loch on the west coast since the 1960s. Other US facilities included the satellite communications and command stations at Forss and West Murkle in Caithness and Mormond Hill in Aberdeenshire, the Naval Security Group surveillance centre at Edzell in Angus, reserve air bases at Stornoway in the Western Isles and Machrihanish in Kintyre and the Military Airlift Command staging post at Prestwick in Ayrshire, but by the 1980s their days were numbered.

For RAF Saxa Vord the end came in the summer of 2005 when the Ministry of Defence announced that the facility would be mothballed and closed in 'all but name', with the loss of around 100 jobs. Operations ceased on 10 October and the base was put on a care and maintenance basis. A year later, in April 2006, the station was finally closed and the sensitive electronic equipment was removed, although the distinctive radome remained in place. At the time fears were expressed by the local community about the economic consequences of the closure and the loss of essential facilities supplied by the RAF such as dentistry and fire-fighting, but help was at hand. The site was bought for redevelopment and opened as a holiday resort, making use of the former RAF accommodation to provide self-catering and hostel accommodation as well as a restaurant and bar. Also included in the site are a small chocolate factory, a brewery and a distillery, and the resort and its attraction feature prominently in Shetland publicity to market Unst as a tourist destination.[6]

Fortunately for defence purposes, the radar head and associated buildings were retained by the Ministry of Defence which announced in the autumn of 2017 that Saxa Vord would be reactivated as a remote radar station to provide improved coverage of the airspace to the north of the UK. The decision was taken in response to increased Russian military activity in the area and to an unexpected surge in incursions by Russian aircraft and submarines. The cost of reactivation was £10 million but for the time being the station would be unmanned, with information being relayed to RAF Lossiemouth and RAF Coningsby, home to the RAF's Quick Reaction Alert flights.[7] Today the electronic paraphernalia, a Lockheed Martin AN/FPS-117 three-dimensional radar set, is contained within a new radome which gives a sense of continuity to the pedigree of the original base. If ever there was a Cold War structure which typified the long-drawn-out confrontation between the Soviet Union and the Western allies, this is it. The former RAF station and its successor stands on the same latitude as Anchorage in Alaska and is further north than the Russian city of St Petersburg, known as Leningrad throughout the Cold War. From the hill above the Burra Firth the visitor looks north across the grey waters of the Norwegian Sea and, ignoring Muckle Flugga and Out Stack, there is no land mass before the Arctic polar cap and the approaches to the North Pole. Seen from that vantage Saxa Vord is the end of all things.

1

Last Shots, First Shots

IN COMMON WITH every other participant in the Second World War, Scotland emerged from the fighting exhausted, battle-weary and anxious to make a fresh start. It had been a long and bruising six years and thanks to wartime conscription few people had been left unaffected by the conflict, with its casualties, hardships and deprivations; yet in spite of those setbacks there was a sense of expectation in the summer of 1945 that things could only get better. Partly this was due to the onset of confidence that accompanies the end of any war, partly it was prompted by a sense of relief that the fighting was over, but the biggest single impulse in creating a feel-good factor was the creation of the Welfare State and the promises that it seemed to hold for the creation of a better life. The election of a Labour government in July in the so-called 'khaki election' only served to underline the anticipation which grew throughout the early summer. Shortly before polling day on 12 July a Gallup poll conducted in 195 of the UK's 640 constituencies gave Labour a narrow lead, but the election itself was followed by the anti-climax of having to wait another three weeks for the result to be known, the hiatus being caused by the delay in counting the votes cast by service personnel. The outcome was astonishing. When the result was announced on 26 July Labour had won 393 seats to the Conservative's 213, while the Liberals all but disappeared with only 12 seats. With 47.8 per cent of the vote Labour had a majority of 146 seats, many of them in southern England, the heartland of Conservative support, and Clement Attlee became prime minister.

There was, of course, still a war to be won, for although Nazi Germany had surrendered on 8 May the fighting against the Japanese continued until atomic bombs were dropped on the cities of Hiroshima and Nagasaki in August. For the Scottish regiments involved in this phase of the war it meant a hard summer campaigning in the jungles of

Burma where the Japanese would fight to the last round rather than surrender to the advancing British and Indian forces. Those killed in Japan during the last days of the war were part of the estimated 57 million people who died during the conflict – the exact figure will probably never be known. Of the estimated 380,000 British war deaths, some 10 per cent would have been Scots, although it is difficult to compute a precise figure as conscription was carried out on a UK basis. All told, some 60,000 civilians were killed in the whole of the United Kingdom, mainly as a result of bombing, and of those 2,520 were killed in Scotland with a further 5,725 injured or detained in hospital. The territorial connections of the Scottish regiments had also been loosened during the conflict and this brought about a reduction in casualties. As the war progressed, reinforcements and battlefield casualty replacements came from all over the UK, with the result that most Scottish infantry regiments contained large numbers of soldiers from outside Scotland and their traditional recruiting areas. As was the case with the First World War, it will probably never be known with any exactitude how many Scots died on active service.

One thing was certain. The war had introduced conscription on a large scale and men and women were anxious to get out of uniform and return to their civilian lives. This proved to be a problem for the incoming Labour government, which had to balance the demands of returning service personnel with an equally pressing programme of social and political reform. Unlike the experience of 1919, demobilisation was carried out more equitably, with a points system based on age and length of service at home or abroad. All service personnel were divided into two categories, Class A, the majority, who had to wait their turn and Class B, who were counted as 'key men' whose skills were needed for the vital work of reconstruction – miners, engineers, teachers, police and so on. Release groups were known in advance and the rules were straightforward and, above all else, fair. As was noted at the time the system had no loopholes and enjoyed 'the main virtues of being clear-cut and unambiguous', with the result that returning service personnel could find very little to criticise.[1]

At the time there were ten Scottish line infantry regiments, each with two regular battalions and a varying number of Territorial Army battalions which had all been actively involved in the fighting on the war's main battle fronts. In the early summer of 1945 their locations were as follows:

India: 1st Royal Scots, 1st Royal Scots Fusiliers, 2nd King's Own Scottish Borderers, 1st Cameronians, 2nd Black Watch, 1st Seaforth Highlanders, 1st Cameron Highlanders, 9th Gordon Highlanders

Palestine: 2nd Royal Scots, 6th Gordon Highlanders

Germany: 7th/9th Royal Scots, 8th Royal Scots, 2nd Royal Scots Fusiliers, 4th/5th Royal Scots Fusiliers; 6th Royal Scots Fusiliers, 11th Royal Scots Fusiliers, 1st King's Own Scottish Borderers, 4th King's Own Scottish Borderers, 5th King's Own Scottish Borderers, 2nd Cameronians, 6th Cameronians, 7th Cameronians, 9th Cameronians, 1st Black Watch, 5th Black Watch, 7th Black Watch, 1st Highland Light Infantry, 5th Highland Light Infantry, 6th Highland Light Infantry, 9th Highland Light Infantry, 10th Highland Light Infantry 2nd Seaforth Highlanders, 5th Seaforth Highlanders, 7th Seaforth Highlanders, 5th Cameron Highlanders, 1st Gordon Highlanders, 2nd Gordon Highlanders, 5th/7th Gordon Highlanders, 2nd Argyll and Sutherland Highlanders, 7th Argyll and Sutherland Highlanders

Italy, Greece and Austria: 6th Black Watch, 2nd Cameron Highlanders, 1st Argyll and Sutherland Highlanders, 8th Argyll and Sutherland Highlanders

There were also three battalions of Scots Guards and the Royal Scots Greys armoured regiment which all ended the war in Germany. Scots also served in the Royal Artillery and specialist corps such as the Royal Engineers, the Royal Signals, the Royal Electrical and Mechanical Engineers, the Royal Army Service Corps and the Royal Army Ordnance Corps, all of which had expanded massively during the conflict. These were in addition to the uncounted numbers of Scots who were serving in the Royal Navy, the Merchant Navy and the Royal Air Force. Given the parlous nature of the UK's post-war economic situation there had to be a good deal of retrenchment, which basically entailed cuts in the defence budget because the possession of large armed forces was a luxury the country could ill afford. Fighting the war had cost the country £3 billion and there remained a high level of debt arising from loans made by the US during and after the conflict; exports had fallen to new low levels and sterling was weak. As a result, in the three armed forces cutbacks and scaling-down became the order of the day. Between 1946 and 1948 the RAF Estimates shrank from £255.5 million to £173 million. The Naval Estimates for 1949 totalled £153 million, a decrease on the previous year's expenditure of £44 million and the government urged further economies on both services in personnel and materiel. Expenditure on the Army was also reduced, from £350 million to £270 million, and Second World War equipment was not replaced in any quantity until the 1950s, forcing Field Marshal Viscount Montgomery of Alamein, Chief of the Imperial General Staff between 1946 and 1948, to complain that 'the Army was in a parlous condition, and was in a complete state of unreadiness and unprepared-ness for war'.[2] By 1951 the size of the infantry had shrunk to 20 per cent of the Army's total size – 88,100 soldiers out of a total strength of 417,800, all line infantry regiments (including the ten existing Scottish regiments), had been reduced to a single battalion by a process of amalgamation, wartime Territorial battalions had been scrapped or amalgamated and the combat units had fallen to 184, consisting of 77 infantry battalions, eight Gurkha battalions, 69 artillery regiments and 30 armoured regiments.

At the same time the country retained most of its pre-war strategic obligations and still needed soldiers on the ground to maintain them. The scale of the commitments meant that manpower became a problem for all three services, especially for the Army, which was in danger of being over-stretched. Although the government had a commitment to demobilise war service men and women it still needed a regular supply of trained soldiers for a wide variety of tasks. Wartime legislation for conscription was therefore kept in place and under a succession of National Service Acts every male citizen was obliged to register at his local branch of the Ministry of Labour and National Service as soon as he became 18 (women were excluded from the legislation). Between the end of the war and the final phasing out of conscription in 1963, 2.3 million men served as National Servicemen, the majority in the Army. In its final form the period of conscription was two years, following two earlier periods of 12 and 18 months and like every other part of the British Army the Scottish regiments benefited from the contribution made by men who were the first peacetime conscripts in British history.

National Service proved to be a mixed experience. Some undoubt-edly enjoyed their time in the armed forces, learned a trade, passed their driving tests or travelled abroad for the first time in their lives. A few gained commissions; others just took to service life and, like Private

Alexander Robb from Aberdeen who did his National Service in 1st Seaforth Highlanders, enjoyed the companionship of barrack life and the character training that came with pride and discipline.

We had three super instructors, Sergeant Rennie, Corporal Le Page and Corporal Baker who were very strict but fair to all. Sergeant Rennie told us that he had never had a squad win the passing-out parade at the end of six weeks' training – at Redford Barracks in Edinburgh there were six Highland regiments, HLI, Argylls, Seaforths, Black Watch, Camerons and Gordons. As none of us had much money, around £1 a week, Saturday was the only day any of us went out, either to Tynecastle or Easter Road to watch football, then a fish supper and a stroll round the centre of Edinburgh before the tram back to Redford. We all decided we would try our best not to let Sergeant Rennie down. We used to practise what we had learned during the day in barrack-room after cleaning our kit. On the two passing out days we won the cross-country run, weapon-training, PT, turn-out and drill and came second in shooting. First overall. As we sat at our passing-out meal – of course we were at the top table – it gave us all satisfaction to see Sergeant Rennie's face completely light up, as proud as Punch.[3]

Of course, in contrast, there were also former National Servicemen who had somewhat different memories of their time in uniform, remembering only bullying NCOs, indifferent food, the loss of liberty and counting the days to demob, but as with so many other things in life it all depended on what the individual was prepared to put into the experience. One major gripe was that many of the conscripts were placed in formations which failed to make use of the civilian skills they could bring to service life. Amongst those who felt that way was Corporal Iain Colquhoun from Glasgow, who ended up in the Royal Engineers but was appalled by the apparent wastefulness of the system he encountered while sharing a billet with 'a cascade of Royal Signals troops' at Longmoor in Hampshire. 'Look at all of us! [said one of the Signallers, a Cockney] A painter, four plumbers, a carpenter, two motor mechanics, a plate-layer, two shipbuilders (I forget all the others) and what do we do? March about the square, stand in queues for kit all day, obey orders from stupid bastards who couldn't get by in civvy street . . . And look around any town in Britain – slums, broken-down buildings, chaotic railways and buses, and where are we, who could fix it all up into a decent country? We're here, saluting snivelling idiots who don't know whether their arsehole's bored or punched!'[4]

As Colquhoun 'slowly grasped the non-technical meaning of entropy', he wryly noted that those men were needed to get the country back on its feet again and should not have been in uniform. A vast rebuilding programme had been instituted to make good the nation's already inadequate housing stock and to repair wartime bomb damage, the tax-funded National Health Service had come into being and there were ambitious plans to nationalise the coal industry and the railways. All in all, the Labour government was intent on creating a 'New Britain' which would make unemployment a thing of the past and introduce a fresh system of benefits under the banner of the 'Welfare State'; this would address poverty, health care and education and in so doing produce 'cradle to the grave security' for the people of the UK.

Even before the fighting stopped and peace of a kind returned to a shattered globe the first steps had been taken to try to ensure that it would be 'a world fit for heroes'. In fact, the theme was much more intense than a simple appeal to the optimism that had accompanied the end of the previous conflict. For the beleaguered British people who had withstood almost six years of continuous warfare, when for much of the time they themselves had been on the front line, the predominant emotion was 'never again'. They had seen what could be achieved when people combined in common cause, and the experience of coalition government with united war aims had provided them with the foundations for a new beginning. Now it was their time and they were determined to make the most of it. Many of their hopes were based on the principles embodied in the radical report *Social Insurance and Allied Services*, which had provided the blueprint for a comprehensive post-war welfare state. Written by the visionary social scientist William Beveridge and published in December 1942 its timing was doubly fortuitous. Not only did it bring the promise of change by challenging the scourges of 'idleness, ignorance, disease, squalor, and want' but it provided hope at the very moment when it seemed that the war could be won following the victories at El Alamein and Stalingrad. Not surprisingly perhaps, because it caught the mood of the moment, it became an instant bestseller with a print run of over 600,000 copies plus many thousands more in a truncated version which was distributed to members of the armed forces. Within a few weeks of publication it was estimated that 19 out of 20 people had heard of the report and mainly understood the gist of its findings. From that point onwards support for the Labour Party began to grow and although the wartime electoral truce held firm and support for Churchill as wartime leader never wavered, there was a distinct shift leftwards in the second half of the war as people dared to dream of a New Jerusalem.

Such attitudes were not altogether surprising. During the war people had become used to a collectivist approach to government. They could see what might be achieved by state interventionism on a grand scale and did not want to return to the laissez-faire free market attitudes of the 1930s which had failed to deliver economic recovery and which seemed to have encouraged the policy of appeasement with Nazi Germany. The coalition government had demonstrated what could be done when the will of the country was bent towards defeating the enemy, and with over 5 million men and women conscripted into National Service they wanted that mood to continue into the peacetime years. Nothing else would do. If the evil of fascism could be extirpated by united national resolve then surely a similar effort could be made to defeat poverty, unemployment and social exclusion. There was, too, the added incentive that thousands of men and women had fought and risked their lives on the front line and were not prepared to see their sacrifices dissipated by political inaction. The real problem, though, had little to do with implementing those hopes; it was finding the money in a world which found Britain economically exhausted and saddled with a huge national debt. Hopes were all very well, but the stark reality was that money was in desperately short supply.

Britain also had to deal with its Empire and to determine its future in the much-changed conditions of the post-war world. In 1945 the Empire remained at the heart of British foreign policy and military strategy and Foreign Office officials now led by former trade union leader Ernest Bevin warned that calls for independence in the colonies had to be balanced by the need to maintain Britain's world position, otherwise the country would be irremediably weakened. In the nearby War Office in Horse Guards Parade maps showed that scores of British military bases still dotted the globe stretching from Gibraltar, Cyprus and Malta in the Mediterranean to Palestine and Egypt, and then beyond the Middle East to India, Burma and across Asia to Malaya and Hong Kong. In Africa, there were British military outposts scattered from Cairo to Cape Town but already in the post-war world nationalist movements across the Empire were making their presence felt and calls for independence from British rule were becoming shrill and insistent.

This applied specially to India, the so-called 'jewel in the crown', and one of the first seismic changes in the post-war world was the decision to quit the sub-continent. During the war it had become painfully obvious that the Indian nationalist movement was not an ephemeral movement but the expression of an overwhelming demand for independence, as was the equally insistent demand for the creation of an independent Islamic state to cater for the aspirations of the Muslim population. Britain was also under pressure from the United States to give way to those claims, and at breakneck speed Prime Minister Clement Attlee pushed through a rapid countdown to independence and the partition of the sub-continent into two new countries, India and Pakistan. Guided by the last viceroy, Admiral Lord Louis Mountbatten, the plans were hurriedly shaped and finalised and on 14 August 1947 the new state of Pakistan came into being followed a day later by the creation of India. Amongst the Scottish regiments present in the sub-continent was 1st Royal Scots, whose war had been spent fighting the Japanese in Burma before moving in January 1947 to Karachi, where they took part in the celebrations by providing the guard of honour and street liners for the ceremony marking the official transfer of power. The occasion could have been marred by a threat to the life of the new leader of Pakistan, Dr Muhammad Ali Jinnah, but both he and Mountbatten agreed that the formal procession and the official opening of the Pakistan Constituent Assembly should go ahead as planned. Mountbatten's words for the occasion were prescient: 'We who are making history today are caught and carried on in the swift current of events; there is no time to look back – there is time only to look forward.'[5] Four months later the Royals were on the move again. In the middle of December the 1st battalion left Karachi, boarding the troopship SS *Empire Halladale* after marching through the city with colours flying, bayonets drawn and the pipes and drums playing.

Due to the need to keep order during the transfer of power, a continued British presence was required in Pakistan, and in those final days in the sub-continent this was provided by 2nd Black Watch, which had served in Burma during the latter years of the war. The battalion remained on internal security duties in the North-West Frontier

Province, scene of so many earlier altercations between British forces and local tribesmen; following independence it was based at Malir cantonment, where it received the news that under post-war defence cuts it would be reduced to cadre form and its soldiers transferred to other Scottish regiments. Meanwhile it would stay in the country until Britain's last interests had been secured. As a result, 2nd Black Watch had the honour of being the last British regiment to leave Pakistan, thereby ending a military connection with the sub-continent which had lasted for the better part of two centuries.

Although depleted by demobilisation, the battalion put on a fine show when the men marched through Karachi on 26 February 1948 with colours flying, bayonets fixed and pipes and drums playing. The commanding officer, Lieutenant-Colonel Neville Blair, had been opposed to an official send-off but at the insistence of Major-General Mohammed Akhbar Khan the battalion left Pakistan with full military ceremonial. Their day began at 9 a.m. when a convoy of trucks took the battalion from Malir to the assembly point in the grounds of St Catherine's School in Karachi. From there, behind the pipes and drums, the men marched through the streets of the Empress Market and down Elphinstone Street to the official residence of the Governor-General, where they formed up and accorded a Royal Salute to the country's new leader, Dr Jinnah. In his speech of farewell Jinnah made the customary remarks about the spirit of friendship which existed between military men of the two countries; then, for a moment he lost his composure and almost broke down. 'I couldn't believe that I would ever be entitled to a Royal Salute from a British regiment,' he confided to a clearly embarrassed Blair.[6]

Once the civil ceremony had been completed the battalion then embussed for the military farewell at Karachi's docks. Their own pipes and drums were silent now but at the dockside waited the massed pipes and drums of two battalions of the Baluch Regiment and the 2nd/16th Punjab Regiment. Also waiting was a huge crowd which had assembled to watch The Black Watch marching off with their colours. With the men formed up in hollow square, facing the troopship the *Empire Halladale*, the speech of farewell was read by General Akhbar Khan and then a be-garlanded Blair asked permission to continue the parade. As the battalion presented arms the colours were marched out of the hollow square and the colour party took up station to the flank and in front of a guard of honour found from the Punjab Regiment. The guard presented arms and, with the massed pipes and drums playing, the colours were slow-marched up the gangway into the grey side of the troopship. It was a simple and impressive ceremony, bringing to an end 167 years of regimental service in the sub-continent. Touchingly, the last set to be played by the massed bands was the slow march, 'Will Ye No Come Back Again?' Before leaving Pakistan, Blair had received news of a further change: 'Amalgamation with the 1st battalion is now our destiny; not reduction – for which we are all thankful,' he noted at the time. 'The future of the battalion's property is thereby partly solved, and its proud history will not be forgotten.'[7] A month later, on 20 March, the *Empire Halladale* slipped up the Firth of Clyde into Glasgow's King George V Docks where trains waited to take them back to Perth. After home leave final preparations were made for the amalgamation with the 1st battalion at Duisberg in West Germany and the 2nd battalion went into a state of 'suspended animation'. (But not for long: it was reconstituted in 1951 during the Korean War.)

It was not as if the armed services had nothing to do. Far from it: peace might have brought an end to the fighting but it had not produced any lasting stability and the threat of further violence was never far away. While India had progressed towards partition and independence and the move had been largely welcomed – not least by the USA, which had pushed for it during the war – there remained similar post-colonial problems in South-East Asia, notably in Indochina (later Vietnam) and the Netherlands East Indies (later Indonesia). Both were former colonies of close allies (France and the Netherlands), both were claimed by indigenous nationalist movements (Viet Minh and Indonesia) and both came under the aegis of Britain's South-East Asia Command, which had to deal with the problem with limited forces and very little American support. In both countries there were violent confrontations and in both countries the British were forced to use Japanese prisoners-of-war to help restore order. Commanding the British garrison in Indonesia was Lieutenant-General Sir Philip Christison, a Cameron Highlander, who had served with distinction in Burma and who was told by Mountbatten that he was 'in for a sticky time'.[8] Under his command was 1st Seaforth Highlanders, which had been training for the invasion of Malaya and had arrived in Jakarta in September; significantly, they were the descendants of the 78th Highlanders, which had taken part in the capture of the island of Java in 1811. In a grim foretaste of what would happen during future decolonisation Christison found himself having to deal with civil disobedience, rioting and violence in which his forces had to hold the ring as Indonesian nationalists fought for their independence from the Dutch, who regarded British involvement as a gross betrayal by a wartime ally. It was the same story in Indochina where the French felt equally let down while the British were 'both unprepared and under-resourced to deal with the rise of Vietnamese nationalism'.[9]

Closer to home there were also difficulties in readjusting to the differing demands of peacetime and the growing needs of people demanding self-determination. Within weeks of the end of the war in Europe the western Allies found themselves confronting their erstwhile comrades-in-arms, the Soviet Union, when British troops were involved in clashes with Communist forces in Yugoslavia and Greece. By far the most dangerous of these incidents was the Trieste crisis which erupted at the end of April 1945 when the first Allied troops of the British Eighth Army (2nd New Zealand Division) entered Trieste in the Italian province of Venezia Giulia to find themselves confronted by the Yugoslav 4th Army which clearly intended to annex the area. Feelings were running high not least because the German forces had no intention of surrendering to the Yugoslavs whom they rightly feared would treat them harshly and Field Marshal Sir Harold Alexander, the Supreme Allied Commander Mediterranean had no clear idea of the policy to be pursued. With good reason he also feared that a clash with the Yugoslavs could either be the last battle of the Second World War or the flashpoint for a third world war. On 1 May Alexander wrote to Churchill warning of the danger facing the Eighth Army: 'If I am ordered by the Combined Chiefs of Staff to occupy the whole of Venezia Giulia by force if necessary, we shall certainly be committed to a fight with the Yugoslav Army, who will have the moral backing at least of the Russians.'[10] He also expressed doubts about the reaction of the troops under his command if he was forced to order his forces to turn their guns on their former Yugoslav allies under the overall command of Marshal Tito, the leader of the wartime Yugoslavian partisans.

In many respects this confrontation was a foretaste of what would lie ahead for the Allies in the aftermath of the final defeat of Nazi Germany as the differences between the West and the Soviet Union became more pronounced. In the case of Trieste Churchill felt that Communist intransigence should be resisted and he was backed by the new American leader, President Harry Truman, who agreed that a strong line had to be taken to prevent further aggression. By the middle of May the problem was resolved when Yugoslav forces withdrew across the Isonzo River, the province was divided into two parts and according to the regiment's Official History 'the crisis died away as if it had all been a great misunderstanding.'[11] Amongst the regiments involved in BETFOR (British Element Trieste Force) during the initial stages were 1st Scots Guards and 1st London Scottish, which were both based at Rossetti. They were replaced in successive years by 2nd Cameron Highlanders, 2nd Royal Scots and 1st Cameronians before the BETFOR deployment came to an end in 1954. As the Official History noted, 'the Italian Campaign had finally ended and the first battle of the Cold War had been won by well-staged deterrence.'[12]

Less satisfying in its outcome was the treatment meted out to the prisoners from the surrendered German Army who belonged to racial groupings hated and despised by the Soviets because of their wartime support for the Nazis. These included 46,000 Cossacks, 25,000 Croats and 24,000 Slovenes plus their families, whose fate had been decided by the Yalta Conference signed on 9 February 1945 – all Soviet citizens liberated by the Allies and all British subjects liberated by forces under Soviet command were to be handed over to their national forces, and this included the Russian Cossacks and the Croats and Slovenes who had become embroiled on the Nazi side in the Balkans. For most of them the decision was a death sentence and it fell to soldiers of the British Army to take part in what the War Diary of one Foot Guards battalion described as an 'order of most sinister duplicity'.[13] Amongst those involved in the operation was 8th Argyll and Sutherland Highlanders, a Territorial Army battalion from Argyllshire, which had fought in North Africa and Italy with the Eighth Army and, much to its disgust, became involved in the 'most unsavoury business' of handing over Cossack prisoners of war to the Red Army at Lienz on the River Drau in the Austrian province of Carpathia. For a battalion which had fought so hard and over so many months it was a dispiriting way in which to end the war.

Equally contentious was the treatment of Ukrainian forces which had served under Nazi colours and fought against the Red Army right up to the dying days of the war and beyond. Of all the displaced persons in post-war Europe the Ukrainians were perhaps the most difficult to understand, basically because there seemed to be two Ukraines. Those from the east of the River Dnieper had been subjects of the Russian

Empire and, later, of the Soviet Union and had practised the Russian Orthodox religion; those from the west, also known as Galicia, had been Catholic subjects of the Austro-Hungarian Empire and later, until 1939, of Poland. That shared history had also been deeply divisive and during the war Ukrainians had been caught between Hitler and Stalin: the majority had been conscripted into the Red Army while many more in the western half had helped the Germans in their policy of exterminating the Jewish population. One of the main formations was the Galicia Division, which was created in Lviv in April 1943 as the 14th Waffen SS Grenadier Division (Galizische Nr. 1) and was regarded as the nucleus of a future independent Ukrainian Army. A year later it was largely destroyed at Brody together with most of German XIII Corps during the Red Army's victorious advance into eastern Europe, and the few survivors joined the Ukrainian Insurgent Army (UPA), which operated in western Ukraine against Soviet forces and was operational as an insurgency force until the early 1950s. The UPA's aim was the creation of an independent Ukraine and the forcible expulsion of all Poles. At one point it numbered 200,000 fighters, many of whom were military police personnel and other militias who used ethnic cleansing techniques learned from the SS – over 60,000 Poles were massacred during the latter stages of the war.[14] By the summer of 1944 there was an all-out conflict between Polish and Ukrainian partisans, the latter led by the ultra-Nationalist Stepan Bandera, and considered to be 'adroit political intriguers and past masters in the art of propaganda', well able to play off rival Western intelligence services.[15]

A different fate awaited other members of the 14th Galicia Division who managed to escape into Austria, where they re-formed as the 1st Ukrainian Division of the Ukrainian National Army under the command of General Pavlo Shandruk fighting against the Soviet Army right to the end of the war. In May 1945 the Division crossed the Alps and surrendered to the British Eighth Army in Carinthia and the men were transferred to the UK in April and May 1947 as 'surrendered enemy personnel', the majority of whom were put to work as agricultural labourers under a scheme known as European Voluntary Workers (EVW) which had been established to create a pool of agricultural labourers to ease post-war manpower shortages. All told, under the EVW scheme 8,128 former members of the Nazi-trained Galicia Division ended up in camps across southern Scotland, some 450 were held at Hallmuir Camp in Lanarkshire, south of Lockerbie, where they built a Ukrainian Orthodox Chapel inside one of the huts. It survives as working church and visitor attraction to this day and the Ukrainians remained in Scotland until December 1948, when a decision was taken to deport about 300 of their number. The order sparked a protest and a general strike of Ukrainian EVWs took place on 28 December 1948. Two days later the Home Office announced that only 81 persons were to leave: 45 who chose to go home, mainly to rejoin family, and 36 with records of unsatisfactory behaviour as prisoners of war. Many of the remainder subsequently merged into the local community or emigrated to other countries abroad.[16] There was, though, a different and more sinister outcome for some 400 'Galizianers' who remained in Scotland to complete the 'civilianisation' process, as it was known: they were detained at the former Amisfield prisoner-of-war camp (Camp 243) outside Haddington in East Lothian, where they were kept under surveillance by MI6 to see if they were suitable for employment as spies behind the Iron Curtain. Eight were chosen and trained near Fort William but on being parachuted into Ukraine they were immediately arrested and executed.[17] Soviet infiltration of British intelligence, notably by the traitor Kim Philby, meant that the Soviet security forces had prior knowledge about the timing and the positioning of the drops and the agents were doomed before they set out on their mission.[18] Some idea of the Allied confusion surrounding the position of the Ukrainians at the end of the war can be seen in a Foreign Office document sent to British military commanders in May 1946: 'It is not possible to provide a precise definition of who are Ukrainians. It can only be said that they are those persons who speak the Ukrainian language and wished to be considered Ukrainians.'[19]

By then the international situation was worsening, with problems in the Middle East where tensions were running high between the Arab and Jewish populations as they struggled to gain the ascendancy in Palestine, which was nominally under the control of a British mandate and which had been designated as a home for the Jewish people in 1917. By the end of the war it was clear that a confrontation was inevitable between them and the Arab population, who resented the steady arrival of European Jews throughout the 1930s, many of them refugees from Hitler's Germany. As a result of the growing friction the Jewish resistance group the Haganah was strengthened and it began to adopt the offensive ethos embedded in the philosophy of Ze'ev Jabotinsky, the founder of Revisionist Zionism, who believed that if a Jewish state were created in Palestine confrontation with the Arabs was inevitable and that the Jews would be forced to fight for, and then defend, their homeland 'behind an iron wall which they [the Arabs] will be powerless to break down'.[20] Standing between the two sides were the 20,000 men of the Palestinian police force backed by 80,000 soldiers of the British Army's 1st Division, 6th Airborne Division and, from March 1947 3rd Division. Amongst the battalions involved in the operation were 1st Argyll and Sutherland Highlanders. It was a deployment which Britain was hard-pressed to make and throughout the period the military units involved in internal security duties were severely overstretched.

Inevitably, fighting an invisible enemy had a demoralising effect on the members of the British security forces. They were able to disrupt terrorist activities and in some cases forestall them, as they did during Operation Elephant in March 1947 when martial law was declared for three weeks in Tel Aviv, Petach Tikva and Ramat Gan, but all too often the men of the 1st Argylls found that they had to react to situations about which they had no prior knowledge and for which they had received no special training. This bred a siege mentality best expressed by the military historian Correlli Barnett, who served as a National Service conscript in Palestine in 1946: 'two British divisions and support troops, some 60,000 soldiers, were stuck in Palestine adding to the balance of payments deficit, carrying out clumsy and ineffective sweeps against the Jewish terrorists who were murdering their comrades, and otherwise doing nothing but guard their own barbed wire.'[21] During the deployment the 1st Argylls was brigaded with 2nd Oxfordshire and Buckinghamshire Light Infantry and 1st Royal Ulster Rifles in 6 Air Landing Brigade. Given the nature of the conflict it was not surprising that there were Argyll casualties: four killed in action, ten wounded and five dead as a result of accidents. It was all in vain. Under sustained international pressure to retrieve the situation the British government admitted defeat in February 1947 and announced that the problem would be handed over to the stewardship of the United Nations. After protracted wrangling in the UN the new state of Israel came into being at midnight on 14 May 1948, the British garrison was finally withdrawn, and the opposing factions emerged into the open to plunge the country into warfare. For all concerned it had been a grim and dispiriting experience. As the commanding officer of 2nd Royal Scots admitted before taking his battalion to Malta, there had been little satisfaction for his men in being forced to act as armed policemen in a struggle not of their making. Most other British sailors, soldiers and airmen felt the same.

The next post-war crisis came on 16 June 1948 where a state of emergency was declared in the British Crown Colony of Malaya due to the outbreak of a guerrilla war against British rule by the Communist Malayan Races Liberation Army, and the resulting confrontation dragged on into the next decade largely as a result of British determination to face down the Communist aggression and to hold onto Malaya's valuable stocks of rubber and tin.

Closer to home, things were hotting up in Germany. Just over a week later and following a period of increasing intention, the Soviet Union took the belligerent decision to cut all land links between West Berlin and western Germany – as part of the post-war settlement Germany had been divided into four zones occupied by the Soviet Union, the USA, Britain and France. At the same time Berlin was similarly divided into four zones with defined air and land corridors to the West. The flashpoint was the decision taken by the Western powers to create the new country of West Germany (properly the Federal Republic of Germany) from their occupied zones and to introduce a new Deutschmark currency, a move which provoked the Soviet Union into closing all rail, road and canal communications with the West. This left the Western powers with the choice of capitulating to the Soviet aggression or to counter it by arranging armed convoys to transport essential goods into Berlin even though that introduced the risk of outright war. Coming on top of an earlier coup in Czechoslovakia in which the Czech Communist Party had seized power with Soviet backing this seemed to be another sign that the Soviet Union was intent on creating a monolithic Communist bloc in eastern Europe even if this provoked confrontation with her former wartime allies. That was certainly the assessment of the UK government's Joint Intelligence Committee (JIC) at the time.

> The fundamental aim of the Soviet leaders is to hasten the elimination of capitalism from all parts of the world and to replace it with their own form of Communism. They envisage this process as being effected in the course of a revolutionary struggle lasting for many years and assisted, should favourable conditions arise, by military action.[22]

The same document also made clear that Soviet land and air forces already had that capacity and were 'sufficiently strong, at the present time, to achieve rapid and far-reaching successes against any likely combination of opposing land forces'. This was not scaremongering but the JIC assessment and its successor papers formed the basis of the UK response to the Soviet threat in 1948, namely that the Soviet Union had a long-term aim of world domination and was fully capable of attacking the West without warning. In that case the Berlin crisis seemed to presage the beginning of a new confrontation which could quite easily provide a *casus belli* for a third world war. For the Western allies there appeared to be two options: to form armed convoys and send them along the autobahn to Berlin (this was briefly considered by General Lucius Clay, the US commander-in-chief in Europe) or to threaten the Soviet Union with the newly developed atomic bomb (by way of underlining the reality of that option three additional squadrons of US Air Force B-29 strategic bombers were deployed in East Anglia in July). As only the US possessed these weapons it was a dangerous moment which could have led to further escalation or, as Attlee was told by his military advisers, the confrontation 'would almost certainly lead to an incident and the opening of World War III'.[23] Fortunately, good sense prevailed. While the bombers arrived, thereby creating a permanent US nuclear presence in the UK from the following year, Clay was ordered to halt all plans to supply Berlin by land and instead planning began for a massive operation to send in essential goods, including fuel, by Allied aircraft. It was a brilliant solution. In June 1,400 tons arrived, by mid-July this quantity was arriving on a daily basis and by the end of the year the daily average was 5,500 tons. The aircraft travelled along three narrow air corridors and flew their cargo into the Berlin airports of Tegel, Gatow and Tempelhof, the bulk of the flights being carried out by the US Air Force and the RAF as well as aircraft flown by civilian contractors such as the newly formed Scottish Airlines, which had been formed at Prestwick in 1946 as a subsidiary of Scottish Aviation. As a historian of the period put it, by the time the Air Lift had come to an end in May 1949 when the Soviets lifted the blockade the operation had 'almost come to seem business-as-usual'.[24]

The Berlin blockade and the success of the subsequent Air Lift also concentrated minds in Western capitals, particularly in London and Washington, about how to deal with the emerging Soviet challenge. The first stage, engineered by the British Foreign Secretary Ernest Bevin, was the creation of the Western European Union which brought the

UK, France and the Benelux countries (Belgium, Netherlands, Luxembourg) into a defensive alliance in March 1948, but this was expanded a year later by the creation of the North Atlantic Treaty Organisation (NATO), which came into being on 4 April 1949, the founding Treaty of Brussels being ratified by the UK, USA, Canada, Belgium, Denmark, France, Iceland, Italy, Luxembourg, the Netherlands, Portugal and Norway (West Germany joined in 1955). According to Lord Ismay, NATO's first Secretary-General, the alliance's main purpose was 'to keep the Russians out, the Americans in, and the Germans down' and there was much truth in that wry observation.[25] Russia had been confronted without a shot being fired and the USA had been drawn into the collective defence of Europe, the treaty's significant Article 5 having stated that 'an armed attack on one or more of them in Europe or North America shall be considered an attack against them all'. As for the UK it deployed ground forces in West Germany in the shape of the British Army of the Rhine (BAOR), which was allotted to the Northern Army Group under the command of British generals and was to remain there until the early part of the twenty-first century. This was Britain's main contribution to the post-war defence of Western Europe and in some respects West Germany came to be regarded, somewhat tenuously, as the Army's successor to India, ideal for training and self-contained in another country. However, even the most enthusiastic promoters of that theory had to admit that the country lacked the conditions, the climate and, it has to be said, the mystique. Soldiers saw it somewhat differently, the standard army joke being that 'We are guarding the Eastern Frontier against the might of the Russian Empire.'[26] (The quip has history behind it: from the days of the Roman Empire the River Elbe running from the Polish–Czech border to the North Sea was regarded as the natural fault line or *Limes Germanicus* between the civilised west and the savagery of 'East Elbia', home to the backward and deeply conservative Junker warrior caste. This was the natural barrier dividing west and east: for the historian Tacitus, the Germania of Roman times was bounded to the north by the North and Baltic seas, to the west by the River Rhine and to the south by the River Danube. To the east lay the vastness of unfathomable distances and unknown barbarism and that perception produced one of the main levers of Western thinking up to and including the Cold War.)

NATO's strategy also embraced a robust maritime element and while its main focus was the Mediterranean, where the US Sixth Fleet was deployed to contain and threaten the Soviet Union's Southern Flank, the north could not be ignored despite the climatological challenges of operating in extreme temperatures, especially in winter. Also, the inclusion of Denmark, Iceland and Norway in NATO meant that the alliance had an obligation to be involved in areas such as the Arctic Ocean, the Barents Sea, the Danish Strait and the White Sea approaches, which had been identified as key operating and training areas for Soviet submarines and which would therefore require the counter-deployment of NATO attack submarines and anti-submarine warfare (ASW) warships and aircraft.[27] In response NATO's first major exercise was Operation Mainbrace, which was mounted in the North Sea over 12 days in September 1952 and involved 9 countries, 80,000 men, over 200 ships, and 1,000 aircraft – the 'largest and most powerful fleet that has cruised in the North Sea since World War I'.[28] Its purpose was to test the defences of Denmark and Norway by reproducing NATO's response to a major Soviet ('Orange') offensive across the Norwegian border as well as an enemy advance into Denmark. This involved NATO ('Blue') air forces supporting ground forces in both areas while naval units undertook shore bombardment as well as amphibious and anti-submarine operations along the Scandinavian coast. A final aspect of the exercise was an escorted convoy from Scottish North Sea ports to Bergen, reflecting the need for the rapid reinforcement and resupply of Norway as part of the response to any Soviet invasion.[29] The RAF bases at Leuchars and Kinloss played roles in handling NATO aircraft and the old flying boat base at Scatsta near Sullom Voe in the Shetlands was reopened for the occasion.[30] The operation was also notable for the substantial number of reported sightings of unidentified flying objects (UFOs) or 'flying saucers' which were observed by NATO personnel at sea and in the air and gave rise to a belief that either the world was under observation from extra-terrestrial visitors or that the Soviet Union possessed unknown secret weapons which were technically superior to anything else known at the time.[31] Sightings of this kind were frequently reported in the years ahead and UFO or flying saucer mania was a by-product of the growing escalation of international tension in the 1950s, spawning a number of sensational newspaper and magazine articles and attracting the attention of Hollywood in movies such as *The Day the Earth Stood Still* (1951) in which Klaatu, an extra-terrestrial alien played by Michael Rennie, lands his space craft in Washington to present a stark warning to humankind from another world: 'Your choice is simple: join us and live in peace, or pursue your present course and face obliteration.' The reference to nuclear weapons and the dangers they posed is unmistakable, but closer to known reality Operation Mainbrace was counted a success. Despite the challenging weather conditions, which limited flying time from the ten participating aircraft carriers, three of which were British, the operation led to the adoption of the defence of the Northern Flank as a vital NATO policy in countering Soviet belligerence in the area.

More than any other factor in the aftermath of the blockade of Berlin, the need to protect this flank put Scotland firmly on the front line throughout the growing confrontation with the Soviet Union and her allies. From Moscow's point of view the strategic situation was quite simple. The Nordic waters were crucial for the Soviet Northern Fleet, which had relocated its main strength from the Baltic to the Kola Peninsula in the period after the Second World War as part of the revised Soviet maritime doctrine which called for the development of naval aircraft, surface ships and submarines with long-range capabilities. It was from there that they would deploy their main submarine force into the Atlantic prior to the outbreak of hostilities or under the cover of land or carrier-based aircraft in time of war and, equally crucially, it was from these northern waters that they would interdict NATO reinforcement convoys from the US as they approached Europe through the crucial Greenland–Iceland–United Kingdom (GIUK) gap. Equally, it was essential that NATO forces contained the Soviet Northern Fleet and in time of war would be well placed to destroy it before it was able to threaten the security of the GIUK gap. While the defence of the Norwegian land mass was the key to all NATO security initiatives senior commanders also recognised that 'Soviet submarines and aircraft based in the Kola Peninsula posed a special threat to the United Kingdom, a vital ally and a key base in any future European war' and that the first land mass they would encounter would be Scotland.[32]

Overall, the central plank in the formation of NATO was the need to keep the US tied in to Western Europe's security structure at a time when the Eastern Bloc had fallen under Soviet domination. That much had already become clear when the Soviet Foreign Minister Vyacheslav Molotov rejected the US European Recovery Programme (better known as the Marshall Plan) at an international conference held in Paris in July 1947. When the Soviet delegation walked out in protest at what they saw as US plans to dominate the whole of Europe by offering

$13 billion in aid, food, raw materials and machinery it was a clear sign that Europe had been divided into two opposing power blocs. To understand Soviet fears, it was only necessary to look back at recent history: twice in the twentieth century the Russian land mass had been subjected to attack by Germany, most recently Hitler's Operation Barbarossa offensive in 1941, and now it seemed to be facing an even deadlier threat backed by the USA. A similar fear drove the Americans, who had been surprised in 1941 by the Japanese offensive against Pearl Harbor. During this period the phrase 'cold war' began to emerge as the way to describe the new bipolar situation, the first recorded use being in a speech made to the South Carolina House of Representatives on 16 April 1947 by financier and presidential adviser Bernard Mannes Baruch – 'Let us not be deceived, we are today in the midst of a cold war'. The other phrase from this period, 'iron curtain', had already been popularised by Winston Churchill when he employed it during a speech given at Fulton, Missouri on 5 March 1946 – 'from Stettin on the Baltic to Trieste on the Adriatic, an iron curtain has descended across Europe'. In time both phrases were useful shorthand to describe the situation in Europe as the Soviets and their allies confronted the NATO alliance at the beginning of what had come to be known as the Cold War.

2

When Cold War Became Hot War

FOLLOWING THE RESOLUTION of the Berlin Blockade and despite the tensions in Europe caused by the creation of two power blocs, the confrontation in Germany never looked as if it would spill over into open land warfare of the kind fought on the continent in 1944 and 1945. Due to the development of nuclear weapons by both sides it soon became clear that any future conflict would be devastating and possibly even terminal, but maintaining the defence of West Germany was an expensive proposition. It cost the British taxpayer £80 million a year to run the British Zone centred on Hamburg and embracing Schleswig Holstein and Lower Saxony, a populous area of 22 million Germans administered by 16,000 British officials. In order to feed them adequately bread rationing had to be instituted in the UK for two years between 1946 and 1948. It was a highly unpopular policy that had been avoided during the war years, but it was considered a price worth paying if it kept the Soviet Union out of Western Europe and Communist influence to the east of the River Elbe.[1] How, then, to deal with the problem of Germany? That was the central question of the day and its solution would influence Britain's relationship with Europe for the rest of the century and beyond. Consider the predicament. In 1945 at the end of a bruising six years of warfare Europe began to take stock and to look ahead to an uncertain future. It was not an attractive prospect. The land mass had been devastated by conflict, heavy industries had been badly damaged, the infrastructure had received a hammering, entire populations were on the move and people were attempting to come to terms with the aftermath of the unimaginable iniquity of the Holocaust. More than anything else the people of Europe were determined that the ceasefire should not be accompanied by further civilian disasters or a renewal of hostilities; no one wanted that.

One possibility was to take steps to make sure that Germany, the war's main instigator, could never again be in a position to threaten the peace. When the victors met at Potsdam in the summer of 1945 to agree how to administer post-war Germany, the main Allies – Britain, France, the Soviet Union and the United States – agreed that Germany's armed forces should be abolished and that its heavy industries should be restricted to prevent the country becoming again the workshop of war. Given the tenor of the times, especially the uncovering of the Nazi death camps and the growing evidence of so much human misery, that made sense, but the Allied powers also remembered that the punitive peace terms of 1919 had led indirectly to the rise of the Nazis. Bearing that in mind it was agreed that German industry would be allowed to continue manufacturing but on a lighter scale and only to 'approved peacetime needs'.

Out of that desire to be pragmatic was born the concept that the raw materials of European heavy industry should be integrated to keep them under common control and to prevent them being used for bellicose purposes. Thus was born in 1951 the European Coal and Steel Community (ECSC), which embraced the main power groupings of Western Europe – France, Italy, West Germany and the Benelux countries (Belgium, the Netherlands and Luxembourg). Its architect was the French Foreign Minister Robert Schuman, who well deserved his appellation of the 'Father of Europe'. Born in Luxembourg in 1886, he was a reformer by instinct who had become active in French politics after the First World War; he was an avid European whose main aim in life was to bring about the creation of an 'organisation putting an end to war and guaranteeing an eternal peace'.[2]

It was an optimistic hope but the first result, the ECSC, was a real breakthrough. Coming at a time when there was heady talk of creating an integrated organisation to run European affairs – Britain's wartime prime minister, Winston Churchill, had already called for the creation of a 'kind of united states of Europe' – the first steps were being taken to put aside past differences and to work together in common cause. Out of this came the Council of Europe founded by the Treaty of London in May 1949 to promote human rights and the rule of law. Suddenly Europe seemed to have come a long way from endless confrontation and the years of continuous warfare followed by a succession of treaties which failed to resolve underlying problems and proved the cause of so much misery. Slowly but surely Europe would be locked

together by economic, financial and cultural bonds which would have
astonished earlier diplomatic architects such as Lord Castlereagh and
Prince Metternich, the creators of the post-Napoleonic peace settlement in 1815. Some visionaries even started talking about a common
defence policy and a single currency. Within eight years the signatories
to the ECSC treaty would sign the Treaty of Rome which brought the
European Economic Community into being but the UK would not be
amongst them, their position having been acutely delineated by the
French diplomat and political economist Jean Monnet, who had come
to the conclusion that the UK had no confidence in Europe's ability to
stand up to Soviet pressure: 'She [the UK] therefore does not wish to let
her domestic life or the development of her resources be influenced by
any views other than her own and certainly not by continental views. If
this, as I suspected, was really what the British felt in their heart of
hearts, we had no hope of convincing them for a long time to come.'[3]

The question of whether or not to throw in her lot with Europe or to
stand aloof was to dominate UK (and Scottish) politics into the following century, but in 1950 it was a question which had an especial
resonance as it also affected the relationship with the Commonwealth
and especially with the USA, which had been a solid ally during the
recent global conflict and had good reason to expect the UK's support
in international affairs. Both countries were beginning to discover that
confrontation with the Soviet Union would not take place only in
Europe; as the Cold War deepened the East and the West soon found
that there were other areas of the globe where their interests were at
odds as they strove for global domination. The collision came in the
early summer of 1950 in the Korean peninsula, which had been annexed
by Japan in 1910 and had remained a Japanese colony until 1945, when
the country had been split into two halves along the 38th Parallel, the
north becoming a Communist autocracy under President Kim Il-Sung
and the south a hastily organised democracy under the ageing dictator
Syngman Rhee, who enjoyed US support. Although the United Nations
entertained hopes that the two Koreas might be united in the future,
the two regimes were antagonistic towards each other and resented the
artificially created barrier which divided them. Any idea that they
might find an accommodation was shattered on 25 June 1950 when
North Korean troops attacked across the border and made easy gains
against the inexperienced and lightly armed South Korean divisions. In
making the assault Kim had the support of the Soviet Union, which

supplied armour, artillery and aircraft that had been transported surreptitiously into the country over the Trans-Siberian Railway through north-west China. Having seen Soviet interests blocked by NATO in Germany, Stalin clearly sought an alternative locus to embarrass the West and at the same time to extend his influence in the Far East, in this case as far as the Sea of Japan.

His plan quickly bore fruit. Shocked by the abruptness of the invasion and aware that American interests were being threatened, the US successfully persuaded the UN to respond – the argument in favour of armed intervention was helped by the absence of the Soviet Union from the Security Council in protest at the UN's refusal to recognise Communist China in favour of the Nationalist regime in the island of Formosa (Taiwan) under the leadership of Generalissimo Chiang Kai-shek. The US acted decisively: General Douglas MacArthur, commanding the US Army in the Far East and a Second World War veteran, was despatched from Japan to appraise the situation and by the end of July the US had four divisions in South Korea. Although the US forces had command of the air and the sea they were powerless to halt the North Korean attack and by the end of August the UN forces were desperately defending the Pusan perimeter, their last line of defence in the south-east of South Korea. Almost immediately Washington decided to request military assistance from those UN members who had backed their call for military intervention; seven responded, notably the UK, which was sorely placed to offer any large-scale help but was still anxious to honour its commitments to its wartime ally.

The initial British response came in the shape of the 27th Infantry Brigade from Hong Kong, which was not in a position to make anything other than a token contribution. By July 1951, the UK was able to create a Commonwealth Division under the command of Major-General James Cassels, a Seaforth Highlander who had ended the Second World War commanding the 51st Highland Division and whose most recent experience of command was with the 6th Airborne Division in Palestine. In its final form the Commonwealth Division consisted of three infantry brigades, 25th Canadian Brigade, 27th (later 28th) Commonwealth Brigade and 29th British Brigade. All told, four Scottish infantry battalions served in Korea at various stages of the war, although, as had been the case in previous conflicts, untold numbers of Scots served in other UK infantry regiments as well as in the Royal

Artillery, Royal Engineers and other support regiments. The Scottish line infantry regiments involved in the conflict were:

1st Argyll and Sutherland Highlanders, September 1950–March 1951
1st Black Watch, June 1952–July 1953
1st King's Own Scottish Borderers, June 1952–July 1953
1st Royal Scots, June 1953–July 1954

Some 66,000 British servicemen fought in Korea from all three armed forces and at least 10 per cent of them would have come from Scotland. Although they were smaller in number than the American contribution of around one million, their role was not without importance. Several RAF pilots flew on attachment with Commonwealth or American units, three squadrons of Short Sunderland flying-boats flew reconnaissance sorties from their bases in Japan, ships of the Royal Navy patrolled the Korean coastline to prevent infiltration and a carrier task force provided air cover for the battle ashore. The main contribution, though, was provided by the Army: in all, sixteen infantry battalions served in Korea, backed up by four armoured regiments and eight regiments of artillery with engineering, ordnance, transport and tactical support. A hurried process of rearmament allowed the Army to expand and as a result 2nd Black Watch was reinstated for the period 1951–6, during which time it served on peacekeeping duties in British Guiana (later Guyana). It was a hard, bruising war with high casualties: 71 officers and 616 other ranks were killed in action, 187 officers and 2,311 other ranks were wounded and 52 officers and 1,050 other ranks were listed as 'missing', of whom 40 officers and 996 other ranks were prisoners-of-war and eventually repatriated. By comparison, 33,000 US lives were lost and the total UN casualty list was 447,697 officers and men killed or wounded in action.

The first support for the US-led forces came in the shape of the weakened 27th Brigade under the command of Brigadier Basil Coad which was based in Hong Kong and consisted of two under-strength infantry battalions, each numbering some 650 men – 1st Middlesex Regiment and 1st Argyll and Sutherland Highlanders. (The personnel shortages were exacerbated by a government decision to ban those soldiers under 19 from serving in Korea.) Getting them there was a taxing business involving two warships, the light aircraft carrier HMS

Unicorn and the cruiser HMS *Ceylon*, and both battalions had been hurriedly reinforced with volunteers from other regiments but, according to the novelist Eric Linklater, who wrote the British official history of the campaign, what they lacked in numbers they made up for in enthusiasm and a reliance on age-old traditions.

> Neither the Middlesex nor the Argylls could muster more than three rifle companies and there was no military principle to justify the despatch of and committing to battle of two weak battalions that had neither their own necessary transport nor their proper supporting arms. It was the desperate plight of the Americans in the Pusan bridgehead that had compelled their sudden embarkation and as military principles were overridden by moral need so were the difficulties of their strange campaign to be overcome by recruitment, as it seemed, from the regimental spirit to which they were heirs. In the months to come both the Middlesex and the Argylls – though nearly half of them were youngsters doing their National Service – were to enhance the pride and reputation, not only of the Diehards and the 91st, but of all the Army.[4]

Such was the urgency of the situation that the Argylls were pitched more or less immediately into the fighting on arrival in Korea at the end of August when 27th Brigade took over responsibility for a 10-mile section of the UN line along the Naktong River south-west of Taegu. At the same time MacArthur was drawing up plans to break out of the perimeter and the offensive opened on 21 September with 27th Brigade on the left flank of the US line where they had been reinforced by the arrival of around 1,000 South Korean policemen and porters armed with a variety of small arms and grenades. However, the brigade had no supporting artillery or armour other than five tanks and two artillery batteries loaned by the US Army and as a later commentator, General Sir Anthony Farrar-Hockley, observed: 'if the NKPA [North Korean People's Army] had attacked this sector decisively the 27th Brigade would not have been able to hold its ground'.[5] Having served in Korea as adjutant of the 1st Gloucestershire Regiment Farrar-Hockley understood the problems facing Coad's force but fortunately the North Koreans were kept at bay by a series of air and artillery attacks.

Even so, the Argylls faced a challenging time when they went into the line: a range of hills to the north was their first objective and they had been given the task of capturing Hill 282 on the left end of the ridge. This was accomplished at dawn on 23 September, with B Company on the right and C Company on the left, but almost immediately the men came under sustained enemy fire and casualties started mounting. At 9 a.m. Major Kenneth Muir, the battalion second-in-command, arrived with stretcher-bearers and stayed on to organise the defences. With no artillery support the situation was in danger of becoming hopeless and the Argylls' commanding officer Lieutenant-Colonel Leslie Neilson requested an air strike on the neighbouring Hill 388, which the North Koreans occupied. This came in at 12.15 p.m but to the dismay of those watching the three US Air Force Mustang fighter-bombers attacked B and C Companies first with napalm bombs and then with machine-gun fire. Recognition panels had been displayed and the aircraft circled the target three times before attacking but still the US pilots pressed home their attack. Only five officers and 35 other ranks from the two companies made good their escape. It was not the end of the incident. Muir led a counter-attack to retake the burning hilltop and although it succeeded, the position could not be held as the Argylls lacked sufficient men and were rapidly running out of ammunition. Throughout the action Muir continued to encourage his men but he was mortally wounded while helping to man a 2-inch mortar. His last words were reported to be: 'The Gooks [North Koreans] will never drive the Argylls off this hill.'[6] For his courage Muir was posthumously awarded the Victoria Cross and the US Distinguished Service Cross. During the action the battalion lost 17 killed and missing and 79 wounded.

The incident was a grim reminder of the problems of forming a unified UN command from scratch; it was also indicative of the untested air–ground liaison during that early stage of the war. In the aftermath the battalion was hurriedly reinforced, many of the new arrivals being National Servicemen. The brigade was also reinforced with the arrival of 3rd Royal Australian Regiment from occupation duties in Japan and in its final form served as 27th Commonwealth Brigade. This was followed by a period of fine weather which allowed US strike aircraft to attack the North Korean positions to good effect and all along the line came reports of the North Koreans surrendering or fleeing north towards the 38th Parallel to fight again. On 27 September the capital, Seoul, was retaken following an audacious amphibious attack on the west-coast port of Inchon and the decision was taken to move UN forces into North Korea until such time as Kim agreed to surrender in advance of the two countries being reunited.

Following a breakout from the Pusan perimeter the UN forces pushed north towards Pyongyang, with 27th Brigade acting as the spearhead for the US 1st Cavalry Division. During this phase the enemy resistance started faltering under the weight and power of the UN advance but it soon became clear that the North Koreans were being reinforced by soldiers from the Chinese Army operating under the title 'Chinese People's Volunteers'. Following an action at the Chongchon River the Argylls started collecting its first evidence that the Chinese were involved in the war when they moved forward to inspect the enemy casualties. In his memoir of that period Colin Mitchell, a future commanding officer of the Argylls but then a young lieutenant, remembered the moment when the discovery was made: 'They were unlike any enemy I had seen before. They wore thick padded clothing which made them look like little Michelin men. I turned one body over with my foot, and saw that he wore a peaked cap with a red star badge. These soldiers were Chinese. I then turned another over and, as I looked down at him, he opened one eye and looked up at me. I shot him with my Luger [pistol], shouting to the platoon, 'they're alive!' It was quickly over and all the enemy lay dead.'[7]

The arrival of the Chinese at the end of October changed everything and once again the UN forces were forced to retire south across the 38th Parallel as the 'volunteers' entered the battle in force. Organised as the XII Army Group, the forces consisted of four armies, each with three infantry divisions, one cavalry regiment and five regiments of artillery, some 130,000 soldiers in all. They also travelled lightly and required little in the way of support: compared to the 60 lbs of supply per day required by the UN soldier his Chinese counterpart needed only 8–10 lbs per day, a significant difference in fast-moving operations.[8] At the same time the bitter winter weather made conditions extremely difficult and the battalion was not unhappy when it was relieved in March 1951 by 1st King's Own Scottish Borderers (KOSB) and shipped back to Hong Kong. It had been fortunate to escape a mauling from the Chinese during the retreat across the 38th Parallel, a disorderly withdrawal that had been accompanied by considerable panic – the Argylls won admiration for their élan, each rifle company being led by its piper – but they too were affected by hunger and exhaustion during the long march south. During the eight months of almost continual fighting in Korea the Argylls lost 35 killed and 136 wounded and a further 9 were killed and 45 wounded amongst those who stayed on to reinforce other regiments in the UN force. A year later 1st Argyll and Sutherland Highlanders returned to Britain, where it became the resident battalion in Edinburgh, responsible for carrying out public duties in the Scottish capital. During its tour of duty, on 26 June 1953, the regiment received new colours from the Colonel-in-Chief, Queen Elizabeth II, whose coronation had taken place three weeks earlier.

For the Argylls it had been bewildering experience which exposed shortcomings in their ability to conduct operations far from home – at one point Lieutenant Colin Mitchell had been forced to use a map torn from a newspaper to brief his men – and revealed to them their reliance on the US armed forces. A few officers had previous experience of fighting against the Japanese in Burma during the Second World War but nothing had prepared them for the conditions they faced in Korea. The British servicemen who saw action in Korea between 1950 and 1953 had to fight their way over a barren, remote and barely known peninsula which was almost as far away across the globe as it was possible for them to travel. Much of the fighting was reminiscent of the trench warfare which their grandfathers had encountered on the Western Front; the weather was usually awful, freezing cold in winter yet hot and wet in summer, and they faced an enemy who asked for, and offered, no quarter, especially the Chinese volunteers who attacked in 'human waves' and were frequently suicidal in their approach. The most common reaction of the men of the Commonwealth Division was bewilderment: bewilderment about the identity of their enemy and bewilderment that they should have been fighting the war in the first place. That feeling was summed up by Lance-Corporal Jim Laird of 1st Black Watch, a young National Serviceman from Glasgow when the battalion was deployed to Korea in the summer of 1952 to relieve 1st Royal Leicestershire Regiment in 29th Infantry Brigade.

I would say that we were totally ignorant of anything that was relevant to the war. I think possibly that at the time we were still thinking of it as a follow-on from the [Second World] War and that in a sense we were fighting for world peace. I think that was really caused by the fact that we were part of a United Nations force. Again, we felt there was a sort of togetherness against the Communist threat, although even from that point of view we were still very mystified about why someone we were fighting on the same side with during the war, an ally, was now an enemy. We were certainly very naïve . . . I don't think it was clear to us what was happening at the time. There was all this mystery about who we were fighting: was it the North Koreans or was it the Chinese? My initial reaction to the country was that it was a great place for a war.[9]

Most of the battalion's National Servicemen had only received 16 weeks' basic training at Fort George followed by a similar period in West Germany, and consequently they had to learn by experience. An article in the regimental magazine commented that two days in the Highland rain showed that the men still had 'a lot to learn about weather-proofing'.[10] When the battalion entered the line in July under the command of Lieutenant-Colonel David Rose, it still contained a number of officers and men who had served in the Second World War (including Rose) but, as Jim Laird remembered, for the rest of his fellow National Servicemen it was a question of falling back on the first tenets of basic training: 'There was no doubting that we were well disciplined. From Day One at Fort George we had been pressured and efficiently processed to run, stand still, jump, salute, obey without question – or take the consequences. We were brimming with an elite Scottish brand of esprit de corps, and this combination of elitism and pride was shown to be sufficient to allow us to be led onto the field of battle without any great doubts that we would stand and defend ourselves when required – without tarnishing the good record of the regiment. The battle training could be safely left to the hard school of bitter experience.'[11]

Laird and his fellow Black Watch soldiers would need all that resilience, and more, when they were involved in one of the most fiercely contested actions of the war, the Third Battle of the Hook, a key position in the UN defence line covering the Imjin valley and the road to Seoul. The fighting began on the night of 18 November 1952 with a series of probing attacks on Black Watch positions in front of the camel-backed hill known as the Hook. The battalion had already served there earlier in the year when the main problem had been torrential rain, but that was nothing compared to the artillery barrage and close-quarter fighting they faced in November. At one stage in the battle which was reckoned to be the most intense enemy attack of the war an advance standing patrol led by 2nd Lieutenant M. D. G. Black had been cut off and was reduced to hurling rocks and fighting off the Chinese with their fists, but this allowed a counter-attack and by dawn the attack had been beaten off. Throughout the fighting Black had shown a cheerfulness which was out of keeping with his and his men's parlous position. Asked by his company commander Major (later Brigadier) Angus Irwin if he was as happy as he sounded over the radio Black replied, 'No! Never have been.' For his courage under fire he was awarded the Military Cross. During the battle the battalion lost 16 soldiers killed, 76 wounded and 15 missing while the enemy's losses were put at over 100 before the task of counting the bodies became intolerable.

A second action was fought over the same ground in May 1953 while peace talks were taking place at Panmunjom to end the stalemate and one of the casualties was Jim Laird, wounded in an explosion which left him paralysed from the waist down. Only the presence of a nearby American Mobile Army Surgical Hospital (MASH) saved his life, 'being one of the few who were aware of the then new attitudes and methods in treating a spinal injury casualty'. Laird, who died in 2007, said that he could never be amused by the US television black comedy series *M*A*S*H* based on the exploits of a US field hospital in Korea as he owed his life to the work of one of their medical teams. Evacuated to Japan, Laird made a long and exhausting journey home by aircraft, arriving in the UK shortly before the coronation of Queen Elizabeth II to be treated at the Wheatley Military Hospital in Oxford and later at Stoke Mandeville, where he was given rehabilitation treatment in preparation for life in a wheelchair. Later he became a well-regarded potter and competitive international archer.

The rest of the battalion left Korea in July 1953, but that did not mean a return home. Instead they were sent to Kenya to take part in the operations against Mau Mau fighters engaged in a campaign of indiscriminate terror against the white population and the Kikuyu people who were largely loyal to the government. During the same period 1st KOSB had arrived in Korea under the command of Lieutenant-Colonel J. F. M. Macdonald to join 28th Commonwealth Infantry Brigade (previously 27th) with 3rd Royal Australian Regiment (Later 1st Royal Australian Regiment) and 1st King's Shropshire Light Infantry (KSLI). It was a time of uncertainty: a flurry of peace talks had suggested the possibility of a truce, but by autumn the political stalemate had again degenerated into armed hostility. That October 28th Commonwealth Infantry Brigade took up new positions beyond the Imjin, successfully dislodging the Chinese from the gaunt slopes of the hills known as Kowang-San and Maryang-San. The ridges formed an arrowhead piercing into the enemy lines and it was there, at the beginning of November, that the KSLI and KOSB faced some of the fiercest fighting of the war. Following a series of probing attacks the Chinese turned the full weight of their assault on the KOSB positions on the Maryang-San ridge. It was there that Private William Speakman, a Black Watch regular attached to the Borderers, won a Victoria Cross after leading one attack after the other on enemy groups on Hill 217.

Private Speakman, known as 'Big Bill', was the 'runner' with B Company in immediate reserve on the reverse slope of Hill 217 and therefore partly protected from the artillery fire. Just as a message came over the radio net that the forward positions were being over-run he was priming the last of some 200 hand grenades ready for throwing. Gathering together a group of six men he handed out the grenades before moving towards the ridge. 'Where the hell do you think you're going?' demanded his Company Sergeant-Major 'Busty' Murdoch. 'I'm going to shift some of them bloody Chinks [*sic*],' came Speakman's succinct if politically incorrect reply as he led his small group in a dash over the crest, at the same time launching a series of grenade charges against the enemy, who had seized the platoon's forward trenches. 'There was no time to pull back the bolt of the rifle,' he recalled. 'It was November, the ground was hard, so grenades bounced and did damage.' He continued this daring but effective tactic against each successive attempt by the Chinese to rush the crest but while leading his group Speakman was wounded in the leg by a mortar fragment. Even that failed to stop him. While his injuries were being tended a medical orderly was hit in the neck helping another wounded man. Angered by this, Speakman waited until the doctor's back was turned and then hobbled back up the hill for what he described as a few more 'dabbles' at the enemy. According to military folklore beer was to play an important part in what happened next but not, as was scurrilously suggested at the time, as an intoxicant. As Speakman's platoon had not used up their ration they were able to utilise the beer to cool the barrels of their weapons and then throw the empty bottles at the enemy. Speakman's conspicuous heroism and powers of leadership stiffened the resolve of B

Company, and against all the odds the Chinese assaults were beaten off
sufficiently to allow an orderly withdrawal from the ridge. The award
of the Victoria Cross was gazetted on 28 December, 1951, the citation
concluding, 'Private Speakman's heroism under intense fire throughout
the operation and when painfully wounded was beyond praise and is
deserving of supreme recognition.' He was the first private soldier to be
awarded Britain's highest award for valour since the end of the Second
World War and the first recipient to receive the award from the new
queen. After the Korean War he remained in the KOSB and served for
a time with the SAS regiment, reaching the rank of Sergeant. 'Big Bill'
Speakman died on 20 June 2018, aged 90.[12]

To the right of the ridge the KOSB positions were held on a feature
called the Knoll by two platoons from C and D Companies which had
come under the command of 2nd Lieutenant William Purves following the wounding of the senior subaltern. Formerly a bank clerk from
Kelso in the Scottish Borders, Purves was a National Service officer
with a reputation for being quiet and retiring, but his effective
defence of the Knoll allowed his men to retire in good order in the
early hours of the morning on 4 November. According to the regimental magazine every wounded man from the two platoons was
withdrawn from the ridge, and despite his own wound, Purves personally oversaw the dangerous operation until all his men had been
shepherded safely off the hill.

> The position on the Knoll held by 2nd Lieutenant Purves's platoon
> of C Company and 2nd Lieutenant Henderson's of D Company
> was obscure owing to communications being destroyed. However,
> at about midnight it was established that this gallant party was still
> holding out though running short of ammunition, that and
> Lieutenant Henderson being wounded, 2nd Lieutenant Purves
> had assumed command of the two platoons. Surrounded on three
> sides, the plight of this party was serious. 2nd Lieutenant Purves
> was ordered to try and fight his way out towards D Company who
> were now holding out on 'Peak', a foothill of Point 317. This
> unpleasant operation was brilliantly carried out under the very
> nose of the enemy on Point 317. This exploit was rendered even
> more remarkable in that 2nd Lieutenant Purves succeeded in
> evacuating all the wounded and the complete equipment of his
> platoon under heavy mortar fire.[13]

For his conspicuous gallantry and devotion to duty 2nd Lieutenant Purves was awarded the DSO, a unique and never-to-be-repeated achievement for a National Service officer. (Later, on completion of his service obligations, he returned to civilian life and became a distinguished banker, crowning his career with a knighthood as chairman of the Hong Kong and Shanghai Banking Corporation.)

The bravery shown by men like Speakman and Purves – and by the entire battalion – allowed 1st KOSB to complete a successful evacuation from the ridge at a low cost in lives. Seven Borderers had been killed and 87 wounded, but after the battle it was estimated that the Chinese 'human wave' tactics had led to the opposition sustaining around 1,000 casualties. The KOSB Mortar Battery fired a total of 4,500 rounds during the night-long engagement. Both the KSLI and the KOSB spent another eight months in Korea, fighting through a winter which saw the war along the 38th Parallel degenerate into a struggle of static defence punctuated by frequent attack which was reminiscent of the Western Front battles during the First World War. From this period onwards the domination of No Man's Land became the crucial test of the war as the stationary armies probed each other's defences. Hardly a night passed without infantry patrols infiltrating the Chinese lines, testing the enemy's strength, collecting intelligence information and attempting the challenging task of capturing Chinese prisoners for interrogation. (This latter duty reaped few rewards as most Chinese and North Koreans managed to commit suicide before – and in some cases, even after – being captured.) Most of the patrols were led by young subalterns, many of them National Servicemen.

The fighting on the Maryang-San ridge was also prolonged by the North Koreans and their Chinese allies as a means of winning ground for the armistice which was clearly in view as 1952 came to an end. Peace talks had been held intermittently throughout the war and the British had pushed unsuccessfully for an exchange of prisoners, but the initiatives faltered on the need of both sides to retain face and get the best possible deal while not giving ground in the field. The death of Stalin in March 1953 gave fresh impetus to the possibility of brokering a peace deal, for by then China, the chief financier of the war, had grown weary of the fighting and wanted a deal which would give them some advantages. The US, too, wanted an escape route and its new leader, President Dwight D. Eisenhower, had come to power with plans to withdraw his country from the fighting. This outcome also suited the UK, which had been ill-placed to mount a campaign in the first place but as General Farrar-Hockley pointed out, 'it sent forces without obligation, acting on the principle with others that aggression would not be tolerated by one state against another'.[14] With a certain degree of inevitability, a ceasefire came into being on 27 July 1953 but the war never came to final full stop and enmity between North Korea and South Korea endured into the twenty-first century along the demilitarised zone which marked the border between the two very different countries. South Korea became a modern developed and democratic state, while North Korea remained a hidden and increasingly bankrupt Communist autocracy. All attempts at the reunion which had been one of the UN's war aims foundered in the face of Korean obduracy and Chinese support for Kim.

One of the main stumbling blocks in finding common ground for agreeing a ceasefire and creating an armistice was the release of prisoners taken captive during the conflict. By far the biggest number of service personnel lost to captivity were South Koreans, while 7,140 Americans fell into enemy hands, of whom, 2,701 died in captivity. The comparable figure for British and Commonwealth soldiers was 1,188 officers and men, of whom an estimated 82 died in captivity.[15] In April 1953 both sides agreed to a limited exchange of sick and wounded prisoners of war (Operation Little Switch) and it was also agreed that those who did not want to be repatriated could refuse to return to their home countries. This had an obvious attraction to the 22,000 Chinese volunteers in UN captivity, many of whom had fought earlier for the Nationalist cause and feared for their safety on being returned to their homeland, but most of the 75,823 Communist fighters, mainly North Koreans, were repatriated in the summer of 1953. During the same process 12,773 UN soldiers (7,862 South Koreans, 3,597 Americans and 946 British) were sent back south across the armistice line and to freedom, but a small handful decided to remain with their captors and ended up in China. These included 327 South Koreans, 23 Americans and a British Marine – Andrew Condron from Bathgate in West Lothian, who chose not to be repatriated and spent the immediate post-war years in China.

The treatment meted out to the UN prisoners of war excited a good deal of comment in the West and attempts to persuade the Chinese and North Koreans to abide by the terms of the Geneva Conventions generally fell on deaf ears. Neither side expected to take prisoners on any great scale and one of the features of the experience was the systematic attempts by the Chinese to convert their UN prisoners to Communist ideology. This led to allegations of 'brainwashing' and there is no doubt that in the Chinese camps along the River Yalu Chinese guards did their utmost to persuade UN prisoners that they had nothing to lose and everything to gain by switching their allegiance and embracing Communism. On occasions this kind of indoctrination was tolerably well-organised and humane, if repetitive and mind-numbingly boring, but all too often it descended into crude violence and brutal physical coercion. To make matters worse, the Chinese approach was always unpredictable and the sudden changes from leniency to viciousness could add to the bewilderment felt by the UN prisoners. The North Korean approach was uniformly barbaric, while it has to be said that the UN forces, especially the US elements, did not use kid gloves and there were instances of North Korean and Chinese prisoners being killed when it was inconvenient to keep them alive. Perhaps the best evidence is provided by the ratio of prisoners' exchanges: far more Chinese and North Koreans opted to stay with their captors rather than return to their homelands, and of the handful of Westerners who decided to stay, most had drifted back by the later 1960s having found that life in Communist China was not for them.

Amongst them was Marine Andrew Condron, who had been taken prisoner during the fighting at the Chosin reservoir in November 1950 and when interviewed later found it relatively easy to change a certain pre-war bolshiness into a respect and admiration for Marxism: 'I had lost my Catholic faith even before I went into the Marines. Perhaps I needed something to latch onto.'[16] As the sole British soldier to take that course of action Condron was excoriated in certain quarters of the military but he attracted little opprobrium from fellow prisoners later in life and attended Royal Marine reunions. In China he went to university, worked as a translator and married Jaquelin Hsiung-Baudet, a Franco-Chinese diplomat's daughter. In 1962 having become disenchanted with the country in the xenophobic atmosphere that sprang up in the heyday of Mao Tse-Tung's regime he returned with his wife to the UK. Condron was not interrogated or prosecuted by the naval authorities even though he had been posted as a deserter.[17] He died in 1996.

The treatment meted out to Western prisoners-of-war spawned one of the most successful novels of the Korean War, *The Manchurian Candidate* (1959) by Roger Condon, which was made into an equally celebrated Hollywood movie starring Frank Sinatra and Laurence Harvey. Its title soon entered everyday speech as shorthand for a brainwashed sleeper, a subject who has been hypnotised and instructed to act when his controllers pull the psychological trigger. (During the 2008 presidential campaign the claim was made against Barack Obama and earlier, in 1962, it was believed that Lee Harvey Oswald, John F. Kennedy's assassin, was also a sleeper.) That such programming is impossible has not prevented it from being absorbed as the truth, but the facts are equally strange and perverse. Of the 10,000 UN soldiers taken prisoner it has been estimated that one in seven offered 'serious collaboration' or were subjected to what became known as 'brain-washing'. One of these was the notorious British double agent George Blake, a Dutch-born diplomat captured by the North Koreans in Seoul in 1950 who was later accused of spying for the Soviet Union and was sentenced to 42 years before escaping in 1966 and living out his life in Moscow.

In the dying days of the war and in the uneasy peace which followed the armistice the last British units arrived in the country to relieve those which were ready to go home and to provide the UN with a continuing military presence at a time when hostilities could have recommenced along the 38th Parallel. Amongst them was 1st Royal Scots, which arrived in June and went into reserve positions near the Imjin River, scene of some of the fiercest fighting earlier in the war. With the nearest enemy positions under two miles away the men began a period of intensive training including live firing with 60 mm mortars and American Browning machine-guns. The battalion's other main activities included the construction of defences but to their consternation no sooner had they arrived than a truce came into effect and the war was effectively over. Ahead lay a year's further service in the country undertaking internal security duties and other necessary administrative tasks. It could have been a boring ordeal but as the commanding officer, Lieutenant-Colonel Mike Melvill remembered later there was 'the curious satisfaction of having to do everything for oneself, the amount of work and time involved, and the amazing versatility shown by the modern young soldier when put to the test.'[18] The deployment ended in July 1954 when the battalion made its way by sea to the Suez Canal Zone with stops at Hong Kong, Singapore, Colombo and Aden.

The conflict in Korea was not the only 'hot' war during the Cold War but it was the one which brought both sides closest to a more direct and more dangerous kind of confrontation. During the difficult first winter of the war when the full extent of the Chinese intervention was being felt, the Americans gave serious thought to using atomic bombs, so much so that in an appraisal of the strategic situation on 24 December 1950 MacArthur submitted a request for 26 such weapons to be made available for use against enemy forces in North Korea, especially air bases, as well as obvious industrial targets. In the summer of 1951 the US Air Force ran a number of tests simulating B-29 bombers flying against North Korean targets equipped with either dummy atomic bombs or heavy conventional weapons. As casualties continued to grow US public opinion was also increasingly in favour of using atomic bombs to protect ground forces and prevent further casualties but the UK government was opposed to any widening of the conflict if it involved the deployment of nuclear weapons. Equally damaging to British interests would have been the introduction of a 'limited war' against China as that would have had damaging repercussions across the Far East. In December 1950 Attlee visited Washington to discuss the situation and while it is doubtful if the atomic bomb was the sole item on the agenda, it is generally agreed that he forged a good working relationship with President Truman. It would be easy, though inaccurate, to claim that his influence restrained the Americans from using atomic bombs in Korea or even against China, but the British tendency to aggrandise the UK's position in the post-war world does not negate the contribution made by the UK at a time when it could ill afford to fight what became a major conflict. There is little doubt that the war effort did place a strain on an already shaky economy, but it is also true to say that the fear of further Cold War confrontation in Europe also encouraged successive Labour and Conservative governments to increase defence expenditure to replace the largely Second World War weapons which had equipped the British forces in Korea. It also strengthened the trans-Atlantic nexus with the USA and created a belief in Washington that, far from being washed up as a global player, the UK was still a partner from whom much could be expected whether the test took place along the River Imjin on the Korean peninsula or guarding the River Elbe in West Germany.

Besides, the Korean War was not the last occasion when the world teetered on the verge of a Third World War: there were several other occasions when conflicts in other parts of the world created conditions which brought the West into confrontation with Communism. Indeed, for the soldiers in the British Army in the Cold War period, 1968 is often cited as the one year – the so-called 'year of peace' – when they were not on active service.[19] In addition to the full-scale military operations in Korea (1950–3), Suez (1956) and the Falklands (1982), which is discussed in Chapter Seven, there were several lesser conflicts, generally classified as 'low-intensity operations' in which the aggressors were usually engaged in an armed insurgency against the state and the Army was called in to provide aid to the civil power. Most of these confrontations occurred as the UK shed its colonial Empire, and depending on one's viewpoint the aggressors were characterised either as 'terrorists' or as 'freedom fighters', but at the same time they were also shaped by the wider events of the Cold War and in some cases were used as proxy conflicts in which opposing sides were backed by the great powers.

Although the war in Korea was conducted under the auspices of the UN and the contributing British forces were drawn from across the UK there was a strong Scottish element, with the presence of four Scottish infantry battalions and the award of two Victoria Crosses to Scottish soldiers. At the time, it was not particularly unpopular and most sections of the UK press supported the UN initiative and believed that failure to do anything would encourage an escalation in global Communist aggression or, as a leader in *The Times* put it, 'separately and together, the free countries have to ask how far the defences they have set down on paper exist in fact'.[20] Such was the interest in the war in its initial stages that by the end of the first year around 270 correspondents from 19 different countries had arrived in South Korea to report on the UN campaign. Amongst them was James Cameron of the *Picture Post* and his photographer Bert Hardy, who had worked in Glasgow in 1948 producing his well-known 'Gorbals Boys' images of young boys living in what was considered to be one of Europe's most deprived areas. They arrived in time to report MacArthur's breakout from Pusan and went on to record the main events of the first winter of the war. Together they made a formidable team. Born of Scottish parentage in 1911 – his grandfather had been a Highland divine – Cameron had started training in journalism as a teenager in Dundee working on the *Red Star Weekly* before moving to the *Daily Express* in 1939. By his own admission he was a subjective reporter who believed that journalists had to be fully engaged to do their job properly. This was not the writer as propagandist; rather, he felt that it was the writer's duty to present their argument and counter-argument as vigorously as possible and then to make sure that their point of view was paramount.

All that commitment was to be put to the test in Korea during the late summer of 1950 following the US landings at Inchon, when Cameron came across incontrovertible evidence that the South Koreans were indulging in atrocities against their own people and that the authorities knew what was happening but were taking no action. The main thrust of Cameron's story was that atrocities of the kind he had witnessed should never have been committed in the name of the UN and that the behaviour of the Rhee regime was a corruption of its values: 'They [the prisoners] are South Koreans whose crime – or alleged crime, since they have not yet had the formality of a trial – is that they are possible opponents of the Synghman Rhee regime. They have for a variety of reasons, and by a variety of people, been denounced or accused – not necessarily convicted – of being politically unreliable, "politically Communist". They have been in jail now for indeterminate periods – long enough, we can say, for lack of information, to have reduced their frames to skeletons, their sinews to strings, their faces to a translucent, terrible grey, their spirits to that of cringing dogs.'[21]

Accompanied by Hardy's photographs, the result was what Cameron called 'a journalistic essay of elaborate moderation', but because it seemed to criticise the UN, *Picture Post*'s owner Edward Hulton refused to have it published and the editor, Tom Hopkinson, was sacked. It was a futile move as a proof of the article was passed to the Communist *Daily Worker* which immediately published it. After resigning and then being reinstated due to staff pressure from his colleagues Cameron quit his job the following year and forged a new career with the liberal *News Chronicle* but his stand caused a sensation at the time and helped to make him one of the best-known journalists of his generation. He later commented that Korea was the prep school for Vietnam and he added to his reputation in 1965 by making a fine documentary about that war called 'Western Eyewitness', which was remarkable for being shot partly in Hanoi. Cameron remained an ardent liberal and anti-imperialist, and was an early member of the Campaign for Nuclear Disarmament. Although he later lived and worked in London, according to his friend the Labour politician Michael Foot, 'his Scottish roots always remained unshaken' right up to his death in January 1985. In time he would despair of the UN's aims and objectives in Korea, which came to be remembered, if at all, as the 'forgotten war'. So it was for many years, but it was not altogether forgotten in Cameron's native country. In 2000, 50 years after the war began, a memorial to those who died in Korea was created by the Lothians and West of Scotland branch of the British Korean Veterans Association as a tribute to the memory of their fallen comrades. Situated at Witchcraig Wood near Linlithgow in West Lothian it consists of an arboretum of 1,114 native Scottish trees, one for every British soldier who died, and a shrine surrounded by two mounds in the shape of the Yin and Yang on the Korean flag. Thirteen years later the shrine was enhanced by the addition of a traditional Korean pagoda containing name boards which list all the British casualties. It is a fitting memorial to a conflict which was certainly heated but never plunged humankind into a third world war.

3

The Yanks Are Coming

FOR ALL THAT the Korean War had been a dangerous flashpoint in which hot words were spoken by both sides, especially during the hard first winter of the war, it never escalated into a nuclear shooting match. It was not as if the weapons were not available. The US had first used atomic bombs against Hiroshima and Nagasaki in August 1945, and by the end of 1948 had an arsenal of 50 similar weapons plus a reliable delivery system in the B-29 Superfortress bomber. The Soviets had tested their first atomic bomb in August 1949 and although the British were not to follow suit until three years later, when they exploded a similar atomic weapon at Monte Bello Islands off the north-western coast of Australia, the UK had been party to the US development of such weapons during the Second World War. This development gave the wartime allies a certain amount of parity – France joined the club in 1960 when it tested a nuclear weapon in the Sahara – but from the outset there were problems with the US–UK partnership. Following the attacks on the two Japanese cities the US began to regard the atomic bomb as its exclusive property and in 1946 legislation was passed restricting access to US nuclear technology – the McMahon Act introduced by Senator Brien McMahon, chairman of the Atomic Energy Commission. As a result of this move, Attlee decided Britain 'had to go ahead on [its] own' and develop its own weapon. At the same time plans were put in place for the development of a new long-range bomber fleet, later known as the 'V-bomber force', to carry the bombs to their targets in the Soviet Union. This strategic objective arose as a result of the Berlin Blockade, which had led the UK to feel that the Soviet Union was the next potential threat. In a private conversation with the US ambassador to London, Lewis Douglas, Churchill, by then in opposition, told him it was his opinion that the only way to make the Soviets see sense over the Blockade was to 'raze their cities'.[1]

The V bombers were the Vickers Valiant, the Handley Page Victor and the Avro Vulcan, which were all originally intended for high-altitude subsonic bombing. The Air Ministry specification required a jet bomber with a range of 3,350 nautical miles, a maximum speed of 500 knots and an over-the-target capability of 50,000 feet. The bombload would be a 20,000-lb capacity and there would be a crew of five. The Valiant was the first to come into service, in 1956, and the last, the Victor, retired in 1993 – a total of 37 years' operational service. A Valiant B1 (WZ366) of 49 Squadron was the first RAF aircraft to drop an operational British atomic bomb when it performed a test drop of a Blue Danube weapon at Maralinga in South Australia on 11 October 1956. A fourth jet-powered strategic bomber, the Short Sperrin, did not get beyond the prototype stage.

It was against that background that the US Air Force deployed its 3rd Air Division to East Anglia in the summer of 1948, basing three groups of B-29s (six squadrons) at RAF Marham, RAF Scampton and RAF Waddington. The arrival of these large and powerful aircraft sent an unmistakable message to the Soviet Union that the US meant business. Not only were the B-29s nuclear-capable, or would be by the end of 1950, but they were within range of Moscow and were highly visible symbols of Western resolve. They were soon joined by the improved B-50, which had a longer range and greater carrying capacity. Initially, the reason for their presence was described as 'operational training' for a 30-day period but this was soon doubled and further bomber groups arrived on a rotation basis. Later, during the initial stages of the Korean War in 1950, the British government allocated four other bases to the US Air Force – RAF Brize Norton, RAF Fairford, RAF Greenham Common and RAF Upper Heyford – leaving them only nominally under RAF control. In all cases the US commander was of a higher rank, leaving the RAF representative as 'little more than a local liaison officer' with no say over operational decisions.[2] While the deployment was effective in giving the US a forward operating base from which its strategic bombers could attack Soviet targets, it was an extraordinary arrangement, based as it was on a 'gentleman's agreement' which had been brokered by Air Chief Marshal Lord Tedder, Chief of the Air Staff, and General Carl Spaatz, head of the US Air Force. In its preliminary stages it seemed to give the US permission to base nuclear weapons in the UK without the British government having any right of veto over their use and in so doing putting the country in harm's way by making it a target for retaliatory raids. Although it was made clear that the deployment was not permanent and had only come about as a result of the Berlin crisis, that was a mere fig leaf. For good or for ill, the arrival of the B-29s in the summer of 1948 presaged a permanent US nuclear presence in British territory and it was not until January 1952 that President Truman conceded that there was no question of these bases being used for offensive purposes without British consent. The official communiqué from the meeting reads 'the use of these bases in an emergency would be a joint decision by His Majesty's Government and the United States Government in the light of circumstances prevailing at the time', but it was a significant turning point in the relationship between the US and the UK when the Cold War began in earnest in Europe. As historian Peter Hennessy has noted, the arrival of the B-29s paved the way for the deployment of future US nuclear delivery systems 'on English runways and Scottish sea lochs'.[3]

At the time, though, Scotland was left relatively undisturbed by this US 'invasion'. Later the country would become the epicentre for the deployment of American nuclear weapons in the UK when the preferred delivery systems changed to missiles fired by strategic submarines, but in the early 1950s the main US interest in Scotland was SIGINT, or signals intelligence, the garnering of information obtained by intercepting foreign communications transmitted by radio, wire or any other electromagnetic media. In pursuit of that aim, in May 1952 the US Air Force established its 37th Radio Squadron (Mobile), later 6952nd Security Group, at Kirknewton in West Lothian, a few miles to the south-west of Edinburgh and a former wartime RAF base. Soon its 35 acres were festooned with a variety of antennae capable of monitoring high frequency (HF) radio messages from all directions, while simultaneously obtaining bearings that could enable the position of a transmitter to be located. Until its closure in August 1966, when the facility moved to Menwith Hill near Harrogate in Yorkshire, Kirknewton housed around 400 US personnel, and one of its responsibilities was the maintenance of the 'hot line' which provided a secure teletype communications link between Washington and Moscow to lessen the threat of an accidental nuclear war. This top-secret line was established in 1963 and ran under the Atlantic from Washington to Oban. From there it proceeded through Kirknewton towards Moscow by way of Denmark, Sweden and Finland.

Amongst the US service personnel was a young man from Louisiana called Jim Haynes, who arrived at Kirknewton in 1956 having requested a posting to 'the smallest possible military base, near a major city and university'. Haynes fell in love with Edinburgh, signed up for a course at the university and quickly immersed himself in the city's cultural and social life, becoming a great enabler and one of the founding parents of the avant-garde Traverse Theatre, which opened in January 1963. While in the US Air Force Haynes described his work as intercepting and analysing international radio links between all the major European cities and passing the results to the headquarters of the National Security Agency (NSA) at Fort Meade in Maryland.

In the early 1950s the US Air Force consolidated its position in the UK, taking possession of 43 air bases plus several support and satellite fields through a new agreement brokered in April 1950 by US Ambassador Douglas and Aidan Crawley, UK Under-Secretary for Air.[4] An administrative headquarters was established at High Wycombe in Buckinghamshire and personnel gradually increased to 45,000 plus dependants. At the same time the first atomic bombs began to arrive in the UK and by 1953 the piston-engined B-29s and B-50s were gradually being replaced by modern jet-powered Boeing B-47 Stratojet strategic bombers which brought Strategic Air Command (SAC) into the jet age following a brief interlude with the massive B-36 Convair 'Peacemaker', which was powered by four jet and six piston engines and had a wingspan of 230 feet. So big and ungainly was the aircraft that it did not inspire much affection amongst those who flew it – one pilot compared his job to sitting on his front porch and 'flying his house around' – but it was grimly effective. To give some idea of this aircraft's power, the B-36 could carry the massive Mark 17 atomic bomb, which was 21.5 feet long and weighed 21 tonnes. But by the mid-1950s it had become easy prey for the new generation of Soviet air defence fighters such as the supersonic MiG-19. By the end of the decade the B-36 had been retired and the B-47 was becoming obsolete; both were gradually superseded by the Boeing B-52 strategic bomber equipped with eight jet engines and with a combat radius of up to 4,500 miles, some examples of which, the H model, survived into the twenty-first century and were still flying in 2018.

The introduction of this giant bomber in 1961 was revolutionary, in that it allowed the US Air Force to maintain a constant presence of 12 B-52s which would be airborne 24 hours a day, 365 days a year, and would be refuelled as needed during their patrols which took them northwards across the North American continent or eastwards across the Atlantic and over the Mediterranean to loiter at points close to the border with the Soviet Union. Code-named Chrome Dome, each aircraft was armed with up to four thermonuclear bombs with pre-assigned targets, and they were reinforced by other aircraft on constant standby, needing only a 15-minute warning to be scrambled and airborne. In addition, the bombers were backed by 182 Titan inter-continental ballistic missiles (ICBMs), which were fully primed and ready for firing in the event of any Soviet attack, not least the dreaded 'first strike', which successive US administrations feared throughout the 1960s. It was not until the Palomares Incident in January 1966, when a B-52 carrying four hydrogen bombs exploded over Spain, drop-ping its weapons (fortunately they were not armed), that the continuous airborne patrols were ended, and new over-the-horizon radar systems took over the task of providing the US with a safeguard to any feared Soviet surprise attack. Alerted to the American superiority in missiles and aircraft the Soviet Union responded by developing its first anti-ballistic missile shield (ABM), which could destroy ICBMs in flight, thereby abnegating the advantage held by the USA, although it has to be said that this early Soviet system was primitive and unreliable.

At the beginning of the Cold War the Soviet Union did not possess any modern strategic bombers other than the reverse-engineered Tupolev-4, which was a direct copy of the US Boeing-29 and was nuclear-capable, but it soon became clear that they would have to develop longer-range strategic bombers capable of attacking targets in the USA. The result was the development of two aircraft which seemed to fit that purpose. The first was jet-powered but short-ranged – the Myasishchev M-4 Bison – but it played an important role in Cold War history by originating the so-called 'bomber gap' which led the Americans to believe that the Soviets had an unassailable lead in the construction of strategic bombers. This was the result of an infamous event in July 1955, witnessed by American agents at the Soviet Aviation Day demonstrations at the Tushino Airfield outside Moscow, when ten Bison bombers were flown past the reviewing stand, flew out of sight, quickly turned around, and then flew past the stands again with eight more. That presented the illusion that there were 28 aircraft in the flyby. Western analysts, extrapolating from the illusionary 28 aircraft, judged that by 1960, the Soviets would have 800. In fact only 93 Bisons were ever built before production ceased in 1963. The other widely recognised bomber from this period was the Tupolev Tu-16 Badger, which was built in many variants and was both jet-powered and nuclear-capable, but if any aircraft personified Soviet air power during the Cold War it was the giant Tupolev-95 'Bear' long-range strategic bomber, which came into service in 1956 and became a familiar visitor in Scottish airspace. With its swept wings and four enormous turbo-prop engines powering eight sets of propellers, it had a top speed of over 500 mph and was originally planned to drop freefall nuclear bombs before being converted to carry long-range cruise missiles. In its maritime reconnaissance role, it is still in service in the twenty-first century and enjoys the same longevity and iconic presence as the US Boeing B-52.

During this period of expansion, which saw SAC increase the number of its UK-based personnel to 11,000 in 1955, Scotland was not considered as a possible site for US strategic bombers although in the next decade they were to be regular visitors at Scottish RAF bases under NATO agreements. Between 1960 and 1962 an existing wartime Fleet Air Arm base at Machrihanish on the Mull of Kintyre was length-ened and its infrastructure enhanced, but no aircraft were stationed there on a permanent basis and it later became a NATO facility for the storage of nuclear depth bombs. (The base was regularly used by RAF Vulcan bombers and by US Navy P-3 Orion anti-submarine warfare (ASW) patrol aircraft which carried nuclear ASW weapons.) This did not mean that there was no regular US air presence in Scotland. On the contrary, at Prestwick in Ayrshire the US Military Air Transport Service, later Military Airlift Command (MAC), opened a staging facility with the deployment of 1631st Air Base Squadron together, with a courier station for storing and handling sensitive documents in transit following in 1963. These units made use of a former RAF wartime facility and Prestwick became a key staging post for US aircraft travel-ling across the Atlantic to and from Europe, as well as supplying a base for the 67th Air Rescue Squadron equipped with the Douglas SC54D Rescuemaster aircraft, which provided air–sea rescue cover for the eastern Atlantic area. It was based on the air-frame of the successful Douglas C-54 Skymaster military transport aircraft. On 3 March 1960 Prestwick received attention of a different kind when the singer Elvis Presley made his only visit to the UK while flying back to the USA to demob after completing his military service in West Germany. The

DC-7 aircraft was flying from Frankfurt-am-Rhein to the McGuire Air Force Base in New Jersey when it stopped at Prestwick to refuel. News quickly leaked out that Elvis was on board and hundreds of fans turned up at the airport to catch a glimpse of him. Although he asked, 'Where am I?' he obliged his fans by being photographed and signing autographs and the visit is commemorated by a plaque in the present terminal building.[5] Also included in the US list of British bases was the RAF airfield at Stornoway, which had been used for transit purposes during the Second World War and by June 1943 had a presence of around 100 US Air Force personnel.

All the while the Cold War was becoming more serious as the two sides became more polarised. Partly in response to the decision to permit the recently formed state of West Germany to join NATO on 14 May 1955, the Soviet Union created the Warsaw Pact of Friendship, Cooperation and Mutual Assistance; consisting of Albania, Bulgaria, Czechoslovakia, East Germany, Hungary, Poland and Romania, it was ostensibly a defensive alliance, although in the opinion of a Scottish infantry officer at the time, for those on the other side 'it was considered a threat by all levels on both the military and political establishment, and not just those with access to considerable intelligence reports'.[6] Albania withdrew from the Warsaw Pact (as it was better known) in 1968, but for the next four decades the Eastern Bloc of Soviet-led nations and NATO were in a state of constant confrontation which could easily have degenerated into open warfare. So serious was this threat that the British Joint Intelligence Committee revised its thinking about the possibility of another global conflict breaking out by bringing forward the possible date from 1957 to 1953 'when American and West German rearmament cannot yet have become fully effective and by which time the Soviet Union will have in part made good some of its major deficiencies and will have accumulated a stock of atomic bombs'.[7] Partly this readjustment had been made because of the recent Berlin crisis, but mainly it was due to a fear that had grown during the Korean War that the Soviet Union might have used US/UK involvement in the Far East to destabilise Western Europe and make a pre-emptive strike using their newly developed atomic bombs.

It was this fear that led the British government to pursue the development of a British atomic bomb and the associated delivery systems, not just the V-bomber force but also the Blue Streak strategic ballistic missile, which was given the go-ahead in 1954 with a budget of £50

million. Developed by De Havilland and due to come into service in
1965, when it would replace the V-bomber fleet, Blue Streak would
have been fired from underground reinforced silos and one of its first
operational bases would have been the old Royal Naval Air Station at
Crail in Fife which had been used for torpedo training during the
Second World War and was built on land suitable for the construction
of silos.[8] Delays and escalating costs – the programme had reached
£300 million by the end of the decade – led to the cancellation of Blue
Streak in 1960. As a result Crail was never developed as an operational
base but it still had a Cold War role when in 1956 it became home to the
Joint Services School for Linguists (JSSL), which had been founded
five years earlier to provide the armed forces with a cadre of bright
young men, many of them conscripts undergoing National Service,
who were given intensive training in Russian, prompted by the need to
provide greater numbers of interpreters, intelligence and signals intelligence officers in all three services. Earlier JSSL sites had been situated
at Bodmin in Cornwall, and Coulsdon Common near Croydon. The
Crail facility remained in being until its closure in 1960.[9] Its principal
task was to train suitable recruits to 'A' level standard in Russian, a task
which took nine months; thereafter those with the best marks and apti-
tude were posted to further intensive courses at the School of Slavonic
and East European Studies at the University of London (Royal Navy)
or the Department of Russian at Cambridge University (RAF). The
rest would be posted to the Intelligence Corps or to intelligence work in
the Royal Navy or RAF, where they were engaged in basic translating
duties relevant to British intelligence such as listening in to Soviet radio
traffic from bases in West Germany and recording the findings. The
exact number of recruits has not survived but it is thought to have been
around 4,200 over a nine-year period. Notable alumni of JSSL include
the former governor of the Bank of England Eddie George, playwright
and novelist Michael Frayn, actor and writer Alan Bennett, dramatist
Dennis Potter and former director of the Royal National Theatre Sir
Peter Hall. The Soviet spy Geoffrey Prime (arrested and imprisoned in
1982) was also a graduate of JSSL at Crail while serving as an RAF
National Serviceman.[10]

Learning Russian in such a short time, and in some cases perfecting
it to degree standard, was a prodigious feat and one which never failed
to draw the admiration of the civilian teaching staff. 'They had to work
hard at their Russian and it must have seemed a real grind,' recalled

Professor G. H. Bolsover, who had charge of one of the courses at London University. 'But they were always conscious of the progress they were making. They knew they were doing something which was worthwhile. Very few of them failed to pull their weight or had to be sent off the course and this in itself was a good indication that the great majority considered the exercise to be worth the effort they were required to put into it.'[11] In addition to the intelligence material accrued at the time there was another unexpected benefit. After years of being considered a specialist, even unlearnable, language, Russian emerged in the 1960s as one of the growth areas in British education. As a result of their training at JSSL centres such as Crail many former National Servicemen returned to the world of education as teachers of Russian and helped revolutionise attitudes to the language and the methods of teaching it. At the time, though, many of the Crail graduates questioned the usefulness of their role, as Leslie Woodhead did when he was posted to RAF Gatow near the East German border in the late 1950s: 'Our job was to trawl key frequencies, listening in on the endless tittle-tattle of Soviet pilots over East Germany. Armed with pencils, we scribbled down changes of direction, bearing and fuel levels onto pads with three carbon copies. As a job, it had all the appeal of full-time train spotting. Like all my co-sleuths, I improvised freely. I recall some squadron call-signs had a soothing, pastoral feel – 'rain' and 'squirrel' and 'birch'. I suppose the grand idea was to know what Ivan was up to, and whether he was about to try and conquer the free world.'[12]

By the time of the closure of JSSL at Crail advances in military technology were bringing fresh challenges to the confrontation between NATO and the Soviet Union, notably in the development of nuclear weapons. In May 1954 the US had made the not inconsiderable leap from atomic to hydrogen bombs by exploding its first dry fuel thermonuclear device at Bikini Atoll in the Pacific; it proved to be 1,500 times more powerful than anything seen previously. (An earlier non-deliverable prototype had been tested two years earlier.) By way of retaliation the Soviet Union responded a year later with the testing of a similar weapon, codenamed Joe 19, at its testing ground in Kazakhstan, which produced a yield of 1.6 megatons. That same year work began on creating British equivalents which were eventually tested three years later at Malden Island and Christmas Island in the Pacific in a trial known as Operation Grapple, thus making the UK the third member of the thermonuclear club.

From these developments emerged the strategy of Mutual Assured Destruction, or MAD, the aptly named concept of finite deterrence which underpinned policy on both sides during the Cold War.[13] It was also to be central to the way in which the US and its increasingly close ally, the UK, viewed their possession of such weapons and the ways in which they might be developed. This was based on the so-called 'special relationship' which had come into being during the Second World War and which was cemented in the late summer of 1958 by the signing of the Agreement for Co-operation on the Uses of Atomic Energy for Mutual Defence Purposes, enabling both countries to exchange classified information with the objective of improving 'atomic weapon design, development, and fabrication capability'.

In addition to working together on improved designs for the bombs as part of the agreement, the US provided a complete nuclear propulsion unit for the Royal Navy's first nuclear-powered submarine HMS *Dreadnought*, which was laid down in the summer of 1959 and commissioned four years later. (The world's first nuclear-powered submarine was USS *Nautilus*, which had been launched in 1954 and in so doing had revolutionised naval warfare.) Although *Dreadnought*'s reactor was similar to those used on the later US 'Skipjack' class submarines, its acquisition allowed Rolls-Royce, in collaboration with the United Kingdom Atomic Energy Authority, to begin work on an independent nuclear propulsion system for future submarines. This was carried out at Dounreay in Caithness at a site adjacent to the civil nuclear reactor, which was created in 1955 to provide the government with a fast breeder reactor to provide electricity for the National Grid. In respect of its origins and purpose, the Admiralty Reactor Test Establishment was recognised as HMS *Vulcan* in 1963 and the subsequent propulsion units for all the Royal Navy's nuclear submarine fleet were developed and tested there until its final closure in 2015.[14]

The arrival of the nuclear-powered submarine was a game-changer in the Cold War. First conceived in 1939 by the US Navy, scientists anticipated using nuclear energy to create steam power to drive the turbines which allow the boat to produce its own oxygen, thereby helping it to stay underwater for longer periods of time. It was not until after the war that work began in earnest and the result was *Nautilus*, whose keel was laid down in June 1952, with the launch taking place one year and seven months later, on 21 January 1954, at a total cost of $100 million. In addition to the traditional armament of torpedoes the boat was air-conditioned and carried such luxuries as a jukebox, a soda fountain and ice-cream machines. Fittingly, the name came not just from a previous US boat which had served with distinction in the Second World War but from the submarine in Jules Verne's futuristic novel *Twenty Thousand Leagues under the Sea* (1870). The implications for the US Navy were enormous. Not only could *Nautilus* maintain an underwater speed of 20 knots almost indefinitely, but its plating shielded the crew from the radiation produced by the onboard nuclear reactor. As a historian of submarine warfare noted, 'here, at last, was true stealth at sea; capable of diving to more than 400 feet, *Nautilus* need never betray herself to ships, aircraft or even "spy in the sky" satellites'.[15] All that was needed was a further development to produce a strategic weapons system which would give the new generation of boats a role beyond sinking other shipping with torpedoes. Almost immediately work began on a nuclear-armed missile with a range of 1,500 miles, which could be launched from a submarine, preferably while submerged.

This was a considerable challenge and initially the US Navy experimented with the development of the Regulus missile, which was essentially a cruise missile powered by a turbojet, and its shape resembled many combat aircraft of the same period. Developed by Chance Vought, it carried a small 40-kiloton nuclear warhead, had a range of 500 nautical miles and first flew in 1951. Two years later it came into service on board the submarines USS *Tunny* and USS *Barbero*. Both were diesel-powered and had seen service in the Second World War, but in 1958, together with three other submarines, they provided the US Navy with its first strategic deterrent patrols. Although it was a workable weapons system, the submarines had to surface to fire the Regulus missiles, which were carried in a deck-mounted hangar and required two auxiliary rockets for take-off, making it unwieldy and vulnerable during the launch phase. At the same time, the US Army began development of a rival missile known as Matador, and later the Jupiter medium-range ballistic missile built by the Chrysler Corporation. With its squat fuselage and relatively short length of 60 feet, Jupiter attracted the US Navy's interest as a possible submarine weapon, and joint development continued until December 1956, when it became apparent that the missile would be too large and too heavy for deployment on surface ships and submarines. Instead, the Navy began development of a new weapon under the Fleet Ballistic Programme. Three years later this emerged as Polaris, a two-stage, solid-fuelled, submarine-launched ballistic missile with a range of 1,200 miles, which was first launched from the Cape Canaveral missile test base in Florida on 7 January 1960. Crucially for submarine operations it weighed only 14 tons and was 28 feet in length. A sophisticated inertial guidance system ensured reasonable accuracy and the first test launch from a submarine, USS *George Washington*, took place on 20 July 1960; five months later the same boat began its first patrol equipped with 16 A-1 Polaris missiles. Initially the missile was expelled from the submerged submarine by compressed air before rocket propulsion took over, but later this was superseded by the use of steam. A second Polaris boat (SSBN) USS *Patrick Henry* was on patrol by the end of the year and in all the US Navy produced 41 SSBNs in five different classes – *George Washington, Ethan Allan, Lafayette, James Madison* and *Benjamin Franklin*, all of which remained operational until the 1980s and all of which were known in US Navy slang as 'boomers'. (The Royal Navy nicknamed their SSBNs 'bombers'.) At the same time Polaris continued to be developed, with the appearance of the A-2 in 1962, which had an enhanced range of 1,500 miles, followed by the A-3 in 1964 with a range of 2,500 miles, and the introduction of three warheads.

With the arrival of Polaris, Regulus was obsolete and a perception grew that this seemingly undetectable underwater missile represented the West's best hope in nuclear technology and gave it an unsurpassed lead in the arms race against the Soviet Union. There was some truth in this belief as the rapid and successful development of Polaris and its SSBNs was an astonishing achievement. At one stroke the US had produced a weapons system which was not only stealthy but provided second-strike capability or the ability to mount a decisive counter-attack, an important part of nuclear strategy. Just as importantly from a government point of view, the presence of the hidden submarines less-ened the possibility of the Soviet Union attacking the US homeland to destroy other counter-measures such as missile silos and air force bases. As the American nuclear strategist Oskar Morgenstern put it when a replacement for Polaris was under discussion, submarine-launched missiles gave the USA a trump card by placing its main retaliatory weapon outside the country in deep oceans where its detection was unlikely: 'We then combine through the use of nuclear-powered, missile-firing Polaris submarines the tremendous advantages of mobility with invisibility; and we can distribute individual units randomly, thereby making surprise attack on any substantial part of that force impossible.'[16] But it was not the only card in the US hand. While the Polaris A-3 missile and its successor Poseidon (introduced in 1971) were lethal weapons in that an SSBN with 16 missiles had the destructive power of all the bombs dropped by the Allies in the Second World War, the USA still needed to hit 'high value' primary targets such as cities. This entailed maintaining a force of strategic bombers equipped with stand-off air-to-ground missiles and developing an accurate and reliable force of intercontinental ballistic missiles (ICBM) and intermediate-range ballistic missiles (IRBM). Together with the SSBN-launched Polaris this would provide the triad of weapons requested by Washington to deter the Soviet Union, which was developing comparable nuclear weapons.

Although US ICBMs were never deployed in the UK, that was not the case with the IRBMs, which needed a European base in order to hit Soviet targets. The result was the Douglas Thor missile, which had a projected range of around 1,500 miles. As with the deployment of the bombers of Strategic Air Command this did not affect Scotland but, under an agreement signed in January 1957, 60 Thor missiles were based in eastern England with four wings of 15 missiles each centred at Great Driffield, Hemswell, North Luffenham and Feltwell. A subsequent deployment was based on four RAF Strategic Missile Groups, each comprising five squadrons armed with three Thor missiles and took the weapons further north into Lincolnshire and Yorkshire. As the historian of SAC in Britain put it: 'sleepy little towns and villages stretching in an arc from Yorkshire to Suffolk did not take long to realise that, in the space of just a few months, they had jumped into the front line of NATO's nuclear arsenal and would be the first to be hit by an enemy strike if war broke out.'[17] Under the terms of the agreement the missiles were supplied by the US and became the property of the RAF, while the UK was responsible for building and maintaining the operating bases; permission for firing depended on a dual-key system which required the agreement of both parties. This arrangement permitted the RAF to initiate a countdown but the launch could only be achieved after the USAF officer armed the warhead, thereby ensuring that both the British and US governments had a veto over the launch of the missile. The missiles were stored horizontally on transporter-erector trailers and covered by a retractable missile shelter. To fire the weapon the crew first opened the missile shelter, then they used a hydraulic launcher-erector to lift the missile to an upright position, where it was fuelled in preparation for launch. The entire launch sequence took approximately 15 minutes, while total flight time from launch to target impact ('flash to bang') was approximately 18 minutes. The nuclear warheads for the Thor missiles were stored securely at RAF Faldingworth in Lincolnshire, a base so secret that its presence was not noted on any civilian map, and defence of the UK bases was entrusted to two RAF squadrons operating the Bristol Bloodhound surface-to-air missile (SAM).

While the deployment of Thor put the UK in the front line, it was a move which suited both London and Washington. To make the missiles effective the US needed forward operating bases in Europe and they got these reasonably cheaply in that they only had to supply the infrastructure plus the training for the RAF crews. For the UK it was also a good deal. Not only did they get an off-the-shelf missile system but as a sweetener the US also offered to assist the development of the Blue Streak missile by providing the engines and guidance systems used in their own Atlas ICBMs. For the new prime minister, Harold Macmillan, the deal was also highly satisfactory as it seemed to indicate that the relationship with the US was back on track following the hiatus of the previous year when the Suez crisis of 1956 had stretched it to breaking point. (The botched military intervention by the UK and France to retake the Suez Canal after its nationalisation by Egypt had led the US to threaten to support the introduction of economic sanctions against both countries.) Agreement for the Thor deal was reached in Bermuda in March 1957 under the code name Project Emily, allowing Macmillan to reassure parliament that there should be no misgivings about dual control as it was 'absolutely untrue to say that the President and not the British Government will decide when these missiles will be launched and at whom'.[18] Even so, the deployment of Thor was only supposed to be a temporary measure to fill a gap until the RAF V-bomber force had been fully modernised. By 1963 the Blue Steel stand-off missile had come into service. This nuclear-armed weapon was carried by the V-bomber force and was rocket-propelled, allowing the planes to launch it while still beyond the range of Soviet missile defences. At the time this was 100 miles away from the target, but that short range meant that the V bombers were vulnerable to improved Soviet air defences, making Blue Steel instantly out of date, and there were only slim hopes of producing an enhanced version with a longer range.

By then, too, the appearance of the Thor missiles had triggered concern in Moscow. Seen from the Soviet point of view, the US deployment of Thor missiles in the UK and Jupiter missiles in Turkey was a direct threat to the Russian homeland at a time when the Cold War was entering one of its periodic times of crisis. In Washington John F. Kennedy had come to power as president while Nikita Khrushchev, 'a fat, vulgar man with his pig eyes and ceaseless flow of talk' (according to Macmillan), had taken control in Moscow. From the outset the two leaders were at loggerheads and theirs was to be an uneasy relationship. In 1957 the Soviet Union had displayed its superiority in ballistic missile technology by launching the first orbital earth satellite, known as Sputnik, which required a huge SS-6 ballistic missile with a 6,000-mile range to get it into space. Taking advantage of that success Khrushchev boasted, quite untruthfully, that the Soviet Union possessed 1,000 missiles of that type thereby claiming an entirely imaginary Soviet lead in its arsenal of ICBMs, a boast which Kennedy believed, so much so that the so-called 'missile gap' became an integral factor in US defence policy and spending and created doubts about the usefulness of the strategic bomber fleet. Later, Macmillan was to claim that the Sputnik revelation had produced a similar impact on the American psyche as Pearl Harbor had done in 1941. There were other irritants. In 1960 the US resumed spy plane flights over the Soviet Union and in April a Lockheed U-2 was shot down and its pilot Gary Powers was put on trial before the Soviet Supreme Court. A year later, in response to the deteriorating international situation and with Soviet encouragement, the East German government constructed a security wall along its border in Berlin to place a physical barrier between east and west. Suddenly the Cold War was becoming ever more serious and in October 1962 the tensions between East and West culminated in the notorious and potentially dangerous episode known as the Cuban missile crisis, which almost provoked a new world war.

This incident came about largely as a result of the Soviet's response to the US missile deployments in Europe and as a means of exploiting Washington's hostile relationship with Fidel Castro, a Communist revolutionary who had come to power in Cuba in February 1959 and had immediately attracted US enmity. In the previous year the Bay of Pigs fiasco – a failed attempt masterminded by the CIA to unseat Castro – had permanently soured relations between the two countries; tensions were exacerbated when the Americans attempted to deny their involvement. Khrushchev saw this state of affairs as an opportunity and in July 1962 he provoked the crisis when he offered Cuba a selection of Soviet missiles, including modern SS-4 and SS-5 IRBMs equipped with one-megaton nuclear warheads which were capable of hitting targets across the US. Also included in the deal were air defence systems and modern combat aircraft including MiG-21 fighters and Ilyushin Il-28 medium bombers, both of which were capable of challenging equivalent US aircraft. The Soviet build-up did not go unnoticed and throughout the summer tensions escalated, with claim and counter-claim from Moscow and Washington – Khrushchev insisted that the weapons were only being deployed for defensive purposes, while Kennedy feared that he was being out-manoeuvred and the USA was being put in harm's way. In the middle of October matters came to a head when an American U-2 spy plane flew over Cuba and returned with firm photographic evidence that the Soviets were constructing launching sites for their medium-range ballistic missiles. Not only did this contradict Khrushchev's claims, but the presence of these nuclear armed missiles put the US at risk of a pre-emptive strike, one of the great fears on both sides during the Cold War. Further photographic reconnaissance revealed evidence of four other missile sites, leaving the US with no option but to respond using either diplomatic or military means.

Fortunately, air strikes were discounted and instead the US instituted a policy of 'quarantine' to prevent the continued import of 'offensive military equipment' by Soviet merchant ships; the word 'blockade' was not used as it would have been considered an act of war. To provide the operation with greater legality the quarantine operation was supported by several South American navies of the Organisation of American States. However, the crisis continued to deepen as the Soviets refused to concede anything and claimed that the US action was an act of war, while Kennedy ordered his own air forces to raise their readiness levels to DEFCON 2 (defence readiness condition), the last stage before nuclear war. At the height of the emergency SAC had at its disposal 1,479 bombers, 182 ballistic missiles and 2,952 nuclear weapons, plus 1,003 airborne tankers for refuelling.[19] This state of preparedness extended to the UK where SAC strategic bombers were loaded with nuclear weapons and their crews were moved to cockpit readiness. The UK also responded. For the first time RAF Vulcan bombers were loaded with nuclear weapons and their crews put on

Quick Reaction Alert, a heightened state of readiness whereby the aircraft were on the runway and capable of being airborne in 15 minutes or less. At the same time 59 Thor missiles were unobtrusively prepared for firing within 15 minutes of receiving the command from the prime minister, having already received their nuclear warheads from RAF Faldingworth. Each warhead was capable of unleashing an explosion 100 times larger than the bomb dropped on Hiroshima.[20] Later, once the crisis was over, it was revealed that six American nuclear-powered strategic submarines had headed out to sea from their forward operating base at Holy Loch on the west coast of Scotland carrying with them an arsenal of A-1 and A-2 Polaris missiles. These were the SSBNs *George Washington, Patrick Henry, Robert E. Lee, Theodore Roosevelt, Abraham Lincoln* and *Ethan Allen*. Three were already on patrol before the crisis erupted and three were made ready to join them at extremely short notice on 22 October. With them went the tender ship USS *Proteus*. Their patrol areas included the Norwegian Sea, the Barents Sea and the eastern Mediterranean.[21]

Suddenly Scotland would have been on the front line if a global conflict had broken out over the confrontation in Cuba. The US Polaris submarines had arrived in Scotland the previous year and according to commanders in the 14th Submarine Squadron it was accepted that the Soviets kept a careful watch on their comings and goings. If any of the squadron's Polaris missiles had been fired against the Soviet Union, retaliation would have been inevitable and the Holy Loch base on the west coast of Scotland would have been a natural target.

The Soviets kept a trawler (AGI), equipped for electronics and communications surveillance, stationed close enough to the Holy Loch to keep track of traffic in and out of the port. Most certainly the Soviet High Command knew there were five SSBNs within range of targets in the Soviet Union with 80 nuclear weapons on board. This must have given the Soviet leadership food for thought.[22]

No missile was ever fired because good sense prevailed. As the world held its breath in expectation of a nuclear holocaust 27 Soviet ships heading for Cuba, presumably carrying military equipment, changed course and began heading back to their home ports in the Soviet Union. With that decision the immediate danger passed but the crisis was not yet over as the Soviet missiles remained on Cuba, still a threat, and Kennedy was under public and private pressure to have them removed. Eventually a deal was drawn up whereby Khrushchev agreed to withdraw the SS-4 and SS-5 missiles from Cuba in return for the US removing its Jupiter missiles from Turkey. This in fact happened the following year but it was a good deal for the US, as by then the American weapons were obsolescent and were due to be retired from frontline service. The Thor missiles, too, were taken out of service, not just because they were nearing the end of their useful lives but also because the UK was about to transfer its main nuclear deterrent from the RAF to the Royal Navy, and the acquisition of the Polaris missile and the US presence at Holy Loch base were integral to the change of policy.

The Polaris saga and how it came to involve Scotland is one of the most convoluted stories of the Cold War.[23] It involved inter-service rivalry on both sides of the Atlantic, it stretched the 'special relationship' to breaking point and it involved a good deal of political chicanery and double-dealing, especially in the UK. The starting point came in March 1959 during talks between Harold Macmillan and Eisenhower held at the latter's summer retreat at Camp David in Maryland, to discuss Soviet policy towards Berlin. By then the Polaris missile had come into service with the US Navy and it was clear that to be effective as a deterrent the George Washington class boats needed a forward operating base in Europe; otherwise up to 14 days would be lost from their operational cycle of 60 days on patrol as they made their way back across the Atlantic to their main bases in the US. According to US Navy operational rules 'each submarine had a Blue and Gold crew that flew back and forth from Charleston, SC [South Carolina]'. Between patrols there was a 25–30 day period when repairs were made and supplies put aboard.

The need for this facility came about as a result of a dramatic change in Soviet policy following the debacle in Cuba. Under the leadership of Admiral Sergei Gorshkov, the Soviet Navy and Air Force produced a five-year plan which increased their presence in the Northern Flank by introducing new air bases for long-range bombers equipped with stand-off missiles and by reinforcing their Northern Fleet in the Kola Peninsula with 209 modern surface ships, amphibious warships and submarines equipped with nuclear weapons, many of which were carried by cruise missiles.[24] From being a home defence force considered to be subordinate to the Army to support a land war in Europe, the Soviet Navy was transformed into a force capable of out-of-area 'blue water' operations with a global reach. The early fruits of Gorshkov's policy was the first Soviet submarine equipped with ballistic missiles, the Zulu class (NATO designations) which appeared in 1956 and carried one S-N-1 with a range of 150 kilometres. This was followed by the improved Golf class, which carried three missiles, the SS-N-4 with a range of 650 kilometres and finally the Hotel class, a nuclear-powered boat capable of firing an SS-N-5 missile while submerged, thereby obviating the need to surface before launching. Later nuclear-powered models were the Echo and November classes, collectively known as HENs, which were succeeded by the more sophisticated Victor, Charlie and Yankee classes, the latter so christened because of its striking resemblance to the American George Washington class.

By 1975 the Soviet Navy had over 300 submarines in service, the majority nuclear powered, and it was apparent that Gorshkov's reforms were predicated on two strategic imperatives – the security of Soviet nuclear forces on the Northern Flank and the need to deploy its submarine force in the Atlantic prior to hostilities or under the cover of land-based aircraft or naval forces in the GIUK gap. In the event of war both would also be used to interdict US reinforcement convoys en route to Europe, hence the need for a robust response to neutralise the increasingly powerful Soviet Northern Fleet by basing US strategic submarines in Europe. Although this represented a radical reform of Soviet naval policy the new fleet operated with serious drawbacks. The nuclear-powered boats were relatively primitive in providing protection against radiation, giving rise to the joke that submariners from the Northern Fleet glowed in the dark, and all were noisy, which meant that they were easily detected. Other problems lay in low morale amongst the crews – the Soviet Navy was a conscript force drawn from across the Soviet Union. Poor pay and indifferent conditions were endemic, training was often haphazard and the presence on board each submarine of a political officer (*zampolit*) was also a disincentive. Nevertheless, the emergence of the Soviet naval threat plus the perceived imbalance of the missile gap concentrated minds in the West and, while the Camp David talks had been arranged to discuss Berlin and the worsening confrontation with the Soviet Union, the British prime minister was determined to investigate the concept of 'interdependence' over the ownership and use of nuclear weapons.

His opportunity came when Eisenhower mentioned the possibility of finding a forward operating base for the US Navy's Polaris fleet on the west coast of Scotland, preferably on the Clyde estuary and with access to the main transatlantic air base at Prestwick, which could be used for transiting the Blue and Gold crews. In return for this concession the UK would be permitted to purchase the Douglas GAM-87 Skybolt, a new US air-launched stand-off missile with a range of 1,000 miles which would replace Blue Steel and extend the life of the RAF's V-bomber force, providing the UK with a credible nuclear deterrent. This was an important offer, as development of the UK's Blue Streak ballistic missile was not only running late despite the arrival of US-supplied Atlas engines but was seriously over budget. It was also considered to be vulnerable to pre-emptive strikes with its slow reaction time and unprotected launch system, and it had not impressed the Chiefs of the Defence Staff. At the same time, development of the mark two Blue Steel missile had also fallen behind schedule, making the Skybolt with its extended range an attractive proposition and one which was eagerly accepted by the Macmillan government.

After the Camp David talks defence officials in London and Washington began negotiations to find a suitable base for the US submarines on the west coast of Scotland and it was during this period that the possibility was first raised of supplying Polaris missiles to the Royal Navy. The suggestion came from Admiral Arleigh Burke, US Chief of Naval Operations, who enjoyed a close relationship with Admiral Lord Louis Mountbatten, shortly to become Chief of the Defence Staff, who was a proponent of nuclear propulsion and enthusiastically endorsed Burke's proposal while understanding his friend's caveat that 'such a decision cannot be made by our [US] Navy alone'. It helped that Burke was close to Admiral Hyman Rickover, the notoriously prickly 'Father of the Nuclear Navy', who was initially suspicious of any involvement with the Royal Navy but soon succumbed to Mountbatten's charm during an official visit to the UK. It was through this nexus, whereby 'the introvert iconoclast from the Ukraine [Rickover] . . . fell under the spell and aura of Queen Victoria's grandson [Mountbatten]' that the US offered the enhanced propulsion plant for HMS *Dreadnought*.[25] From the Cabinet papers it is clear that from the outset the US demand for a Scottish base was coupled to the provision of the Polaris missile system, although this linkage was not mentioned overtly in the early days of the negotiations, one problem being that it would have exacerbated inter-service rivalries by shifting the management of the UK nuclear arsenal from the RAF to the Royal Navy.

However, for a variety of reasons, finding a suitable base on the west coast proved to be no easy matter and a number of options were discussed and rejected, two being Loch Ewe or Loch Linnhe, which were considered to be too remote, before settling on four possibilities on the Clyde – Rothesay, Largs, Rosneath in the Gare Loch and Holy Loch on the Cowal peninsula opposite the port of Gourock. All sites possessed the main criteria, namely a sheltered anchorage but with easy access to open sea, relative proximity to an international airport and sufficient shore facilities to provide housing for military personnel and their families. There was, though, a political problem which had nothing to do with the special relationship but everything to do with local sensibilities. Before a final decision could be made Macmillan began to get cold feet about the project because of growing public protests about the possession of nuclear weapons, and he began to fear that the arrival in Scotland of the American submarines would be a step too far. 'It would surely be a mistake to put down what will become a major nuclear target so near to the third largest and the most overcrowded city in this country [Glasgow],' Macmillan wrote in a letter to the president in June 1960, when the US was putting pressure on London to locate the base at Gare Loch. 'From a security point of view a robust population of three or four thousand Highlanders at Fort William [Loch Linnhe] is much more to my taste than the rather mixed population of the cosmopolitan city of Glasgow.'[26] Unable to make a quick decision about a Clyde base, other sites outside Scotland were briefly considered by UK officials – Falmouth in Cornwall, Milford Haven in Wales and Bremerhaven in West Germany – but eventually the Holy Loch was chosen, and the decision was announced in parliament on 1 November 1960. The first depot ship USS *Proteus* arrived early the following year with a crew of 980 officers and men and 500 dependent families. Also part of the US deployment was the USS dry dock *Los Alamos*, which became operational by the end of the year. The Yanks had arrived in Scotland, albeit not to a universally warm welcome due to the presence of anti-nuclear demonstrators, and the plan to bring them, codenamed Operation Lamachus, had finally been fulfilled.

Although the Americans were satisfied with the decision, the question of the UK's independent nuclear deterrent remained an open issue. Shortly after Mountbatten became CDS the Blue Streak ballistic missile was finally cancelled, leaving the UK with Skybolt as the only viable alternative; it would have been operated by the RAF as part of its V-bomber force. However, its future as a practical frontline weapon was already in doubt in the US following several test failures and the arrival of the Polaris system. It also has to be said that the US Defense Secretary Robert McNamara was opposed to a bomber-based delivery system and not only thought Polaris superior in every respect but also placed great faith in the development of the Minuteman ICBM, which had an improved range and better guidance system to enable it to hit hardened military targets. His view eventually prevailed and on 22 December 1962 President Kennedy cancelled Skybolt, leaving the UK without a nuclear deterrent other than freefall bombs delivered by the V-force. This delivery system was already becoming obsolete due to the advances in Soviet air defence technology, notably the arrival of the SA-75 surface-to-air missile. The American decision caused consternation in London as the UK had cancelled all other nuclear options to concentrate on Skybolt, and Macmillan was much criticised in parliament for failing to protect UK interests. The crisis was also fuelled by the knowledge that the UK had provided the US with the Holy Loch base in return for receiving Skybolt, leaving Macmillan with an urgent need to find a replacement. By then it was clear that submarines had the edge over bomber fleets when it came to deploying nuclear weapons, and the prime minister quickly came to the conclusion that the only solution would be delivery of Polaris, and he made it clear that he would 'not be fobbed off with anything else'.[27]

The relationship between Macmillan and Kennedy has been much discussed and examined. Both came from wealthy patrician families and both had experience of war. Macmillan's wealth came from his family's publishing empire (they had started as farmers on the island of Arran but by the end of the nineteenth century were well established in London), and his wife Dorothy was a daughter of the Duke of Devonshire. During the First World War Macmillan had seen frontline service in the Grenadier Guards and was wounded three times. Entering politics as a Conservative MP in the 1920s he rose steadily if unspectacularly up the ranks and became prime minister in 1957 at a time when, to use Dean Acheson's memorable description, Britain was losing an empire and struggling to find a role in the world. Kennedy's father, a wealthy businessman, had been US ambassador to the UK during the Second World War, when Kennedy had served in the Pacific as a naval lieutenant commanding a motor torpedo boat. Encouraged by his ambitious father he entered politics as a Democrat in 1947 and was elected president 13 years later, the youngest American to be elected to the post.

Two men from broadly similar backgrounds, but there the comparisons ended. By the time of the Skybolt affair Macmillan was in his late 60s and his moustache and tweed suits seemed to belong to another age, or as one recent commentator put it, he was 'almost a caricature of an aging politician'.[28] Kennedy, on the other hand, was 20 years his junior and suffused with glamour, having presented himself during his election as a youthful president for a new generation. Not only was he energetic and good-looking but his wife Jackie was equally photogenic and well-connected, and in the Kennedy White House those attributes counted for a great deal. It was in that unlikely ambience that Macmillan saw his chance to rebuild a relationship with the USA and to use his avuncular charm and his experience to overcome the younger man's doubts, shared by many in his administration, about dealing with a Britain which was in decline and becoming an increasingly needy ally. Macmillan also wanted to position Britain as Greece to America's Rome in the confrontation with the Communist world, as exemplified by the Soviet Union. In building the transatlantic connection the British prime minister was helped by the fact that he had an American mother, and through his wife he was related to Kennedy, albeit tangentially – Dorothy's nephew Lord Hartington was married to Kennedy's sister Kathleen.

From the outset of Macmillan's time in office he made it his goal to revive the British relationship with the USA and one early success was his ability to persuade Washington to repeal the terms of the McMahon Act in respect of the UK, thereby enabling renewed nuclear cooperation between the two countries. The cancellation of Skybolt gave him the chance to build on that unexpected breakthrough. During the fast-moving crisis Macmillan met Kennedy at an emergency summit in Nassau in the Bahamas in the week before Christmas 1962; they agreed that the UK could buy the A-3 Polaris missiles from the US while the UK would supply British-built warheads and would begin building the submarines to carry the missiles. These were to be four Resolution class submarines based on the Valiant class hunter-killer or attack boats which had evolved from the first nuclear submarine, HMS *Dreadnought*, and would be extended to allow the addition of a compartment capable of carrying up to 16 Polaris missiles, each armed with three warheads. They were built by Vickers Armstrong in Barrow-in-Furness (*Resolution* and *Repulse*) and Cammell Laird in Birkenhead (*Renown* and *Revenge*) between 1964 and 1968 and remained in service until 1996. The option for a fifth boat, to be known as *Ramillies*, was cancelled in 1965. As a result of this change, the RAF lost primacy in defence priorities for the first time since the 1930s but the historians of the chiefs of staff noted that for the UK the Nassau agreement was a bargain: 'the Air Staff felt outmanoeuvred, detecting the hand of Mountbatten at work behind the scenes but it cannot be said that the decision was wrong'.[29] Although the four Resolution class submarines and their Polaris missiles were assigned to NATO's Supreme Allied Commander Europe (SACEUR), they remained independent due to the nature of NATO command and control systems, which allowed British commanders to communicate with both NATO and UK authorities and as a result, SACEUR orders could be overruled in defence of the national interest. In the first instance, the creation of the UK's Polaris squadron was regarded as the prelude to the emergence of a NATO multilateral nuclear force which never came into being.[30]

A suitable base had also to be found, and given that the desiderata were similar to those demanded by the US Navy it was not surprising that the Clyde was chosen. The two main requirements were an operational base plus accommodation for the submarines and their crews and an armaments depot nearby for the storage of missiles and their warheads. Deep water and easy access to the ocean were also important. Although the claims of Rosyth and Plymouth were considered the choice fell on Faslane, a former Second World War base at the eastern end of Gare Loch just to the north of Helensburgh, with the armaments depot sited at Coulport on the eastern shore of Loch Long, about 13 miles away by sea. The announcement was made on 24 April 1963 and the House of Commons was told that Faslane 'offers on balance the greatest advantage for a Polaris operating base'. It was also announced that work would start immediately on what came to be known as HMS *Neptune*, and that the estimated cost would be in the region of £20–£25 million.[31] Within the space of little more than a decade, thanks to the arrival of the US Navy and the Royal Navy's acquisition of Polaris missiles, Scotland found itself on the frontline of the Cold War.

The new relationship also spelled doom for Britain's nuclear V bombers. another expensive and highly controversial initiative which had been created to provide the RAF with big four-engine jet bombers capable of hitting targets in the Soviet Union with freefall nuclear bombs. Warning of an impending enemy attack came from the Fylingdales radar station in Yorkshire and it gave the bombers exactly four minutes to get airborne, which meant that the quick reaction squadrons had to be on high alert 24 hours a day, 365 days a year, a procedure they maintained for over 15 years. But when the country's nuclear deterrent was switched to submarine-launched Polaris missiles there was no place for the V bombers. The workhorse Valiant which dropped the bombs at Christmas Island was scrapped, the beautiful delta-winged Vulcan was given a conventional role while the futuristic Victor, which looked as if it came out of a Dan Dare comic, became an airborne fuel tanker.

With the V bombers went the last of the secrets surrounding the post-war development of Britain's super-weapons. Although it was never revealed at the time for fear of damaging morale, the bombers did not carry enough fuel to hit their target and then return to base, which meant that they were on a one-way ticket to eternity. One pilot was simply advised to 'keep going east and settle down with a nice warm Mongolian woman'.[32] The crews' on-board safety was also an afterthought. While the pilot and co-pilot had ejector seats, the three electronic warfare crew members had to take their chances with their parachutes and escape hatch. Not that the pilots got off easily. Following the attack run they had to face the inevitable blinding nuclear blast. Their protection? Each pilot wore a single eye-patch which meant that he could use his good remaining eye for flying the bomber out of the area. It was a fitting metaphor for the secretive and duplicitous development of Britain's nuclear weapons – in the country of the blind the one-eyed man really was king.

4

Frontline Scotland

SCOTLAND WAS NO stranger to being on the front line in time of war. The nation's history is bloody with battles, some fought against the nearest neighbour, England; many more fought amongst the Scots themselves, family against family, clan against clan. Even the land mass could be said to have been fashioned for warfare. Whichever way the topography of Scotland is examined, it makes ideal territory for the training of service personnel. First, much of the terrain is rugged high land which offers challenging conditions for adventurous training, while the bottom land is open and reasonably flat, with good internal communications. Secondly, the surrounding waters provide a variety of sea conditions and, thirdly, and perhaps most importantly, most of the land and coastal waters, especially those on the western side of the country, were beyond the prying eyes of a European enemy, at least in the days before the advent of long-distance aircraft and satellite surveillance technology. From the military point of view, therefore, Scotland has always provided defence planners with a number of possibilities and opportunities. The land mass sprawls over 7.7 million hectares; one-third the size of the UK, it consists largely of high land and rough grazing. Less than 2 million hectares is made up of pasture or arable land. Some idea of the extent of the area can be gauged by superimposing Scotland upon England: Scotland then stretches from Aldershot in the south to the borders in the north, and from Liverpool in the west to Scarborough in the east, even before the Western and Northern Isles have been taken into account.

But there is one problem with the lie of the land: physical barriers like the Mounth (the mountain massif which includes the Cairngorms) and the Southern Uplands make north–south and east–west communications difficult. Historically, the high lands provided a refuge in time of danger and helped, therefore, to preserve Scotland's independence.

Invaders from the south were forced to use the eastern coastal route to bypass the Cheviots or the difficult upland terrain in the west through Annandale. Other problems are posed by the length of the coastline, which is the longest in the UK – over 0.4 million hectares of foreshore – and much of this consists of long sea lochs and broad open firths. Most of the high ground is sparsely populated or uninhabited, and the weather conditions are often harsh and unpredictable. Rivers and inland lochs also provide barriers, and the pattern of north–south roads was determined by the presence of glens and mountain passes, some of which, like the Pass of Drumochter on the main route between Perth and Inverness, rise up over 450 metres. In short, from a military standpoint Scotland offers most of the advantages to the defenders and provides a serious test to those intent on invasion. By its very nature, it is a terrain which was also made for demanding military and naval training.

In 1991, as the Cold War was coming to an end, Scotland provided the Army with 208,000 man-training days, not just for soldiers north of the border but also for formations based in England. To meet that need the Army maintained major training areas or ranges at Garelochhead in Argyll, Barry Buddon in Angus, Cultybraggan in Perthshire and Castlelaw in Midlothian.[1] Low flying training by the RAF was regularly carried out across the Borders and Dumfries and Galloway but the most intensive use of the land mass for this purpose took place in the Highlands Restricted Area north of the Great Glen, where military aircraft regularly flew at heights below 500 feet. Inevitably there were near-misses and accidents – one account claims that between 1978 and 1983 at least 18 crashes were caused by low flying, but the problem was partially resolved in 1992 when low flying was scaled back by 30 per cent.[2] The waters off Scotland's coast provided ideal sea conditions for training in minehunting and minesweeping as well as amphibious operational training, and these often provoked clashes with other sea users, notably the fishing community, but the most controversial impact came from submarine operations off the west coast and in the waters of the Firth of Clyde, which provided an ideal environment for testing and training officers seeking promotion to command submarines.

By and large, there was a peaceful coexistence between the people of Scotland and the economic benefits that accrued from the Cold War. The main exception was, as previously noted, the presence of the nuclear weapons at the submarine bases on the Clyde, which were the focus of frequent protests. Another significant concern came from within the fishing industry – once a staple of the country's domestic economy but in recession by the 1970s. Between 1961 and 1971 the full-time workforce in the fishing industry dropped from 9,460 to 8,390 as the industry struggled to come to terms with the need for modernisation, especially in the deep-sea trawler fleet, which was still largely coal-fired. The public's tastes were changing too, leading to the decline of the herring industry in the 1970s. After the UK joined the European Economic Community (EEC) in 1973 the acceptance of the European Common Fisheries Policy opened up EEC waters for common use by all member states and brought fresh challenges for the Scottish fishing community. Due to the implementation of this policy rationing was introduced, with a fixed 'Total Allowable Catch' (TAC) set by species and allocated between member states based on a quota system. This came as a disadvantage to Scottish fishery workers, who had to compete against highly industrialised factory ships from Spain and the Soviet Union and it was not long before cod became an endangered species.

During the latter stages of the Cold War the Scottish fishing industry shifted towards inshore fishing, and shellfish became an increasingly popular alternative. By 1993 there were almost as many shellfish boats over 10 metres long (640) as there were pelagic (herring, whiting, mackerel) and demersal (cod, haddock, halibut, ling and turbot) boats combined (692) and the sector was growing at 2 per cent per year.[3] Profitability was also high, ranging from 19 per cent to 24 per cent, and the sector's growth was assisted by an increasing number of whitefish boats that turned to creeling and potting when their own quotas were not filled. While this provided a boost to inshore fishing, the increase also prompted clashes with other sea users and the most controversial impact came from submarine operations, notably in the Irish Sea, off the west coast of Scotland and in the Firth of Clyde.

Soviet and American submarines were also involved in incidents with British (mainly Scottish) and Irish fishing boats, with the result that within the fishing community the Irish Sea gained the nickname 'submarine highway'. All too often, the rival submarines were involved in their own cat-and-mouse war games and although these resulted in damage to fishing gear there were also too many unexplained incidents, such as the sinking of the Kirkcudbright scallop trawler *Mhairi L*, which took place in February 1985 in calm weatherwith the loss of all five crew, whose bodies were never recovered. At the time the sinking was blamed on the boat snagging an underwater telephone cable – a claim denied by British Telecom – but there were persistent rumours that the fishing boat or its gear had been struck by a submarine.

Throughout the 1970s and 1980s there were numerous reports of fishing boats 'catching' submarines in their nets and being dragged at speed through the Irish Sea. In one highly publicised incident in 1982 the crew of the Irish fishing boat *Sheralga* escaped injury when the vessel capsized and sank off the coast of Dublin on 18 April after the Royal Navy diesel-electric submarine HMS *Porpoise* became entangled in its nets. Initially the Admiralty denied that any submarine had been in the area and it took two weeks for them to acknowledge responsibility, perhaps because the submarine involved was designed for silent running and was therefore used for clandestine operations involving the secretive Special Boat Service.[4] Five years later another Irish trawler, the *Summer Morn*, was dragged backwards by an unknown American nuclear-powered submarine for up to 20 miles during a terrifying incident lasting about three hours. The skipper retrieved a sonar device which proved the identity of the offending submarine but only later did the US Navy admit that the boat was 'one of ours'.[5]

These deep coastal waters also provided an ideal environment for testing and training officers seeking promotion to command submarines, and this led to one of the most high-profile incidents involving a fishing boat and a submarine with an officer under instruction – a procedure which involved up to a dozen candidates and took place twice every year. Known as the 'perisher' due to its demanding nature and low success rate, the submarine command course had to be carried out under realistic wartime operational conditions, a difficult task when the same waters were being used by fishing boats, and that was a contributory factor in what happened during the incident in question. On the night of 21 November 1990, while operating in deep water known as the Arran Trench in the Bute Sound, the newly commissioned hunter-killer submarine HMS *Trenchant* was engaged in a realistic training exercise simulating laying mines while being attacked on the surface by a Leander class frigate, HMS *Charybdis*. During the operation, *Trenchant* snagged the nets of the Carradale-based fishing boat *Antares*, a small pelagic trawler operating in the area, which capsized and sank with the loss of all four hands. Although the submarine surfaced and a trawl net was found on the hull the crew could see nothing amiss as two other boats, *Heroine* and *Hercules III*, were fishing nearby and it was assumed that the fishing gear belonged to one of them. Since everything seemed to be normal *Trenchant* continued with the exercise and it was only later the following day that *Antares* was reported missing and the wreck was found in the same position that the snagging had been heard. An official report by the Marine Accident Investigation Branch said that there had been 'a partial breakdown in the watchkeeping structure and standards' on board the submarine and blamed faulty operational procedures.

It also has to be borne in mind that the 'perisher' course was extremely intense and failure rates were high. If at any time a candidate failed to come up to the mark he would leave the course immediately and would never again serve in the submarine service. In 1967, officer-in-charge Sandy Woodward (known simply as 'Teacher') told candidates on the course: 'We need to know your personal limitations under pressure. It's an unrepeatable offer, to drive yourself and your submarine to their limits. It's an opportunity to find yourself and you must use it. If you don't you won't get through the course.' Woodward was one of the most experienced submariners of his generation and crowned his career commanding the carrier task force sent to the Falklands in 1982. He retired from the Royal Navy seven years later as Admiral Sir John 'Sandy' Woodward. Understandably, there was much speculation that the candidates on *Trenchant* were being pushed to their limits and that this was a factor in the incident, but the main problem seems to have been the secrecy which understandably surrounded the perisher courses.

When the report's findings became public, the Clyde Submarine Base agreed to provide fuller information to local fishermen when exercises were taking place.[6] Previously, at the height of the Cold War, information of that kind had been kept secret for reasons of national security but according to the Clyde Fishermen's Association there were at least 20 cases of submarines snagging the nets of trawlers in Scottish coastal waters between 1970 and 1990. The *Antares* incident showed in tragic detail the consequences of two very different types of vessels operating in the mid-waters of the Arran Trench, which were ideal for the activities in which they were both engaged but fatal for the smaller and fragile fishing boat whose crew was unaware of the dangers that lay beneath them as they went about their lawful business.

Throughout the *Antares* investigation there was considerable public interest in the role of the armed forces in Scotland, particularly that of the Royal Navy. The country was a vital cog in the homeland defence of the UK and beyond that of the NATO alliance during the Cold War. Responsibility for naval affairs was vested in the position of Flag Officer Scotland and Northern Ireland (FOSNI), in the 1980s a three-star appointment (Vice Admiral) with responsibility for the Royal Navy's main presence on the Clyde and the Forth together with 36 other shore establishments (45 Commando at Arbroath came under the direction of the Commandant, Royal Marines). In 1992 there were 10,000 naval personnel based in Scotland together with 52 warships. While FOSNI did not command the Clyde submarine base, whose commander reported to Flag Officer Submarines at Northwood, his role was 'double-hatted' – he had both UK and NATO responsibilities. On the home front he was the sea area commander for UK waters from Morecombe to the Wash and the Atlantic westward to Greenland and north to the high Arctic, while his NATO tasks made him subordinate commander for Allied Command – Atlantic and Allied Command Channel.[7]

The facility on the Clyde already had a connection to the Royal Navy, having been designated a military port (together with Cairnryan near Stranraer) in 1939. Its depth of water and proximity to the railway gave it obvious advantages for use in emergency – its intended wartime use – and these were exploited in the post-war world when Faslane became the base of the Royal Navy's Third Submarine Squadron. From 1946 the port was also home to Metal Industries Ltd, which dealt with shipbreaking and became the last berth for many famous British ships including the Cunard transatlantic liner RMS *Aquitania* (1950) and the last Royal Navy battleship, HMS *Vanguard* (1962). Ironically, both had been built at John Brown's at nearby Clydebank. With the arrival of the new submarine base Metal Industries had to give up its lease, which had a yearly rental of £12,500, but because the surrender was not due to take place until 1966 the company demanded compensation of £1.5 million for the loss of jetty space, and the negotiations prevented any public announcement until March 1964.[8] However, it was not until the further extension of the base in the 1980s that the company finally moved out of Faslane, with their docking facilities at the north end being taken over for later development by the Royal Navy for the next generation of Trident submarines. Even so, the scale of the Polaris project was impressive and involved a workforce of 2,000, who were on site from 1964 until 1968 as the base's three principal areas

took shape – the docks for two Resolution class submarines, three attack
submarines and one frigate, accommodation for 1,700 officers and
men, and administrative offices for running the base.[9] The entire cost
for the introduction of Polaris was £370 million and the project was
described by the Ministry of Defence as 'the largest single industrial
undertaking that this country has ever attempted within a given times-
cale'.[10] Unlike other submarine bases such as the American facility at
nearby Holy Loch, there was no need for a depot ship at Faslane and
the base was built to be largely self-contained, with its own purpose-
built 'Polaris School', which opened in 1966 at a cost of £8.5 million
and was used for training and refresher courses.[11] At the same time
work commenced on building the Royal Naval Armaments Depot at
Coulport, which consists of 16 reinforced concrete bunkers on the hillside above Loch Long for storing missiles and their nuclear warheads
and which opened for business in June 1968 when the first Polaris-
equipped boat, HMS *Resolution*, went on patrol.

By then the submarine had been commissioned into service and had
already visited Cape Canaveral in the USA, where both Port and
Starboard crews had successfully fired a Polaris A-3 missile into the
downrange area off the Florida coast. In common with the American
squadron at Holy Loch, each submarine had two crews, Port and
Starboard, in each case with 13 officers and 131 ratings. According to
Royal Navy publicity literature in 1966, it was a well-regulated system
with patrols lasting eight weeks before returning to Faslane 'for a month
to change over crews and maintain, after which the opposite crew will
go to sea for eight weeks'. At any one time at least one of the boats
would be on an operational patrol. The other members of the class were
launched in 1967 (*Renown* and *Repulse*) and 1968 (*Revenge*) and they
were all fully operational by the following year. As happens in the introduction of any new weapons system, there were snags. The first
operational submarine patrol had run into problems when it was discovered that *Resolution*'s carbon dioxide ventilating plants ('scrubbers')
were not working effectively, forcing the submarine to rise to periscope
depth at night so that the snort inlet and ventilation mast could be
deployed. There were also scares over welding and these were magni-
fied in April 1963 following the loss of the USS *Thresher*, a modern
American attack submarine which disappeared during a test dive in the
Atlantic. But by and large the Polaris project had arrived on time and
within budget and the Royal Navy not only had a formidable weapons

system but also a modern one, allowing their publicists to claim: 'for the first time in 50 years the MOD (N) have had the opportunity to build a completely new base with the right facilities for work and play'.

The writer also noted approvingly that there was a good variety of married quarters, with two estates in Helensburgh and one in Rhu providing various types of quarters, a community centre, shops, welfare offices and a school. In all cases the houses were designed and built by the semi-official Scottish Special Housing Association, with the result that there was no tendering from private firms which were therefore denied the opportunity of making money from the opportunity.[12] Over the years this was to become a common complaint as it had been assumed that the construction of the base and the arrival of the submarines would provide financial benefits for the local community, but the reality was somewhat different. Due to the specialised nature of much of the construction work, the bulk of the workforce came from outside the area, as did most of the skilled workers. True, there was the spending power generated by the base and its family quarters, but the amounts were frequently disputed, and the economic benefits became a regular matter for debate in the years ahead. One thing was certain: Polaris was in Scotland to stay even though its presence was not universally welcomed and in time it spawned a large and influential protest movement. But as the historian of the Royal Navy in Scotland noted, at the time feelings were relatively muted and 'on the whole the [Conservative] government was proud that it was creating work in a high-unemployment area of Scotland'.[13]

It was not just in Faslane that the Polaris project set down roots. From the outset the government agreed that there had to be a separate naval dockyard facility for refitting and refuelling the submarines and that it was not feasible to site these in the private shipyards at Barrow and Birkenhead, where the boats had been built. Other possibilities were the existing naval bases at Portsmouth and Devonport but they did not score well in evaluating the risk factors caused by any nuclear accident. That left the dockyards at Chatham in Kent and Rosyth in Fife, the former created in 1567, the latter in 1909. Both had solid claims to be selected and both scored well in evaluating possible dangers. Both also had history on their side, Chatham being both a refitting yard of many years' standing and a more recent builder of submarines, Rosyth being a frontline naval base in the two world wars with large modern dry-docks and a Cold War naval presence. But both had drawbacks. The sea approaches to Chatham were not advantageous for easy navigation and the River Medway was prone to silting while Rosyth was in a zone of high unemployment and lacked a skilled workforce. Eventually the superior infrastructure at Rosyth told against Chatham and the Fife dockyard was chosen as the lead base for refitting and refuelling the Polaris boats. There was some suspicion of a political carve-up which worked in Scotland's favour, as Chatham was in an area of high employment within the relatively prosperous southeast. There was some consolation for the Medway town when its dockyard was chosen to refit the new generation of hunter-killer submarines. HMS *Dreadnought* arrived at Rosyth for refit in 1968 and *Resolution* followed two years later. In 1984 it was announced that the dockyard at Chatham would be closed as part of defence cuts but it was reborn as a Historic Dockyard tourist attraction which claims to be the 'world's most complete dockyard of the Age of Sail'.

For the submariners the introduction of the nuclear submarine changed everything. For all that modern diesel-electric boats such as the Porpoise and Oberon class were admired in their day, they possessed operational limitations and the crews' quarters were cramped and uncomfortable. On long-range missions fresh water could become scarce and food could run out, with obvious knock-on effects for the physical and mental health of the crews. In comparison the new nuclear-powered boats had good supplies of water and food and the supply of scrubbed air was not a problem. Hot showers were always available, and the galley provided nutritious food with carefully rationed supplies of beer. Compared to the old diesel-electric boats the Resolution class SSBNs and their attack, or hunter-killer, stable-mates (SSN) of the Valiant, Churchill, Swiftsure and Trafalgar classes seemed to provide sheer luxury but the world inhabited by submariners was circumscribed and could be claustrophobic. There were also operational differences. Whereas the main duty of the SSNs was to seek out potential enemies in the shape of surface ships and rival submarines, the duty of the SSBNs was the exact opposite. Before each patrol every crew member was given the option of being told if anything untoward happened to their families but most refused as they could do nothing about it. As one SSBN commander, Captain Mike Hawke explained the issue in a television interview in 1983: his job was to keep his submarine (HMS *Repulse*) undetected, 'to go into the oceans of the world and disappear, totally disappear'. As the Royal Navy only had one Polaris boat on patrol at a time (at most two), operational secrecy was paramount; if it was detected by the Soviets the ramifications would have been 'shattering'. Before each patrol Captain Hawke's orders arrived in a sealed envelope carried in a battered briefcase 'for his eyes only', and throughout the patrol only he and a handful of senior officers knew exactly where the submarine was located.[14] With him he also carried a sealed envelope with a letter from the prime minister providing the orders for carrying out a nuclear attack in the event of an outbreak of hostilities. With no means of communicating with naval headquarters, one of the last tests to discover if the UK had suffered a catastrophic nuclear attack was the absence over several days of BBC Radio 4's *Today* programme. This was the metaphoric 'finger on the button', but in the event of a nuclear war the orders could have represented a decision from the grave.[15]

In other words, once on patrol Polaris boats were on their own and nothing could divert the mission – neither a crew member's serious illness nor an accident beneath the waves. Radio silence had to be complete and absolute, although incoming messages could be received through a complicated system of towing an aerial, hundreds of feet long, on the surface to receive essential low-intensity transmissions. While there were sound operational reasons for maintaining that strict security regime the crews understood that nothing was allowed to compromise the boat's security for the eight long weeks of an SSBN patrol: 'Year after year they took their vessels out on deployment, disappearing beneath the surface of the sea for weeks, if not months, at a time. Between the last time they saw their homeland and the next, babies were born and loved ones died. Wars might be fought or peace and goodwill reign. Deep in the oceans, throughout every personal tragedy and triumph, each world-shaping event, they hovered, unseen and ignored by the majority of Mankind, on the edge of the abyss.'[16]

Such an eventuality visited the Polaris-equipped HMS *Revenge* in July 1978 when she was on an operational patrol whose whereabouts still cannot be revealed even though the senior engineering officer, Eric Thompson, wrote a comprehensive account of what happened. A sudden steam leak threatened disaster: the reactor would have to be shut down, leaving *Revenge* without a power source and therefore effectively 'dead'. Faced by that outcome, which would require the boat to surface and await rescue, Thompson also realised that the result would be 'national humiliation' at a time when the Labour government was 'riven by anti-nuclear sentiment . . . if the deterrent appeared to fail, Britain's nuclear strategy would be holed below the waterline'. Fortunately, a solution of sorts was cobbled together, the submarine did not require assistance and was able to continue a further eight weeks on patrol, although with remarkable candour Thompson admitted that everyone on board recognised that they 'would be walking a tightrope; one machine failure could bring everything tumbling down'.[17] Later in his career Thompson, who had been brought up in Coatbridge, became Commodore of the Faslane base and his account of the accident on board HMS *Revenge* is one of the most candid and thought-provoking descriptions of life on the front line during the Cold War.

Operating in an environment which meant that the crew were as isolated as they would have been in deep space brought enormous challenges. Not only did crew members have to adapt to being in a confined and occasionally claustrophobic space where they were often 'living on top of each other', but they also had to remain operationally effective, able to react immediately to any orders coming from fleet headquarters at Northwood. Whereas the submarine service had acquired a buccaneering ethos during the Second World War which continued to a certain extent in the post-war diesel-electric boats, the advent of the nuclear-powered submarines changed everything. These were multi-million-pound vessels which carried the country's nuclear deterrent, and which were in a constant state of readiness while on patrol – there was no room for a cavalier approach. To combat the effects of isolation and possible ennui the Navy had developed a system whereby the working day was divided into three watches – eight hours on duty when the crew had to be prepared for any eventuality, including the firing of the missiles, eight hours' rest and sleep and eight hours' recreation, when they could devote themselves to leisure activities such as reading, watching films (all latest releases) or applying themselves to hobbies such as modelling. One submariner recalled that there was a sophisticated Scalextric model racing car set up on board the Polaris boat HMS *Revenge*. There was, of course, a darker side. Given the nature of the crew's operational duties the use of nuclear missiles capable of causing thousands of deaths could have caused misgivings, but this seems not to have been the case, the general feeling being that the responsibility 'went with the job'. One SSBN commander, Toby Elliott, later chief executive of the charity Combat Stress, was quoted as saying that during a period of high tension with the Soviet Union in 1981 he would have been fully prepared to fire his Polaris missiles from HMS

Resolution had he been ordered to do so.[18] On that score there was regular vetting on nuclear issues by the security services but the main anxiety seems to have been claustrophobia and in severe cases suffering crew members were removed from the submarine service.[19]

The arrival of the US Navy at Holy Loch and the consolidation of Faslane marked the end of the first phase of the UK's acceptance of the nuclear deterrent and the beginning of a period characterised as 'economic decline and defence retrenchment'.[20] In 1965 Mountbatten's period as CDS came to an end and he was succeeded by a soldier, Field Marshal Sir Richard Hull. Under Mountbatten's watch the Ministry of Defence had been changed utterly, having been streamlined into a modern organisation whose senior personnel embraced a 'tri-service' ethos while retaining the tribalism of the three separate forces. Moving into a unified building in Whitehall greatly eased the process. There were other changes. In May 1963 the last National Serviceman left the Army, thus ending peacetime conscription and leaving the all-volunteer forces very much in the job market at a time when they still had a global role to play with reduced resources and fewer personnel. In October 1964 Labour won the general election with a narrow majority and found itself having to confront the realities of a constrained budget, necessitating successive 'defence reviews' which quickly revealed themselves to be exercises in a never-ending search for economies. Amongst the most hotly debated issues were the UK's commitments outside Europe, particularly in Singapore and the Gulf, a policy loosely known as 'east of Suez', harking back to the days of Empire – which Labour was determined to abandon. It was able to do this in January 1968 following the previous November's sterling crisis in which the pound had been devalued, forcing the introduction of austerity measures. To his credit the prime minister, Harold Wilson, was able to resist US requests for the UK to send forces to assist in the Vietnam War, as it had done in the earlier Korean War. This long-running war in southeast Asia escalated after President Lyndon B. Johnson came to power in November 1963 following the assassination of John F. Kennedy in Dallas, and the Vietnam War came to be considered one of the most dangerous proxy conflicts of the Cold War.

Keeping Washington sweet continued to be a preoccupation for British politicians and defence chiefs alike, and in no other area was the special relationship put under greater strain than in the Vietnam War in the period between 1964 and 1969 when Wilson's Labour government was in power in London and Johnson was US president. Throughout that time Johnson kept up a stream of demands for military aid, famously asking Wilson in December 1964 for the provision of the Black Watch (Royal Highland Regiment) 'even a few pipers would be better than nothing'.[21] The request was made privately in the White House Rose Garden and Wilson was able to deflect it by falling back on the familiar argument that the UK could not involve itself in Vietnam as it co-chaired the 1954 Geneva Convention on ending the war in Indo-China, but the truth was that the prime minister would have ended his political career had he offered any support to the Americans, so unpopular was the war in Vietnam. All this mattered because the UK was an unequal partner in the relationship and Wilson was uncomfortably aware that the country's trade deficit could have been wiped out if he asked for US financial help; at one stage he was advised by one of Johnson's officials that he possessed a powerful bargaining chip, that 'a British brigade could be worth a billion dollars'.[22] He was also aware that not only was the war extremely unpopular with the British people but any support would have alienated the Labour left on whom Wilson had come to depend following the 1966 election, which had given him a majority of 97. If they had defected it would almost certainly have brought down his government. At the same time Wilson managed to pull off the tricky balancing act of dissociating Britain from the US bombing of Hanoi and other targets in North Vietnam while upholding Britain's support for Washington's overall policy in the country. However, covertly, he allowed the provision of some weaponry including napalm and signals equipment, and the SAS Regiment provided training for US special forces in Vietnam.

Equally secretive and pervasive was the arrival in the UK of American signals intelligence (SIGINT), the electronic spying, surveillance and code-breaking activities which were a vital adjunct of the nuclear partnership. To this should be added C³I (Command, Control, Communications and Intelligence) the Pentagon's designation for the network without which no war could be fought. Many of these installations were sited in Scotland and while they did not create the awe-inspiring or frightening spectacle of the Polaris-armed submarines on the west coast, they were central to the creation of the UK as the most important American forward operating base in Europe. This became increasingly important in the late 1960s when the NATO strategy of waging any future nuclear war was moving away from the concept of mutually assured destruction (that is, short, sharp and terminal) to the more likely outcome of flexible response (that is, deliberate escalation so that the first conventional shots would not necessarily lead to a nuclear exchange). Under the terms of the latter strategy, second strike capability was all-important – the ability to respond to a nuclear attack with overwhelming nuclear retaliation if all else had failed. It followed that the ultimate aim of flexible response was to prevent an enemy from launching a massive first strike aimed at demolishing the target country's nuclear arsenal, hence the importance of preserving SIGINT and C³I. In that scenario Scotland became a crucial site for US facilities which were established mainly in the north and north-east.

Perhaps the most important of these, because it was 'probably the base in Scotland which the USA would least wish to lose' was RAF Edzell in Angus.[23] In common with other similar US facilities the use of RAF in the base's name was pure camouflage. Although it was a former RAF airfield which had seen service in both world wars and had been used as a motor-racing circuit in the 1950s – the future world-champion driver Jim Clark had competed there – the US Navy moved in to re-establish the base in 1960 as the US Naval Security Group Oceanographic Monitoring Station. Opened for business on 1 July, its task was to monitor the North Sea and the European continent listening for radio transmissions from the Soviet Union and its allies. RAF Edzell was part of a network of 16 high frequency direction finding (HF/DF) facilities located around the world that monitored the electromagnetic spectrum from 2 to 32 megahertz. The base was situated on 440 acres, including a stretch of water known as Loch Wee, and by the 1970s had a strength of 700 service personnel and civilians, the latter thought to have included members of the US National Security Agency (NSA) and the UK's Government Communications Headquarters (GCHQ). The land on the north-west end of the base contained the housing area, the enlisted men's barracks, the officer and enlisted men's clubs, mess hall, medical office, store, post office, three hangars containing technical shops, and administrative buildings. To the south-east lay the Second World War airfield, sports fields and the communications building located in the centre of the airfield. This had two levels below ground housing a computer and communications centre and was surrounded by a circular multi-directional Wullenweber antenna array known as the 'elephant cage'. This was the heart of the station's activities, which were recalled with considerable warmth by Seaman Daniel Flanagan from Baltimore, who added the salient fact that a posting to Edzell was highly prized and limited to those cryptologic technicians who passed out with the highest marks from the US Navy's Class 'A' Communications School at Corry Field in Pensacola, Florida.

> During the cold war, Navy and Marine Corps personnel stationed at RAF Edzell monitored the HF radio frequency spectrum for clandestine communications from Soviet land-based stations and the Soviet Navy and merchant fleet. During my tour of duty, there were a few occasions when we listened for satellite telemetry signals just prior to satellite re-entry into the atmosphere. The communications facility was manned 24 hours a day, 7 days a week with rotating watches. There were four watch sections that rotated through a daily schedule. The eve[ning]-watch (4 p.m. to 11 p.m.), and the mid-watch (11 p.m. to 7 a.m.) and the day-watch (7 a.m. to 4 p.m.). After completing a round of eve, mid and day watches one had 80 hours off duty before repeating the cycle.[24]

In 1966 a Petty Officer Academy was established at Edzell to enhance cryptologic training and to provide a professional career structure for this increasingly vital aspect of US intelligence gathering. In the 1970s Edzell's importance was increased by the introduction of satellite technology known as 'White Cloud', which allowed ground operatives to detect Soviet ships by their heat signatures and differing types of radar emissions. Connected to Edzell were microwave relay facilities at nearby Inverbervie (with an associated bunker), Kinnaber and Clochandighter near Portlethen in Aberdeenshire. Other US surveillance and communications included the vital US Navy communication facilities at Forss and West Murkle in Caithness, which were constructed between 1963 and 1965 to provide secure low frequency command and control communication with Polaris submarines operating in the North Atlantic, a duty that was shared with a similar facility at Londonderry in Northern Ireland, at least until 1974, when the entire operation was switched to Thurso. Both Caithness stations relied heavily on satellite communications as part of the US World Wide Military Command and Control System and at the height of their operations employed 152 personnel.[25] These intelligence-gathering sites or 'listening posts' were recognisable by their masts, aerials or 'golfball'-style radomes but perhaps the most obvious installation of this type was the US Air Force's North Atlantic Relay System on Mormond Hill south of Fraserburgh, which operated as Station 44 in the US North Atlantic Radio System, an early warning facility which ran from Iceland to Fylingdales in Yorkshire. In this guise it shared the space with the US Navy's microwave dishes and NATO's saucer-shaped dishes, which provided secure communications across Western Europe. This was the sophisticated ballistic missile early warning system (BMEWS) which, together with the US Air Force bases at Thule in Greenland and Clear in Alaska, provided the USA and UK with round-the-clock warning of an impending Soviet attack. It was better known as the 'four-minute warning' which was a central motif of the Cold War years and much parodied in popular culture – not least in Scotland during the late 1980s, when a sketch on the BBC Scotland programme *Naked Video* contained a mock announcement warning of an imminent nuclear attack with the punchline of 'except for viewers in Scotland', a sarcastic reference to the fact that many UK programmes were not always screened in Scotland. In addition to these manned sites there was also a US presence in unmanned though highly visible early warning facilities at Latheron (Caithness), Craigowl Hill (Angus), East Lomond (Fife), Kirk o' Shotts (North Lanarkshire), Browncarrick Hill (South Ayrshire) and Sergeant Law (Renfrewshire).

It was not just the US presence that made itself felt across Scotland during the Cold War. The UK's armed forces also recognised the importance of the country's topography and strategic position for training purposes and for siting bases. In addition to the naval facilities on the Clyde and the Forth for the use of nuclear submarines and surface ships there was the secretive defence munitions centre in Glen Douglas on Loch Long, which was constructed in the early 1960s as a NATO facility for storing conventional weapons in 56 underground chambers built into the hillside, the whole area covering 650 acres. With its razor-wire high security fences it was widely supposed to store nuclear warheads but this was not the case, even though it was busy enough with a large fleet of lorries and a jetty at nearby Glen Mallen on Loch Long which was used regularly by Royal Fleet Auxiliary ships to collect conventional weapons and ammunition for use by all three services. There were two other munitions centres in Scotland which catered mainly for the Royal Navy; these were situated at Beith in north

Ayrshire and Crombie on the Firth of Forth in Fife and both were substantial local employers with 500 civilians at the former and 200 at the latter.

Throughout the Cold War the main RAF bases in Scotland were at Kinloss, Leuchars and Lossiemouth where a total of 10,000 personnel were based. They too had expanded during the Second World War, the first two under RAF Coastal Command and the third as a Royal Naval Air Station. Until 1968, when Strike Command was formed to unify the RAF's operational duties, the three main commands were Bomber Command, Coastal Command and Fighter Command. Of the three Scottish bases during the Cold War, Leuchars had the highest public profile because at the time it was the UK's most northerly fighter airfield and was home to the Quick Reaction Alert flight. This entailed two interceptor aircraft being on constant duty at immediate readiness 24 hours a day in a hardened hangar with aircrew fully dressed in the close-by Ready Room – 'about the size of a seaside bungalow' – in order to carry out 'a standing instruction that they must be off the ground within ten minutes of an alert indicating a possible enemy air attack on the United Kingdom.'[26] QRA became a symbol of the RAF's preparedness to defend the country from attack by Soviet bombers but the reality was that the majority of the 'scrambles' were to investigate reconnaissance aircraft flying in support of Soviet naval exercises in the Atlantic or transport aircraft going about their legal business in international skies. Other QRA flights were based in England at Binbrook, Coningsby in Lincolnshire and Wattisham in Suffolk, but Leuchars retained its mystique as the RAF's Northern Watch which was always on alert as it carried out its operational duty of intercepting Soviet aircraft above the Norwegian Sea, mainly Tu-95 Bear and Tu-16 Badger maritime reconnaissance aircraft. Aerial photographs of these huge aircraft being escorted by RAF fighters soon became iconic images of the confrontation with the Soviet Union and the results were much used for propaganda purposes.

For the QRA crews it was a long and debilitating duty, with two pilots and two navigators sitting for hours on end clad in their heavy and stifling hot immersion suits – known as 'goon suits' – which would keep them alive if they had to eject into the bitterly cold northern waters. They were on duty for 24 hour shifts, with each squadron providing QRA cover for six months at a time; the biggest gripe from the air crews was that 'unavoidably they stink of body odour in their thirty-pound gear'.[27] That discomfort came with the territory, as did the expertise. All QRA air crew were highly trained professionals and although they acknowledged that most of the scrambles led to frustrating cat-and-mouse encounters with their Soviet counterparts the operation was a real enough component in the defence of the UK homeland. As one commanding officer of the Leuchars-based 111 Squadron explained long after the Cold War had ended, each mission was packed with imponderables: 'What we're going to intercept, the height and the speed. Then there's the weather, or we could be wearing night-vision goggles. You get an adrenaline kick. Equally, there's apprehension. Then the training kicks in and you manage the aircraft in the way you've been taught. Every scramble is different though, so you never really get into a routine. The aircraft you're intercepting could also be providing challenges: descending or climbing, flying through cloud, changing course, all at somewhere around 400 mph.'[28]

To meet those demands Leuchars never lacked teeth. During the Second World War it had come under the control of Coastal Command (224 and 233 squadrons) but in 1950 it passed to Fighter Command with the arrival of the first jet fighters, the Gloster Meteor F8s of 222 Squadron and 43 Squadron. The Leuchars Wing was completed in September with the arrival of 264 Squadron equipped with De Havilland Vampire night fighters. In July 1954 the Meteors were exchanged for swept-wing Hawker Hunters and the delta-wing Gloster Javelin night and all-weather fighter arrived in 1957 until it was replaced in 1964 by the dramatic lines of the English Electric Lightning, the RAF's first supersonic fighter. Five years later 43 Squadron was re-equipped with the US McDonnell Douglas Phantom using Rolls-Royce Spey engines, which proved to be better suited to long-range operations over the North Sea than the thirsty Lightning. It was destined to be the last American-built jet fighter in RAF service during the Cold War and was gradually replaced in the 1980s by the Panavia Tornado F3, the versatile air defence version of a pan-European aircraft that gradually became the RAF's mainstay, operating in three primary variants: the Tornado IDS (interdictor/strike) fighter-bomber, the suppression of enemy air defences Tornado ECR (electronic combat/reconnaissance) and the Tornado ADV (air defence variant) interceptor aircraft. With the introduction of more modern aircraft possessing greater endurance the horizons of flight crews were also extended. At the end of the Cold War the Air Officer Scotland and Northern Ireland

(AOSNI), Scotland's senior air force commander, was Air Vice-Marshal Allan Blackley who had been educated at Perth Academy and Glasgow University where he took a degree in aeronautical engineering. Although he had fond memories of learning to fly in gliders at Edzell when he was an air cadet, he came to understand that the Scottish RAF bases under his command were part of the jigsaw that made up the doctrine of Allied air power.

In the old aeroplanes like Meteors or Hunters by the time you got to the end of the runway, it was time to come back; you couldn't go anywhere and people thought locally. The modern young airman isn't like that. Although they're based in Scotland they do see the world; they see a great deal of it and they think like that. On any particular day you might get a chap out of Leuchars and he might fly off to the north of England and land at a base in Lincolnshire . . . or he might go off and take a tanker and five hours later they're flying in Mediterranean skies. So their minds are being stretched: they don't just think of their backyards.[29]

During that same period Lossiemouth was a naval air station operating as HMS *Fulmar* between July 1946 and September 1972 when it was closed for major building works. When it reopened under RAF command it became the main UK base for operational conversion to the British-French SEPECAT Jaguar ground attack aircraft. Lossie (as it is usually known) was also home to Avro Shackleton airborne early warning aircraft as well as Blackburn Buccaneer maritime strike aircraft and in the post-Cold War years it emerged as one of the largest and busiest fast jet stations in the RAF, operating Tornado and Typhoon aircraft. Its close neighbour, RAF Kinloss, retained its wartime Coastal Command traditions by continuing to operate maritime patrol aircraft such as the Shackleton and Nimrod MR2 which carried out long-range anti-submarine patrols aimed at tracking Soviet operations in the North Atlantic and Norwegian Sea. However, not every RAF facility was concerned with operational flying during the Cold War. The strategic maritime headquarters at Pitreavie Castle also housed the location for the RAF's Search and Rescue (SAR) organisation and its yellow Sea King and Wessex helicopters were a familiar sight in Scottish skies, especially along coastal and upland areas. Responsible for providing SAR cover for millions of square miles of ocean and for the whole of the UK land area, Pitreavie's Rescue Co-ordination Centre and its counterpart at Plymouth were on permanent alert to assist aircraft and shipping in distress, while RAF Mountain Rescue teams at Kinloss and Leuchars were immediately available to assist at major incidents in the Scottish hills and mountains. Although their primary task was to assist at aircraft and ship-related incidents, some 95 per cent of their work was generated by civilians who found themselves in difficulties, one area in which ordinary people received a positive return for defence expenditure.

The Army in Scotland was equally well established and entrenched within the fabric of Scottish society. In 1939 Scottish Command had its headquarters at Edinburgh Castle and was divided into two areas, Highland and Lowland, each with two nominal Territorial Army divisions plus supplementary reserve units and various supply and service formations. Much of this administrative order survived the war and the division between Lowland and Highland was maintained with the creation of administrative brigades which lasted until 1968, when the Scottish Division was formed as the training and administrative organisation for the eight Scottish line infantry regiments. In 1955 Army Headquarters Scotland moved to a modern site at Craigiehall to the west of Edinburgh. During this period the GOC Scotland had 92 separate military locations under his command, with 2,500 regular service men and women plus 8,800 members of the Territorial Army, all told representing 14 per cent of the UK total. Much of this estate had its origins in the Second World War and anyone aged over 25 in 1960 would have remembered that wartime military presence or been reminded of it by the clusters of derelict buildings which still dotted the landscape. But the creation of that command structure had taken place in a time of national emergency, when the country was fighting for its life against a determined enemy and the threat of invasion was never more than a heartbeat away. Now, in the 1960s, the opposition was not only nameless and unseen, though widely known to be the Soviet Union and its Warsaw Pact allies, but the arrival of so much firepower seemed to put the bulk of the population in harm's way or, in extremis, in danger of nuclear annihilation.

Perhaps the most controversial Cold War development in Scotland was the creation of the Royal Artillery Range Hebrides, which came into being between 1957 and 1958, with the main sites being built in Benbecula and South Uist. Associated to the range was a remote radar

tracking station on the uninhabited island of St Kilda, some 40 miles to
the west. When it was first proposed the range met with considerable
local hostility; a campaign against it was led by Father John Morrison,
the influential priest of Ardkenneth, who quickly became known to the
media as 'Father Rocket'. He argued that the development would
destroy the local community and put in jeopardy the intrinsic Gaelic
culture – the original proposal envisaged the construction of a new
military town together with facilities for the construction of missiles
similar to the Army's existing training area on Salisbury Plain. This
would extend from Sollas in North Uist to Bornish in South Uist, with
its centre in the parish of Ardkenneth, and as a result of its construction
people were to be 'removed' from the military area. Partly as a result of
the campaign the project was scaled back and in April 1959 the government announced that the development would be for missile testing only
and that most military personnel would be temporary visitors during
the summer months. There was to be no 'new' town and no forcible
removal of people, although there was further expansion in 1968 when
the base was expanded to test the new battlefield tactical missile, the
nuclear-capable MGM-52 Lance operated by 50 Missile Regiment
Royal Artillery. Based in Menden in North Rhein-Westphalia,
Germany, the regiment spent two weeks each year on South Uist
test-firing the Lance on the range south of St Kilda. Serving with
BAOR the Lance missiles were nuclear-capable, but the summer firings
used dummy warheads

The range was a substantial development and over the years it
became a solid fixture which made a significant contribution to the
local economy, so much so that when it was threatened with closure in
June 2009 with the loss of 125 jobs there was local outrage. Local MP
Angus MacNeil (SNP) raised the matter in parliament, claiming that
'Uist people have given their full cooperation to the bases over the
decades and now deserve fair treatment in return.' It was a far cry from
the complaint put forward by one of his predecessors, Malcolm
Macmillan (Labour), in 1957 when he asked Defence Secretary
Duncan Sandys if he realised that the rocket range development had
'caused the utmost disturbance to local people, that it has put some out
of their homes and land, and some out of jobs?'[30] Interestingly, both
MPs used similar arguments to back their case: Macmillan that the
arrival of the range would damage the local community and almost 50
years later MacNeil that its closure would damage that same

community. In response to the local uproar the government decided to rescind the decision in September 2009, allowing Scottish Secretary Jim Murphy to claim that the range was 'here to stay'.

In its half-century existence, the range occupied three main sites: Balivanich (West Camp) on Benbecula, camp accommodation and support services; South Uist, Rueval (Range Control Building), range control functions; and South Uist, western shore (Range Head), target operations and weapons storage. There were other associated presences across Benbecula and South Uist.[31] Initially the range was used for testing first-generation tactical missiles such as the MGM-5 Corporal and its replacement, the MGM-29 Sergeant, but it was also used for testing smaller anti-aircraft missiles such as the Rapier and Blowpipe. Inevitably the military presence sparked a good deal of local curiosity and although the protocols for firing the missiles were strict for both safety and security reasons, there were occasions when rogue missiles had to be detonated in mid-flight. There were several reports of unconfirmed and unexplained explosions on hillsides in other parts of the Western Isles and in neighbouring Wester Ross on the Scottish mainland. The most serious incident came in 1979, when high levels of radioactive cobalt-60 were found on the range. Used in missile nose cones to ensure accuracy, the discovery of the leaks was kept secret and the findings were not released until 25 years later.[32] Inevitably, too, the presence of space-age technology in a remote island community attracted wider interest and became the inspiration for Compton Mackenzie's novel *Rockets Galore* (1957). A sequel to his popular novel *Whisky Galore* (1947), which was set in the Second World War on the fictional Hebridean island of Todday and had as its plot the islanders' attempts to hijack a shipwrecked cargo of whisky, the plot of the sequel was equally farcical and amusing as the inhabitants opposed the construction of a missile range. That fate was eventually evaded by the islanders painting seagulls red and claiming that the result was a new and unique species which had to be protected. According to Mackenzie's biographer Andro Linklater, the message was clear: 'the preservation of a habitat for birds counts for more than a habitat for people'.[33] Both novels were made into equally successful films although *Whisky Galore* was the more enduring – a remake appeared in 2016 – and with the passing of the Cold War *Rockets Galore* became little more than a historical curiosity. Later, in the twenty-first century, control of the range passed from the Royal Artillery to QinetiQ, which is the privatised part of the former UK government agency, Defence Evaluation and Research Agency (DERA).

Putting Scotland on the front line was not just a case of maintaining military and naval bases for offensive and defensive purposes. During a period when all-out nuclear warfare threatened mass civilian casualties and the colossal disruption of everyday life, thought was also given to the provision of shelters not just for individuals but also for the government. Although it was never admitted at the time, no one really thought that there would be large numbers of survivors from a nuclear attack on the densely populated UK and as a result there was no attempt to replicate the supply of domestic and public air-raid shelters of the Second World War. In 1980 a Home Office working party reported that it would cost £70 billion to provide shelter spaces for the whole population. Home defence reviews were carried out on a regular basis between the 1950s and the 1970s – notably the Strath Report of 1955, which predicted that ten hydrogen bombs could kill 12 million people – but as one author pointed out, the reality was that 'the idea of a plucky Brit with a first aid kit and a shovel already belonged to a bygone age'.[34] Fanning the sense of general unease, in 1965 the BBC refused to screen *The War Game*, a realistic docudrama written and directed by Peter Watkins which depicted the horrifying effects of a nuclear strike on Kent and the dire effect it had on the undefended and defenceless local population. According to the BBC it was considered 'too horrifying for the medium of broadcasting' and was only seen in a number of private cinema clubs such as the Cosmo in Aberdeen and Glasgow.[35] The controversial film was eventually broadcast by the BBC on 31 July 1985 in the week preceding the fortieth anniversary of the Hiroshima bombing.

However, during this period there was in theory a workable civil defence structure and a plan, codenamed 'Turnstile', to ensure the governance of the country in the event of nuclear annihilation. After any attack the country would have been governed by regionally based commissioners from 18 Regional Seats of Government (RSG) led by Commissioners of Cabinet Minister rank backed up in each location by up to 300 essential staff. These would be housed in secret fortified bunkers with the Scottish RSG being sited at Barnton Quarry in west Edinburgh plus three subsidiary bunkers, North Zone at an underground air defence bunker in Anstruther in Fife, East Zone using the former war room at Kirknewton and West Zone taking over a former

the central belt to Shetland in the far north. In such an attack the central belt would have been devastated, especially the Clyde basin, and targets to the north from Fife to Shetland would have been 'taken out' by multiple ground-burst nuclear strikes. What this would have meant for the local populations can be gauged by one of the few contemporary physical descriptions produced for the UK Cabinet describing the effect of a plutonium bomb exploding above London at a height of between 500 feet and 1,000 feet and creating a crater 450 yards in diameter:

> Total collapse of all buildings including multi-storey framed struc-tures is to be expected up to a distance of about 600 yards from ground-zero . . . and heavy internal damage, probably resulting in fires up to at least 1,500 yards . . . suburban houses . . . would be destroyed or would require demolition . . . to a distance of about 1,400 yards from ground-zero and would be rendered uninhabita-ble . . . Severe flash burns will occur on the unprotected parts of the bodies of people in the open at a distance of up to 2,000 or 3,000 yards from ground-zero . . . Gamma radiation from an airburst will cause death to people caught in the open at a distance of about 1,400 yards from ground-zero.[42]

That spare description was written in 1948 and related to the kind of bomb detonated over Nagasaki three years earlier. It is not too difficult to transpose those findings from London and to apply them to Edinburgh or Glasgow – an air burst above either city would have destroyed the central business area and caused huge collateral damage in outlying residential suburbs such as Morningside and Kelvinside. With the advent of thermonuclear weapons in the 1950s the destructive power would have been increased 1,000-fold, according to the findings of the American testing of a thermonuclear weapon at Bikini Atoll in March 1954 and comparing it to the weapons used against Japan. Not only was this bomb deadlier, with an equivalent explosive power of 15 million tons of TNT, but its effects reached further afield and touched innocent parties – 90 miles away the crew of the Japanese fishing boat *Lucky Dragon* were caught in the fallout and as a result developed radi-ation sickness which affected the entire crew and killed one of their number. With the advent of these new powerful weapons it became clear that human beings in a wide radius of an explosion would also be killed or maimed by blast and fire and that they would go on suffering from higher incidences of leukaemia and cancer, not to mention psychological trauma. In such circumstances the health services would be hard-pressed and only a handful could expect to receive any help. This too was part of the terror of the new nuclear age ushered in by the hydrogen bomb. Fortunately, the world will never know what would have happened if such a weapon had been used in modern warfare: although atomic bombs were used against Hiroshima and Nagasaki, thermonuclear devices have never been used in anger, and hopefully never will be.

5

Ding Dong Dollar:
Opposing Armageddon

EVEN BEFORE THE Americans arrived in the Holy Loch it was clear that they would not be universally welcomed in the UK. This was especially true in the growing peace movement which had come into being in 1957 with the emergence of two separate groups, the National Committee for the Abolition of Nuclear Weapons Tests (NCANWT) and the Direct Action Committee (DAC) Against Nuclear War both of which in different ways opposed the Conservative Party's 1957 White Paper on Defence outlining a nuclear policy for the UK's armed forces. Out of these was born the Campaign for Nuclear Disarmament (CND), which came into being on 17 February 1958 at a public meeting in Westminster's Central Hall and was attended by 5,000 people. The writer and philosopher Bertrand Russell was elected its president, Canon John Collins, Dean of St Paul's Cathedral, its chairman, and doughty peace campaigner Peggy Duff from NCANWT its organising secretary. It immediately attracted a large following of like-minded supporters, including scientists, religious leaders, academics, journalists, writers, actors and musicians. Its first action was to organise an Easter march from London to the Ministry of Defence's Atomic Weapons Establishment at Aldermaston near Reading, the centre for the development and production of the UK's nuclear warheads, and this attracted 10,000 marchers. (Subsequent marches were from Aldermaston to London and by the early 1960s attracted up to 100,000 participants.) From the outset CND called for unilateral nuclear disarmament in the UK, believing that if it did so other countries would follow suit. Accordingly, it set out its stall with a policy statement which was clear and unambiguous:

We shall seek to persuade British People that Britain must:

(a) Renounce unconditionally the use or production of nuclear weapons and refuse to allow their use by others in her defence.

(b) Use her utmost endeavour to bring about negotiations at all levels for agreement to end the armaments race and to lead to a general disarmament convention.

(c) Invite the co-operation of other nations, particularly non-nuclear powers, in her renunciation of nuclear weapons.[1]

Three months later opinion polls showed that 25 per cent of the British people supported the aim that the UK should give up its nuclear weapons 'even if other countries did not do so'.[2] Two years later the number had grown to 33 per cent and the CND was in business but already there were tensions between the two founding bodies, with former DAC members advocating a more robust approach or 'civil disobedience' as it came to be known, while the NCANWT faction favoured using its influence to put pressure on the main political parties, especially Labour, to change their policies of support for the existence of a UK independent deterrent. As one of the founder members Bruce Kent put it, Labour's support was essential because if it 'could be persuaded to give up aspirations for a British nuclear bomb, then this example would set in motion a worldwide shift in attitude about nuclear weapons.'[3] The debate became public in 1960 when Russell resigned as president of CND and formed the Committee of 100, which advocated non-violent action such as sit-ins to make high-profile protests against nuclear weapons. Amongst the founder members were the writers Doris Lessing, Arnold Wesker and Hugh MacDiarmid, who all spoke at the first meeting held in Trafalgar Square on 18 February 1961. The principal objective of the committee was to have as many people apprehended as possible and this did not exclude Russell, who was arrested and imprisoned for a short period in Brixton, an event which attracted a wave of sympathetic publicity and international outrage: 'The sight of the frail but defiant and distinguished philosopher being sent to prison was a major propaganda coup for the anti-nuclear movement, and throughout the 1960s the image of Russell – impossibly old, white-haired, small and bony, his jaw jutting out in implacable defiance – became a familiar and popular icon of political protest.'[4]

From the outset there was interest in Scotland, with the formation in 1957 of the Scottish Council for Abolition of Nuclear Tests and the later founding of Scottish CND in Simpson House, Edinburgh on 22 March 1958. This initiative chimed in with CND's attempt to make separate protests across the UK so that the message was spread across the country and was not seen as a London-based movement. Although there was little support in East Anglia, where American bombers were based, it was different in Scotland. The arrival of the US Navy base at Holy Loch provided the impetus for action and persuaded Scottish members that they should follow the Committee of 100's example. It is also possible that Scottish support for CND was fired by the country's left-wing traditions, especially the memories of 'Red Clydeside', the Marxist-inspired strike movement of the First World War. When the news of the American deployment was announced in parliament on 1 November 1960, 30 Labour MPs, mostly representing Scottish constituencies, tabled a motion of opposition, arguing that the arrival of Polaris not only imperilled Scotland but was also an abnegation of responsibility, as the government had no control over the use of the nuclear weapons. That point was reinforced by an exhibition of contemporary art which opened at the McLellan Galleries in Glasgow in January 1961 with the telling title 'Count Down' and attracted widespread interest in the press and elsewhere.[5] Despite the publicity nothing changed government policy, although notice had been given that the Polaris submarines and their crews were unlikely to be welcome guests in Scotland. And so it proved. In the original plan the American submarine tender ship had been due to arrive in Holy Loch shortly before Christmas but due to industrial action in the USA this was postponed until 3 March 1961. The delay allowed the US Navy and the Royal Navy to make detailed plans to mark the occasion, having overcome British government concerns about generating the wrong kind of publicity. It also allowed Scottish CND to fine-tune its own plans for a campaign of civil disobedience.

As it turned out, both sides achieved their objectives. The arrival of the submarine tender USS *Proteus* was carefully choreographed. When it arrived off Cumbrae in the early morning it was greeted by two small naval vessels carrying accredited reporters and photographers who followed the ship, now pulled by tugs, to its mooring buoy off Kilmun on the north shore of the Holy Loch. After local dignitaries had arrived there was a press conference on board the ship and that same evening there was a reception in the Queen's Hall in Dunoon followed by a public dance. The expected demonstrations did take place but the number of canoes and dinghies was too small to cause any inconvenience. It was not until the following day, 4 March, that CND showed its hand with a march of 1,000 protestors from Dunoon to Holy Loch, with some protestors carrying banners with the hopeful message 'Killers Withdraw!' while others carried the douce warning 'Americans we like you but not Polaris'. This was followed by further demonstrations when the first submarine, USS *Patrick Henry*, arrived on 8 March. Again, there were seaborne protests and one canoeist was arrested while the submarine was berthing but still managed to board the *Patrick Henry*, where he climbed onto the top of the after fin. All this was a prelude to a larger demonstration held over the Whit weekend which involved around 2,000 protestors whose aim was to board the *Proteus* or the recently arrived supply ship *Betelgeuse*. On Sunday 14 May the protest march was organised by Glasgow District Trades Council, Glasgow City Labour Party and Glasgow and District Cooperative Association and it was led by William Scholes, Scottish Secretary of the Transport and General Workers Union, accompanied by Michael Foot, the prominent Labour MP and unilateralist.[6]

Inevitably, perhaps, the relationship between the political left and CND led to allegations that members were Communist sympathisers and even that the protest movement was funded by Moscow. From the outset, therefore, MI5 took a close interest in CND's activities and in 1985 a former intelligence officer, Cathy Massiter, revealed that these investigations were in fact politically motivated and were not prompted by any fears of an actual threat. 'We were violating our own rules,' she told Channel 4's *20/20 Vision* programme on 8 March. 'It seemed to be getting out of control.' Amongst those accused of having an 'unhealthy intimate relationship' with East Germany was Bruce Kent, at the time chaplain to the University of London and later (1979–85) General Secretary of CND and so upset was he by these allegations, which were current in the 1960s, that he had offered a reward of £100 to anyone who could prove that any link existed between CND and Moscow. It was never claimed.[7]

Meanwhile, on the waters of the Holy Loch on the day of the first major protest, 12 canoeists set off towards the *Proteus* supported by a motor launch and a converted house boat bearing a Red Cross and a banner stating 'Life not Death'. At the same time boats crewed by local sailors attempted to thwart the demonstrators and there was a brief moment of hilarity when two police launches collided, one of them, according to the *Glasgow Herald* 'carrying senior police and naval officers'. The newspaper also reported a number of minor clashes between CND demonstrators and local residents who accused the former of being 'Communist stooges' and invited them to carry out their demonstrations in Moscow.[8] There was also a confrontation between Scholes and the well-known pacifist Pat Arrowsmith, who was representing the Committee of 100 and had marched from London with other campaigners. On their arrival Scholes offered the advice that 'the best help she [Arrowsmith] can give us is going back to London' and 'that we will achieve our object through the democratic machinery of this country and will not be influenced by cranks or anyone of that nature'. For her efforts Arrowsmith was arrested and sentenced to three months' imprisonment at Gateside Prison in Greenock, where she was force-fed after going on hunger strike. Although the demonstration began relatively light-heartedly the use of fire hoses introduced a tougher note and an official report on the incident claimed that the '[police] action seemed unnecessarily vigorous' while the reporter from *The Times* noted that 'marine skirmishing of this enthusiastic nature probably had not been seen in these parts since the Danes were here'.[9] (This was a reference to the Norwegian attack on Scotland in 1263, in which King Haakon Haakonsson attempted to assert Norwegian sovereignty over the western seaboard of Scotland. It culminated in the indecisive Battle of Largs.)

Undeterred by the forceful response the protestors set up camp on the north shore at nearby Kilmun, where they were determined to make their presence felt. Later, many of those who took part in the demonstrations would recall the warmth and camaraderie generated by the occasion, and above all they remembered the boisterous but good-humoured singing. This was the period of the folk revival and the gatherings were enlivened by protest songs such as 'Ding Dong Dollar', which became the anthem of the anti-Polaris movement with its rousing chorus:

> Oh ye cannae spend a dollar when ye're deid
> No ye cannae spend a dollar when ye're deid
> Singing, Ding Dong Dollar, everybody holler
> Ye cannae spend a dollar when ye're deid.

The song had its origins in a chance remark by the Rev. Dr George MacLeod of the Iona Community, who told a meeting in Glasgow that he had a simple response to the argument that the Americans would bring wealth into the area: 'Of course, you cannot spend a dollar when you are dead.' This was heard by a songwriter called John Mack who put the phrase to use in an embryonic chorus sung to the tune 'She'll be coming round the mountain'. Later, as revealed by folklorist Gordon McCulloch in *The Bottle Imp*, it was reworked and refined by the group of singers and writers who collaborated with the activist and teacher Morris Blythman.[10]

Unofficially known as the 'Glasgow (or Glesga) Eskimos', they were an informal grouping of protestors who were also involved in the burgeoning folk music scene in Scotland and were members of the influential Glasgow Song Guild. They included Morris and Marion Blythman, Josh MacRae, Jim McLean, Jackie O'Connor, Nigel Denver, and Jackie Keir. MacRae and Denver both enjoyed successful careers as singers and entertainers but the driving force behind the Eskimos was Morris Blythman, born in 1919, whose house in Balgrayhill Road Springburn was a meeting place for like-minded people interested in socialism, literature and music and passionately opposed to nuclear weaponry. A highly respected teacher at Allan Glen's School in Glasgow, Blythman wrote poetry under the pen name 'Thurso Berwick' and was widely admired for the energy and commitment he brought to radical politics and the folk revival in Scotland. It was in Blythman's house after the Whit protests at Holy Loch that the notion of the Glasgow Eskimos came into being and the impetus was provided by none other than the commander of the submarine depot ship USS *Proteus*, Captain Richard B. Laning. At a press conference following the first demonstration against the deployment in March 1961 he was asked what he thought about the protestors in their canoes and kayaks. Unwisely and unwittingly he responded: 'They don't bother us, they're just a bunch of goddam Eskimos.' Not only was this a dismissive comment meant to denigrate the demonstrators but Laning was not to know that a popular Glasgow children's street song of the period contained the following verse sung to the tune of the well-known Edwardian Cockney music-hall song 'Let's all go down the Strand':

> Ma Maw's a millionaire (hiv a banana)
> Blue eyes and curly hair.
> Doon amang the Eskimos,
> Playin a gemme o' dominoes
> Ma Maw's a millionaire.

It was from that seemingly unpromising beginning that the Eskimos were born and the fact was celebrated in a song which was almost certainly written by Blythman but then put through the collaborative ethos which he brought to most of his output. It was sung to the rousing American Civil War tune of 'Marching through Georgia' and would have been recognised by the sailors whenever it was sung at the Holy Loch.

> It's up the Clyde comes Lanin [sic], a super-duper Yank,
> But doon a damn sight quicker when we cowpt him doon the
>   stank,
> Up tae the neck in sludge and sewage fairly stops yuir swank
> – We are the Glesga Eskimos.
>
> CHORUS:
> Hullo! Hullo! We are the Eskimos,
> Hullo! Hullo! The Glesga Eskimos,
> We'll gaff that nyaff caa'd Lanin
> We'll spear him whaur he blows
> – We are the Glesga Eskimos

By coincidence the tune was also used for an equally popular song called the 'Brigton Billy Boys' which emerged in the 1930s to commemorate the Glasgow razor gang leader Billy Fullarton and for many years was an unofficial anthem of supporters of the Rangers football club.[11] As a Marxist Blythman was opposed to the sectarian divide in Glasgow – the hostility between Protestant and Catholic – and although he was frequently criticised for using so-called 'Orange' tunes his friend and colleague Janey Buchan, herself no mean folklorist and radical spirit, pointed out that he only used them as parodies of both Protestant and Catholic songs.[12]

In any case, the collaboration between anti-nuclear protestors and the folk movement in Scotland produced a rich harvest and a string of songs flowed out from the Eskimos or were inspired by the activities of the protestors at the Holy Loch base. These included 'We Dinna Want Polaris' (sung to the tune of 'Three Craws' and containing the memorable chorus 'tell the Yanks to drop them [Polaris] doon the stanks') and 'Boomerang' (sung to the tune of 'Bless 'em all' with its invitation 'just send them back whaur they belang').[13] In all it has been estimated that around 80 protest songs of this kind were composed, and they reached a wider audience when an album (LP) entitled *Ding Dong Dollar* was issued by the US label Folkways. The sleeve notes were written by Blythman and the poet and folklorist Hamish Henderson (without attribution) and give a good idea of the sense of protest, optimism and reforming zeal which the Eskimos brought to the cause.

> Everything was thrown into the pot: the missionaries first to give it the bite, army ballads from World War II, football songs, Orange songs, Fenian songs, [F. J.] Child ballads, street songs, children's songs, bothy ballads, blues, skiffle, Australian bush ballads, calypsos, [Ewan] McColl and [Alan] Lomax, [Burl] Ives and Leadbelly, Dominic Behan, SRA songs, IRA songs, [Woody] Guthrie and [Cisco] Houston, pantomime and vaudeville, Billy Graham, Scottish Land League songs, Gaelic songs, mouth-music, Wobbly [Industrial Workers of the World] songs, spirituals, mountaineering and hiking ballads, [Ramblin' Jack] Elliot and [Pete] Seeger, mock-precenting, the Royal Family, Roddy McMillan and Matt McGinn . . . and as a result of this genial eclecticism, we finished up with a banquet.[14]

The songs also made their way into the public domain through the medium of print, using the long established publishing method of chapbooks with titles such as *The Rebel Ceilidh Song Book* and *Ding Dong Dollar Song Book*, and all bore the Blythman imprimatur of collaboration without individual attribution to reflect the collectivist ideals of the movement, or as he described the process, putting the work through the 'collective mincer': 'One of the most unusual features of this whole movement was the way in which many of the songs were born. Workshop techniques were employed, and as a result, many of the songs had a communal authorship. In at least one song as many as twenty people contributed to the final production . . . I have always believed in mass creation.'[15]

The inspiration behind 'Ding Dong Dollar', George MacLeod, was one of the most original and most committed supporters of the CND in Scotland. A Christian socialist, he came from a long line of influential Highland ministers of the Church of Scotland; according to his biographer it was a genealogy that included six Moderators of the General Assembly of the Church of Scotland, seven Doctorates of Divinity, two Deanships of the Chapel Royal, two Deanships of the Order of the

Thistle and four Royal chaplaincies.[16] Even so, despite such a distinguished lineage, MacLeod was very much his own man and had emerged in the 1930s as a charismatic preacher and a passionate reformer with a rare capacity to get on with everyone who came into his orbit, especially young people. His upbringing was that of an anglicised Scot – he was educated at Winchester and Oriel College Oxford – and his family enjoyed considerable wealth, his mother being the daughter of a successful Lancashire cotton manufacturer, but MacLeod always had a common touch. During the First World War he served as a front-line infantry officer with the Argyll and Sutherland Highlanders, winning a Military Cross in 1918, and then returned to Edinburgh to read Divinity. Very quickly he rose to prominence as a preacher and in the 1930s he took up his ministry in Govan, a deprived working-class area in Glasgow where he was greatly offended by the poverty and hardship suffered by most of his parishioners. As a result of that experience he conceived the idea of founding a revivalist community on Iona, the birthplace of Christianity in Scotland, and slowly evolved the notion of creating a church based on 'Celtic Christianity'. The result was the Iona Community, which he founded in 1938 and whose members went on to rebuild and refurbish the ruined abbey on the island. As MacLeod was also a committed pacifist it was only natural that he would lend his considerable support to the CND and it was entirely in keeping that he should have provided the impetus for the song 'Ding Dong Dollar'. However, while MacLeod had been a founder member of CND and agreed with its principles he rejected Russell's invitation to join the Committee of 100 because he believed that it would be divisive and that the spiritual ground for such a move had not been prepared.

And faith would be needed, because in spite of the Whit weekend success – which had produced a huge amount of publicity – there was still a great deal of work to be done. That September the Committee of 100 planned its largest demonstration to date with simultaneous protests at the Holy Loch and in London's Trafalgar Square, although the latter was banned by the government it still went ahead, leading to the arrest of 1,314 protestors. The Holy Loch demonstration faced other problems in the shape of a Force 8 gale on Saturday 16 September and while it too went ahead as planned there was inevitable disruption. The Sunday demonstration at the US Navy pier at Ardnadam was more successful in that campaigners managed to block the surrounding roads, a move that led to the arrest of 351 of their number, many of whom were fined £10, the alternative being a prison sentence of 60 days. Amongst those who were arraigned at Dunoon Sheriff Court was Bob Starrett, a young shipyard worker from Glasgow who was a member of the Young Communist League. Like many others he believed that the American deployment in Scotland was illegal; he was determined to join the demonstration, which he described as being peaceful and non-confrontational, at least in the initial stages: 'It was a non-violent protest because we felt that if things turned violent we would lose the argument. But many were arrested and when they came out four days later some found out they'd lost their jobs.' Fortunately for Starrett his fine was paid for him by one of the founder members of the Committee of 100, Compton Mackenzie.[17] Later in life Starrett became a political cartoonist and never forgot the sense of common purpose which engulfed those who took part in the demonstrations of the early 1960s.

Even getting to the US submarine base took time, energy and determination as Keith Bovey, a leading CND member and Glasgow lawyer, remembered 50 years later: 'To get to the Holy Loch, we'd take a train to Gourock and cross on the ferry, then march from Dunoon to Ardnadam where the pier was for the US base. I remember once getting a ferry to Kilmun pier, which is the wrong side of the loch– only about four miles away. I hitched a lift, but when I asked for Ardnadam the driver realised I was a CND demonstrator and threw me out – against a mild protest on his other passenger's part.'[18]

Despite disappointing numbers – as far as the organisers were concerned – the demonstration made its point by creating a well-publicised CND presence at the Holy Loch and reminding US naval personnel about the strength of the opposition to their presence. That was an important point because the US reaction to the protests tended be muted and bemused. A visiting American journalist reported that the sailors 'treated the situation with good humour, looking upon the anti-bomb crowd as more weird than alarming'.[19] It was a reasonable response, as despite the energy and commitment put into the demonstration there was no way that the USA or the UK would give way on the development of Holy Loch. In 1963 the increasingly obsolescent *Proteus* was replaced by the purpose-built depot ship USS *Hunley* and the number of submarines at the base was increased to four at any one time.

However, far removed from the claims of realpolitik it was also clear that the CND in Scotland was making another kind of point, namely that their protests could be both good-humoured and reasonably effective. In the former respect it helped that the demonstrators were backed by songs that were catchy, irreverent and made full use of Glasgow vernacular, all in stark contrast to the kind of protest songs popular in England – such as Ewan McColl's 'Song of Hiroshima' or John Brunner's 'The H-Bomb's Thunder' – which seemed to owe more to Puritan or Leveller traditions and were consequently regarded as being worthy but joyless. While Scottish CND's activities did nothing to persuade the government, far less the Labour Party, to change policy over the possession of nuclear weapons, the demonstrations at the Holy Loch did ensure a steady stream of publicity throughout 1961 when the issue was rarely off the front pages, ensuring that this period was the high-water mark of CND's early activities in Scotland. Later in the decade support for CND began to dwindle across the UK, partly due to the 1963 Test Ban Treaty which prohibited testing of nuclear weapons in the atmosphere and partly due to a growing preoccupation with the war in Vietnam.

It was not just protest groups that objected to the basing of nuclear weapons in Scotland; so too did other parts of civic society. As was only to be expected, principal amongst these was the Christian church in Scotland which in the 1960s still had a membership of some 60 per cent of the adult population, 25 per cent them being adherents of the Presbyterian Church of Scotland and 13 per cent being members of the Catholic Church.[20] Although these numbers would decline in the decades that followed, at the beginning of the 1960s both churches influenced Scottish life and helped to set the moral tone with the result that both were under pressure to reach a conclusion on the presence of nuclear weapons in the country. In the Church of Scotland the example of George MacLeod was strong and his name was listed as a sponsor of the Scottish CND when its executive committee met in Edinburgh on 15 April 1958. Other noteworthy sponsors were the novelists Naomi Mitchison and Compton Mackenzie, the actor James Robertson Justice and the veteran nationalist campaigners Oliver Brown and R. E. Muirhead. When MacLeod was elected Moderator of the General Assembly of the Church of Scotland for the period 1957–8 much was expected of him in pacifist circles, for although he had refused to join the Committee of 100 he was closely associated with CND. It was too much to hope that he would persuade the General Assembly, the church's governing body, to pass any motion proposing abolition but in his opening address he argued that the production and testing of nuclear weapons was out of control and that the church had a responsibility to face up to that fact and confront 'the vast oblong blur of Christian indecision in this, the eleventh worsening year of the Atomic age'.[21] By contrast, at the same time Archbishop (later Cardinal) Gordon Gray of St Andrews and Edinburgh told the Secretary of Scottish CND that there was no impediment to Catholics supporting CND but he thought it would be 'imprudent for a priest to be publicly associated with the movement'.

In addition to MacLeod there were other members of the Church of Scotland who took advantage of the annual General Assemblies to promote the cause of nuclear disarmament. Principal amongst these was Roger Gray, an optician from Skye whose shop in Portree became a well-known peace centre, and who was a tireless supporter of unilateral nuclear disarmament. His interventions at the General Assembly made him a kenspeckle and much-admired figure. He was also firmly opposed to the war in Vietnam, a subject he raised on three separate occasions (1966, 1967 and 1970) and his approach was made abundantly clear when he first addressed the General Assembly as a commissioner in May 1965 on the topic of nuclear disarmament: 'I have long been convinced that if the world Church, with its vast potential, and its peculiar access to the power of the Holy Spirit, had been in the vanguard of the peace movement, already the possibility of nuclear annihilation would be almost as remote as a return to cannibalism.'[22]

Ten years later Roger Gray returned to the subject, the intervening period having been spent on his opposition to the Vietnam War, when he moved a motion urging the government to renounce the possession or use of nuclear weapons 'by us or on our behalf'. Although this failed to get the necessary support the question remained on the General Assembly's agenda and it became customary to hold prayer vigils on the eve of debates on the issue. Ahead lay a long and rocky road but Gray's hopes were fulfilled in May 1982 when the General Assembly passed a motion put forward by a former Moderator, the Very Reverend George Reid, urging the church to oppose the construction of nuclear weapons and to press for arms control: 'Recognising the dangers inherent in the arms race and in recent developments in the actions and attitudes of the great powers, the General Assembly believe that particular efforts are called for at this time to reduce international tension and to start the process of disbarment.'[23]

The motion was passed by 255 to 153 votes, leaving Gray to claim: 'It's like ten miracles piled on top of each other. And it just came out of the blue, out of a totally ordinary Assembly.'[24] Four years later there was further reform when the General Assembly accepted a motion put forward by George MacLeod, who was by then in his ninetieth year: 'As of now this General Assembly declare that no Church can accede to the use of Nuclear weapons to defend any cause whatever. They call on HM Government to desist in their use and further development.' After 30 years of sitting on the fence and being unable to decide between the claims of those who supported disarmament and those who preferred the policy of deterrence the Church of Scotland came down firmly on the side of nuclear pacifism and that became the accepted policy in the years ahead. That same year, Roger Gray died on Iona while attending a meeting. As his fellow campaigner, the Rev. Alastair Ramage, summed him up, 'Roger Gray's name is one that deserves to be much esteemed in the involvement of the Church of Scotland in the peace movement.'[25]

There was also a political aspect to the process. Nuclear weapons were first developed under the post-war Labour government and this policy was continued after the Conservatives came to power in 1951 with a defence policy which was heavily weighted toward the use of nuclear weapons and the development of missile technology. Between then and 1958, 21 above the ground atmospheric tests of British nuclear bombs were carried out in Australia until the Partial Test Ban Treaty came into being in 1963, putting an end to the practice. When the Conservatives were in power during this period agreement had been reached with the USA on the use of the Polaris missile and the Holy Loch was granted to the US Navy as a forward operating base for its own Polaris-equipped submarines. It followed, therefore, that possession of nuclear weapons was central to Conservative defence orthodoxy and this was confirmed in 1958 when Prime Minister Harold Macmillan chaired a meeting of the Cabinet Defence Committee, which made it explicit that such weapons underpinned UK aspirations to be a great power. The main desiderata were:

(a) To retain our special relation with the United States and, through it, our influence in world affairs, and, especially, our right to have a voice in the final issue of peace and war.

(b) To make a definite, though limited, contribution to the total nuclear strength of the West – while recognising that the United States must continue to play the major part in maintaining the balance of nuclear power.

(c) To enable us, by threatening to use our independent nuclear power, to secure United States co-operation in a situation in which their interests were less immediately threatened than our own.

(d) To make sure that, in a nuclear war, sufficient attention is given to certain Soviet targets which are of greater importance to us than to the United States.[26]

While the Conservatives were in office there was little likelihood that CND's aims would ever be achieved, with the result that great hope was put on Labour returning to power because several prominent left-wingers such as Michael Foot were unilateralists, as was the bulk of the trade union movement. The key would be winning over the party's annual conference, but that day seemed far off. Two elections in quick succession, in February 1950 and October 1951 saw the Conservatives return to power as they did again in 1955 when they won 36 of Scotland's 71 seats, a feat they were never to repeat. In 1959 Labour won 38 seats to the Conservatives' 32 in Scotland, although the latter remained in power at Westminster having increased their UK majority by over 100 seats. However, with the economic situation declining in Scotland, the writing was on the wall and in the 1964 election the Conservatives lost heavily, winning only 24 seats, while Labour took 43 seats to help them secure a tiny overall majority in London – Labour had 317 seats, the Conservatives 304 (including the Speaker), and the Liberals 9. This gave hope to Labour unilateralists that there would be a change of nuclear policy but the new prime minister, Harold Wilson, was minded to retain the nuclear deterrent. A pragmatist who believed in fudging most difficulties, he was at heart an Atlanticist who supported the special relationship with the US and was in favour of the NATO alliance and a multilateralist approach to disarmament. Wilson was also uncomfortably aware of the way in which the Labour Party's attitude to nuclear weapons had badly affected the leadership of his predecessor Hugh Gaitskell – in 1960 the party conference had rejected the official policy document on defence thereby causing an internal crisis – and his response had been to ignore the anti-nuclear feeling within the party, which had been mainly articulated by the trade unions. Here he was helped by winning the next general election in 1966, turning his dissolution majority of three into a more impressive 97 and Labour remained in power until 1970, when it lost to Ted Heath's Conservatives.

With Labour unwilling to support the aims of unilateralism, by rights the left could have turned to the Communist Party of Great Britain (CPGB), which had a reasonably high profile in Scotland in the post-war period. Of the party's membership of 45,000, one-quarter were based in Scotland, two recent General Secretaries were Scots (J. R. Campbell and John Gollan) and it enjoyed considerable prominence and influence in the Scottish Area of the National Union of Mineworkers (NUM).[27] The Communist Party was also well represented in the trade unions generally in Scotland but the Scottish District (as it was termed) was part of the CPGB, which in turn was part of a worldwide movement and as such it is difficult to discern any separate or distinctly Scottish identity or modus operandi. The general orthodoxy as expressed in the party's official history is that 'after initially opposing the unilateralism of the Campaign for Nuclear Disarmament (CND) when it was formed in 1958, the party had thrown its weight behind it from 1960.'[28]

The subject is still a matter for debate, with claim and counter-claim about the strength of the relationship between CPGB and CND in the early years. It is certainly a vexed subject, for while the connection was not formalised until early in 1960 that cannot be the whole story. Many Scottish Communist members belonged to trades councils or trade unions which supported the aims of CND, and many members of the party's youth section, the Young Communist League, would have participated as individuals in the pre-1960 demonstrations. It is not over-stretching the facts to believe that by 1960 the CPGB had to come to an accommodation with CND because to remain on the outside of the peace movement would not only have threatened its own credibility but it would also have looked ridiculous. In any case, even before CND came into being the CPGB maintained its own British Peace Committee, which had a youth section as well as a Scottish section and was active in anti-nuclear activities, its white dove on a blue background being particularly notable at demonstrations. Part of the problem is that as far as the CND was concerned the CPGB was simply too small to influence events as a political power bloc even though its effect at grass roots level was not insubstantial. When the Labour Party conference of 1959 voted to reject the party's defence policy and embrace unilateralism the decisive vote came from the unions and there is little doubt that the NUM vote was ensured by the Scottish contingent, many of whom would have been CPGB members.

In the decade that followed there was to be another political grouping which influenced the debate about 'banning the bomb', as unilateralism had come to be known in the media. This was the Scottish National Party (SNP), which had come into being in 1934 and had enjoyed mixed fortunes in the polls. At the start of the 1960s party membership stood at around 2,000 and the party's influence in Scottish politics was negligible but all that was to change as the decade unfolded. By its end of the decade the SNP had become news and was no longer considered a joke or a haven for idealists. There were several reasons for this upturn. The first was an internal reorganisation of the party's structure which resulted in a growing membership; funds were raised and activists worked long and hard to get the message across to doubting voters, who responded by taking the SNP seriously, regarding it as a viable alternative to the existing larger parties. The second change was the emergence of a new leadership, with Ian Macdonald as the first full-time national organiser and William (Billy) Wolfe, a committed and thoroughly decent man, who stood for West Lothian in a by-election in 1962 when he came a creditable second to the Labour candidate Tam Dalyell, an Old Etonian socialist whose ancestral home, the House of Binns, was in the constituency and whose ancestor, also Tam Dalyell, had founded the Royal Scots Greys cavalry regiment in 1678.

Although not elected Wolfe had come to prominence and this led to him being chosen as vice-chairman and essentially deputy leader and then chairman in 1969. Not only did Wolfe institute a top-to-bottom review of the party structure, but he was instrumental in moving it to the left and embracing radical policies such as land nationalisation and nuclear disarmament – it helped that Wolfe was a member of Scottish CND and later served as its treasurer. All this appealed to a younger generation of voters who were disenchanted with Labour and the Conservatives, were opposed to the Polaris submarine base at Holy Loch and disliked the tacit British support for the US war in Vietnam. In 1963 the SNP adopted its thistle-looped logo, which soon became as recognisable as the equally ubiquitous CND peace symbol based on the semaphore symbols for 'N' (two flags held 45 degrees down on both sides) and 'D' (two flags, one above the head and one at the feet, forming the vertical line) for 'Nuclear Disarmament' within a circle. The electorate responded well. At the 1966 general election the SNP contested 23 seats and although none was won the party's profile had been raised. A year later the party contested Glasgow Pollock in a by-election and won 28 per cent of the vote, allowing the Conservatives to win, unthinkable in a seat once solidly Labour. That same year in the local elections the party won 200,000 votes and gained 69 seats. It was clear that momentum was growing.

All this was a prelude to the SNP's breakthrough at Hamilton in November 1967 when Winnie Ewing, a lawyer by training and a nationalist by conviction, won the seat with a handsome majority – 46 per cent of the vote – and in so doing put Labour in second place. Echoing a popular musical of the day, *Stop the World, I Want to Get Off*, her first words passed into legend – 'Stop the world, Scotland wants to get on' – and it is not stretching the facts to claim that her victory caused a sensation across the UK. Not only was it the beginning of a new era in nationalist politics but it also marked the end of the SNP's time in the doldrums. After Hamilton anything seemed possible and even though Ewing failed to hold the seat in the 1970 general election, when the sole SNP seat was won in the Western Isles by Donald Stewart, the party had arrived as a formidable force in Scottish politics and won 11 seats in the October 1974 general election. Unfortunately, it was then hobbled by a period of internal factionalism which lasted until the election of Alex Salmond as leader in 1990. Throughout this period, the SNP was also opposed to the presence of nuclear weapons in the country, regarding them as 'immoral, ineffective and expensive' and for many years it was hostile to the notion of an independent Scotland becoming a member of NATO on the grounds that under certain circumstances the alliance would permit a first strike using nuclear weapons. Long after the Cold War had ended the SNP altered its stance at its annual conference in October in 2012, when it agreed by a narrow margin that NATO membership would be sought by an independent Scotland 'subject to an agreement that Scotland will not host nuclear weapons'. By then the SNP had become the predominant force in Scottish politics and was able to ignore the anomaly that under NATO's nuclear policy US Navy submarines of the Ohio class armed with Trident missiles could exercise their right to continue using the Clyde Submarine Base at Faslane.[29]

Cultural events also forced a change of attitude and encouraged people to widen their horizons. If any event typified the transformational and progressive ethos of the post-war world in Scotland it was the staging of the first Edinburgh Festival in August 1947. As the recently demobbed poet Maurice Lindsay put it in his memoirs, 'it is impossible to exaggerate the impact the Festival made upon us in that long-ago sunny summer, when Europe was still in the process of dragging itself out of the shadows of war'.[30] It helped that the sun shone throughout the event and the closing concert by the Vienna Philharmonic was hailed as a manifestation of 'the unconquerable spirit of European civilisation'. Certainly, no one who heard Kathleen Ferrier singing Mahler's *Das Lied von der Erde* to Bruno Walter's conducting ever forgot the experience. Despite occasional financial and organisational vicissitudes and local carping the Festival never looked back, to become in time one of the world's great civilising celebrations and one of the brightest ornaments in Scottish cultural life.

The first ever Edinburgh International Festival was a triumph and its existence during the Cold War years was a reminder of the redemptive power exercised by the arts and the ways in which culture can overcome political boundaries. As evidence the Leningrad Symphony Orchestra appeared at the Festival in 1960 with four outstanding concerts, each one containing a work by Tchaikovsky, and this was followed by a second Soviet appearance six years later with the arrival of the Moscow Radio Orchestra. Amongst the pieces played was the first European performance of Prokofiev's cantata *They are Seven*, which involved a collaboration between the Moscow-based orchestra and the newly formed Edinburgh Festival Chorus. It was no easy matter to arrange as the choir had to learn the words phonetically but they did this to great effect and the result was a stream of excellent reviews. As the Festival's historian observed, 'music can break all boundaries'.[31]

In its early days the Edinburgh International Festival was a reaffirmation of what the leader-writer of the *Manchester Guardian* called 'the unconquerable spirit of European civilisation', and its birth was a cultural rebuff to the depredations of the Second World War.[32] In that sense it was very much a child of conflict but in time it also came to be regarded as a means of transcending cultural and political boundaries and building bridges between divided peoples, especially at moments when the world came perilously close to plunging over the edge. For example, in 1962, the year of the Cuban missile crisis, the Soviet composer Dmitri Shostakovich was the guest of honour in Edinburgh and he responded by admitting that never before had he heard so many of his pieces being played over such a short space of time – 16 works in the three-week period of the Festival – but not everyone was entranced by his appearance in Edinburgh. Writing in the *Catholic Herald* the critic Colm Brogan sparked a lengthy correspondence after objecting to the presence of a programme 'heavily weighted with Iron Curtain performers and material', including the presence of Shostakovich as guest of honour. Calling Shostakovich a 'pretty abject creature' who had betrayed his artistic beliefs for political reasons – in 1960 he joined the Communist Party in order to become General Secretary of the Soviet Composers Union – Brogan gave the reasons for his dismay at the Festival's invitation to the great composer: 'There is one quality we can and must demand in every artist of international standing before we do him honour. That quality is integrity. An honourable man living in a suffocating tyranny has the alternatives of protest or silence. If he chooses to lick the tyrant's boots he loses his honour. That is what Shostakovich did.'[33]

It should not be thought that there was no wide-ranging dialogue between the two sides during the Cold War. On the contrary, throughout the confrontation there were meetings of interested minds at cultural or academic level, and some of these involved Scotland. Principal amongst these was the Scotland–USSR Friendship Society, which was founded in June 1945 to 'promote friendship and mutual understanding between the peoples of Scotland and the USSR'.[34] It was born out of the admiration felt for the people of the Soviet Union during the long fight against Nazi Germany during the Second World War, but that respect prospered during the Cold War years and became a focus for maintaining connections with the Soviet Union at a time when the Society's president, John Kinloch, said that there were three alternatives for the world – 'annihilation, peaceful coexistence based on a fear of the Bomb, or friendship'.[35] While opening its headquarters, Freedom House in Belmont Crescent in Glasgow, in May 1955 Kinloch made it clear that he preferred the third option. Amongst the Society's many supporters were leading representatives from Scotland's cultural life, including the poet Hugh MacDiarmid, the artist J. D. Fergusson and the actor Duncan MacRae. Amongst other activities, the Society was responsible for arranging cultural and delegate exchanges between the two countries, the high point being 'Months of Friendship' which were held across Scotland during the difficult year of 1956 when the Soviet Union invaded Hungary, an incident which divided opinion in the West. Most intellectuals deplored the invasion and many resigned from the Communist Party of Great Britain which had supported the Soviet move, but one exception was MacDiarmid, who took the opportunity to write to the General Secretary John Gollan voicing his support and informing him that 'the time has come for me to express my complete agreement with the line taken by your Executive and to renew my membership of the party'.[36] MacDiarmid's decision puzzled many of his friends and admirers, but this was, after all, the poet who had written of himself in his long poem *A Drunk Man Looks at the Thistle*:

> I'll ha'e nae hauf-way hoose, but aye be whaur
> Extremes meet – it's the only way I ken
> To dodge the curst conceit o' bein' richt
> That damns the vast majority o' men.[37]

At the time MacDiarmid was travelling extensively in eastern Europe and China and, as he explained to those who deplored his decision to rejoin the Communist Party, the experience had had a profound effect on him: 'Everything I have seen in these countries and all my intercourse with their public men, their writers and other artists, and their ordinary folk, has abundantly strengthened and confirmed my Communist faith.'[38] And MacDiarmid knew what he was talking about. In 1957, at the invitation of the Chinese Ministry of Culture, he travelled to Beijing by way of the Soviet Union and Czechoslovakia to celebrate May Day as part of a delegation of the British–Chinese Friendship Society which included the novelist Graham Greene. In addition to finding the visit invigorating MacDiarmid was fired by the sense of purpose he encountered in the country. Five years later, at the time of the Cuban crisis, he wrote a mawkish poem of 32 quatrains entitled 'The Chinese Genius Wakes Up', one of which gives full voice to his admiration:

> In the dawn of history the Chinese
> With their arts and inventions glorified Man.
> Now at this crisis in human affairs
> It's good to see them again in the van.[39]

As Scotland's leading poet MacDiarmid was often visited by writers from the Soviet Union and Eastern Europe, one of the most notable being Yevgeny Yevtushenko, who made an early trip to his house Brownsbank near Biggar in May 1962. The Russian poet himself was no stranger to controversy, having written in the previous year what would become perhaps his most famous poem, 'Babi Yar', in which he denounced the Soviet distortion of historical fact regarding the Nazi massacre of the Jewish population of Kiev in September 1941.[40] In the same year that Yevtushenko visited MacDiarmid his friend Dmitri Shostakovich set 'Babi Yar' as the opening movement of his 13th Symphony with four other Yevtushenko poems forming the basis for its other movements, making a cumulative portrait of the mood of the times.

That kind of cultural cross-fertilisation was a vital element in the relationship with the Soviet Union and for many Soviet visitors at its centre was the eighteenth-century Scots poet Robert Burns, who seemed to represent an abiding interest in individual liberty and a concern for the poor and the oppressed as expressed in works such as 'A Man's a Man for a' That' and 'Love and Liberty'. Burns became some-thing of a cult figure in the Soviet Union: his work was translated widely into Russian and was taught in schools. In 1956 official postage stamps were issued to mark the 160th anniversary of the poet's death. Much of the enthusiasm was created by the translator, Samuil Marshak, whose original translation of Burns's poetry sold 600,000 copies and who first visited Scotland in 1955 to attend the International Burns Festival organised by the Burns Federation and the Scottish Tourist Board. While in the country he attended several events and during a visit to a primary school in Cumnock in Ayrshire he delighted pupils by reciting the nursery rhyme 'Humpty Dumpty' in Russian. There was a serious side to his visit, and while at Ayr Academy – where he tearfully listened to a recital of Burns' songs – he reminded his young audience of the importance of Burns in the Soviet Union.

> The poetry of Robert Burns is part of our daily life. Our young people quote him in their love letters. Our best composers – Shostakovich, Kabalevsky, Sviridov, – have set his lyrics to music and these songs come over the radio intermingling with the hum of our work-days and the merry-making of our holidays. Volumes of his poetry are to be found in the studies of intellectuals, the cottages of collective farmers, in the apartments of workers, on the tables of students.

Burns creates links between people in defiance of all who would keep nation apart. And it must not be forgotten that it is in human hearts, not museums or monuments that his poems will be preserved.[41]

One of those listening was 12-year-old Ronnie (R. D. S) Jack, later Professor of Scottish and Medieval Literature at Edinburgh University, who was also asked to recite 'Scots Wha Hae' – so that Marshak could get a sense of the dramatic power of spoken Scots. As a result of that encounter Jack became a leading Burns scholar and an enthusiastic Burnsian who spoke regularly at Burns Suppers and never forgot his meeting with Marshak, who called him 'a fine little soldier'.[42] During this time in Scotland Marshak renewed his acquaintance with MacDiarmid and, while visiting Burns' Cottage at Alloway, where the poet had been born in 1759, he again delighted his audience, this time by reciting 'A Man's a Man for a' That' in tandem with the cottage's curator Thomas McMynn, each man reciting in turn a line in their own language. The visit's success renewed public interest in the Soviet Union and in 1961 the Scotland–USSR Society founded Sovscot Tours Ltd, which allowed many thousands of Scots to travel directly from Scotland for holidays in the Soviet Union, explaining that 'while the literature of a country can evoke something of its reality there is no substitute for physically going there and directly experiencing the life of its people'.[43]

While visits of that kind were generally welcomed and engendered considerable publicity, from a propaganda point of view they were probably more useful to the Soviet Union and as a result critics of the Scotland–USSR Society (the word 'Friendship' was quietly dropped in the 1960s) were not slow to query its political affiliations, especially its 'predictable ties to the Soviet Embassy'.[44] There were also justifiable fears that delegate exchanges were useful covers for intelligence-gathering or simply to allow Soviet officials to shop in the West – the charge on both counts was levelled against Anatoly Melnikov, who ran the British desk in the Soviet Writers' Union and was a frequent visitor to Scotland and the UK.[45] The problem was made more difficult in Scotland by the existence of the quite separate Foreign Office-funded Great Britain–USSR Association, founded in 1959, whose Scottish committee was chaired by Arthur Woodburn, Secretary for Scotland in Attlee's post-war government. For a time its Secretary was Elizabeth

Smith, wife of John Smith MP, later leader of the Labour Party. The two Scottish bodies were diametrically opposed from an ideological point of view and frequently at odds with one another as the younger UK organisation followed a more cautious line in its dealings with Moscow; its director, John Roberts, handled these. He had learned Russian during his National Service, knew the country and its culture intimately and from the evidence of his memoirs handled relations with Moscow, especially the Soviet Writers' Union, fairly but robustly throughout the Cold War. In that role he was a frequent visitor to the Soviet Union, memorably in 1987 in the company of the distinguished and bestselling novelist John le Carré, who had expressed a wish to visit the Soviet Union for research purposes – this would emerge in his novel *The Russia House* (1989). The author described Roberts as a man of 'forthright integrity of spirit', quite capable of seeing through the officials' 'double-think, their necessary self-deceptions and rather hopeless lies'.[46] Roberts' task was made less easy by the fact that the Association's allocated main partner in Moscow was the USSR–Great Britain Society, which worked out of the House of Friendship, home to the Union of Soviet Societies for Friendship (SSOD), and was widely held to be in league with the KGB.

Under most circumstances it might have been supposed that opposition to nuclear weapons would have come from Scotland's cultural community, but that turned out to be not wholly the case. It was not that Scottish writers and artists did not have public positions about the subject – many did. One such was the poet Alan Jackson, who served as Secretary of the Scottish Committee of 100 and organised the 1962 sit-down protest at the Holy Loch. Born in Liverpool in 1938 to Scots parents, Jackson was a popular performer of his poetry throughout the 1960s and 1970s and attracted large and responsive audiences. Several other leading Scottish authors of that generation were members of CND or produced articles that were critical of nuclear weapons and the threat they posed to the future of humanity, but apart from the 'Scottish Writers Against the Bomb' committee, which was chaired by the bestselling novelist Joan Lingard, there was no formal literary grouping. This committee had come into being as a result of a widespread dislike of Conservative defence policies following the election of Margaret Thatcher in 1983, the year in which US cruise missiles were sited at RAF Greenham Common in Berkshire, but the impetus came when Lingard's youngest daughter was arrested while protesting on behalf of CND – her 'crime' was putting up posters for a CND jumble sale. Undeterred, she went on to protest the siting of cruise missiles in the UK and was eventually arrested for obstruction; sentenced to a fine, she refused to pay and was sent to Holloway Prison in London for eight days. The incident provided the inspiration for Lingard's novel *The Guilty Party* (1987), which describes a similar occurrence – in this case the construction of a nuclear power station – and is one of the few novels written by a Scot to take its theme from contemporary Cold War events. Later, Lingard admitted that *The Guilty Party* was 'the most polemical book I've ever written'.[47] One novel that dealt specifically with the American presence in Scotland – *Holy Loch* (1964) – was written by a former US Merchant Marine radio officer called Robert Franklin Mirvish who died in 2007. Stripped of its contemporary naval background this was a basic love story featuring two American submariners who vie for an unhappily married local girl.

The lack of many literary works addressing the Cold War should not suggest apathy or indifference; at the time there were so many rival topics in the wider political spectrum, notably the war in Vietnam and the troubled internal politics in the UK (the miners' strikes, growing unemployment and increased social and economic inequality, to name but a few of the main domestic issues). Nonetheless, the Cold War could not be ignored and opposition to nuclear weapons was a specific ingredient of the folk revival in the 1960s and informed the work of writers such as the poet and folklorist Hamish Henderson, who refused the award of an OBE in December 1983 due to his opposition to the government's 'suicidal defence policies'. His refusal was front-page news and the following year he was voted BBC Scotland's 'Scot of the Year'. Henderson also wrote 'The Freedom Come-All-Ye', which was dedicated to 'the Glasgow Peace Marchers, May 1960' and appeared on the Folkways LP. Sung to a retreat air of the First World War called 'The Bloody Fields of Flanders' and composed by Pipe Major John McLellan, this was written in response to the anti-Polaris protests at the Holy Loch and it quickly became an unofficial anthem for CND and for the Scottish left in general. Although composed in the format of a traditional song, 'The Freedom Come-All-Ye' creates a synthesis of emotion and intellect which lies at the heart of pure poetry or, as the singer Sheila Douglas put it, 'sometimes a song is crafted by a poet that marries new words and an old tune into something that expresses our highest aspirations; the result is a song to carry like banner.'[48] Henderson provided notes for the preferred performance style which read: 'Non-workshop, much richer language. The Scots has been wedded, after the Gaelic fashion, to the pipe-tune. Style: rebel-bardic.' The second verse excoriates the military traditions which Henderson believed had darkened Scotland's history and its last line is a fitting condemnation not just of the injustices of apartheid (its intended target) but also subconsciously of the arrival of nuclear weapons in Scotland:

> Nae mair will the bonnie callants
> Mairch tae war when oor braggarts crousely craw,
> Nor wee weans frae pit-heid and clachan
> Mourn the ships sailin' doon the Broomielaw.
> Broken faimlies in lands we've herriet,
> Will curse Scotland the Brave nae mair, nae mair;
> Black and white, ane til ither mairriet,
> Mak the vile barracks o' their maisters bare.[49]

Opposition to Polaris also found its way into the thinking of novelist Naomi Mitchison who was a founding patron of Scottish CND and a lifelong opponent of the use of nuclear weapons in war. To the end of her long life – born in 1897, she died in 1999 aged 101 – Mitchison remained 'opposed to nuclear weaponry and . . . fearful that science would destroy, rather than enrich, mankind'.[50] As a socialist and liberal reformer, she was naturally suspicious of the establishment and she conformed very much to the Scottish tradition of philosophical quizzi-cality which holds that reason and science are the best protection against economic mismanagement, arbitrary rule and the creation of human misery.

Rather different was the line taken by her near-contemporary Eric Linklater, a novelist and historian who had served in both world wars and who had an abiding affection for the regimental system, having served in the Black Watch. Such was his literary reputation and so strong were his links with the Army that he was invited to visit Korea during the war to write an account of the role played by the British Army. He carried out the task with the temporary rank of lieuten-ant-colonel. His novel, *The Dark of Summer* (1956) drew on those experiences to give a vivid account of the fighting in the 'wild land-scape of steep brown hills' which 'echoed and re-echoed the rattle and bursting din of battle' but the narrative is not just about the war in

Korea; it also covers the other wars which moulded its main protago-
nist, Tony Chisholm. One of the great Scottish fictional soldiers,
Chisholm has been marked by warfare: his father won a Victoria Cross
in the First World War and he himself was wounded during the retreat
to Dunkirk in 1940; later he discovers that his younger brother was shot
for cowardice during the same action. Chisholm goes on to fight in
North Africa and Italy and, being a career soldier, ends up in Korea. He
later serves as a staff officer with NATO, planning for nuclear war in
the initial stages of the Cold War. Although not strictly a product of
that conflict, Linklater's novel deals with many of its preoccupations in
the character of Mungo Wishart, a patriarchal Shetland laird, nationalist and traitor who commits suicide when he fears being uncovered by
Chisholm. Much of the novel is set in Shetland and the Faroe Islands
while Chisholm is on a counter-espionage mission, but the main thrust
of the plot is Chisholm's attempt to find some quietus in his inner life,
especially in the relationship with his hero-father and his remorse for
Wishart's death. Above all, he yearns for a future when, as he tells
himself, 'I could rid myself of guilt and go free'.[51] Having witnessed the
death of Wishart's son Olaf in Korea and married his daughter Gudrun,
he eventually finds what he is seeking by settling in Shetland with 'the
North Sea on the one side, the Atlantic on the other'.[52]

Linklater was very much an establishment man, for all that he
described himself as 'an old peasant with a pen'.[53] Very different in his
approach was a younger poet, Tom Buchan, who declared in 1969 that
'the only possible role for the writer today is a subversive one'.[54] Born in
Glasgow in 1931, the son of a Church of Scotland minister, Buchan
taught in Scotland and India before becoming in 1958 warden of
Community House, the Glasgow headquarters of the Iona Community.
He emerged in the 1970s as a poet and playwright and spent much of
his life struggling to find an alternative path and develop his radical
voice. As a longstanding member of the Iona Community he supported
the ideals of CND and the idea of opposing nuclear weapons was never
far away in his poetry, which was first collected in 1969 under the title
Dolphins at Cochin. In his poem 'The Low Road' Buchan, a keen hill-
walker, imagined a nuclear air burst over the munitions depot at Glen
Douglas near Loch Long in Argyll:

> . . . the fireball of which will deforest Inchclonaig,
> vaporize Cailness and Rowchoish, fry

the Glasgow councillors fishing for free
on Loch Katrine and kill all the spiders
and earwigs between here and Crianlarich
and me (he thought) . . .[55]

This is typical of Buchan's approach. Buchan never quite lost the view of himself as a mischievous and maverick outsider, but it is the serendipitous tone of the poem which gives it resonance. 'There is someone somewhere aiming a missile at me,' muses Bohannan, the narrator, at the beginning of the poem as he walks across a mountain 'drilled with caves each one crammed with nuclear hardware'. In the 1970s Buchan became the epicentre of a group of like-minded writers in Glasgow such as Tom McGrath, Tom Leonard, Alan Spence and Alasdair Gray; the latter became a strident critic of the Trident missile system which replaced Polaris and Poseidon later in the century. Tom Buchan died in 1995.

One other writer dealt with the perils of nuclear warfare and created probably the best-known poem of that particular genre – the much anthologised 'The Horses' by Edwin Muir, which was first published in *The Listener* in March 1955 and later collected in the volume *One Foot in Eden* (1956). Set in a future dystopian world which has been destroyed by a short and violent global conflict, presumably nuclear – the 'seven days war that put the world to sleep' – the survivors are made to come to terms with the fact that the modern age has broken down and that its artefacts were probably to blame for the disaster in the first place. Forced to live without technology and to adjust to the unexpected silence, those left behind turn to an older way of living and working. Into that apocalypse (for so it seems) come the 'strange horses' from another simpler and almost long-forgotten age when humans and horses worked together in simple harmony:

We did not dare go near them. Yet they waited,
Stubborn and shy, as if they had been sent
By an old command to find our whereabouts
And that long-lost archaic companionship.[56]

The poem ends on a note of optimism with the thought that the arrival of the horses was a turning point for the survivors of that dreadful war and gives them a second chance: 'Our life is changed; their coming our beginning.' In the preface to Edwin Muir's *Selected Poems* (1965) T. S. Eliot described 'The Horses' as 'that great . . . terrifying poem of the "atomic age"' and it is a fair description; Muir's poem is one of the most recognisable literary works from the Cold War period, not least because it does not shy away from vividly describing the awesome terrors produced by nuclear warfare such as silent radios and 'a warship heading north, dead bodies piled on the deck'. The symbolism is also rich and rewarding, the mention of the seven days war reflecting the period of the Creation of Genesis and assimilating themes of nuclear annihilation, industrialisation, renewal and mankind's relationship with the animal world. Muir had some inkling of those horrors, having served as Director of the British Council Institute in Prague between 1945 and 1948 and witnessed the Communist takeover in February 1948, one of the key moments in the onset of the Cold War. Because of that experience perhaps, he wrote some of his best poetry in later life – as a younger man he was better known as a critic and translator – and 'The Horses' is rightly considered one of his finest achievements, with its symbolic representation of the Fall of Man and the consequent loss of innocence leading to a rebirth of faith. No less rewarding but less well known is Muir's 'After a Hypothetical War', written shortly before his death, in which he reveals a preoccupation with the possibility of a disastrous global war which shatters not just the world but also humankind's responsibility for its well-being. Whereas 'The Horses' bred the possibility of hope and renewal with the arrival of the 'fabulous steeds', 'After a Hypothetical War' is a deeply pessimistic vision revealing a post-nuclear world imbued with chaos and decay and shorn of any kind of humanity:

> . . . Poor tribe so meanly cheated,
> Their very cradle an image of the grave.
> What rule or governance can save them now?[57]

In different ways both poems argue the necessity of a return to more elemental values and a rejection of the scientific advances which had led to the creation of the atomic bomb, but both contain stark warnings of the possibility of a total social and political breakdown should nuclear war ever break out. These were themes which infused much of Muir's later work, a fact he recognised in a letter written to his friend and fellow poet Kathleen Raine from Harvard in 1955, in which he admitted that he had been 'writing some very queer poetry since I came, with a good deal of new horror in it'.[58] Muir always wrote movingly and convincingly about mankind's fall from grace and the pain of being expelled from Eden, which he equated with his childhood experience of leaving his native Orkney to live in the slums of Glasgow; in these final poems he also showed that he understood the equally elemental horror of lethal destruction brought about by the use of nuclear weapons.

The literary response to the Cold War helps to illuminate Scotland's condition as the post-war period gave way to the 1960s and beyond. There has been a tendency to see the 1950s and 1960s as 'dead decades' in which little happened in Scottish culture, except for the Edinburgh International Festival, and it has been argued with considerable conviction that the liberalising influences of the Swinging Sixties were not felt in the country until the following decades.[59] While there is some truth in that contention, it is not the whole story. The connections with the Soviet Union, limited though they were, and the revival of interest in anarchic and irreverent anti-nuclear folk culture, reveal a lively and disinterested capacity by writers and musicians to engage in intellectual debate about matters of seminal importance not just to them but to Scottish cultural life in the longer term, at a time when the threat of nuclear annihilation was never far from people's minds.

6

The Past Is a Foreign Country: Families on the Front Line

AT THE HEIGHT of the Cold War there were over 200 military installations in Scotland. These ranged from radar and communications facilities to major locations such as the US Navy and Royal Navy submarine bases on the Clyde and the three RAF airfields in the east and north-east of the country. In most cases the service personnel were accompanied by their families or dependants, and provision was made for their accommodation. For those serving in the British armed forces Scotland was simply another posting but for the Americans it was 'abroad', just one part of the US global network of bases which numbered 1,139 in 1947 but had dropped to 794 in the dying days of the Cold War. Due to the confrontation with the Soviet Union most of these, 627, were in Europe, Canada and the North Atlantic. At the height of the Cold War the US had around 300,000 military personnel based in Europe alone. The next largest deployment, 121 bases, was in the Pacific and South-East Asia. Most of these had been acquired during the Second World War but the dominant trend had been to reduce the commitment, with the result that by 1949 half of the US basing structure had been cut and there was no significant rise until the outbreak of the Korean War in 1950.[1] Generally speaking, the size and spread of the US overseas basing structure depended on need, but as the Senate Committee on Foreign Relations conceded on 21 December 1970: 'Once an American base is established it takes on a life of its own. Original missions may become outdated, but new missions are developed, not only with the intention of keeping the facility going, but often to actually enlarge it.' This policy was aided and abetted by what was known as 'strategic denial', which meant that no base could be abandoned if it implied any advantage to the Soviet Union.

The American presence in the UK became part of that equation in the late 1940s. In England the major contribution was provided by the US Air Force with all bases, as we have seen, coming under the nominal command of the RAF. Initially the majority were Strategic Air Command bases with long-range bombers such as the B-29, B-50 and B-36 rotating regularly from their home stations in the US but a French decision in 1966 to loosen its ties with NATO by closing all alliance bases in the following year increased the US presence in England. As part of the relocation plan US fighter aircraft began arriving in the UK, with fighter wings taking up residence at RAF Alconbury, RAF Bentwaters, RAF Lakenheath, RAF Mildenhall, RAF Upper Heyford and RAF Wethersfield. In the first instance these operated North American Super Sabre F-100 and Republic Thunderchief 105 aircraft but they were superseded by the Lockheed Phantom F-4 in the 1970s and were augmented by the arrival of nuclear-capable General Dynamics F-111 strike aircraft and the Fairchild Republic A-10 Thunderbolt close-support aircraft. Visiting aircraft included C-5 Galaxy, C-141 Starlifter and C-130 Hercules transporters as well as the top-secret SR-71 Blackbird supersonic reconnaissance and intelligence-gathering aircraft, a regular sight at Mildenhall, which became the UK headquarters of the US 3rd Air Force in 1972. Despite their different purposes, all these aircraft were manufactured by Lockheed, the largest US defence contractor during the 1970s before it became mired in allegations that its officials had paid millions of dollars in bribes while negotiating the sale of aircraft to foreign governments, most notably the supersonic interceptor F-104 Starfighter.

None of these deployments affected Scotland, at least not until the 1980s, when US plans were revealed to extend and improve the existing bases at Prestwick and Stornoway for reinforcement in time of war. The former airport had had a US presence since the end of the Second World War and even though its usefulness for refuelling transatlantic flights between the USA and Europe had declined, with the introduction of longer-range aircraft it was still a Military Airlift Command base and was used regularly by contracted civilian airliners for transporting the Blue and Gold crews returning to the US from the Holy Loch submarine base. All that changed in 1982, when a US Air Force team visited Ayrshire to survey Prestwick for the construction of a 20,000 square foot 'Forward Storage Warehouse', which would be an integral part of a proposed European Distribution System (EDS)

designed to reinforce and resupply US forces in Europe should war
break out with the Soviet Union. It was estimated that the building
would cost $1.82 million to build, and although the funds would come
from the US defence budget and were approved by Congress in January
1983, no approach was made to the British government. The outcome
was farcical. As reports about the project began to appear in the Scottish
and UK press the Ministry of Defence denied all knowledge of the
proposals and the Secretary of State for Scotland, George Younger,
even claimed that the reports were 'irresponsible and misleading'. At
the same time officials in Washington confirmed that the construction
would take place, thereby suggesting either that Washington took UK
permission for granted or that there had been a major breakdown in
communications between the two allies. Whatever the real reason, the
revelations and the resulting scandal meant that the project was doomed
and the expansion at Prestwick was quietly dropped that April with the
EDS project being switched to RAF Kemble in Gloucestershire.

There was equal confusion and murkiness surrounding a similar
proposal to develop the airport at Stornoway in Lewis, which had been
transferred to the ownership of the Ministry of Defence in 1971.
Although nominally a civil airport under the control of the Civil
Aviation Authority, this change allowed it to be used as a forward
operating base for RAF aircraft and aircraft from other NATO countries. The US was also interested in using the base for reinforcement
flights in time of war as part of its EDS system and this was made clear
to the local authority in a presentation in 1979. As a result, the runway
was extended, hardened aircraft shelters were built and new navigation
aids introduced, with the funding coming from NATO's Infrastructure
Programme, but the plans met with sustained opposition locally from
both the Western Isles Council and also from a vigorous 'Keep NATO
Out' campaign. During the consultation stage there was a fair amount
of obfuscation and double-talk and the opposition to the scheme at a
public inquiry was overruled by the Secretary of State for Scotland as
being against the national interest. Insult was added to injury at the
beginning of 1983 when it was revealed that the US Defense Nuclear
Agency was considering Stornoway as a site for anti-ship cruise missiles
to attack Soviet shipping passing through the choke-point in the GIUK
gap.[2] Although the missiles would be armed with conventional
warheads, they were nuclear-capable and could have been used in that
role in time of war. This revelation was denied by the UK government

but it only fuelled local fears that the Western Isles would become a primary target in the event of nuclear war.

Although Stornoway airport played host to several types of visiting NATO aircraft during the 1980s it never became a fully fledged Cold War base except in the imagination of novelist Tom Clancy, whose 1986 novel *Red Storm Rising* is partly set on the island and became a firm favourite of President Ronald Reagan, who urged the British prime minister, Margaret Thatcher, to read it. The plot is complex and based on real-life possibilities such as an energy crisis involving terrorists in Azerbaijan, thereby creating an energy crisis in which vital Soviet oil supplies are destroyed. During the ensuing confrontation with the Soviet Union which escalates into all-out war, RAF Stornoway becomes the NATO headquarters for directing operations in the North Atlantic and against Soviet forces in recently invaded Iceland. In common with all of Clancy's novels the action is fast-paced and realistic with well-drawn characterisation, but there is little in the way of local physical detail to place Stornoway in the Western Isles and the novel ends on an optimistic note with a last-minute intervention to prevent the outbreak of a strategic nuclear war following conventional skirmishes across northern Europe. No nuclear weapons are ever used, although the threat is always in the background. In that sense *Red Storm Rising* is more of an allegory and it is hardly surprising that it achieved equal popularity as a video simulation game centred on the fictional USS *Chicago*, a hunter-killer submarine operating in the Norwegian Sea whose task is to interdict Soviet forces, especially ballistic missile-equipped submarines. Based on an episode within the novel this is an imaginative and thought-provoking use of modern media and the game was well received when it was launched in 1988, ironically the year in which the Cold War was coming to an end.

It was also apposite that the game focused on submarine warfare, for if any weapon symbolised the US presence in Scotland it was the dark hulls of the ballistic missile submarines of Submarine Squadron 14 which inhabited Refit Site One at the Holy Loch. Known in US Navy argot as Sub Ron 14, the squadron was established on 1 July 1958 and its main task was to develop operational procedures and doctrine for the new class of nuclear-powered submarines which would carry the Polaris missile and form a vital part of the US nuclear deterrent during the Cold War. Its first commander was Captain Norvell G. Ward USN, and it was under his direction that the first naval vessels were deployed in Scottish waters in March 1961. As we have seen, they arrived to find an uncertain welcome, with protests about the nuclear presence balanced by polite indifference and some counter-protests from those who supported the American presence and regarded the demonstrators as Communist stooges. There were also more protests later in the year, followed by the siting of a tented 'peace camp' at Ardnadam but as the 1960s progressed the objections died down, with the next major demonstration being directed at the arrival of the USS *Hunley*, which replaced the *Proteus* as depot ship in March 1963. But by and large the reaction of the people of Dunoon was one of discreet curiosity mingled with a desire to be reasonably welcoming. The provost of the day, Miss Catherine McPhail, set the tone by admitting that although she had had initial misgivings these had been overcome and she pledged that 'Americans will get a hospitable welcome from all of us, no matter how any of us feel about the policy which brought them here.'[3] It helped that the base was set amongst spectacular scenery, described by one visiting American reporter as 'a misty out-of-the-world retreat' which seemed to have come out of the fantasy movie *Brigadoon* and offered various outdoor sporting facilities including sailing and several golf courses, whose clubs made US sailors welcome. It helped too that by then US forces felt at home in the main frontline areas of the Cold War – Western Europe and Japan – and that any lingering resentment from the immediate post-war occupations had long since dissipated. This was an important point, as during the Second World War Scotland had been spared any large-scale American military presence, the bulk of the estimated 3 million US service personnel in the UK being based in southern England and the East Anglian bomber counties. By contrast, during the Cold War occupation the figures were considerably lower and more equally divided – 46,000 across the UK during the early 1950s dropping to 30,000 later – and of these fewer than 4,000 were based in Scotland, most of them in the Dunoon area.[4]

In that sense the Holy Loch was regarded by most US service personnel as 'a good occupation' which was mainly beneficial, and which was being carried out as part of Washington's global policy of containment and deterrence. Anything else would have been considered unAmerican and unpatriotic and for many years there were rumours that the first US crews had been carefully vetted and selected before arriving in Scotland. Certainly, in the early years the Americans made a determined effort to fit in and worked hard at building relationships with the local community. In 1964, acting on the suggestion of Captain Walter F. Schlech, a Polaris tartan was designed by Alexander MacIntyre of Strone for the use of officers and men based at the Holy Loch and it continued in use by the pipes and drums of the US Naval Academy, Annapolis. The missile's name was also used for a sailing cup in the local regatta and over the years some American sailors represented Scotland at various sports – Mark Mallory was the Scottish Light Middle Weight boxing champion in 1981 and Marine Leigh Mallory ran in the Glasgow marathon two years later, raising money for a local charity. Add on the countless social occasions involving both communities and it is clear that the US presence was broadly welcomed by the people of Dunoon and the Cowal peninsula. As a Dunoon Grammar School pupil and future Labour politician, Brian Wilson noted in his recollection of that period that he felt it was important to differentiate between ordinary Americans and the policies pursued by their government.

In any case, the Holy Loch was always presented as less of a base and more of a naval facility, the only permanent fixtures being the depot ship and the huge dry dock, the USS *Los Alamos*, which arrived in four sections in June 1961 and was assembled by 500 'Seabee' engineers of the Mobile Construction Battalion Four (MCB-4). At any one time it would have one submarine on board being refitted with another four alongside between patrols, for by the end of the 1960s Sub Ron 14 had reached its full complement of ten submarines. In that respect the American presence was largely unobtrusive, with no US flags or Navy signs dominating the seascape and few men in uniform. Apart from the depot ship, which received drinking water and a telephone link from the shore but was otherwise self-sustaining, the submarines and associated vessels offered limited and transient accommodation. Naval personnel who wanted to live ashore ('on the beach'), especially if they had families, had to rent or purchase houses or flats and this led to greater integration, not least when American children started attending local schools in Dunoon. More than any other factor this helped to break the ice, especially at the local secondary school, Dunoon Grammar, where the young American pupils soon integrated and, following initial curiosity, quickly became part of school life, taking a full part in classroom and sporting activities. However, few Scots pupils forgot the casual elegance of bobby socks, penny loafers, plaid skirts and crew cuts which seemed to be so exotic and different from the sartorial standards remembered by the future novelist William McIlvanney. While on holiday from boyhood Kilmarnock he was 'a seasonal sophisticate in Arran where I danced with my girlfriend into the early hours, suave in shirt, shorts, woolly socks and sandshoes'.[5]

In May 1962, the US Navy purchased the old Ardnadam Hotel and transformed it into an Enlisted Men's Club, a kind of NAAFI, but otherwise the message was that integration was the order of the day. To assist that aim the Ministry of Defence appointed a local liaison officer and there was a joint community relations council chaired by Sir Fitzroy Maclean, a well-known local landowner, author and former soldier, but otherwise it was left to the good sense of the naval personnel and civilians who lived in the community and owned or rented some 500 houses at the height of the US presence.[6] Later, in the mid-1970s, purpose-built housing was constructed for some of the sailors and their families in Sandbank and as a result some of the closeness between the two communities was dissipated, so much so that it was possible for some Americans to complete their posting without having met local people.

Throughout the deployment at Holy Loch the economic benefits prompted frequent debate and in the years since the US departure the subject is still a matter for conjecture despite (or perhaps because of) the number of reports which have been produced on the subject.[7] The divided opinion can be summarised in the following way: either there was very little bearing on the local community as the incomers purchased most of their needs from the Commissary, 'a non-profit-making supermarket run by the US government', or the arrival of the Americans with their dollars and high spending habits were bound to effect Dunoon and the Cowal peninsula with its fragile economy based on agriculture, forestry, fishing and seasonal tourism.[8] When the site closed at the end of the Cold War reports in the US media claimed that the American presence in Dunoon had produced 3,100 jobs and contributed an annual $100 million to the local community but this was countered by other claims that the economic spill-over into the local community had been negligible because there had been no big infrastructure projects and the American presence had been mainly self-contained. Both sides of the argument have their supporters but much of the oral evidence from the period seems to show that the influx of so many US service personnel into a small maritime coastal area did have a financial impact. They were young men (mostly) who were far away from home in an alien environment and they had considerable spending power at a time when the US dollar was strong and the local economy in the west of Scotland was weak. And perhaps more than any other factor, as local girl Sarah Cairns remembered, the Americans brought with them a whiff of glamour and high living: 'I clearly remembered the night before the ship [*Proteus*] sailed in. There was a huge full moon and I remember my sister said everything would be bigger and better because the Americans would be here soon. She was joking but I believed that life would be like the films, everyone would be glamorous and wearing fabulous clothes . . . their diet was extravagant by our terms – T-bone steaks bought in the Commissary, mince was something they used to make burgers.'[9]

Most Scots took their ideas of the US from Hollywood, and against that background there was bound to be an economic stimulus mingled with some exploitation on the part of the local population. This was particularly true of the housing market, which by its nature was limited to what was available, and there were very few options for expansion. Because Dunoon and the surrounding villages in the Cowal peninsula were geared towards providing seasonal holiday accommodation for summer visitors – most of them from Glasgow during the July trades holidays – there was ample 'bed and breakfast' provision in private houses, but the American sailors were looking for something more permanent. This allowed local landlords to rent out their properties, often at exorbitant rents, and in the early days when the families started arriving it was 'bonanza time . . . with demand far outstripping availability'.[10] Although it could not have been foreseen at the time, the change of emphasis came as a lifeline: by the end of the 1960s package holidays in Europe were becoming increasingly popular and as a result seaside resorts such as Dunoon were starting to go into a steady decline.

The business dealings seem not to have led to any undue bad feeling as it was a learning experience for both sides, with most Americans happy to live ashore away from the confines of their working environment, but it did produce a certain culture shock. In the Scotland of the 1960s and 1970s central heating and double glazing were rarities, yet most Americans took such facilities for granted and were astonished by the array of coal fires and paraffin heaters which provided the heating in most houses. By the same token most Scots were equally amazed by the levels of heat produced in houses occupied by Americans – many young Scots were taken aback by seeing their American counterparts wearing short sleeves indoors in the depths of winter and this style of living produced incredulity and condemnation in equal measure. Gradually, too, the Americans started importing their own furniture and motor cars and this too caused bemusement as large Chryslers and Buicks made heavy weather of the narrow country roads in the vicinity. Otherwise sailors tended to use local taxis to get around and this led to an explosion in their use as new firms came into being to take advantage of the rise in business. At one stage there were thought to be 140 taxis operating in Dunoon, rumoured to be the largest concentration of such vehicles in any town in the UK.[11]

Another widely believed story was that Holy Loch operated as a kind of marriage market, with 25 per cent of the single sailors based there marrying local girls. Oral indications suggest that marriages of that kind were not uncommon but the only hard evidence comes from the local registry office, which recorded that between 1961 and 1974, nearly 36 per cent of the marriages registered in Dunoon were between non-US women and US Navy personnel.[12] From a different perspective the site also became a magnet for prostitutes from Glasgow and elsewhere, and according to contemporary local evidence they were usually recognisable by their appearance – beehive hair-dos, excessive make-up, fishnet stockings and high-heeled winkle-picker shoes. So disreputable did the trade become that in October 1963 a Dunoon councillor, Ann Melville, moved that only married US personnel with families should be allowed into the 'town of shame'. However, no one could be found to second her motion and a week later she was rebuked by a former provost, E. J. Wyatt, who wrote to the press saying that Dunoon had not been corrupted and that there was little evidence to suggest that it had become a second Sodom and Gomorrah although he did concede that the police were investigating 'two boarding houses of ill repute'.[13] Later, in the following year, a call-girl business in Dunoon was uncovered involving 22 girls.[14]

Another flashpoint in the relationship between the people of Dunoon and the US Navy came from allegations of sexual relations with local girls under the legal age of 16, a concern that led to a deputation being sent to Captain Lanning, who introduced a curfew for his sailors in the spring of 1962 while his spokesman offered the palliative but ineffectual comment that 'our men are expected to behave like gentlemen, but whom they date is a matter of personal preference'. This cut little ice with worried local fathers, one of whom complained to the local paper that 'anything the Captain would say to this type of man would be as ineffective as singing hymns to a tiger'.[15] Other signs of the times were the opening of a venereal diseases clinic at Dunoon Cottage Hospital in the summer of 1963 and the revelation that the illegitimacy rate for Dunoon had increased from 6.3 per cent of births in 1961 to 15.3 per cent the following year, the second highest increase in Scotland. Although illegitimacy rates are an inexact indicator of sexual morality, the correspondence columns of the *Dunoon Observer* in the early 1960s bear witness to the concern voiced by local families about the unwanted changes in young people's behaviour occasioned by the US presence. No one seems to have raised the obvious fact that young men far from home and involved in a dangerous business would be interested in engaging with the opposite sex. As one anonymous submariner told the author G. G. Giarchi, who researched the impact of the US presence on the Cowal peninsula, 'Imagine what it's like to come from that tin box in the dark deep where your eyes see nothing for weeks but nuts and bolts, to see a real sexy "broad" in the daylight!'[16]

By then the police were also dealing with other types of criminality, the most common being drunk driving or brawls between sailors and local men, often fuelled by the excessive consumption of alcohol. The majority of the cases were trivial and of the kind found in most Scottish police courts on a Monday morning, but in July 1961 there was one incident which turned nasty when a black sailor slashed his assailant's throat during a fight after being called a 'nigger'. He was acquitted on a majority verdict. Towards the end of the same year a US petty officer was stabbed in a Dunoon street in broad daylight and a local man was charged with the crime and duly convicted. The first American to be severely punished was Gerald Austin Grimes, who was court-martialled for the crime of bigamy, while the first man to receive a jail sentence from a Scottish court was Petty Officer Michael Edward Beece, who was sent to prison for driving under the influence of alcohol. It was a rare occurrence as there was a tendency to deal with criminal behaviour under the terms of the Visiting Forces Act of 1952, which exempted US military personnel from being tried for any offence if it occurred in the line of duty. Under this jurisdiction and associated orders US Navy personnel could be removed from the justice system if the offence 'arose out of and in the course of duty'. Perhaps the most notorious case of this kind occurred in November 1965, when an American sailor drove his car into a local mother and her baby, killing the latter and severely wounding the former. At the insistence of the US Navy he was not handed over to the Scottish courts but was court-martialled and fined $100 for 'negligent homicide'.[17]

By the 1970s drug-taking had become as much a problem as misuse of alcohol and was to remain a difficulty for the remainder of the US deployment at the Holy Loch. Drug use was thought to have been behind an incident in October 1973, when a serious race riot broke out involving black and white American sailors as well as local youths. After order was restored – shop windows in the town centre had been smashed – ten American sailors, seven of them black, appeared in court on charges of mobbing, rioting and police assault; on being sentenced one gave a 'black power' salute in court.[18] Much of this kind of behaviour reflected changes in society as recreational drugs such as marijuana and cannabis became more freely available – in the final decade of the Cold War a US medical report suggested that an estimated 100,000 young Americans were under treatment for abusing cannabis but, as the same report conceded, that was a small proportion of those addicted to drugs.[19] In the US Navy the figures would have been even smaller, but in 1981 court martial papers found in a rubbish dump near the Holy Loch revealed that five years earlier an American sailor had only been fined and sentenced to four months' hard labour after being found guilty of selling drugs in the Harmony House bar in Dunoon, a regular haunt for off-duty US sailors. Equally worryingly, the papers showed that drug use was not an abnormal occurrence and that in some cases drugs had been loaded on board nuclear submarines in their US bases before departing on operational service.[20]

This should have come as no surprise to the US authorities, because although they had robust procedures in place to deal with drug-taking in the armed forces recent history showed that the problem was a bit of a Trojan Horse created as a result of the long-drawn-out conflict in Vietnam. Quite apart from being extremely unpopular, this has been described as the first 'pharmacological war', so called because the level of consumption of psychoactive substances by military personnel was unprecedented in American history.[21] In 1971, a report by a Senate Select Committee on Crime revealed that from 1966 to 1969, the armed forces in Vietnam had used 225 million tablets of stimulants, mostly Dexedrine (dextroamphetamine), an amphetamine derivative nearly twice as strong as the Benzedrine widely used in the Second World War as a stimulant and performance enhancer. Throughout the war in Vietnam the annual consumption of Dexedrine per person was 21.1

pills in the Navy, 17.5 in the Air Force, and 13.8 in the Army, with little attention given to recommended dose or frequency of administration.[22] In addition to the authorised use of various stimulants the forces had to contend with a rise in the use of illegal recreational drugs, initially marijuana, grown all over Vietnam and freely available, and then high-grade heroin, which could be smoked with less chance of detection. In the same year, 1971, a Senate Staff Report on Drug Abuse in the Military explained that as the military police cracked down on easily detected marijuana, 'GIs who had been smoking only "grass" turned to heroin, which was initially passed off to them as non-addicting cocaine. They reasoned that the substance itself, heroin, and the smoking of it were more easily concealed from prying eyes and noses than mari-juana.' It was also cheaper and more readily available, costing up to $3 for plastic phials of 96 per cent pure heroin, which were easily obtained from Vietnamese civilian workers at most US bases in the country.[23]

Drug use in Vietnam by US armed forces has been fully documented and is a well-attested phenomenon, especially in the last years of the war, although doubts remain about whether it had much impact on a soldier's ability to carry out orders or wage war. Because a standard tour of duty in Vietnam was 12 months, it has been estimated that at least half of those involved in the fighting would have been exposed to and experimented with illegal drugs, and by June 1971 the problem was serious enough for President Nixon to announce the creation of the Special Action Office for Drug Abuse Prevention. It is on that commission's findings that most of the evidence on wartime drug usage is based.[24] Against that background, it would have been surprising if the crews in the Holy Loch had not been exposed to recreational drugs and in 1983 the Ministry of Defence admitted that 20 US sailors had been convicted of drug offences in Dunoon sheriff court.[25] In his study Giarchi claimed that soft drugs were easily bought from sources in the local community or from dealers in Glasgow and elsewhere, but it should also be pointed out that Sub Ron 14 was part of an elite 'silent service' which expected very high standards of its personnel.

Apart from a brief period in the 1970s, when there was a recruitment crisis in the American armed forces and drafting men into unpopular branches was the order of the day (women were not employed in submarines until the twenty-first century), all submariners were volun-teers who not only had to pass stringent tests but also had to undergo an intensive security screening process before being accepted for training.

To get into the service required high academic skills, determination, application and the ability to stand up to 'hazing' – described as being subjected to 'blistering, sarcastic, insulting and demeaning interrogations' during training. Before that stage every potential submariner had to serve at sea aboard a surface ship before spending six months at submarine school and a further year of onboard training. Only then, following further oral and written tests, would he be awarded the coveted pair of gold dolphins which signified membership of the elite club of submarine sailors. It was not just the US Navy which imposed such high standards. During this same period testing for the submarine service in the Royal Navy and Soviet Navy was equally rigorous and concentrated, and from the available evidence there were similarities in the style of training, with newcomers being treated as outsiders and denied privileges until they were found to have fitted in. Once that had been achieved they found that they had received life membership of the fraternity of submariners.[26]

In 1990, the 90th anniversary of the formation of the service, there were 55,000 submariners serving in the US Navy, all of them volunteers, with 17,560 serving aboard America's 123 active nuclear-powered submarines at any given time.[27] That gave them a good conceit of their abilities and in common with any elite grouping within the armed forces they placed a high premium on mutual trust and unwavering team loyalty. As a former Cold War submariner explained, this was the essence of his profession: 'In each submarine there are men who, in the hour of emergency or peril at sea, can turn to each other. These men are ultimately responsible to themselves and each to the other for all aspects of the operation of their submarine . . . This is perhaps the most difficult and demanding assignment in the Navy. There is not an instant during his tour as a submariner that he can escape the grasp of responsibility.'[28]

All elites like to think that they are the best, but given the tasks undertaken by submariners during the Cold War years – operating stealthily in unknown waters for long periods, managing nuclear propulsion and armed with weapons of mass destruction – there was little slack in the US submarine service to allow widespread drug abuse. The cases which have come to light are not so numerous as to suggest that there was a serious epidemic; certainly, after 1980, the US Navy pursued a rigorous campaign against drug-taking, and in 1982 a policy of zero tolerance was introduced and enforced by frequent random drug testing. Supporting this, sniffer dogs were based at Holy Loch under the control of the Naval Investigative Staff. Service personnel caught using drugs faced dishonourable discharge and even criminal prosecution. Officially the stance in Sub Ron 14 was that any sailor caught in possession of drugs would be sent back to the US for trial but there were constant rumours that this policy was being disregarded or bypassed, and these fears were exacerbated by the failure of the US Navy to make a definitive statement on the subject. There was a serious accident in 1981 which was rumoured to have been caused by an American sailor who was either drunk or under the influence of drugs. On 2 November a Poseidon ballistic missile was dropped 13 to 15 feet following an error by the crane operator while it was being moved aboard the submarine tender USS *Holland* (AS-32). Although the fall was arrested by a safety brake the missile did strike *Holland*'s side with sufficient force to spark fears of an explosion – on board the tender an alpha alert state was put in place and crew were ordered to go to radiation-protected areas. If there had been an explosion the consequences could have been disastrous, as the warhead used an unstable conventional plastic explosive called LX-09 which provided the trigger for the multiple nuclear warheads carried by the Poseidon missile. Although this would not have caused a nuclear explosion it would have dispersed radioactive material over a wide area which would have threatened Glasgow and the lower Clyde to the south. Given the open position of the Holy Loch facility and the presence of American sailors in Dunoon it would have been impossible to keep the incident secret, but the US Navy issued no statement other than to insist that 'there was no damage done, no injuries occurred; there was no danger to personnel'.[29] It also refused to confirm or deny that a nuclear warhead was involved but in the following year it was forced to confirm that the missile had struck *Holland* and that LX-09 would be withdrawn from service.[30] The matter was also raised in the House of Commons by Labour MP Harry Ewing who received an emollient (and untruthful) reply from the defence minister, Geoffrey Pattie, that due to mechanical malfunction there had been a 'minor incident' involving a missile but that 'standard procedures were successfully carried out and the missile's descent was halted'.[31]

The drug or drink allegation involving the crane operator was never satisfactorily addressed but the incident encapsulated many of the long-standing fears of the release of radiation from a submarine reactor or nuclear warhead. A worst-case scenario envisaged the accidental explosion of a nuclear weapon and while the Clyde Local Liaison Committee insisted that such an incident was unlikely, fears of an environmental hazard involving radioactive pollution refused to go away. There was good reason for the concern despite the assurances of the Committee, which had been established to allay local fears but was little more than a cosmetic exercise with no power to act independently. In August 1965 the Ministry of Defence admitted that there were unusually high levels of radiation in the Holy Loch as a result of American submarines discharging excess coolant water from their reactor into the loch, leading to the contamination of the shoreline.[32] While these produced no danger of immediate death they did create a health hazard and it was hardly a good advertisement for the US Navy, not least because shortly after the arrival of the USS *Proteus* Captain Lanning had assured journalists that it was possible to drink the coolant waters from the submarines' reactors.[33]

From the outset it was obvious that the Holy Loch would have been a target for Soviet attack by nuclear weapons but that seems to have been a matter of little concern to the local community, with only 20.4 per cent voicing that fear in interviews conducted in 1974. One local woman expressed the thought in fatalistic terms: 'If anything does happen to the people of Cowal, they'll be lucky, because they'll all go up to the pearly gates together.'[34] The threat of nuclear annihilation was also accepted by the resident American community as part of the equation of their service. Every time one of the Polaris boats went on patrol the crews did not know if they would be called on to fire their weapons and the same holds true for the families who waited at the base. The first time there was a genuine frisson of fear came in October 1962, when the depot ship *Proteus* and the resident submarines slipped out to sea. One local girl, Mary Paton, who later married an American sailor, watched the departing vessels from Ardenslate school and thought that it must have been 'purgatory for the families when all leave was cancelled and everyone in the area felt that we were very close to destruction'.[35] A week later the *Proteus* returned to the Holy Loch but the episode had been a grim, if temporary, reminder that the black-hulled submarines were agents of destruction and that Soviet retaliation would have been instant and deadly, a fact recognised in parliament by Home Office Minister Monty Woodhouse, who admitted on 5 December 1962 when the crisis was over that 'we were very near the edge'.[36] Later, it was revealed that throughout the crisis Kennedy's hand had been strengthened by information provided by one of the first Soviet defectors, Oleg Penkovsky, who had supplied irrefutable evidence that the 'missile gap' was in America's favour, thereby helping the US president to decide that Khrushchev could only be bluffing and that his hand could be called. It was against such margins that disaster had been avoided.

The US presence at Holy Loch lasted 31 years, and although government officials on both sides of the Atlantic stuck to the line that it was a refit facility for submarines based on the east coast of the US, with their headquarters at Norfolk, Virginia, to all intents and purposes it was nevertheless an American installation. 'Like roses,' claimed Professor A. P. Dobson of Dundee University in his survey of the US deployment, 'bases by any other name are still bases.'[37] In time the differentiation became blurred and over the course of almost four decades initial opposition (where it existed) gave way to acceptance. Amongst the early protestors was a Dunoon Grammar School pupil called George Robertson, whose father was a senior policeman who was 'less than enchanted by his son and namesake's political adventure'. Later, George Robertson entered politics and became a distinguished Labour politician and statesman who crowned his career as Secretary-General of NATO, but he acknowledged that his interest in politics was kindled by his experience of life in Dunoon and the arrival of the American nuclear deterrent. 'I grew up politically very fast. I got politics into the bloodstream. I became absorbed in knowing about one of the great issues of our age, which has dominated my career and interests. In addition I was to gain immense self-confidence from being about people with such strong views.'[38]

Quite early on, Robertson had realised that while 'Ban the Bomb' was a good campaigning slogan it did not form a basis for dealing with international affairs and that his teenage support for the CND was youthful idealism, in support of which he joined the 'ban the bomb' SNP. It was an outlook he shared with Brian Wilson, who joined the same party and later said that his life and political outlook had been transformed by the arrival of the Americans. Wilson eventually became a Labour MP and government minister, yet as a young man in Dunoon he had been at the forefront of many anti-Polaris demonstrations. In that sense while the 'American Years' (as they came to be known) influenced a handful of people, the period was a phase which left very little lasting wider impact, not least because the influence was only felt in a small area of Scotland. This was in contrast to the larger arrival of émigré Polish soldiers and airmen during the Second World War, which created a permanent imprint on the Borders and the east of Scotland, mainly because many of the Poles stayed on and settled in Scotland after the conflict to become a recognisable part of the Scottish community.

A similar sense of commonality surrounded the second-largest US deployment in Scotland at Edzell in Angus. The former Air Force station retained its identity as RAF Edzell but it was run by the US Navy as NSGA Edzell, the first commanding officer being Captain John S. Lehman, USN. When the station was handed over on 11 February 1960 there were blizzard conditions and the advance party was housed in the Glenesk Hotel, known locally as the 'Glennie' to distinguish it from the 'Pannie' or Panmure Arms Hotel at the other end of the town. (In between the two was the Central, whose proprietor George Wedderburn won many American friends by inviting them to his 'Saturday Night After Hours' parties which allowed special guests to remain in the lounge bar long after the official closing time of 11 p.m. to enjoy 'good conversation and a song or two'.)[39] With the RAF gone there was accommodation available for the 400 enlisted men who would serve there, including 54 houses, but as happened at the Holy Loch, many American sailors decided to live off-base and rented or bought accommodation locally. Their children went to local schools, mainly in nearby Brechin and Laurencekirk, but as the numbers were always small they did not make a deep impression on the local community and seem to have been quickly assimilated. The same was true of their parents, who threw themselves into local life with commendable enthusiasm – so much so that the base won the coveted Ambassador of the United States of America Award for Community Relations in 1966, 1969, 1972, 1974, 1978, 1982, 1983 and 1995. It also won the equally prestigious US Navy League London Award for Community Relations six times between 1977 and 1993. Americans enjoyed attending quintessentially Scottish celebrations such as New Year festivities and Burns Suppers and reciprocated with Independence Day and Thanksgiving parties. Golf, too, provided a link, especially as there were several courses and clubs nearby, all of which welcomed visiting American service personnel. A glimpse at the base newspaper *Tartan Log* reveals a comprehensive list of activities aimed at cementing ties with the local community – from Navy Day Balls and Square Dancing Clubs to engineering assistance, with the construction of the restored railway line between Brechin and Bridge of Dun.

On that level the 37-year occupation of Edzell could be counted a success and in the aftermath of the closure in 1997 considerable effort went into maintaining links between the Angus community and former service personnel, many of whom had married local girls during their stay in Scotland. (At least 300, according to the last commanding officer in her farewell speech in 1997.) The Enlisted Men's Club ('the EM') encouraged relationships, with social nights on Saturdays involving local pop groups and girls bussed in from Dundee, known to the sailors as the 'Dundee Runners'. In the memoir of his time in Edzell Seaman Daniel Flanagan seems to have enjoyed his tour of duty, having taken the opportunity to travel further afield in Britain and Europe and made full use of the base's amateur radio facilities or 'ham shack' to develop his interest in wireless technology. His memories are a reminder that whereas some Scots resented the US bases in their country it was often very different from the perspective of the American personnel who were based in Scotland and grew to love the place.[40] Some idea of the importance of the relationship can been seen in the fact that, like their compatriots at the Holy Loch, the sailors at Edzell created their own tartan in 1985 from a design provided by the Strathmore Woollen Company in Forfar. Somewhat earlier, when the base redesigned its official seal, a motto in Gaelic was adopted – *Os-cean na h-uile* ('above them all', or 'second to none') – below a crest featuring the distinctive Dalhousie Arch through which the town of Edzell and the hills beyond can be seen.

The creation of the motto was not without its problems as it proved difficult to find an exact Gaelic rendition of 'second to none' and so it was decided to adopt 'above them all'. Much later, in the 1980s, a visiting British brigadier (nameless but with a sense of humour) decided to tease the US commanding officer Captain Isaiah C. Cole by saying that the Americans had been duped. He spoke Gaelic and explained po-faced that the motto meant 'party-throwers from across the sea'. Clearly this was a joke – the brigadier saw a connection between *os-cean* and 'ocean' and *na h-uile* and 'hooley' – but his words and laughter caused sufficient consternation for inquiries to be made and an anxious call to be made to West Germany, where the original designer was then based. The episode also seemed to reinforce the commonly held notion that Americans and the British are not only divided by an ocean but also by a common language and, in this case, by a sense of humour as well.

Unlike Holy Loch the US presence in Angus did not produce any significant crime other than minor traffic offences. Partly this was due to the small size of the base, which never had more than 400 sailors and marines plus dependants at any one time, and partly to the specialised cryptologic nature of the work, which encouraged a concern for maintaining security – it was after all a top-secret listening base – but it was also due to the surroundings. Rural Angus was (and is) a quiet backwater dominated by agriculture and with a modest transport infrastructure while Edzell itself is a pleasant and picturesque small town set in the lea of the Grampians, with a ruined sixteenth-century castle and walled garden and some fine Victorian domestic architecture. It was not until the exploitation of oil in the North Sea in the 1970s that there was any appreciable change as the nearby port and city of Aberdeen became a magnet for a different kind of American working in the oil industry, who caused some friction largely due to their spending power. As mentioned by one sailor in the base newspaper *Tartan Log*, the presence of the oil workers threatened to undo the good work done by the US Navy in building up a good relationship with the community: 'Part of the problem with the oil folks was their ability to buy whatever they wanted regardless of the cost.'[41] That may be special pleading, as the discovery of oil in the North Sea led to an unexpected boom in the north-east which benefited north Angus as well, although it was said at the time that the short-term approach to this bonanza gave 'a greater boost to the economy of Texas than to that of Scotland'.[42]

A similar point could be made about the development in the 1970s of a short-lived oil platform construction yard by the Sir Robert McAlpine civil engineering firm at Ardyne Point at the east end of Loch Striven on the Cowal peninsula. Although only three platforms were ever built and the project was an economic failure, the arrival of the 400-strong workforce caused consternation in Dunoon with uneasy comparisons being made between the 'Yanks' and the 'navvies' (as they were called locally). On one level, there were similarities. The workers at Ardyne brought with them considerable spending power, but unlike the Americans they were uninterested in joining the local community. On the contrary their drinking habits and occasional raucous behaviour were a source of antagonism and they made a nuisance of themselves on the ferries which brought them into work. There were also problems with women and sex as 'vice girls' from Glasgow started returning and illegitimacy rates in Dunoon doubled from 7.1 per cent of births in

1972 to 14.4 per cent in 1973.[43] Many of the problems were caused by the presence in a small community of a large workforce consisting of fit young men doing hard and dangerous work and being well rewarded for it; the local police were hard pushed to deal with the attendant problems of excessive drinking and brawling. Sometimes there were fights between the McAlpine workers and off-duty American sailors; in conversation with US Navy officers Giarchi noted that they felt that the Ardyne workforce had done them a good turn. 'The locals are now too annoyed about the navvies to concern themselves about us,' said one at a lunch on board the USS *Canopus* which was the tender ship between 1970 and 1975.[44] The main difference was that whereas the McAlpine workers were only at Ardyne for a fleeting time and made no attempt at integration, the Americans were in the Holy Loch for over 30 years and made every attempt to do the exact opposite.

7

The Watch on the Rhine:
Scots in Germany and on Other Fronts

THROUGHOUT THE COLD War the main battleground was always envisaged as the north German plain, where UK forces came under the overall command of NATO. It was here that the decisive land battle would have been fought if the Soviet Union and its Warsaw Pact allies had ever decided to attack westwards towards the Rhine, the Low Countries and the English Channel. With its open terrain of rolling farmlands and good road infrastructure the landscape was made for tank warfare and encouraged rapid movement and manoeuvre whereas further south lay rough, heavily wooded terrain which favoured the defenders and only the Fulda Gap revealed the possibility of attacking toward Frankfurt-am-Rhein; further south the Hof Corridor provided the same opportunity for any assault on Munich. It was territory already well-known to the British Army for it was in the Länder of Westphalia, Lower Saxony and Schleswig Holstein that the regiments of King George II had campaigned in the eighteenth century and where many of them had won the battle honours emblazoned on their colours. In that sense at least, it was very much a home from home, especially for the Scottish regiments, most of whom could trace their histories back to that period and had taken part in those historic campaigns.

Known as the British Army of the Rhine (BAOR), the main British component was 1st British (BR) Corps with its headquarters at Bielefeld, consisting of 55,000 soldiers together with some 200,000 dependants and civilian supporting staff; formed in 1952, this consisted initially of four divisions until the early 1980s, when the 2nd Division was returned to York to act as a reinforcement force and in time of war would be used to guard the lines of communication and the general rear area. Above that was the headquarters of the Northern Army Group (NORTHAG), which had its headquarters at Rheindahlen under the command of a four-star British general and at any one time it was made up of the British Corps, a West German (GE) Corps (HQ Münster), a Dutch (NL) Corps (HQ Apeldoorn) and a Belgian (BE) Corps (HQ Köln-Junckersdorf) plus various supporting US formations. Further south were the four corps of the Central Army Group (CENTAG) drawn from the US and West German armies plus a Canadian division. Perhaps the truest expression of the British military presence in West Germany was to be found at Bielefeld on the edge of the Teutoburger Wald, where the corps headquarters was ringed by its main garrisons at Herford, Detmold, Sennelager, Paderborn, Münster and Osnabrück. It was in this area that the main British field army would have deployed in the event of an attack by Warsaw Pact forces, with the Dutch and the Germans to the north and the Belgians to the south. In the words of the historian Anthony Beevor, who served in an armoured regiment in West Germany during the Cold War, it was a coherent location which gave the British Army the priceless advantage that in the event of a conflict they would be fighting on territory over which they had already trained and which they knew intimately: 'its front would be less than a hundred kilometres broad, with two of the three armoured divisions deployed forward, each screened by an armoured reconnaissance regiment'.[1] The other main British presence was the 3,000-strong autonomous Berlin Infantry Brigade (Berlin Field Force from April 1977), which included amongst its responsibilities a contribution to the four-power guard on Spandau Prison. This held a number of Nazi leaders, including the deputy leader Rudolf Hess, who did not die until 17 August 1987. After his death Spandau Prison was demolished to prevent it from becoming a Nazi shrine. The British brigade consisted of three infantry battalions and an armoured squadron which rotated every two years.

Together with the air power provided by 2nd Tactical Air Force (later RAF Germany), which operated six main bases at Brüggen, Geilenkirchen, Gütersloh, Jever, Laarbruch and Wildenrath, this was Britain's contribution to the post-war defence of Western Europe and in some respects West Germany became the real home of the British Army during the Cold War. Infantry regiments were stationed in West Germany for up to five years at a time, armoured regiments for ten years or more, while artillery, engineer and logistic regiments were based in the country more or less permanently; at the same time, from 1960 the RAF maintained a round-the-clock nuclear strike capability with English Electric Canberra bombers followed by Blackburn Buccaneers, SEPECAT Jaguars and Panavia Tornados. Accompanying the service personnel were their families and while the married quarters, with their schools and shops, took on a German identity the ambience was resolutely British: not for nothing was BAOR also known as 'Little Britain across the Rhine'. During the early months of peacetime the British pursued a vigorous policy of non-fraternisation through a civilian Control Commission composed of 26,000 administrators, many of them retired colonial civil servants who wanted to rule the country as if it were a protectorate peopled by an alien and ungovernable race. To that end they issued a handbook giving specific warning about the people under their control: 'You are about to meet a strange people in a strange enemy country. When you meet the Germans you will probably think they are very much like us. They look like us except there are fewer of the wiry type and more big fleshy types. But they are not really as much like us as they look.'[2]

By 1948, though, the policy of non-fraternisation had been found to be unworkable and for the rest of the Cold War relationships between the British Army and the local population were reasonably good, even though initially the attitude of many older soldiers was 'sometimes little better than that of a benign occupying power'.[3] All ten (later eight) Scottish infantry regiments plus the two battalions of the Scots Guards and the Royal Scots Greys (later Royal Scots Dragoon Guards) served in BAOR throughout the Cold War, and for the personnel their experience depended on where and when they were stationed in the country. For example, the Gordon Highlanders undertook several tours with BAOR but their first time in immediate post-war Germany was a grim experience. The end of hostilities in Europe was greeted with widespread relief – Nazi Germany had proved to be an obstinate and unyielding enemy – but all three of the Gordon Highlanders' operational battalions (1st, 2nd and 5th/7th) were involved in the complicated peace-enforcement and peace-making duties facing the Allies in post-war Germany. The bulk of these fell on the 1st Battalion, which had ended the war in Bremerhaven as part of XXX Corps and was destined to remain in post-war Germany until 1950. At the beginning of 1946 it moved to Muna Camp near Zeve, then on to Verden before a more permanent posting to the industrial city of Essen on the Ruhr. Home to the huge Krupp industrial complex, the city had been the target for heavy aerial bombardment throughout the war and the damage to the infrastructure made life difficult for the Germans and the occupying forces alike. The 1st Battalion was housed in the Meeanee Barracks, which one Gordon Highlander, writing with some feeling in the regimental magazine, described as 'a heap of steel, bricks and mortar'.[4] After the excitements of the final weeks of victory it was a huge anticlimax and it proved to be a taxing time for the battalion under the command of Lieutenant-Colonel B. J. D. Gerrard, who was destined to be the battalion's last commanding officer. Eventually sporting activities were increased and the introduction of new and regular training routines kept men on their toes, but the time at Meeanee Barracks was described by the regimental historian as 'monochromatic' and it tested to the full the battalion's *esprit de corps*.[5] In 1948, as part of a War Office plan to reduce the size of the infantry, all regiments lost their 2nd battalions through amalgamation – since September 1945 the 2nd battalion had been based in Libya – and thus it was in July that the Gordons' two battalions were amalgamated to form the new 1st Battalion The Gordon Highlanders under the command of Lieutenant-Colonel V. D. G. Campbell, who had started his army career in the Cameron Highlanders.

A vivid description of the conditions faced by the Gordons during this period can be found in the private letters of the future novelist James Kennaway, who served with the battalion as a National Service subaltern. The son of a Perthshire lawyer and factor, Kennaway had been commissioned as a Cameron Highlander in 1948 but due to the desperate shortage of junior officers had been posted to 1st Gordons. While his letters recorded the improving state of affairs in West Germany – rough shooting for the officers and cheap drink and cigarettes for every soldier – he could not ignore the local conditions and in one letter to his mother he described a little boy in Essen tripping over a boot in the snow: 'then picking himself up, brushed his knees and ran on, assuredly that might happen in England and to any child. Only the boot still had a foot in it'.[6] Kennaway later wrote about his time with the Gordons in his first novel, *Tunes of Glory*, whose plot centres on the clash of personalities between two officers – Jock Sinclair, an officer from the ranks with a superb wartime record, who is replaced as commanding officer by Basil Barrow, a pre-war regular officer. Although the setting is Scotland the regiment is undeniably the Gordons and most of the characters were based on officers Kennaway had known in West Germany. Before the novel was published he sent the manuscript to be read for accuracy by a brother officer, John Durbin, who replied that he could identify every single one of the officers in the fictional Campbell Barracks (loosely based on Queen's Barracks, Perth). Later the book was made into a memorable and highly acclaimed film of the same title, with Alec Guinness playing Sinclair and John Mills playing Barrow.

By coincidence, the 2nd Gordons also had a future novelist amongst its young officers, namely George Macdonald Fraser, who had fought during the war in the 9th Border Regiment as a private soldier before being commissioned in 2nd Gordons. The creator of the *Flashman* novels – named after the bully in Thomas Hughes's novel *Tom Brown's Schooldays* (1857) – Fraser also produced the equally memorable character of Private McAuslan, 'the biggest walking disaster to hit the British Army since Ancient Pistol'. Although Fraser claimed that 'the Highland battalion in this book [*The General Danced at Dawn*] never existed, inasmuch as the people in the stories are fictitious' it is equally clear that he based it on his time spent with 2nd Gordons. Reviewing Fraser's first collection of short stories in the *Sunday Times*, Bernard Fergusson, a distinguished Black Watch soldier and himself an author, said of McAuslan's creator: 'twenty-five years have not dimmed Mr Fraser's recollections of those hectic days of soldiering after the war'. Later, in 1988, after publishing his third collection, *The Sheikh and the Dustbin*, Fraser finally acknowledged the debt he owed to his old regiment in the creation of his short stories when he dedicated the volume to his commanding officer, Lieutenant-Colonel R. G. Lees, following a chance meeting at a book signing in London. It too is part of the literature of the Cold War.

In the first years of the occupation the rationale for being in post-war Germany, by then divided into western and eastern sectors, was not always apparent to soldiers but following the blockade of Berlin in 1948 the confrontation between NATO and the Soviet Union became increasingly belligerent. For many of the soldiers the posting was a bit of an eye-opener. Not only were most of the barracks well-appointed and modern, especially those from the Nazi era, but they were self-contained units with ample facilities for off-duty leisure activities. The Army Kinema Corporation provided recent releases of popular films; the British Forces Broadcasting Services, founded in 1942, was an acceptable alternative to the BBC World Service, with its British Forces Network Germany broadcasting a cosy mixture of record request

Cold War long stop: RAF Saxa Vord. Home to No. 91 Signal Unit, its task was to monitor the skies to the north as part of the UK's air defences and to intercept potentially hostile aircraft. Closed in 2005, it was reactivated in 2017 in response to an unexpected surge in incursions by Russian aircraft and submarines as a new Cold War threatened.

The Berlin Blockade in 1948 was the first test of Western resolve when the Soviet Union closed all rail, road and canal communications between West Berlin and West Germany. A massive air lift of essential supplies was organised – and it worked. An RAF Dakota is being unloaded at Templehof airport with army lorries standing by to take supplies into the city.

The Cold War almost became hot between 1950 and 1953 when the USA led a UN coalition army to oust North Korean forces from South Korea. Lieutenant-Colonel David Rose, commanding 1st Black Watch, greets three visiting US generals during the fighting.

Above. In March 1961 the US Navy began a three-decade-long occupation of Holy Loch near Dunoon, when Submarine Squadron 14 took up residence with its Polaris-armed nuclear submarines. As seen in this photograph, the floating dock *Los Alamos* was used to service and repair the boats. The base was closed in 1992.

Right. The Royal Navy acquired Polaris the US-built submarine-launched ballistic missile in June 1968, when HMS *Resolution* test-fired the weapon off Cape Kennedy. Polaris remained in service until 1996, when it was superseded by Trident.

Below. The arrival of nuclear weapons in Scotland sparked large and vociferous protests. The Campaign for Nuclear Disarmament (CND) was founded in 1958 and enjoyed widespread support on the left. This protest against the US presence at Holy Loch was mounted by the STUC in Paisley in March 1961.

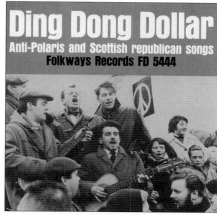

Ding Dong Dollar
Anti-Polaris and Scottish republican songs
Folkways Records FD 5444

Left. This was the period of the folk revival and the CND protests were enlivened by songs such as 'Ding Dong Dollar', which became the anthem of the anti-Polaris movement. The songs reached a wider audience when an LP of the same name was issued by the US label Folkways.

Above. At Holy Loch, off-duty American sailors used local taxis to get around. At one stage there were thought to be 140 taxis operating in Dunoon, rumoured to be the largest concentration of such vehicles in any town in the UK

Left. In March 1960 Elvis Presley made his only visit to Britain while flying back to the USA after military service in West Germany. When his DC-7 aircraft stopped at Prestwick to refuel, and although Presley was temporarily bewildered, asking, 'Where am I?', he obliged his fans by signing autographs and posing for photographs.

Inside the nuclear bunker at RAF Turnhouse in 1987. The underground building was designed to monitor fall-out levels in the event of a nuclear attack on Edinburgh and was demolished in 1997.

Edinburgh-based Ferranti was Scotland's largest defence contractor, with eight plants operating across the central belt, all built on successful defence contracts as the company invested heavily in the development of inertial navigation equipment and weapons guidance systems for the new generation of jet-powered aircraft.

Royal Scots on patrol in Belfast during the first year of the 'Troubles' in 1970. Led by Lance Corporal Sneddon, a patrol of B Company receives orders while standing in front of their Humber 'Pig' armoured vehicle.

The British Commanders-in-Chief Mission to the Soviet Forces in Germany, better known by its acronym BRIXMIS, was officially an overt operation designed to 'to maintain liaison between the Staff of the two Commanders-in-Chief and their Military Governments in the Zones' but in reality 'their job was official spying'. Although no lives were lost, there many close calls such as this incident when a BRIXMIS car was rammed by a massive NVA Tatra148 truck in August 1982.

In the 1950s and 1970s a series of maritime disputes between Iceland and the UK flared up over the right to fish in Icelandic waters. Although it was not a war in the technical sense it was an ugly and acrimonious confrontation in which expensive British naval assets were damaged in collisions with smaller Icelandic patrol vessels. Damage to the frigate HMS *Diomeid* is assessed at Rosyth after returning to port.

Beware the Bear: a huge Soviet Tu-95 aircraft takes off on a mission which could take it across Scotland and over the Atlantic. Used in the bomber and maritime reconnaissance roles it was a regular visitor to UK air space and despite its age is still in service today.

Above. The instantly recognisable delta-wing Avro Vulcan nuclear bomber kitted out in white anti-flash paint to protect it from thermal radiation following a nuclear explosion. This restored version, Vulcan XM603, is on display at the Avro Heritage Museum, Woodfield Poynton in Cheshire.

Right. Scramble! Squadron Leader MacGillivray and his crew race towards Handley Page Victor B.1 XH592 of 15 Squadron, during a demonstration scramble at RAF Cottesmore, in June 1959.

Below. Throughout the Cold War the Soviet Navy operated at a disadvantage because its submarines were noisy and difficult to disguise. This Foxtrot diesel-electric vessel was not retired until 1995; altogether 74 of the class were completed.

Code-named Sabre, the SS-20 IRBM missiles were game-changers in the Cold War arms race. Not only were they powered by solid fuel, making them safer to operate and more reliable, they were mobile, being transported and fired from large wheeled portable launchers to avoid detection.

The Cold War thaws. In December 1984 the new Soviet leader Mikhail Gorbachev visited the UK at the invitation of Margaret Thatcher. His trip included a visit to Edinburgh, where he met Scottish Secretary George Younger and Foreign Office Minister of State Malcolm Rifkind (left, wearing glasses).

The protestors' question was not rhetorical: throughout the Cold War and beyond one of the most contentious issues was the secretive transportation on public roads of nuclear warheads from Aldermaston and nearby Burghfield to their destination at Coulport. These heavy convoys travelled north and returned south up to eight times a year – a round trip of 900 miles.

Arriving too late for the party. Designed for firing Trident missiles, HMS *Vanguard* was rolled out at Barrow-in-Furness on 4 March 1992, but by the time it came into service and arrived at its home port of Faslane the Cold War was long over.

programmes and military gossip; and the ubiquitous NAAFI made every posting a home-from-home. It was also possible to meet Germans and visit local pubs, even though the required linguistic ability was usually little more than '*Zwei Bier, bitte*'. Still, it was a welcome change as it provided a unique occurrence of living abroad at a time when overseas travel was difficult and expensive and anything 'foreign' was considered a novelty. (At that time travel between the two countries was mainly confined to rail and ferry, commercial air flights being prohibitively expensive and, in the early years at least, currency controls were strictly imposed.)

For most British soldiers West Germany was largely a pleasant and trouble-free experience but there were obvious tensions too. The outrage caused by the revelation of the Nazi concentration camps had excited public indignation in the UK and the policy of non-fraternisation had not encouraged peaceful coexistence. On the other hand, many Germans resented the foreign presence in their country, just as had happened in Scotland with the arrival of the US Navy. Throughout the 1950s and 1960s trouble between local youths and British soldiers was a niggling problem, although most of the tension amounted to little more than coldness towards service personnel and their families in pubs and shops. Occasionally this bad feeling erupted into violence and one of the worst incidents occurred in Minden in April 1962, when there was a mass brawl in the local Coliseum bar between German youths and soldiers from 1st Cameronians (Scottish Rifles), which had just completed a demanding tour in Kenya and the Middle East. Once the fight had been broken up 17 soldiers were arrested and two of them were sent for court martial. At the time the incident attracted little interest – squabbles between BAOR soldiers and Germans were commonplace – but a few months later the British press took up the story and a reporters and television camera crews descended on Minden. During the investigations, the word *Giftzwerg* (poison dwarf) was used by some of the locals to describe Cameronian soldiers, and it stuck. It has to be said, too, that within the battalion it caused no little amusement and was even regarded as a compliment, but the adverse publicity was harmful not just to the Cameronians but to all Scottish regiments. It mattered not that the battalion had been engaged on local community projects; for the press, all that seemed to count was a bar-room brawl which had achieved widespread notoriety. Not that it was an uncommon occurrence: 20 years later an officer in an armoured regiment in BAOR revealed that little had changed and that soldiers still turned to alcohol when off-duty: 'Human frustration manifested itself as violence or drunkenness, usually both, helped along by the cheap duty-free drink which the Army makes available as a safety valve. Fights, marital breakdowns, alcoholism and car crashes are among the direct and common consequences. Drinking may become the only escape from the soul-destroying life in hideous garrison towns like Sennelager or Hohne.'[7]

To counteract the threat of bad behaviour, itself a by-product of idleness or boredom, a posting to West Germany offered a variety of sporting activities – from yachting in the north to skiing in the south with familiar field sports such as football, rugby and hockey in between – but it should not be thought that army life in BAOR was a round of fun and games. Far from it: the military year was dominated by a strict training regime which was tough and realistic, even though its regularity made it somewhat predictable. Whatever else, it was intensive, as Lieutenant-Colonel (later Lieutenant-General Sir) Robert Richardson insisted when he took over command of 1st Royal Scots in May 1969, at that time based in Osnabrück where the battalion was serving in 12 Mechanised Brigade in the 2nd Division: 'We are to spend more time this year on basic skills as infantrymen, particularly shooting and to become fully trained in air defence, nuclear, biological and chemical warfare and German language, while not forgetting our APC [armoured personnel carrier] skills. To ensure we remain fully trained we are faced with taking part in over thirty exercises ranging from Jutland to Berlin and Bavaria.'[8]

At that time field exercises were designed to be representative of the kind of fighting that would take place if the Warsaw Pact were to decide to invade from the east. This was made easier by the open terrain of the North German plain and by the tolerance of local farmers to allow large-scale armoured manoeuvres on their land and by the willingness of NATO to pay generous compensation for any damage done. Just about every soldier involved has stories of farmers ushering destructive armoured vehicles onto the land in the hope of getting funds from this unexpected 'second harvest'. This became more prevalent in the late 1960s, when infantry battalions started converting to the mechanised role using the new FV-432 tracked fighting vehicle or armoured personnel carrier, which was capable of taking a section into battle; in so doing it transformed the face of the modern battlefield. As Captain (later

Colonel) Robert Watson, Signals Officer of 1st Royal Scots, described the transition to the new vehicle it was a revolutionary moment which involved a huge change in tactics and procedures: 'The FV-432 was essentially an "armoured taxi" whose role was to move the infantry, with a degree of protection, to a point from where they could dismount to assault on foot. The only armament on the vehicle at that time was a pintle-mounted machine-gun, manned by the vehicle commander, who had to expose himself out of his hatch to use it.'[9] Due to the existence of the 'arms plot', a complicated system by which infantry battalions were periodically rotated to various locations and trained for different roles, all the Scottish battalions trained in armoured or mechanised warfare at some point during their deployment in West Germany. And as one infantry corporal explained, despite any drawbacks, most soldiers felt that they were doing a necessary job which was the result of Cold War confrontation with the Soviet Union and their Warsaw Pact allies: 'Our role is to protect our part of Germany against threat from the other side. We have to be ready, just in case, because we can never properly tell with the Russians. Yes I do honestly believe there is a threat. You could easily wake up one morning and find they were here, they'd just come across like that before you could do anything about it. That's why they teach us recognition of Russian arms and tanks and uniforms, so that we can spot them immediately: you need to be able to do it through binoculars, to tell whether a soldier in an unfamiliar uniform is one of our side or one of theirs.'[10]

While based in the country soldiers also became used to the regular rhythms of the training year, which began with all-arms exercises involving live-firing practice; areas such as Soltau, Sennelager and Haltern became familiar, even over-familiar, parts of the Lower Saxony landscape. By agreement with the West German government the extensive Soltau range was used by British and Canadian forces with 30,000 soldiers and 1,500 armoured vehicles training over it each year during the 1970s. The high point of the year came with the autumn manoeuvres, which were held 'in an atmosphere of intense competition, rivalry and scrutiny' and were designed to be as realistic as possible to replicate the stresses and strains of modern armoured warfare.[11] During these periods, all armoured regiments in 1st British Corps had to be prepared at four hours' notice to move with 90 per cent of their assets ready and available for instant action. Added realism came from unannounced inspections by NATO teams, usually in the middle of the night, the

purpose being to test the fitness of soldiers to carry out their tasks and
the professionalism of their officers to command them. In West Berlin
the call-out exercise was called 'Bear Defender' and took place four
times a year, two of which were unannounced and were designed to test
a formation's readiness. As remembered by one participant, Major
Richard Nunneley, 1st Black Watch, even in the late 1980s the accent
was on realism: 'We didn't just play at soldiers; we regularly reconnoi-
tred our wartime positions had it come to war with the Russians. There
were a number of scenarios, one was closing the corridors to planes,
trains and vehicles. This included exercises at Battalion level like Bear
Defender but also at Divisional and NATO levels.'[12] The Army also
used alternative training areas in Libya and further afield in Canada, at
the British Army Training Unit at Suffield near Medicine Hat in
Alberta. These sites were ideal from the point of view of terrain but
both had drawbacks. The Canadian facility was not only hugely expensive to maintain but it could only be used in the summer months, and
the Libyan rights to use a range at Tobruk were withdrawn in 1971
after Colonel Muammar Gaddafi came to power having unseated King
Idris I, a long-time British ally.

Nunneley's commanding officer, Lieutenant-Colonel (later Lieutenant-
General Sir) Alistair Irwin, recalled that he did not know if these
call-outs were real or not and before departing he always advised his
wife that in the event of war she should take the family back to Scotland
and somehow or other he would make his way back to the country to
find them.[13] Whole careers could be changed by an unsatisfactory
report and that sense of competition added to the frisson created during
the culmination of the training year, although some critics became
concerned that winning competitions became an end in itself and was
not particularly helpful for learning new skills. There were also local
difficulties. As time went by the Germans became less enamoured of
the military exercises and by the 1980s there was considerable resistance to the annual dislocation of life in the area around the Soltau
range, so much so that in 1988 there was serious disruption to the
autumn exercises, with the blocking of local roads as well as the railway
loading ramp at Rheinsehlen Camp.

Fortunately, the Cold War in the North German plain never turned
to hot war but there were moments when the temperature fluctuated
alarmingly, and it seemed inevitable that the opposing armies would be
committed to a ground war which was probably unwinnable. During

the 1950s, in the early years of the confrontation, it was a case of all quiet on the Eastern Front and there was little likelihood of real conflict. Even a student rising against Soviet control in Hungary in 1956 failed to attract much official condemnation in the West, largely because it coincided with the furore over a widely condemned British and French initiative to invade Egypt after the Suez Canal had been seized by Colonel Abdel Nasser. As the US vice-president of the time, Richard Nixon, explained later: 'We couldn't, on one hand, complain about the Soviets intervening in Hungary and, on the other hand, approve of the British and the French picking that particular time to intervene against Nasser.'[14]

However, in the following decade a number of crises created a climate of growing anxiety in the West, beginning with Berlin in 1961 when the East German government ordered the construction of a border wall in an attempt to stop the flow of emigrants to the West. This was followed in the following year by the Cuban missile crisis and matters were exacerbated by the escalating war in Vietnam, which prompted endless protests across Europe. At the end of the decade tensions were heightened in 1967 by the Six-Day War in the Middle East, fought between Israel and an Arab alliance of Egypt, Jordan and Syria and then again in 1968 when Warsaw Pact forces invaded Czechoslovakia to crush the liberal reform movement led by Alexander Dubček. All these crises were unsettling for NATO leaders and threatened Europe's stability. Moreover, throughout the 1960s there was growing awareness that NATO's inferiority in numbers, especially in the British-led northern sector, might call for the early use of nuclear weapons to stem any Warsaw Pact attack.

Most strategists believed that an assault from the east could only be contained for a fortnight before NATO forces were overrun, opening the way to the Low Countries and the English Channel. Some estimates reckoned that the Soviets and their Warsaw Pact allies would reach the Rhine 'within a matter of days, even from a standing start' and that NATO forces were little more than a tripwire rather than a purely defensive wall. Faced by that scenario NATO commanders would have had no option but to resort to the use of tactical nuclear weapons such as nuclear landmines and battlefield missiles in the hope that this would bring the opposition to the negotiating table before deadlier strategic weapons were employed and doomsday beckoned. It was a grim outcome but given the existence of nuclear weapons, it was also one which was predictable and seemed to mock the presence of enormous conventional forces on both sides of the divide. As two young analysts, both former army officers with experience of NATO service, put it at the time: 'The cold fact of the matter is, then, that the greater part of the British Army is dedicated to losing a two-week battle in Europe.'[15] If that was a policy of despair it merely delineated a truth that was rarely admitted. While NATO forces were arguably better equipped and trained, they were smaller in number: by the 1980s the Warsaw Pact had numerical superiority of 1.4:1 in personnel, 3:1 in artillery, 2.4:1 in anti-tank weapons and 2:1 in combat aircraft.[16] This excluded American forces in the USA, which could be used to reinforce those in the European theatre – however, the operation to bring them across the Atlantic would have taken weeks to implement and would be hindered by any early Warsaw Pact advance westwards. In short, because it was considered likely that NATO ground and air forces would have been unable to resist their opponents' numerical superiority, 'the use of nuclear weapons would then have been inevitable.'[17] So ingrained was this belief that NATO exercises usually ended with an order authorising the use of ADMs (tactical nuclear weapons) once the Orange (Warsaw Pact) forces had taken possession of the main battlefield, thereby neutralising the Blue (NATO) defenders.

The conundrum exercised the minds of all senior commanders and strategists throughout the Cold War. On the one hand opponents of nuclear weaponry such as Chief of the Defence Staff Field Marshal Lord Carver argued that reliance on 'the early use of nuclear weapons is no answer as the West would come off second best in any nuclear exchange and would simply be "cutting off its nose to spite its face".' This did not mean ignoring their own deterrent capacity. On the contrary, like Sir Michael Howard, Professor of Modern History at Oxford University, Carver believed that the Soviet threat could be contained by conventional means provided that they were 'lethally efficient' and were backed up by political resolve. Both men were veterans of the Second World War and had ample reason to mistrust Soviet intentions and expressions of good faith but for many younger soldiers the idea of nuclear war starting in Europe seemed far-fetched and even risible. To counter it they put their trust in NATO's policy of flexible response, which evolved in 1966–7 following France's decision to remove itself from the alliance's command structure and which NATO itself summarised thus: 'The deterrent concept of the Alliance is based on a flexibility which will prevent the potential aggressor from predicting with confidence NATO's specific response to aggression and which will lead him to conclude that an unacceptable degree of risk would be involved regardless of the nature of his attack.'[18]

What this meant in practice was that the British-led northern forces would engage the enemy when it crossed the border into West Germany, both to make NATO's position clear and to discover the direction and weight of the assault. It would also buy time for a strong defensive position to be created further back and for political negotiation towards a ceasefire and cessation of hostilities. By then, too, there was a growing school of thought that in the initial stages a nuclear exchange could be survivable provided that a balance could be found between using limited violence and maximum diplomacy.

In 1978 General Sir John Hackett published *The Third World War*, an apocalyptic fictional future-history which envisaged a short, sharp nuclear conflict between the Soviet Union and NATO breaking out in August 1985; it quickly became an unexpected publishing triumph, selling over 3 million copies and being translated into ten languages. A second, revised edition appeared in 1982 to reflect changes in the Cold War. Hackett, a soldier turned author and academic, knew what he was talking about – he had ended his military career as commander of NATO's Northern Army Group and commander-in-chief of BAOR – and his book had been co-authored by several senior soldiers and academics, but he was keen to drum home the message that, given proper resources, with conventional weapons NATO could repel a Warsaw Pact assault and preserve peace in Europe. In *The Third World War*, following a Soviet-instigated outbreak of hostilities, the cities of Birmingham and Minsk are annihilated by nuclear weapons but both sides survive after the government of the Soviet Union implodes. His descriptions of the nuclear exchange are stark and horrifying but are balanced by an argument that a war conducted on those terms need not be terminal provided full scope is given to diplomatic initiatives.

There are several points in Hackett's narrative when both sides have to take decisions about whether to use nuclear weapons. Within the NATO command structure subordinate commanders argue for the early use of tactical nuclear weapons against Soviet ground and naval forces but this is refused as it would only encourage Soviet retaliation. On the Soviet side the decision is made relatively quickly after their conventional forces start losing the battle in Europe, and the decision is taken to drop a one-megaton nuclear warhead on Birmingham. In response, the US and UK decide on an instant 'limited' nuclear attack on Minsk using submarine-based missiles, but this turns out to be the end game. Just as the Soviet leadership is considering further escalation, a coup occurs in Moscow and fortuitously the war ends with the collapse of the Soviet Union, thereby foreshadowing real events which happened two decades later. This 'happy ending' was much criticised at the time but it reflected the book's aim of arguing that NATO had to be strong enough not only to defeat a Soviet attack but also to prevent it happening in the first place. In other words, without additional investment in NATO the alliance risked failure before any shot was fired.[19] It also allowed Hackett and his team to reflect on what might occur in the 1980s – the destruction of two cities – if Europe were to become a nuclear battleground: 'Only much later would the question arise why such an appalling disaster should ever have been invited and who was to blame. There will probably never be an answer. What is sure is that it should never have happened and must never be allowed to happen again.'[20]

No account of the confrontation in Europe would be complete without mention of the Soviets' *spetsnaz* (special purpose) troops, which operated alongside elements of the regular army and navy and were an integral part of their order of battle. Always small in number – an estimated 30,000 served in Europe – and highly secretive, their role was to conduct reconnaissance and sabotage operations behind enemy lines and in time of war to destroy command and control sites related to the operation of nuclear weapons. They were also trained to identify and eliminate the opposition's political and military leadership and to make contact with Soviet agents behind enemy lines. Operating in small teams of five, they received special forces training and had access to modern and sophisticated weapons and communication systems. Naval *spetsnaz* also received specialist training and used underwater weapons such as the SPP-1 pistol and the Piranha midget submarine, which allowed them to operate autonomously and for lengthy periods without supervision. Following an incident in 1956 when a Royal Navy frogman called Lionel 'Buster' Crabb was caught and killed while investigating the hull of the Soviet Sverdlovsk class cruiser *Ordzhonikidze,* naval *spetsnaz* troops were also trained in underwater unarmed combat. Unlike British special forces such as the SAS regiment, the *spetsnaz* were not given training in hostage release; their primary role was to engage in deep penetration operations during the run-up to any outbreak in hostilities and to carry out targeted demolitions and assassinations.

The British response to this threat was the creation of the Home Service Force (HSF), a home guard-type formation which was formed in 1982 from volunteers with previous military experience in the 18–60 age group and equipped with modern weapons. Their role was to guard key points and other installations vulnerable to *spetsnaz* attack, thereby freeing up regular troops for other duties. A pilot study showed that volunteers with more than two years' previous military duty could be quickly brought up to operational effectiveness and the new HSF companies served with Territorial battalions wearing that parent formation's cap badge. In Scotland the pilot study was undertaken by Z (HSF) Coy 1st (V) Bn, 51st Highland Volunteers, The Black Watch (The Royal Highland Regiment). Its headquarters were in Perth and much of the weekend training was carried out on the Barry Buddon range in Angus. Within two years the HSF had expanded to 5,000 soldiers with a UK-wide presence, but the HSF never quite shook off its 'Dad's Army' image – a reference to the popular BBC television series about the misadventures of a Second World War Home Guard company – and it never really gained the acceptance of sceptical senior army officers, who doubted its effectiveness against well-trained professional *spetsnaz* soldiers.[21]

It was against that uncertain strategic background that Scottish regiments served in BAOR during the Cold War and a posting to West Germany was endured both as a necessary evil in an unstable world and as part of the daily round of soldiering in the modern Army. Besides, at the end of the 1960s there was a worrying new development which saw violence break out in Northern Ireland and it would soon involve every regiment in the British Army. The trouble in the province began in July 1969 with the breaking-up of a civil rights march in Londonderry in which the Protestant paramilitary police (B-Specials) used extensive force against the largely Catholic protestors. As the violence spread and Catholics across the province found themselves under attack by groups of Protestants the decision was taken to reinforce the Northern Ireland garrison with additional soldiers acting 'in aid of the Civil power'. Initially they were made welcome, especially by the Catholic community, but the good relations did not last, especially after the rump of the Irish Republican Army (IRA) entered the fray – in December it split with a group of young hardliners establishing the Provisional IRA (PIRA or 'Provos') with a political wing called Sinn Fein ('ourselves alone'). Those who remained called themselves the Official IRA, popularly known as 'Stickies' and by May 1971 they too were in action against the British military presence. Trouble was also fomented by unionist terrorist groups such as the Ulster Volunteer Force (UVF) and the Ulster Freedom Force (UFF), the paramilitary wing of the Ulster Defence Association (UDA).

The first Scottish battalion to deploy to Northern Ireland in what would become regular four-month (later six-month) roulement tours was 1st Royal Highland Fusiliers, which was based in Armagh between February and May 1970 even though the feeling had been 'they'll never send a Scottish regiment' to Northern Ireland as the Fusiliers recruited from Glasgow and Ayrshire and the religious breakdown amongst the men was 60:40 Protestant to Catholic, a statistic that could have been troublesome in Northern Ireland.[22] Similar sentiments had been expressed by the 1st Royal Scots before they deployed to Belfast from their base at Osnabrück. They were the first infantry unit to arrive from BAOR and when they arrived in Belfast in March 1970 they found that they were responsible for security in the south of the city, deploying in an area of some four square miles where they attempted to separate the Protestant and Catholic communities along a hastily built 'peace line'. 'We were shocked by the burnt-out houses and deterioration in the Falls and Peace Line area but pleasantly surprised by the normality in most other areas,' remembered their commanding officer, Robert Richardson. 'However, it was clear that we had to train for any eventuality.'[23] He also remembered that facilities were very ad hoc and that little in the way of direction came from Army headquarters at Lisburn. An added problem was that the battalion had no transport, having operated as a mechanised battalion in West Germany. During this first tour the battalion had to deal with substantial rioting in the city, especially along the Falls Road which the Provisionals tried to turn into a no-go area using a policy of continuous rioting and confrontation. One of the worst riots took place at the beginning of July in the Lower Falls area of the city, which had been sealed off during the imposition of a curfew to allow arms searches to be made. When the battalion arrived in Northern Ireland there was still a sense of optimism that the worst of the violence would be over by Easter but by the time the Royal Scots returned to Osnabrück in August it was noticeable to one young officer that they were leaving 'a city with a deep wound of hatred and suspicion which has been there for many centuries . . . now again it is wide open and will take many years to close and heal again'.[24] The truth of that comment can be seen in the fact that 'The Troubles' (as they became known) lasted until the summer of 1997, when the IRA signed a final ceasefire leading to the Good Friday agreement of April 1998 which committed Dublin and London to 'partnership, equality and mutual respect as the basis of relationships within Northern Ireland, between North and South, and between these islands', and effectively brought peace to Northern Ireland.[25]

Fortunately, and unlike later experiences in the 1970s, there were no fatalities during the Royal Scots' first deployment in Northern Ireland. While several soldiers were wounded, some seriously, by the stones and bottles thrown by demonstrators, none had been killed and there were no casualties from a Scottish regiment until 9 March 1971 during a second tour by 1st Royal Highland Fusiliers, when three young unarmed soldiers were lured into a 'honey trap' by the PIRA while wearing civilian clothes and executed. They were John McCaig, his brother Joseph McCaig and their friend Dougald McCaughey; they were the fourth, fifth and sixth British soldiers to be killed in Northern Ireland and the first of 63 Scots to die in the conflict.[26] The first civilian to be killed by the Army was Danny O'Hagan, who was shot dead by 1st King's Own Scottish Borderers on Belfast's New Lodge Road during street disturbances on 31 July 1970. All of Scotland's infantry regiments took part in at least one tour of Northern Ireland but by the end of the 1960s their number had been reduced due to defence cuts to eight, plus the two battalions of the Scots Guards. In 1959 two Lowland regiments, The Royal Scots Fusiliers and The Highland Light Infantry had been amalgamated to form The Royal Highland Fusiliers while two years later The Seaforth Highlanders and the Cameron Highlanders had been amalgamated to form the Queen's Own Highlanders. Both amalgamations had caused a good deal of upset within the Army in Scotland and attracted adverse publicity across the wider Scottish public. By contrast, when a further regiment had to be cut a decade later the Cameronians chose a different course of action.

In 1964 a Labour administration came to power under Prime Minister Harold Wilson, with Denis Healey as Secretary of State for Defence. One of its first actions was to begin a Defence Review to consider policy in the light of the country's unfavourable economic circumstances and the reduction in colonial commitments east of Suez. A second election in 1966, also won by Labour, hastened the process of change still further and the worsening economic situation made more cuts in the armed forces inevitable. Although expensive projects such as the TSR-2 strike aircraft and CVA-01 fleet carriers were cancelled, the Army was made to bear the brunt of the manpower cuts with a reduction in strength from 200,000 to 165,000: this entailed the loss of four armoured, four artillery, one engineer and eight infantry regiments. This decision affected two Scottish regiments, both of which had managed hitherto to keep their separate identities. Scotland's only cavalry regiment, the Royal Scots Greys (2nd Dragoons) had never been amalgamated but on 2 July 1971 it joined forces in Edinburgh with the 3rd Carabiniers to form the Royal Scots Dragoon Guards, a heavy armoured regiment in NATO equipped with Challenger main battle tanks. The second was the Cameronians (Scottish Rifles), which had come into being in 1881 as a result of the amalgamation of the 26th Cameronian Regiment of Foot and the 90th Perthshire Light Infantry. Amalgamation with another regiment was one option but joining forces with another Lowland regiment, most likely The King's Own Scottish Borderers, was not a course the regiment was willing to take. When the news arrived in 1967 shortly after the battalion had returned from a successful tour in Aden, soundings were taken within the battalion and the regimental family and the decision was taken to disband in the following year. A similar decision was taken by The York and Lancaster Regiment (65th and 84th), which traced its history back to 1756. These were the first disbandments since 1922, when the Army's five Southern Irish regiments were removed from the Army List as a result of Irish independence.

Northern Ireland was not the only distraction, but it was the one that caused most headaches for BAOR brigade and divisional commanders, who frequently resented the loss of operational effectiveness due to the temporary absence of a mechanised battalion taking part in counter-insurgency warfare in Northern Ireland. A bigger problem was caused in the early part of 1982 by an emergency which came out of the blue after the Argentine military junta led by General Leopoldo Galtieri set in train a series of moves leading to the invasion of South Georgia and the neighbouring Falkland Islands, which had enjoyed British sovereignty since 1833. The background events which led to the outbreak of hostilities between Britain and Argentina on 2 April are now well enough known not to require any elaborate reiteration: the basic issue at stake was the sovereignty of the Falkland Islands and the determination of the British prime minister, Margaret Thatcher, not to give in to the illegal behaviour of the Argentine military junta. A naval and military task force was despatched to the South Atlantic, the ground force component being an expanded 3 Commando Brigade, but from the outset it was clear that further land forces would be needed, and this had an impact on BAOR.

There was considerable discussion about the composition of this force and what its remit might be. The designated Strategic Reserve for such tasks was 5 Infantry Brigade, which was based at Aldershot, but it was not fully established and had been denuded by the decision to remove 2nd Battalion Parachute Regiment and 3rd Battalion Parachute Regiment to reinforce 3 Commando Brigade. Its surviving infantry element was 1st Battalion 7th Duke of Edinburgh's Own Gurkha Rifles. There were also conflicting ideas about the rationale for such a force and the impact it would have on the UK's NATO allies. The Ministry of Defence had already decided not to weaken BAOR by withdrawing an infantry brigade from West Germany and reducing Britain's NATO commitments. Consideration was given to using 1 Infantry Brigade, the United Kingdom's Mobile Force based at Tidworth, but this was rejected on the grounds that it was a NATO-designated brigade. That left 5 Infantry Brigade as the only viable alternative and its deficiencies were made good by the addition of 2nd Battalion Scots Guards and 1st Battalion Welsh Guards, both 'first-class battalions', according to Chief of the General Staff, General (later Field Marshal) Sir Edwin Bramall. Both had recent experience of Northern Ireland, neither had any NATO obligations and apart from public duties in London both were available and ready for the intensive training in the Brecon Beacons that would be needed prior to deployment.

Three, later five, Royal Navy submarines also played a role in the war, albeit one which was not widely publicised at the time – HMS *Spartan* (Commander James Taylor), HMS *Splendid* (Commander Roger Lane-Nott) and HMS *Conqueror* (Commander Chris Wreford-Brown). None were Polaris boats but all were modern nuclear-powered attack submarines of the Swiftsure or Churchill class. First to arrive in the war zone was *Spartan*, which had been taking part in Exercise Springtrain in the North Atlantic before Taylor received an urgent message ordering him to proceed to Gibraltar to be stored for war.

Later he recalled that when he passed on the news to his heads of department they all responded, 'War with whom?'[27] *Conqueror* was still at Faslane, while *Splendid* was in the Western Approaches tailing a Soviet Victor class submarine when Lane-Nott received a similar message. All three travelled south knowing that the Argentine fleet was at sea and that it included four diesel-electric submarines, six warships equipped with sophisticated and deadly Exocet missiles, an aircraft carrier, the *25 de Mayo*, formerly the Royal Navy Colossus class carrier HMS *Venerable* and the cruiser *General Belgrano*, formerly USS *Phoenix*, but to the dismay of all three commanders there was little specific intelligence about the South Atlantic's hydrography and conditions around the Falklands and the Argentine coastal shelf, an area that had last been surveyed in the eighteenth century by Captain James Cook.

Shortly after the Argentine invasion the UK had established a 200-mile maritime exclusion zone around the Falklands and on 30 April this was upgraded to a total exclusion zone, which meant that any ship within it or approaching it could be attacked. Patrolling the zone were the three Royal Navy submarines, each given a separate sector. Two days later, in the darkening evening light on Sunday, 2 May *Conqueror* sighted the *Belgrano* and fired three torpedoes at the cruiser, two of which hit her, causing massive damage and sinking her within an hour. The worsening weather and the failure of the escorts to notice that something was amiss contributed to the death toll of 323, and only 772 sailors survived. It was noticeable that Wreford-Brown used Second World War-vintage Mark 8 torpedoes in preference to the newer but less reliable Mark 24 Tigerfish version. It was the first time since 1945 that a British submarine had sunk a ship in anger and later the sinking caused considerable political controversy. It was deemed necessary at the time as the cruiser posed a threat to the British fleet and seemed to be part of a pincer movement which included the carrier *25 de Mayo*. Later *Belgrano*'s commanding officer, Captain Hector Bonzo, admitted as much when he stated: 'It was absolutely not a war crime. It was an act of war, lamentably legal.'[28] Whatever the rights and wrongs of the case it was a decisive moment – as a precaution the rest of the Argentine Navy returned to port and played no further part in the fighting.

The submarine force was reinforced by two other SSNs, HMS *Valiant* and HMS *Courageous*, and also by the diesel-electric HMS *Onyx* for special forces' operations inshore closer to the Argentine coast but in the latter stages of the conflict their work was largely confined to picket duties, providing much-needed information about Argentine military and air force movements. On returning to Faslane Wreford-Brown caused further controversy when he flew a Jolly Roger flag from the submarine's flagpole, a tradition which had been started during the First World War to signify a successful engagement with the enemy. (The incident had happened in September 1914 when HMS *E9*, commanded by Lieutenant Max Horton, successfully torpedoed and sank the German cruiser *Hela* off the coast of Helgoland. Horton, a future admiral, initiated the idea of the Jolly Roger partly in response to an earlier comment by a senior naval officer that submarines were 'underhanded, unfair and damned un-English' and that their crews should be hanged as pirates.)

During the fighting around the Falklands the Royal Navy lost six ships to enemy bombing or missile attack and several more were moderately or badly damaged; there was a further setback when the LSL *Sir Galahad* was hit by bombs while unloading Welsh Guardsmen at Port Pleasant near Fitzroy, leaving 48 crew and soldiers dead and many more terribly injured. The short, sharp campaign in the Falklands ran close to catastrophe but ended triumphantly when the Argentine forces surrendered on 14 June. A key moment in the advance to Port Stanley was the capture of Mount Tumbledown, one of the highest peaks in the area, in which the leading infantry force was 2nd Battalion Scots Guards under the command of Lieutenant-Colonel (later Major-General) Michael Scott. Fought for the most part in total darkness, some of the fighting was hand-to-hand and the Argentine defenders proved to be determined and brave. Like the rest of the campaign, the battle tested ingenuity and capabilities but proved that they could be mastered by the unchanging standards of British infantry soldiering. Not everything went the force's way. The fleet was prey to Argentine air power, there was a shortage of helicopters and the logistical tail of 8,000 miles could have proved fatal in a lengthier conflict, but the victory came as a fillip to Britain's armed forces at a time when they were under threat from government cutbacks.

Although the Soviet Union played no significant part in the war it did pay close attention to what was happening, and one result of the victory was a need for them to reassess the fighting quality of the UK's forces, which had proved beyond doubt that they still provided a serious threat. The Soviet Navy also noted that up to five British SSN attack submarines had been deployed in the South Atlantic, and this meant that they were not being used in their traditional role in northern waters – intercepting Soviet submarines or escorting British SSBNs. This was both a challenge and an opportunity and the Soviets took up both. When one operational patrol undertaken by HMS *Resolution* had to be carried out without SSN escort, the Soviets did their utmost to discover its whereabouts and the patrol was subsequently described as being 'unusually testing'.[29] The war in the South Atlantic had also created an opportunity for Moscow to open a new sphere of influence in Latin America, but this was balanced by Soviet distaste for seeming to support the Argentine military junta, and the Falklands never became one of the Cold War's proxy conflicts. There is also circumstantial evidence to suggest that in the 1970s the left-wing strand in the IRA's leadership attempted to secure Soviet support for its political agenda and this led to PIRA becoming the beneficiary of Soviet funding, training and materiel support through proxies in Libya, South Yemen, East Germany and other governments and groups in the Soviet Union's sphere of influence

Ironically, it was in the dying days of the Cold War that British forces in West Germany were able to put their training to the test, not in the north German plain but in far-off Kuwait and Iraq. The move was made as part of Operation Granby, the British contribution to the US-led United Nations coalition forces under General Norman Schwarzkopf which had been despatched to Saudi Arabia following the illegal invasion and occupation of Kuwait by Iraqi forces on 2 August 1990. This was the 1st Armoured Division commanded by Major-General Rupert Smith and consisting of two armoured brigades, an artillery brigade and supporting elements all drawn from BAOR. There was a significant Scottish representation – Challenger main battle tanks of the Royal Scots Dragoon Guards (7 Armoured Brigade), 1st Royal Scots equipped with Warrior fighting vehicles (4 Armoured Brigade) and the Prisoner of War Guard Force which included 1st Royal Highland Fusiliers, 1st King's Own Scottish Borderers and 1st Queen's Own Highlanders. Regiments which supplied reinforcement and battle casualty replacements included the Scots Guards, and medical assistants and drivers came from the bands of the Royal Scots Dragoon Guards, the Scots Guards, The Royal Scots, The Royal Highland Fusiliers, Queen's Own Highlanders and The Gordon Highlanders. The war was also fought in the air and at sea and Scottish-based assets included mine countermeasure vessels from RN Rosyth and aircraft from RAF Kinloss (Nimrod), RAF Leuchars (Tornado) and RAF Lossiemouth (Buccaneer and Jaguar).[30]

There followed a lengthy game of diplomatic cat-and-mouse between the UN Security Council and Iraq's leader President Saddam Hussein which culminated with the issue of Resolution 678, which gave the Iraqis until 15 January 1991 to pull out of Kuwait. When they failed to comply, the coalition forces went into attack, with the British armoured division fighting on the right flank of VII US Corps. Although the actual battle was short and sharp the fighting was intense, with the Royal Scots Dragoon Guards engaging and knocking out large numbers of Soviet-made Iraqi tanks while 1st Royal Scots fought a traditional trench battle, often clearing Iraqi positions at bayonet point. During the conflict, which ended with the defeat of the Iraqi forces on 28 February 1991 and their expulsion from Kuwait, the British Army had deployed 43,000 soldiers and 2,500 armoured vehicles and by the end of the six-week war just about every regiment was represented in Smith's Armoured Division and its supporting forces. In many respects, the Gulf War (as it came to be known) was a curious affair, but it sent an unmistakable message to Saddam and other leaders in the Middle East. Despite fears of large casualties, not least as a result of Saddam's suspected store of chemical and biological weapons, these were kept to a minimum thanks to coalition air power and superior artillery; although the Iraqis often fought fiercely the actual land battle was almost a walkover. It helped too that the Cold War confrontation in Germany was at an end, and the victory proved that the NATO forces which formed the bulk of Schwarzkopf's army could be used as a force for good in the new world order which was emerging. As the historian John Keegan pointed out in the Official History of the campaign, there was a direct connection between the training in places like Soltau in West Germany and the practice in the sands of the Kuwaiti desert: 'the victory was the result, above all, of the dedicated training to fight an all-out war against the Warsaw Pact in Central Europe in which the British and American units that went to the Gulf had involved them-selves for many years'.[31]

The third 'off-piste' confrontation involving British forces were the so-called 'Cod Wars', a series of maritime disputes between Iceland and the UK which flared up in the 1950s and 1970s over the right to fish in Icelandic waters. Although it was not a war in the technical sense, it was an ugly and acrimonious confrontation in which live ammunition was used – if only as warning shots – and expensive British naval assets were tied up in the operations in the Atlantic. At the height of the hostilities in the 1970s the Royal Navy had 37 warships deployed and there were several incidents in which they were damaged in collisions with the smaller Icelandic patrol vessels. There was also a Cold War aspect in that Iceland was strategically placed in the Greenland–Iceland–UK(GIUK) gap and was home to the major US air force base at Keflavík, which housed the US 85th Air Group, radar stations and anti-submarine warfare units as well as US Search and Rescue units. The country was also a member of NATO, albeit a reluctant and frequently contentious ally whose leaders were not unaware of the leverage they could exert, especially in their relationship with Washington. This certainly proved to be the case during the Cod Wars, the first of which broke out in September 1958 over a dispute concerning the right to fish in Iceland's territorial waters – the Exclusive Economic Zone, or EEZ. Earlier in the year a Law of the Sea Conference held in Geneva had proposed a six-mile limit, but no agreement was reached and Iceland unilaterally brought in a 12-mile limit to prevent British trawlers working close to their shore and taking advantage of the rich fishing grounds. There was also a conservationist aspect to the Icelandic decision as they believed that fish stock, especially cod, was being depleted by over-fishing, but inevitably the confrontation between the squat Icelandic gunboats and the Royal Navy's sleek modern frigates took on the aspect of a contest between David and Goliath. To enforce the law Icelandic coastguard gunboats attempted to arrest British vessels fishing within the EEZ and the UK responded by sending Royal Navy warships to protect the fishing fleet, if necessary by using force. The dispute lasted until March 1961 and there were 84 serious incidents, including a number in which live rounds were fired across the bows of trawlers. A further conference failed to resolve the dispute but the UK agreed to accept the 12-mile limit and peace of a kind returned to Iceland's coastal waters.

Ten years later, in July 1971, hostilities returned when a left-wing coalition government came to power in Iceland and took steps to protect Iceland's fisheries by cancelling the agreement with the UK and by extending the EEZ to 50 miles. This was intolerable to the British government, which again ordered the Royal Navy to intervene; the Iceland coastguard vessels responded by becoming increasingly aggressive in their efforts to remove British and other European trawlers from the EEZ. Any which refused to obey coastguard instructions had their nets cut using a technique similar to those used in mine clearing and during the ensuing confrontations there were 56 incidents in which Royal Navy warships were rammed, causing serious structural damage. Part of the problem for the Royal Navy was the lack of political direction; another was the disparity between their ships, which were mainly anti-aircraft or anti-submarine warfare frigates designed for Cold War operations, while the four Icelandic gunboats and two armed trawlers were more like fishing boats than warships, or as one senior Royal Navy officer described the situation during the operations in the Atlantic, 'Icelandic gunboats, designed for the work, confronted British frigates which were decidedly not'.[32] One of those involved in the 'Cod Wars' was Hugo White (later Vice-Admiral Sir) who commanded the frigate HMS *Salisbury* in 1976; in an interview, he recalled the necessity of keeping any collision on the port side as that conformed with maritime law.[33] Later in his career he was Flag Officer Scotland and Northern Ireland, the senior naval officer in Scotland in the dying days of the Cold War. His headquarters at Rosyth was not only the base for the Navy's minor war vessels, including the Fishery Protection Squadron, but was also home to various destroyer and frigate squadrons.

It was at this stage that the Cod Wars entered their third phase, 1975–6, and the matter became more serious, with neither side prepared to back down. In November 1975, the Icelandic government announced its intention to extend the EEZ to 200 miles and the Royal Navy responded by increasing the level and intensity of its protection operations, including the particularly aggressive ramming of a gunboat by HMS *Falmouth* on 6 May 1976. At this point the Icelandic government made a representation to the US government to purchase modern Asheville class gunboats but when that failed a further approach was made to the Soviet Union to purchase Mirka class light frigates. This too was rejected but the Icelandic government was not finished: when it became clear that they would not receive external help they broke off diplomatic relations with the UK and threatened to close the NATO base at Keflavík, a move that would have been disastrous for the alliance's strategy in containing the Soviet air and sea threat through the GIUK gap. Although it was most unlikely that Iceland would have carried out that threat – the country was generally pro-West and it also benefited financially from the NATO connection – the fact that it had been made was enough to concern Washington. That probably accounts for the NATO mediation which ended the confrontation in June 1976 through a compromise agreement which allowed the UK to keep 24 trawlers within the 200-mile EEZ for six months and to limit their catch to 30,000 tons per year. By any standards, the 'Cod War' represented a defeat for the UK. Not only did it show that naval power was not enough to enforce policy as it had done in the past, but it marked the end of distant water fishing and the ports of Hull, Grimsby, Fleetwood and Aberdeen were badly affected by the subsequent economic downturn. Over 1,000 fishermen were made redundant, plus many shore-based workers; their trawlers were laid up to be scrapped or sold and to add insult the promised government compensation payments were not made until three decades later. By then, too, the fishing industry in Scotland had also been adversely affected by the UK's entry into the European Economic Community and its membership of its successor, the European Union.

8

Ploughshares into Swords:
Profiting from the Cold War

IF THE NAME of any of the Royal Navy's capital ships captures the essence of the Cold War arms race it is HMS *Vanguard*. The name has an honoured place in naval history, having been first introduced in 1587 for a heavily armed galleon of 500 tons in time for her to take part in the destruction of the Spanish Armada a year later. Laid off in 1629, she was followed by nine other ships bearing the same name, all of which gave distinguished service to the Royal Navy, the sixth being Nelson's flagship during his decisive victory over the French fleet at the Battle of the Nile in August 1798. Her successor was less fortunate, being an iron-hulled and partially steam-powered battleship which was lost in the Irish Sea in September 1875 after being involved in a collision in extremely foggy conditions with her sister ship, HMS *Iron Duke*. Although all the crew was saved the ship's captain, Richard Dawkins, was later court-martialled for negligence and never received another command. To add to the indignity his pet Jack Russell dog was drowned during the incident. The eighth *Vanguard* had an equally unhappy ending. A St Vincent class battleship with ten 12-inch main guns, she was commissioned in 1910 and took part in the Battle of Jutland six years later; she was lying at anchor at Scapa Flow in July 1917 when for no explicable reason one of her magazines exploded and she sank immediately, with the loss of 843 of the 845 men aboard. But it was the ninth and tenth *Vanguard*s that had the most resonance for Scotland during the Cold War.

The first of these modern vessels was also the last battleship to enter the service of the Royal Navy. Launched in November 1944 at John Brown's yard at Clydebank, HMS *Vanguard* was the only Lion class battleship to be completed and once she had entered service it was planned that she would join the British Pacific fleet in the war against

Japan. However, her construction was delayed by labour shortages and by the time she was commissioned in 1946 the Second World War had come to an end, which meant that the Navy's largest and fastest battleship never fired her guns in anger. In 1947 she was in the news after transporting the Royal Family to South Africa for a state visit but much of her life was spent with the Home Fleet, being flagship between 1952 and 1954. However, she was becoming obsolete and too expensive to maintain and her short career ended in 1960 when she was laid off and towed from Portsmouth to Faslane to be scrapped only a few miles away from where she had been built. Four decades later the name returned to the Royal Navy and to the Clyde when the first Trident missile strategic submarine was commissioned on 14 August 1993, having been built by Vickers at Barrow-in-Furness. The boat also gave her name to the class of four similar submarines which carried the UK's nuclear deterrent from the 1990s into the twenty-first century, the others being *Victorious*, *Vigilant* and *Vengeance*. Both *Vanguard*s were emblematic of the arms race which fuelled Cold War defence expenditure and had an impact on Scotland, the battleship because she was the last of her class and the largest warship ever built by a Scottish yard, the submarine because she was the first of the most potent warships in naval service and for her entire working life her home port was the Clyde submarine base at Faslane.

Between the launch of the battleship and the arrival of the strategic submarine the building of warships in Scotland underwent a radical change. Initially there was a hint of an Indian Summer as the main yards on the Clyde prospered from the boom brought about by the need to make good shipping losses from the war years. All told, 23,651,000 tons of Allied shipping had been sunk or irreparably damaged, not just warships but also freighters and passenger liners, and there had been considerable destruction of the infrastructure due to enemy bombing, particularly during the Clydebank 'blitz' of 1941 when the German Luftwaffe attacked the industrial west of Scotland. Just as importantly, foreign competition, especially in Europe, had also been damaged by war action and their shipyards were temporarily unable to compete in the international marketplace. Companies such as John Brown entered the post-war period with healthy order books and a government report in August 1945 predicted that in the decade to come shipbuilders could expect to produce 10 million tons of new shipping, most of which would be commercial.[1] In the summer of 1946 an aerial photograph was taken at the Tail of the Bank off Gourock which summed up the position facing the John Brown company that year. In the background is the instantly recognisable Cunard liner RMS *Queen Elizabeth*, which was being refurbished after her war service as a troop carrier and in the foreground HMS *Vanguard* steams past on her way to her speed trials, the largest British warship passing the largest British ocean liner. Within the next quarter of a century both ships had passed into history, one to the breaker's yard at Faslane and the other to an equally dismal end as a burned-out wreck in the harbour of Hong Kong; they were victims of an economic climate which could not support hugely expensive and vulnerable battleships or equally costly and out-of-date luxury ocean liners. It was not exactly the end of the line, as in the 1960s John Brown would go on to build the Cunard liner *Queen Elizabeth 2* (*QE2*) and the assault ship HMS *Intrepid*, which was destined to be the last warship built by the company, but it was a harbinger of the uncertain future that lay ahead for shipbuilding on the Clyde. In 1945 the workforce numbered 98,000 but 30 years later it had contracted to 24,000 and in time would get even smaller.[2]

Significantly, there was a downturn in warship construction, once the staple of shipbuilding on the Clyde but by the early 1960s in sharp decline. Partly this was linked to government defence policy and expenditure, partly it was due to the gradual contraction of the Royal Navy, but it can also be traced to a lack of investment and foresight by management. During the two world wars few of the Clyde yards had specialised in the construction of submarines, preferring to concentrate on surface ships designed and built to Admiralty specification. Only Scott of Greenock had any experience of submarine construction, having taken their first steps in 1909 by building three Italian Fiat-Laurenti submarines under licence as S class boats for the Royal Navy, as well as HMS *Swordfish*, an experimental steam-powered boat, in 1913. The enterprise prospered and continued until the last days of the yard. Between 1962 and 1978 Scott of Greenock built 11 (out of a total of 27) Oberon class diesel-electric submarines, which were rightly regarded as the most sophisticated conventional boats in naval service during the Cold War.[3] Even so, Scott had come to depend on overseas orders for this class of submarine; their last vessel of that type for the Royal Navy had been HMS *Opportune* in 1964.

By then the Admiralty had decided that all future submarines should be nuclear-powered, and when the Royal Navy started tendering for the second batch of the first four strategic submarines to carry Polaris missiles Scott attempted to form a consortium with John Brown and Fairfield to win the contracts for HMS *Renown* and HMS *Revenge*. By early summer a joint company had been formed by Scott and John Brown which would have seen one submarine being built at each yard but the contract went to Cammell Laird in Birkenhead, the first two Polaris boats having been built by Vickers Armstrong at Barrow-in-Furness. All this made sense as both firms were long established as the Admiralty's main submarine specialists, along with the Royal Dockyard at Chatham but at the time there was a good case for considering the claims of the Scott consortium. Not only were there question marks over Cammell Laird's management skills, but Scott had an unblemished record in bringing orders in on time and within budget. A further imponderable was the desire not to present Vickers with a monopoly, the Barrow firm having insisted that they were fully capable of building all four Polaris submarines. Politics also played a part, as shipbuilding on the Clyde was falling into recession: of the 51 warships built in the UK between 1952 and 1965 only two had been built in Greenock, including the Leopard class frigate HMS *Puma* and the Leander class frigate HMS *Eurylaus*. It was perhaps inevitable that the Scott bid would fail, as even with the addition of John Brown the infrastructure was limited and the workforce lacked experience for a project involving innovative and untested technology.[4] According to John Brown's historian, the decision 'highlighted Clydebank's lack of involvement in that [submarine] market'[5] but the failure of the effort to attract the Polaris submarine order was the beginning of the end for Scott, one of the best respected yards on the Clyde. It had been founded in 1711, making it the longest surviving firm in British shipbuilding and probably the oldest established shipbuilding enterprise in the world. In 1967 it merged with Lithgows of Port Glasgow to form Scott Lithgow, which continued to build Oberon class submarines for the Royal Australian Navy and in October 1971 was awarded an Admiralty contract to construct two Royal Fleet Auxiliary supply ships. It was only a temporary reprieve as the company was nationalised in 1977 by British Shipbuilders and ceased to exist in 1993.

Throughout this troubled period Admiralty decisions about constructing other warships were being delayed by political considerations as the overwhelming majority of the 13 firms in the Ministry of Defence's Warship Group of private builders, including Scott, were located in areas of relatively high unemployment. This group comprised: John Brown, Denny, Fairfield, Stephen and Yarrow on the upper Clyde; Scott on the lower Clyde; Vickers Armstrong at Barrow and on the Tyne; Cammell Laird at Birkenhead; Swan Hunter and Hawthorn Leslie on the Tyne; Thorneycroft and J. Samuel White at Southampton and Cowes respectively; and Harland and Wolff at Queens Island, Belfast.[6] Following lengthy prevarication over a decision to replace the Royal Navy's aging aircraft carrier fleet, a type of ship which would have been a natural fit for the Clyde yards, the Ministry of Defence decided in 1966 to cancel the three proposed CVA01 carriers together with the Type 82 Bristol class destroyers which would have acted as their escorts. This had a knock-on effect on the Clyde, where John Brown had built the wartime carrier HMS *Indefatigable* in 1944 while Fairfield had built her sister ship HMS *Implacable* that same year, but it was clear that earlier traditions were no protection against the increasingly harsh economic climate. As the Far East began to emerge as a significant player in the international shipbuilding market the UK's share dropped from 50.2 per cent in 1947 to 8.3 per cent in 1964, and this led to the loss of famous names – Denny Brothers of Dumbarton and William Hamilton of Port Glasgow in 1963 followed by the Blythswood Shipbuilding Company of Scotstoun a year later. The contractions produced further turmoil in the industry, leading to the creation of two consortia backed by heavy government funding under the Shipbuilding Industry Act of 1967, which recommended the rationalisation of the UK's shipyards into regional groupings backed by government investment. On the Clyde this led to the creation of Scott Lithgow on the lower reaches of the river and the formation of Upper Clyde Shipbuilders (UCS), an amalgamation of five existing shipbuilders – Fairfield in Govan (Govan Division), Alexander Stephen and Sons in Linthouse (Linthouse Division), Charles Connell and Company in Scotstoun (Scotstoun Division) and John Brown and Company at Clydebank (Clydebank Division), as well as an associate subsidiary, Yarrow Shipbuilders, in which UCS held a controlling stake of 51 per cent. In the same year, 1968, the Caledon Shipbuilding Company of Dundee merged with Henry Robb of Leith to form Robb Caledon as the main east-coast shipbuilder, the other main yard Burntisland Shipbuilders in Fife being declared bankrupt a year later and subsumed within the new east-coast grouping.

Given the flagging economy and the parlous conditions facing the shipbuilding industry the creation of these consortiums seemed to make sense as they combined resources and achieved economies of scale, the better to allow them to compete in the international marketplace; but from the outset there was something of the spatchcock about them and UCS in particular was soon in trouble. The main problem was that it was a shotgun marriage involving five different managements and workforces which had to be merged into a single identity, with a new administration exercising stringent financial control as the firm attempted to attract new orders in an increasingly tight market place. A second problem was that the component parts of UCS had suffered from years of loss-making and production-line inefficiency caused mainly by weak management and would be hard pushed to achieve profitability. The third problem was the dire economic climate with inflation creeping upwards due to rising prices and increasing demands for higher pay. Bad industrial relations also played a part, with the number of working days lost in Scotland's heavy industries being 55 per cent higher than the UK national average.[7] To compound the problem there were delays and power malfunctions during the acceptance trials for *QE2*, whose public failure attracted widespread and hostile media interest not least because the maiden voyage had to be postponed by four months.

The first cracks in UCS appeared at the beginning of 1969 with an urgent cash-flow problem leading to redundancies amongst the workforce and a need for additional working capital. Later in the year Yarrow announced that they wanted to leave the consortium and the Scotstoun yard returned to private ownership in April the following year. When the Conservatives won the general election on 19 June 1970 the incoming government led by Prime Minister Edward Heath made it clear that they would provide no further guarantees, thereby precipitating the final crisis. According to the UCS directors, £5 million was needed to save the consortium and initially they were encouraged by an earlier decision to nationalise the bankrupt Rolls-Royce engineering giant but when the government rejected their appeal the fate of UCS was sealed. Having run out of funds and with the government minded not to support another 'lame duck' industry UCS went into liquidation on 14 June 1971 with the estimated loss of 8,500 jobs. The decision was a body-blow to shipbuilding on the Clyde and the news was met by shock and disbelief not just in Scotland but across the world, where the term 'Clyde built' was synonymous with quality engineering and high professional standards in shipbuilding. There was a reprieve with the famous 'work-in' at John Brown's yard organised by the unions and led by shop stewards Jimmy Reid and Jimmy Airlie, which captured the public imagination and generated a huge amount of publicity with mass meetings attended by up to 80,000 people. It also succeeded in changing government policy: in February 1972 Heath's government did a U-turn and announced that two yards would be retained and another would be sold. As a result, Govan Shipbuilders came into being at the old Fairfield yard, Yarrow continued in private ownership at Scotstoun while John Brown was eventually sold to Marathon Engineering of Texas, building oil rigs for work in the recently discovered North Sea oil fields. The overall cost to the government was £35 million but it came at the higher price of loss of public confidence in the government: the episode showed that intervention of this kind had more to do with politics and less to do with simple economic facts – the public was clearly not ready to allow large industries to go to the wall.

From a defence point of view the outcome was good for the Royal Navy as warship construction remained on the Clyde and in fact prospered. During the later stages of the Cold War British naval doctrine called for a fleet of anti-submarine and air defence frigates and destroyers to search for and destroy Soviet submarines and surface warships in the North Atlantic. In the fleet's final form, the result was the construction of 14 Type 42 destroyers and 26 Leander class frigates (succeeded in the late 1970s by 8 Type 21, 14 Type 22 and 18 Type 23 frigates). Several of the frigates were built on the Clyde, beginning in 1964 with the Leander class HMS *Aurora* at John Brown – all the destroyers were constructed elsewhere – but the biggest beneficiary was Yarrow Shipbuilders, which had begun life in London in 1865 before migrating to the Clyde in 1906. After leaving the ill-fated UCS consortium it concentrated on building 21 frigates of all types for the Royal Navy and several overseas navies, thus reinforcing the Clyde's reputation by constructing these well-made, seaworthy and, it must be admitted, elegant ships. In 1977, under the terms of the Labour government's Aircraft and Shipbuilding Industries Act, Yarrow became part of British Shipbuilders but returned to private ownership in 1985, when it was purchased by the General Electric Company (GEC) to become Marconi Marine (YSL). During the later stages of the Cold War the yard's main output was the construction of Type 22 and Type 23 frigates for the Royal Navy, both of which were designed by Yarrow in conjunction with the Admiralty's Ship Department in Bath. Such was the strength of the umbilical cord between shipbuilder and warship that Yarrow built six of the first seven Type 23s commissioned by the Royal Navy and it came as a shock in 1989 when the government awarded the contract for the next three to Swan Hunter on the Tyne. Normal service was resumed in January 1992 when Yarrow won the next frigate contract 'by a reportedly handsome margin'.[8]

It was not just shipbuilding that felt the pinch in the 1960s and 1970s: productivity was also falling in other heavy industries such as steel, coal and heavy engineering, for long the backbone of the country's economy and now dependent for survival on government investment. In 1958 funds were made available to the long-established firm of Colville (founded 1871) to develop a hot strip steel mill at Ravenscraig in Motherwell and a cold strip mill at nearby Gartcosh, even though the project was stymied from the outset by the prohibitive cost of importing ore through the port of Hunterston on the Clyde and the even higher cost of transporting strip steel to the English Midlands, where most of the UK motor industry was concentrated. However, it was not all one-way traffic as in 1961 the British Motor Corporation (BMC) built a factory at Bathgate in West Lothian to manufacture trucks and tractors while two years later the Rootes group opened a plant at Linwood in Renfrewshire to produce Hillman Imp saloon cars. In 1963, at Corpach outside Fort William in the West Highlands, Wiggins Teape opened a pulp mill which represented the biggest industrial development in the Highlands since the Second World War. Under the auspices of the Highlands and Islands Development Board, created in 1965, government money was used to fund an aluminium smelter at Invergordon on the Moray Firth, which employed 900 workers, and the creation of a fast breeder nuclear reactor at Dounreay in Caithness, which supplied electric power to the National Grid and brought the atomic age to Scotland. By the end of the century, due to a variety of economic and political factors, all had foundered and disappeared from Scotland's industrial landscape: Corpach in 1980, Invergordon and Linwood in 1981 (following Rootes's takeover by Chrysler), Gartcosh and Bathgate in 1986 and Ravenscraig in 1992. Only Dounreay could be counted as a success, although when the reactor was decommissioned in 1998 it was found to have an alarming number of health and safety issues.

Coal, too, was in a sorry state with old seams, especially in Lanarkshire, being worked out and new seams, especially in Fife, failing to become productive as the industrial world moved away from using coal to operate furnaces and railway engines. By the 1960s the industry was facing competition from other fuel sources such as petroleum, natural gas, and nuclear and hydro-electric power. At the same time, the government's Clean Air Acts of 1956 and 1968 dramatically reduced the use of coal for domestic heating and by the 1980s the number of working pits had been reduced from fifteen to two, at Monktonhall in Midlothian and Longannet near Kincardine on the Firth of Forth. Both were deep mines created in the 1950s to provide fuel for nearby power stations but that did not save them. Monktonhall closed in 1997 following the failure of a miners' buy-out and Longannet met a similar fate in 2002 after its underground workings were flooded, thereby ending Scotland's centuries-long involvement in underground coal-mining. No more forlorn example of successive governments' failures in addressing the role of the coal industry can be found than the creation of the Rothes Colliery in Fife in 1957. Built on land to the west of Thornton, an established village south of Glenrothes new town, the mine was promoted as a key driver in the economic regeneration of central Fife and a source of employment for the new conurbation. However, repeated flooding and unforeseen geological problems in the area, combined with a lessening demand for coal nationally, had a significant impact on the viability of the mine and led to its eventual closure in 1965. Ironically, miners who had worked in older deep pits in the area had long warned against the development of the Rothes Pit for these very reasons. The futuristic structure was closed, leaving the huge enclosed concrete wheel-towers standing at Thornton for many years as a pitiful symbol of the collapse of the so-called 'super pit'. They remained in place until 1993 when they were pulled down and the area was returned to agriculture.

It would be easy to write off these failures as a symptom of industrial decline and a failure of government policy as successive administrations attempted to address the challenge of rising inflation, growing unemployment and industrial discontent by investing public funds in shipbuilding, coal and steel, largely for political rather than economic reasons, but it was not all failure. As heavy industries declined so did the electronics industry come into its own, often related to defence expenditure, and by the 1980s it was employing 47,000 workers in Scotland.[9] While this was not quite the volume obtained by the older heavy industries, by 1988 electronics accounted for investments worth

£200 million and Scotland soon became a substantial exporter of equipment, especially computers.[10] The trend can be traced back to the Second World War, when the Manchester-based electronics firm of Ferranti opened a facility at Crewe Toll in Edinburgh in 1943 for the manufacture of gyro gunsights for the RAF's Spitfire aircraft and stayed on to expand in the post-war world, employing a 1,000-strong workforce by 1950, thereby becoming the founding parent of Scotland's electronics industry. Amongst others which followed in Ferranti's wake were Hewlett-Packard (South Queensferry), IBM (Greenock), Burroughs (Cumbernauld), Honeywell (Newhouse), NCR (Dundee), Digital Equipment (Ayr), Motorola (East Kilbride), National Semi-Conductors (Greenock) and NEC (Livingston).[11]

These mainly worked in the growing field of electronic data processing, including the manufacture of personal computers, laptops and later mobile phones, and were part of a global industry dominated by the USA and Japan, with Scotland being perceived as a branch plant economy which soon became known as 'Silicon Glen', a nickname self-consciously inspired by Silicon Valley in California, the San Francisco Bay area and Santa Clara Valley which became the global synonym for high-tech innovation.

Although this was good for Scotland's domestic economy their work had little direct bearing on the Cold War period – unlike two electronics companies which prospered from the outset due to their involvement in defence-related products. These were Ferranti and the Glasgow-based opto-electronics firm of Barr & Stroud which manufactured electro-optical instruments, thermal imaging devices and other defence systems and was considered to be one of the world's leaders in specialist military technology.[12] Formed in 1893 by two academics who gave their names to the firm, Barr & Stroud specialised in the development and manufacture of naval range-finders, fire control systems and high-powered binoculars. Their factory in Anniesland soon became a centre of scientific and engineering excellence, and during the Second World War the workforce increased from 2,000 to 6,000. During the Cold War period the company expanded further, developing laser rangefinders and thermal imaging devices for tanks and supplying advanced electro-optics for the guidance system in the British Aircraft Corporation's Rapier surface-to-air missile which came into service in 1972 and was the British Army's primary defence system against aircraft for most of the Cold War. In 1972 Barr & Stroud was taken over by the Pilkington Group and 20 years later operations moved from Anniesland to a new plant in Linthouse on the site of the former Alexander Stephen and Sons shipyard. In 2001, long after the Cold War, the company became a subsidiary of the French defence contractor Thales but the name and heritage live on as part of Optical Distribution Services, supplying quality binoculars and scopes mainly made in China.

By then, Ferranti had also disappeared from the scene due to a high-profile financial scandal in 1987 following the purchase of International Signal and Control (ISC), a US defence contractor based in Pennsylvania which developed and manufactured electronic missile sub-assemblies, navigation components, proximity fuses and grenade technology. On paper it looked a good deal – ISC had a healthy sales record and was well regarded within the international defence community – but its profits were non-existent, and its sales figures turned out to be fraudulent, based as they were on illegal arms sales. For Ferranti it was a disaster and by 1991 the firm was declared bankrupt having been defrauded of around £215 million on non-existent contracts and incorrect valuations. The Scottish operation, having become Ferranti Defence Systems in 1984, was bought by GEC-Marconi as the company struggled to find buyers for its beleaguered specialist divisions but to all intents and purposes the Ferranti name was at an end. It was a sad outcome for an engineering-led firm which had come to epitomise Scottish expertise in the highly skilled world of defence avionics and precision electronics and was central to the country's economy. In the 1980s Ferranti was Scotland's largest industrial employer and its commercial success underpinned the entire group, whose profits had risen to £27.5 million by the time of its fateful acquisition of ISC. Ferranti Defence Systems had also branched out of its Crewe Toll headquarters and by the end had eight plants operating across the central belt of Scotland, all built on successful and remunerative defence contracts as the company moved away from the magnetic compass to the inertial navigation equipment for airborne weapons aiming in the new generation of jet-powered aircraft.

It had not been a straightforward progression but one which depended on vision, hard work, enterprise, managerial flair and technological innovation. After the end of the Second World War there had been an unsurprising reduction in the demand for the gyro gunsights produced by Ferranti in Edinburgh and the workforce had been reduced from

1,000 in 1945 to fewer than 400 in 1949 but under the direction of Jack (later Sir John) Toothill the Scottish operation became leaders in the field of onboard radar and inertial guidance systems, with the result that most of the jet-age aircraft supplied to the RAF were equipped with Ferranti avionics. Of particular note was the development in 1958 of the Airborne Interception Radar and Pilot's Attack Sight System (AIRPASS) which was fitted to the supersonic English Electric Lightning interceptor and eliminated the need for the pilot to take his hands off the controls while making an interception because the radar and gun sight controls were situated on the control column and throttle lever instead of elsewhere in the cockpit. Using that system the pilot could press home the attack at supersonic speed and because the aircraft was radar-guided could make the attack 'blind' in all kinds of adverse weather conditions. All told, the firm sold over £13.5 million of AIRPASS and the Lightning was regarded as one of the fastest and most effective interceptors of the Cold War, albeit with a limited range. A second version of the system was developed for the controversial TSR-2 strike and reconnaissance aircraft and after its cancellation in 1965 it was adapted for use as 'Blue Parrot' in the Royal Navy's Blackburn Buccaneer carrier-borne subsonic strike aircraft which later saw service with the RAF. In the 1960s inertial guidance systems were also developed for the revolutionary vertical take-off Hawker Siddeley Harrier 'jump jet' and the British–French SEPECAT Jaguar strike aircraft. Later still, Ferranti played a leading role in developing the avionics for the Panavia Tornado multi-role combat aircraft which was designed and built in the UK, West Germany and Italy and which was in many respects the ultimate Cold War aircraft, a twin-engine variable wing aircraft capable of working in strike, reconnaissance and air defence roles. The fighter variant of this versatile aircraft used Ferranti's Foxhunter on-board radar, which was ordered in 1979 and produced business worth £50 million, thereby reasserting the company's 'dominant market position'.[13] It was fitting, perhaps, that one of Ferranti's last and most satisfying contributions to aviation technology should have come in the dying days of the Cold War when the company, operating as GEC-Ferranti, accelerated production of its revolutionary thermal imaging airborne laser designator pod (TIALD), which was rushed into service with the RAF's Tornado GR1 aircraft during the Gulf War of 1990–1. According to Defence Secretary Tom King the deployment of this laser-guided weapon 'showed a major new capability and important enhancement on the Tornado for medium altitude precision bombing' and proved itself to be a true force multiplier.[14]

What made Ferranti's success more remarkable was the parlous state of the UK aircraft manufacturing industry at the time. Having emerged from the war with a string of successful aircraft such as the Spitfire and Hurricane fighters and the Lancaster and Halifax bombers, not to mention mould-breaking aircraft such as the all-wood Mosquito strike aircraft, the UK's main firms embraced the jet age and emerged with a succession of world-beating aircraft, in so doing giving the country a technological lead which seemed to confirm British skill and enterprise. It was also largely illusory. Although the UK developed the world's first passenger-carrying jet-powered airliner in the De Havilland Comet and the RAF brought jet-powered fighters such as the Gloster Meteor and the Hawker Hunter into frontline service at a satisfying rate, the aircraft industry was under-funded, diffuse and dependent on uncertain government funding for the development of new military models and tended to bring them into service too quickly. Both the Hunter and Javelin had elegant designs and looked the part but were hustled into service before they were fully developed, with the result that early models were exceptionally accident-prone: in an eight-month period in the winter of 1956–7, 42 air crew were killed in 34 accidents, an attrition rate of one fatality every six days.[15] Even so, despite the problems, from a commercial point of view firms such as Hawker, Supermarine, Gloster and Handley Page could match similar firms in Europe, the USA and the Soviet Union but they were stymied by successive government defence policies which were themselves governed by the need to staunch haemorrhaging costs, especially in aviation.

In 1957 this became abundantly apparent when the Conservative government under Prime Minister Harold Macmillan and his abrasive defence minister, Duncan Sandys, introduced one of the most radical defence reviews of modern times. Coming in the aftermath of the previous year's Suez debacle, Sandys's White Paper on Defence was presented to parliament in April 1957 and its aim was quite simple: to save costs in a bloated defence budget by ending National Service and placing reliance on missile systems for air defence and for the delivery of nuclear weapons. Under that scenario the days of manned aircraft would be numbered, and the Navy was given the vaguely phrased responsibility of 'bringing power rapidly to bear in peacetime emergencies and limited war'.[16] Although the review succeeded in making economies the opposition of the chiefs of staff meant that manned aircraft were retained – development of the Lightning interceptor continued in production, as did, temporarily, the TSR-2 – and not only did the Navy keep its global reach but the first steps were taken with the USA to give it nuclear capability. Only the abolition of National Service achieved substantial savings, but in so doing the Army was reduced to 185,000 soldiers without any concomitant reduction in operational commitments. Nevertheless, the aviation industry was badly rattled by Sandys's White Paper; in its aftermath the industry was rationalised through a series of mergers, takeovers and amalgamations which saw the emergence in 1960 of the British Aircraft Corporation (English Electric, Vickers Armstrong, Percival, Bristol, Supermarine and Hunting) and Hawker Siddeley Aviation (De Havilland, Blackburn, Folland, Gloster, Avro, Hawker and Armstrong Whitworth). Later, in 1977, these two groups were nationalised as British Aerospace, which in turn became BAE Systems in 1999 following a merger with Marconi.

The historian James Hamilton-Paterson has argued that 'Whitehall's lack of direction was to have fateful consequences for the way the surviving industry functioned', and the upheaval in turn had a deleterious consequence for key suppliers to the aviation industry such as Ferranti by creating uncertainty and hampering investment.[17] For the Edinburgh-based firm and its England-based divisions the crisis came in the summer of 1974 against a rapidly disintegrating national economic situation, with balance of payments deep in the red, galloping inflation and a rash of industrial relations problems across the UK. In common with many family-owned firms, Ferranti had always suffered from cash-flow problems which came about due to expenditure outstripping income and the need to manage existing overdrafts. An urgent injection of funds was needed to maintain liquidity – some suppliers were refusing to undertake orders unless they were guaranteed payment – and in July Ferranti looked to their bankers, National Westminster (NatWest) to extend their overdraft facilities. Not only was this refused but the bankers insisted on a thorough and independent assessment of Ferranti's accounts, which recommended a harsh choice between calling in the receiver or accepting government investment through the Department of Industry under the direction of Tony Benn MP, described by the firm's historian as 'one of the more radical socialists in a Labour Party that was still committed in principle to public ownership of the means of production and distribution.'[18]

For a family-run firm with a proud heritage this could have been a disaster and the negotiations were not helped when confidential papers were leaked to the *Sunday Times* and published on 13 September 1974. A second general election that year and the need to deal with the public ownership of the giant car manufacturer British Leyland, employers of 170,000 workers, also held up the negotiations but eventually an agreement was reached on 12 May 1975 whereby a total of £15 million was injected into Ferranti in return for reform of the board and the appointment of a new managing director to replace Sebastian de Ferranti, who had held the post since 1958. As the firm's titular head he was opposed to government interference, having had his fingers burned in 1964 when Ferranti was the subject of a parliamentary inquiry into the alleged profits made on the £12 million contract for the Bristol/Ferranti Bloodhound surface-to-air missile used to defend V-bomber bases and as a result had to repay £4.25 million. Although Sebastian and his brother and co-director Basil were criticised for being 'more interested in science than profits' and for maintaining the idiosyncratic management style and attitudes to risk of what was still very much a private company, by 1978 Ferranti had reported record profits and two years later returned fully to the private sector through a placing of the government shareholding with City institutions.[19] It is worth placing on record that Sebastian Ferranti was opposed to the ill-fated takeover of ISC in the following decade.

All this change took place against the background of the discovery of substantial oil and natural gas supplies in the North Sea. Both could provide benefits for Scotland, particularly the 'black gold' of oil which appeared to offer the panacea of an untold supply of wealth. So it seemed to many at the start of the 1970s when it became clear that the Forties field in the North Sea was ripe for affordable exploitation, creating expectations that an oil bonanza was in the offing. At first that was the case and the UK economy benefited as a result. In 1985 production peaked at 122 million tons and North Sea Oil recorded a balance of payments surplus of £8 billion. By then the UK was the world's fifth largest oil-producing country and by the 1990s one in twenty Scottish jobs was oil-related.[20] However, the lure of untold wealth was largely misleading. Many of the jobs were taken by workers from outside Scotland and in the initial stages of the development Scottish heavy industry was unable to take full advantage of the benefits produced by the need to exploit the North Sea fields. Only in the north-east, where

Aberdeen emerged as Scotland's de facto oil capital, and in Orkney and Shetland through the revenues generated by the construction of the terminals at Flotta and Sullom Voe, was there a beneficial impact on local communities. A recession in 1986 put the brakes on the development and two years later the industry was shaken by the explosion of the Piper Alpha platform, which cost 167 lives and reawakened existing fears about safety in the unforgiving environment of the North Sea.

Such a valuable resource also needed protection and from the outset there were justified fears that the North Sea installations could be a target for Soviet *spetsnaz* special forces which were being formed for reconnaissance and sabotage purposes behind enemy lines in advance of the outbreak of any hostilities in Europe. To counter that threat the Royal Marines created Comacchio Company in 1980, a specialist counter-terrorism group of 300 Marines, based at RM Condor, Arbroath in Angus. Its role was to provide force protection for the North Sea rigs and platforms and it was named after a Second World War battle in Italy in which the Royal Marines had played a significant part.[21] (Fought by 2nd Commando Brigade in April 1945 at Lake Comacchio, the battle was part of the Allies' successful spring offensive.) In 1996 Comacchio Group (as it had become) was rerolled as the Fleet Protection Group (later 43 Commando Fleet Protection Group RM) to provide enhanced security for the Navy's nuclear warheads and moved to the Clyde Submarine Base at Faslane. Further protection for the oil fields was provided by the Royal Navy from Rosyth using Island class patrol vessels which could operate in the frequently hostile environment of the North Sea and were similar in design to deep-sea fishing boats. Built originally for the Scottish Fisheries Protection Agency by Hall Russell of Aberdeen, they lacked speed and helicopter facilities and were superseded in 1981 by the larger and faster Castle class vessels HMS *Dumbarton Castle* and HMS *Leeds Castle*, also built in Aberdeen. Also available to the Navy for North Sea protection duties were nine Ton class coastal mine sweepers based at Rosyth. In 1980 these were replaced by the more sophisticated Hunt class mine countermeasure vessels, at the time the largest warships, with hulls built of reinforced plastic. Two of the class (HMS *Middleton* and HMS *Cottesmore*) were built at Yarrow on the Clyde; the remaining eleven were the products of Vosper Thorneycroft in Southampton.

All told, industry in Scotland benefited from the Cold War in that much of it was related to defence expenditure through electronics and shipbuilding. While there was no boom of the kind that was created during the First World War, when Glasgow and the west of Scotland deserved the appellation of being the workshop of empire, in the second half of the twentieth century Scotland emerged at the cutting edge of innovation in shipbuilding and the new inertial technology in aviation, albeit with much smaller workforces. Although this gave the economy in Scotland a healthy appearance, the prosperity was highly reliant on defence spending, with an estimated 150,000 jobs in 1988 dependent on decisions made in Whitehall. Research and development was also part of the equation and the associated costs could cause problems, as Ferranti found when it was forced to balance diminishing budgets with the need to continue pursuing innovative engineering solutions. As one seasoned economics commentator put it when the Cold War was winding down, this reliance could cause difficulties: 'A great preponderance of research and development in Scotland's high-tech industries is dependent on the business of war, as is a high proportion of output. Scots may have become accustomed to seeing their electronics sector as a sleek producer of desktop technology, but around a third of turnover is financed out of defence budgets.'[22] That was both a strength and a weakness; as long as the Cold War produced threats to the West's security UK defence budgets were relatively unscathed, but whenever there was a thaw they became vulnerable and nothing was untouchable, except perhaps expenditure on the nuclear deterrent and its delivery systems.

By contrast, the Soviet Union had an almost cavalier approach to the development of military aircraft and missile systems. In the aftermath of the Second World War the Soviets were heavily reliant on German technology and employed the talents and expertise of captured German designers and engineers. As a result, early jet-powered interceptor and attack aircraft bore a marked resemblance to existing German models. The first response to the government's requirement for a jet-powered interceptor was the La-150 which was based on the Messerschmitt Me 262 and used the same Junkers Jumo 004 turbojet. It first flew in September 1945 but needed so many modifications that it was obsolete before it could enter service. In the second prototype, the La-152, the engine was moved further forward but it proved to be under-powered for its operational duties and after several crashes the project was cancelled. A third prototype, the La-160, was introduced to examine the problems of high-speed flight and although only one was built it proved that the Soviet aircraft industry could produce fast, up-to-date aircraft. But there was one significant difference. Not only did the La-160 have swept wings but it was powered by the British Rolls-Royce Derwent V jet engine, which powered the Gloster Meteor and was the forerunner of the more powerful Rolls-Royce Nene jet engine.

This came about due to a remarkable trade deal made between the Soviet Union and the UK in 1946 when the Soviet aviation minister, Mikhail Khrunichev, and aircraft designer A. S. Yakovlev suggested that the country's lack of a workable jet engine could be made good by buying 55 Derwent and Nene engines off the shelf from the UK. Although Stalin scoffed at the idea – 'what kind of fools would sell their secrets?' – the deal went ahead as a gesture of goodwill under Sir Stafford Cripps, president of the Board of Trade, on condition that they were not used for military purposes.[23] As the Nenes were serviced at the Rolls-Royce factory at Hillington outside Glasgow this clearly had a beneficial effect in Scotland. However, as soon as the engines arrived Russian engineers set about reverse-engineering them as the Klimov VK-1 which powered the new MiG-15 interceptor. Piloted by Soviet aircrew, its performance in the Korean War allowed the Chinese and North Koreans to gain early air superiority over American aircraft and Washington was rightly furious about the sales, even though they had arranged a separate deal which allowed the Nene to be built under licence by Pratt & Whitney to power the Grumman F9F Panther carrier fighter-bomber in 1948. All that can be said in the UK's favour is that at the end of the Second World War the country was facing a massive financial deficit and needed all the trade deals it could get. There was another consequence. The performance of the MiG-15s proved to the RAF that their own jet aircraft were fast becoming obsolete and that the Meteor and the Vampire were no match for modern swept-wing fighters. In 1952, before the arrival of the Hawker Hunter, the government was forced to shop abroad and purchased 428 Sabre Mk 4 aircraft built under licence by Canadair, which was described by one British test pilot, Eric 'Winkle' Brown, as 'the Spitfire of the jet age'.[24]

The purchase of the Rolls-Royce engines produced a step-change in Soviet aircraft design and the success of the MiG-15 in Korea paved the way for a succession of capable modern fighter aircraft, all of which were the equal of anything produced in the West. From the 1950s onwards the main Soviet design bureaus (OKBs) – Antonov, Ilyushin, Lavochkin, Mikoyan, Sukhoi, Tupolev and Yakovlev – introduced a wide range of military and civil aircraft, some of which bore resemblances to existing Western models. (For example, the Ilyushin Il-62 airliner looked remarkably similar to the Vickers VC-10, both of which were powered by four tail-mounted engines, while the Tupolev 154 tri-jet airliner enjoyed conceptual similarities with the Boeing-727 and the Hawker Siddeley Trident, but it had a higher speed and was equipped with an oversized landing gear to enable it to operate from less sophisticated airports.) Not unsurprisingly, developments in Soviet aircraft interested – and frequently alarmed – the West. It also happened vice versa. The existence of high-flying U-2 aircraft was known to the Soviets from the early 1960s and they knew that it was out of range of their existing interceptors. Its successor, the SR-71 Blackbird which flew at over 80,000 feet, caused the Soviets equal problems and these were intensified in the 1960s with the introduction of the Convair B-58 Hustler, a high-speed, high-altitude bomber capable of flying at Mach 2 which could out-fly all existing Soviet interceptor aircraft. Concern was intensified by the knowledge that the Americans were already developing the futuristic North American B-70 Valkyrie, which was planned to fly at Mach 3 with a 70,000-foot cruising altitude. This led to the development of the MiG-25 Foxbat, one of the largest and fastest fighters ever built, but by the time it came into service the Hustler had been retired and development of the Valkyrie had been cancelled. Although the MiG-25 was never used in its intended role it entered service as an interceptor and reconnaissance aircraft with the Soviet Union and several of its allies. At one stage in 1971 a MiG-25 was tracked flying over Egypt at Mach 3.2 but the experience damaged the aircraft's engines and that particular plane never flew again. Nevertheless, the introduction of the MiG-25 encouraged the US Air Force to speed up development of the speedy and manoeuvrable twin-engine McDonnell Douglas F-15 Eagle and the Grumman F-14 Tomcat, the largest and heaviest fighter to operate from an aircraft carrier. During fighting in Lebanon in 1979 Israeli F-15s got the aircraft's first kills when they shot down 13 Syrian MiG-21s and two Syrian MiG-25s, thereby demonstrating the importance of proxy wars to planners on both sides during the wider Cold War confrontation.

Both sides relied heavily on exporting arms to allies and friendly countries, not just to boost income but also to gain influence and prestige. It was also big business: in 1982 the Library of Congress reported that for the first time the USA had overtaken the Soviet Union in conventional weapons sales to Third World countries, earning $7.6 billion compared to $7.2 billion that year.[25] The prevalence of proxy wars throughout the period assisted this process by creating a market for weaponry and for the training programmes and tactics which were generally part of the package. Because much of this demand came from developing countries where there was a relatively low level of technical and scientific competence, Soviet and Western experts were usually required to assemble and maintain the newly arrived weapons and to instruct local military personnel and technicians in their use. In some cases, these specialists were also employed as military advisors and assisted local armed forces in the field, frequently assuming command of technical aspects of the fighting such as electronic warfare and air defences. Such proximity also allowed them to assess the effectiveness, or otherwise, of their own equipment and quite often the results were staggering. By the 1950s the Soviet Union had become embroiled in the Middle East by supporting Egypt, whose radical leader, President Gamal Abdel Nasser, had become disenchanted with the USA over their refusal to offer loans to finance his Aswan High Dam project. He played off the Americans against the Soviets and the deal was cemented with the supply of modern military equipment which was supplied through Czechoslovakia in 1955. It made Nasser the hero of Arab nationalism, yet during the Six-Day War with Israel in 1967 Egypt lost some 60 per cent of their aircraft fleet, largely because of Israeli pre-emptive bombing attacks. All had been supplied by the Soviet Union, but the sorry truth was that the Egyptian aircrews had shown themselves to be no match for the superior skills of their Israeli counterparts.[26]

The war was a disaster for Egypt and its Arab allies. In the north, Syria lost the Golan Heights, the strategically important plateau which forms the border with northern Israel. In the east, Jordan lost its West Bank, the more prosperous part of the Hashemite Kingdom and which, like the Golan Heights, was immediately settled by Israelis. In the south, the Egyptians lost the Gaza Strip and the whole of the Sinai desert and peninsula. As a result, Nasser initiated a 'war of attrition' against Israel – mainly occasional artillery barrages and commando raids across the Suez Canal – and the Soviet Union began supplying Egypt with improved air defences, including the sophisticated SA-6 surface-to-air missile, but it was clear that these measures were only a prelude to a renewed outbreak of hostilities. When it came on 6 October

1973 the Yom Kippur War, so called because it broke out on the Jewish day of atonement, created the most dangerous confrontation since the Cuban missile crisis 11 years earlier. The United States gave massive military support to Israel, while the Soviet Union did the same with their proxies, Egypt and Syria, and sent a large fleet into the Mediterranean to challenge the US Sixth Fleet. In the opening rounds Egypt and Syria achieved complete surprise against Israel and suddenly the Middle East became a new locus for superpower confrontation as the battle ebbed and flowed. Ceasefires took effect and collapsed as Washington and Moscow struggled to find a way out of the impasse. Matters came to a head when the Israelis cut off the Egyptian Third Army in Sinai, prompting the Soviet leader Leonid Brezhnev to threaten that he would act unilaterally to save it. The US responded by issuing a global nuclear alert, DEFCON 3, the highest since Cuba, and once again the world held its breath. In the event mediation held sway as the US Secretary of State Henry Kissinger began a process of shuttle diplomacy, flying between Moscow, Tel Aviv and Cairo, to persuade all participants to back down and accept a ceasefire which came into being on 25 October. Disengagement followed relatively quickly but the most important long-term effect of the war was Egypt's decision to begin direct peace negotiations with Israel, culminating in the Camp David Accords in 1979. No formal treaty was ever signed between Israel and Syria.

No one 'won' the Yom Kippur War but as happens after every conflict, lessons were learned and weaponry was assessed. On this occasion the Arab air forces performed better than in the previous conflict largely because they were able to get their aircraft into the skies to fly combat missions. Even so, they generally avoided direct air-to-air combat although the MiG-21, MiG-19 and Sukhoi-7 all matched the Israelis' US-supplied Phantom and Skyhawk interceptors and French-supplied Mirages and Super-Mystères. In the air war the big winner was the SA-6 missile, which accounted for the bulk of Israeli casualties and because no battery or firing platform ever fell into the opposition hands the Americans and Israelis failed to discover the technicalities of its guidance system and were unable to introduce electronic counter-measures to block its radar. Three years after the war Anwar Sadat, who had succeeded Nasser as President of Egypt in 1970, admitted that this had been the decisive factor: 'one-third of their [Israeli] Phantoms and everything they boasted of came down because of the ground-to-air missiles. We are in a missile era. Ground-to-air missiles deprived

Israel of its supremacy.'[27] Sadat's argument was strengthened by the evidence of US losses in the Vietnam War, which ended in 1973 with the withdrawal of American forces and the unification of the country under Communist control two years later. During the air war the US forces lost thousands of aircraft – the exact number is disputed – the majority falling victim to anti-aircraft defences, notably the ubiquitous SA-2 missile, many of which were operated by Soviet crews. To the F-4 Phantom falls the unhappy distinction of sustaining the highest number of losses over Vietnam – 529 (naval, marine and air force). By contrast the Israelis lost 32 Phantoms out of 99 during the Yom Kippur War, mainly shot down by anti-aircraft defences, albeit over the period of a month and therefore at a higher rate of attrition.[28]

Because the conflict had been a proxy war in the sense that Israel possessed equipment used by NATO countries and the Arabs were equipped with Soviet weapons the October 1973 fighting was of immense interest to the Americans and the Soviets. If the Cold War had ever turned hot these same weapons systems would have been used in Europe and both sides wanted to know how they would perform. The Americans examined the conflict in great detail and two years later the CIA produced a lengthy secret report which was finally released in a heavily redacted form in 2012. The biggest surprise was the lack of an efficient command and control system for the deployment of Israeli armour, one of the success stories of the 1967 conflict but a pale shadow six years later: 'Within the first hours, the Israelis made two costly mistakes. Their experience in the 1967 war led them to believe they could use tanks alone to fight infantry. They did not take adequate account of the effect of antitank missiles in the hands of now better-trained, more highly motivated Egyptian troops. The Israelis compounded this error by sending unaccompanied tanks to rescue the isolated garrisons of their canal-side defensive barrier called the Bar Lev Line. When the Israeli tanks attacked alone on 6 and 7 October, they were badly mauled.'[29]

In the CIA's view not only had Israeli armoured commanders come to believe their own reputations but they had failed to recognise the impact on the modern battlefield of a new generation of anti-tank missiles, notably the Soviet-made AT-3 Sagger, which had already proved its worth in the Vietnam War in April 1972 when a North Vietnamese Army patrol clashed with South Vietnamese tanks in Quang Tri Province near the 17th Parallel and quickly knocked out an

American-made M48A3. In Sinai Egyptian gunners also used the Sagger missile to destroy Israeli US-made M-60 tanks and British-made Centurion tanks. On the first day of the fighting Israel had 293 tanks in Sinai and half of them were out of action within 36 hours. Three days later the Israelis had moved around 700 additional tanks into Sinai, but fewer than half of them were operable. By then the Israelis had rediscovered the lesson from 1967 that the best results came from using a coordinated tank–infantry team: the infantry protected the tanks against missile-carrying enemy infantrymen, while the tanks defended the Israeli infantrymen against enemy armoured attacks and provided fire support. In other words, when the Israelis went back to first principles they managed to overcome the 'flaws' and the 'untidy' response of the early hours of the fighting and 'the situation was saved by the training of the troops and by standardised procedures that allowed [tank] crews to be scrambled without degrading performance'.[30]

Apart from noting innovations such as the SA-6 surface-to-air missile, the Sagger and the shoulder-fired RPG-7 anti-tank missile, which 'represented a new and dangerous presence on the battlefield', the CIA's conclusions about weaponry contained few surprises as most of the equipment under discussion was already in frontline service in both the Warsaw Pact and NATO forces. The main lesson learned was the need for vigilance, preparedness and the absolute necessity of reading and understanding intelligence data: this had an obvious application for NATO forces in Europe. It also led to the acceleration of US wire-guided anti-tank missiles such as the BGM-71 TOW, which was introduced in Vietnam in 1972 and by May had 24 confirmed 'kills' of North Vietnamese T-54 tanks, the missiles being fired from Bell Huey attack helicopters. At the same time the UK developed the Swingfire wire-guided missile which could be fired from armoured vehicles or Lynx helicopters. Both came into service with NATO forces in Europe during the latter stages of the Cold War and both are reminders of how proxy wars hastened weapons development on both sides of the divide.

9

War in the Shadows

FOR THE FIRST time in modern warfare the Cold War confrontation was as much about gaining intellectual or mental control as it was about waging a physical war of attrition. If a land war had broken out in the northern European plain – the most likely theatre of operations – it would have caused immense bloodshed as the rival armies fought one another using the tenets of armoured warfare backed by artillery and air power, but of necessity it would have been brief and the steady escalation would have led to the need to use nuclear weapons. That in turn would have introduced the possibility of global destruction as each side unleashed their nuclear arsenals in a vain attempt to achieve dominance, however appalling the outcome would have been. That was the conundrum that prompted the intelligence war: both sides needed to know the other's intentions, capabilities and plans of action in the event of an outbreak of hostilities. And in the nuclear age which had been ushered in after 1945 that meant gaining information about top secret matters such as uranium availability, the production of highly enriched uranium and plutonium, nuclear warhead research, development and testing, and the capacity to construct nuclear weapons and their delivery systems. Information of that kind enabled analysts to gauge the size and capacity of the opposition's stockpiles and arsenals and therefore their ability to wage nuclear war. To find answers, both sides consumed huge resources, creating an elaborate infrastructure of intelligence gathering in order to interpret information from the main elements of modern intelligence warfare – SIGINT (signals intelligence), COMINT (communications intelligence), ELINT (electronic intelligence) and HUMINT (human intelligence). Of the four elements HUMINT created the most public interest, especially when it was allied to breaches of security or defections when security personnel in positions of trust betrayed their principles and their countries by yielding to greed or lust or by exhibiting previously unknown characteristics which had been masked or not identified earlier in their careers. Throughout the Cold War there was a steady exposure of such incidents, the 'Cambridge spies' being the most scandalous and newsworthy example. It created deep suspicions in the relationship between London and Washington in the initial stages of the Cold War, although it has to be said that the Soviet Union and the USA also suffered from the problem of double agents and treachery, which was all too prevalent throughout the confrontation.

At the beginning of the nuclear age, when the UK and the US were partners in developing the first atomic bombs, there was a sense of co-operation and working in common cause but that soon evaporated in the post-war years after the passing of the McMahon Act in Washington in 1946 which restricted foreign access to US nuclear technology. Matters did not improve with the revelation of the Cambridge spies in the following two decades – Donald Maclean, Guy Burgess, Kim Philby, Anthony Blunt, John Cairncross and their hangers-on – whose treasonable activities with the Soviet Union caused great harm to the relationship with the USA and which took many years to restore, especially in the field of counter-intelligence. Their story has been related in several historical accounts and has provided the basis for several dramatised films such as Alan Bennett's *An Englishman Abroad* (1983) which centred on Burgess, played by Alan Bates, with the film being shot largely in Scotland, locations in Dundee and Glasgow providing the backdrop for Moscow. In most of these productions attention was generally focused on the first four members of the circle, who seemed to be touched by a certain glamour – Philby was a plausibly smooth operator, Burgess and Maclean were perceived as a devious double act and Blunt was a distinguished art historian and Surveyor of the Queen's Pictures – but little attention was paid to Cairncross even though the KGB believed that he was the real star of the group, which they christened the Magnificent Five: 'he successfully penetrated a greater variety of the corridors of power and intelligence than any of the other four'.[1] Cairncross was certainly different from the others. According to the philosopher and wartime intelligence officer Stuart Hampshire, who knew him as a student, Cairncross seemed to be a gauche outsider whom he regarded as 'an absurd and rather untidy scholar, very bright and academic. He was socially from the lower rather than the higher, very talkative, sort of chaotic.'[2] The social class overtones are only too apparent in that spare description – Hampshire had been educated at Repton and was a fellow of All Souls Oxford – but even Cairncross's Soviet handler Yuri Modin admitted that while he admired the man for his energy and expertise in providing leaked information, he found him 'anti-social and a wretched hand at making friends'.[3]

Compared to the other members of the Cambridge spy ring who were English, public-school educated and socially secure, Cairncross came across as a man with a chip on his shoulder, was uneasy in company and had a 'broad accent', unsurprising as he was born a Scot in 1913 in the Lanarkshire village of Lesmahagow, the son of an ironmonger.[4] But he certainly had brains. Like his brother Alec (Sir Alexander Cairncross), who became a renowned economist, he displayed a precocious intelligence and after education at Hamilton Academy won a scholarship to study French and German at Glasgow University before proceeding to the Sorbonne and Trinity College Cambridge, where he flirted with the Communist Party. A career as a civil servant followed and it was during this period that he was recruited by Soviet intelligence. One reason was that while working on the Enigma decrypts at Bletchley Park during the Second World War he was outraged to discover that the intelligence was not being shared with the Soviet Union, a wartime ally; this omission he set about rectifying by leaking sensitive information about the German Army's order of battle and other crucial papers about weaponry which was of immense help to the Red Army in the decisive Battle of Kursk in July 1943. Another reason was that unlike the other Cambridge spies, who had a variety of motives, he was a genuine ideological convert who believed implicitly that he was doing the right thing. In 1979 Cairncross was revealed as the so-called 'fifth man' in the ring – Burgess and Maclean defected in 1951, as did Philby in 1961, while Blunt was exposed in 1979 – but he continued to claim that he had never provided any information such as nuclear secrets which might have harmed his country.[5] He died in Herefordshire in October 1995 aged 82.

Because of the activities of the Cambridge spies, the Americans took the view that the British were not to be trusted with military secrets and that the UK's security services, especially MI6, were either corrupt or dupes of the Soviet Union; it was not until the CIA suffered a series of similar breaches that relations returned to a more even keel. (For example, Christopher Boyce and Andrew Daulton Lee, who were involved in the American defence industry, were both imprisoned in the mid-1970s for selling sensitive documents to the Soviet Union, but their motives seem to have been inspired as much by greed as by misplaced altruism.) Betrayal became a leitmotif of much Western literature of the period, most notably in the novels written by John le Carré who, as David Cornwell (his real name), had served with MI5 and MI6 before writing some of the best-known and bestselling novels on the intelligence war including the 'Karla Trilogy' – *Tinker Tailor Soldier Spy* (1974), *The Honourable Schoolboy* (1977) and *Smiley's People* (1979). The trilogy's plot is driven by the search for a Soviet mole and the rivalry between George Smiley, the head of Britain's security services, and his Soviet opposite number codenamed Karla, whose identity is never revealed. As with all le Carré's Cold War novels the action is thoughtfully muted and determinedly unheroic, in stark contrast to the fantastic action-packed James Bond novels of his contemporary Ian Fleming, which le Carré dismissed as 'candyfloss'. Even the central character Smiley is low-key in manner and appearance, being envisaged by one American critic as 'one of those ashen Englishmen . . . who seem to be permanently 60 years old'.[6]

Nevertheless, the shadowy world of Cold War espionage provided a backdrop for many novels, films and television adaptations from that period, so much so that work by le Carré and others, including Tom Clancy, Len Deighton and Frederick Forsyth, came to be regarded as exemplars of the West's view of the Cold War with its mutual misapprehension, fear and mistrust; a world governed by the difficulty of separating reality from illusion and over-shadowed by the ever-present dread of impending destruction. They are also written from a Western point of view, with the result that characters from the opposition are often little more than cyphers with code-names, thereby reinforcing the notion that while those in the democratic West were able to discuss the anxieties of nuclear annihilation or the moral ambiguities of loyalty and treachery, those held in the thrall of Soviet Communist autocracy were not. While there was some truth in such an assertion during the Stalinist period, with its purges and indiscriminate trials, when millions of lives were lost and intellectuals were singled out for punishment, there were phases of lucidity and calm even at the start of the Cold War as the Soviet Union began to grapple with the new reality of the nuclear age and its own position as a global power. During those years the world of espionage held little appeal to Soviet readers or movie-going audiences, but the authorities could not ignore the mass appeal of the James Bond franchise or the more cerebral attraction of George Smiley and his colleagues in le Carré's 'Circus' – so named because the author sited the fictional headquarters of the UK's secret services in Cambridge Circus in the west end of London. One result of this interest was the emergence of the Bulgarian novelist Andrei Gulyashki, whose 1963 novel *The Zakhov Mission* brought him to the attention of Soviet authorities as the likeliest candidate to create a Soviet literary rival to James Bond. Three years later, with the collusion of the KGB, he visited London to ask Fleming's publisher for permission to use Bond as a character in his next book, but this was refused. Nothing daunted, the KGB then turned its attention to another writer, Yulian Semyonov, whose novel *Seventeen Moments of Spring* was published in 1969 and was then produced as a television mini-series at the start of the 1970s, attracting audiences of over 50 million and introducing the character of Stierlitz as the Soviet's first marketable spy. So credible was *Seventeen Moments* that the future Russian President Vladimir Putin has often credited the show as the main reason why he joined the KGB as a young man. 'What amazed me most of all,' he was quoted as saying, 'was how one man's effort could achieve what whole armies could not.'[7]

That, though, was fiction and according to John Roberts, director of the Great Britain–USSR Association, who encountered Semyonov at a meeting in Moscow in 1987, the creator of Stierlitz was not exactly an attractive proposition; he described the author as 'an ugly figure with a chunky diamond ring and [dressed] in army combat fatigues'.[8] However, by the time that Semyonov's literary reputation had been sealed in the popular imagination the Soviet Union had found itself in need of something more potent to defend its borders than a credible fictional spy. As had become embarrassingly clear during the 1950s, Western advances in nuclear technology meant that the Soviet Union had to introduce measures to keep their own nuclear programme a closely guarded secret. During its early years, under the codename 'Task Number One', the cover-up was directed by Lavrentiy Beria, the head of the Soviet NKVD (*Narodnyy Komissariat Vnutrennikh Del*, People's Commissariat of Internal Affairs), which in 1954 became the KGB (*Komitet Gosudarstvennoy Bezopasnosti*, Committee for State Security), the country's main security agency. Beria was the longest serving and most successful of the heads of security who served Stalin and he had a deserved reputation for single-minded ruthlessness which had been cemented during the purges of the 1930s and culminated in the infamous mass executions of 22,000 members of the Polish intelligent-sia in 1940, known to history as the Katyn Massacres. In this new task as keeper of the country's nuclear secrets, Beria was equally thorough, and nothing was taken for granted as he set about controlling the country's nuclear industry. State security generals were appointed to key management positions at all nuclear research institutes and production plants and the NKVD was instrumental not only in planning those nuclear facilities but also running them, using a workforce drawn from the Gulag (*Glavnoye Upravleniye Ispravitelno-trudovykh Lagerey*, Main Administration of Corrective Labour Camps and Settlements), a vast network of prison camps for enforced labour which existed between 1923 and 1961. As a result, the development of the Soviet nuclear programme was swathed in paranoia and suspicion – quite early on, Beria warned the physicists and scientists that they faced execution if they failed in their appointed task to produce a workable nuclear weapon, first an atomic bomb (achieved in 1949) and then a hydrogen bomb (achieved in 1953). 'Leave them in peace,' cautioned Stalin. 'We can always shoot them later.'[9]

The threat was never put to the test as Beria himself was executed on 23 December 1953, nine months after the death of Stalin that same year. The subsequent purges of many former and active NKVD/KGB officers reduced the state security presence in the nuclear complex, but it was not the end of the matter as the interference continued long after the programme was reorganised to become the Soviet Ministry of Medium Machine Building (*Minsredmash*) and then the Ministry of Atomic Power (*Minatom*) which was responsible for running the entire Soviet military-industrial complex, including the construction of nuclear warheads. The main aim was to thwart foreign intelligence operations by creating an elaborate, multi-layered system of denial and deception which included a blanket restriction of access to nuclear facilities and the strict vetting of all personnel, from scientists to management. Such measures and countermeasures were strictly enforced in similar facilities in the West, but the Soviets took their restrictions to a new level by creating what amounted to a separate and hidden society for the nuclear industry, including the construction of ten closed nuclear cities in densely forested areas deep within the Soviet Union's huge land mass. These ghost cities were not marked on maps and existed in non-secret documents only as post-box numbers together with the names of nearby small towns, which made them virtually anonymous.

Most were situated beyond the Urals or in western Siberia and they were known collectively as ZATOs (*Zakrytye Administrativno Territorial'nye Obrazovaniia,* closed administrative territorial entities). The principal frontline closed city was Sarov (*Arzamas-16*), some 250 miles from Moscow where the first atomic and hydrogen bombs were developed, and which was considered to be the Soviet equivalent of the USA's Los Alamos facility in New Mexico, so much so that it was nicknamed Los Arzamas. Others in that category were Ozersk (*Chelyabinsk -65*), Novouralsk (*Sverdlovsk-44*) and Lesnoy (*Sverdlovsk-45*). Second-tier facilities were sited at Snezhinsk (*Chelyabinsk-70*), Trekhgorny (*Zlatoust-36*), Seversk (*Tomsk-7*), Zheleznogorsk (*Krasnoyarsk-26*), Zelenogorsk (*Krasnoyarsk-45*) and Zarechny (*Penza-19*). All had similar characteristics: they occupied a large and heavily guarded restricted area which possessed common facilities listed in official documents as: 'a town for the facility workforce, large wooded areas, and several isolated technical areas that housed primary research and production facilities, testing areas, and support infrastructure. Technical areas within the restricted area were surrounded by their own double or triple fences, which were patrolled by armed guards.'[10] In other words, despite their geographical isolation, they were self-sufficient and communication with the inhabitants was either strictly monitored or non-existent.

Given the restrictions and the secrecy surrounding the Soviet nuclear programme a premium was placed on making sure that the sites remained secure, especially from prying eyes in the West. This crackdown forced Western intelligence agencies to rely on their operatives working under diplomatic cover or agents entering the country through other legitimate channels such as tourism, scientific meetings and cultural exchanges. It also made aerial surveillance more important, especially as satellite photography was still in its infancy and NATO could only make use of the American development of spy planes to discover if the Soviets were pushing ahead in the nuclear arms race. In May 1960, an American U-2 spy plane piloted by Francis Gary Powers flew over the facility at Ozersk and photographed it from 70,000 feet while on a CIA mission over the Soviet Union codenamed 'Grand Slam', which would take it from Pakistan over the Soviet Union to Bodo in Norway, but the flight was rudely interrupted by the notorious incident in which the aircraft was shot down over Sverdlovsk when an SA-2 missile exploded near it and caused it to crash. Powers was put on trial and sentenced to ten years' imprisonment after the USA claimed untruthfully that the U-2 was on a meteorological mission and had flown off course but he was later released in one of the Cold War's many spy swaps. The incident resulted in the cancellation of a summit meeting planned to take place in Paris and also forced both sides to rethink their capabilities and procedures. In the aftermath, the CIA temporarily suspended flights over the Soviet Union and to protect its British ally removed RAF personnel from its Adana base in Turkey, where they formed the top-secret B detachment: a UK crew section consisting of four pilots, all of whom were decorated with the Air Force Cross – Squadron Leader Robert Robinson and Flight Lieutenants Michael Bradley, David Dowling and John MacArthur. For their part the Soviets increased the intensity of their counter-intelligence operations, the aim being to reveal and arrest 'enemy intelligence officers under diplomatic cover and other foreigners under suspicion of being affiliated with the enemy's special services'.[11] It was during this period that KGB surveillance of British and Canadian diplomatic activity in Moscow led to the arrest and subsequent execution of the KGB double agent Oleg Penkovsky, whose leaking of information had been so vital during the Cuban missile crisis and who was regarded by both the CIA and MI6 as a 'dream spy', with access to the most closely guarded Soviet secrets on missile technology.[12]

The secrecy on both sides surrounding the nuclear issue meant that all information about arsenals, especially warheads, aircraft and missile delivery systems, was the gold dust of the intelligence war. But such was the all-pervading suspicion and distrust that any evidence, however run-of-the-mill or innocuous, was always analysed as so little was available through conventional channels. For most of the Cold War most of the population of the Soviet Union was starved of information from the outside world due to the jamming of English-language broadcasts and the unavailability of most Western newspapers and journals other than those which had official approval, such as the London-based *Daily Worker*, founded in 1930 by the Communist Party of Great Britain and renamed the *Morning Star* in 1966; this enjoyed bulk sales to the Soviet Union until 1989. The paucity of written or published information led to the use of extreme measures by both sides, especially when the papers being scrutinised were from official sources. Most of the material gained in this way came from miniature cameras such as the Minox, which was used by agencies on both sides and the CIA, MI6, the KGB and the East German Stasi became adept at producing sub-miniature cameras and microdot cameras in a variety of disguises which were widely and successfully used – the latter type could photograph and reduce whole pages of information onto a tiny piece of film the size of a sentence full-stop. One of the most infamous spies using this method was the British traitor John Vassall, an Admiralty clerk who was compromised by the KGB – he was homosexual at a time when it was illegal in the UK – and blackmailed into supplying the Soviets with substantial quantities of photographed secret documents relating to the development of radar, torpedoes and anti-submarine warfare equipment. Arrested in 1962 following the defection of Soviet spymaster Yuri Nosenko he was sentenced to 18 years' imprisonment but was released in 1972 and died in 1996 aged 72.

Even more damaging was the espionage committed by a group of agents known as the 'Portland spy ring', which was arrested in January 1961 after a tip-off from a Polish double agent codenamed 'Sniper' (Michael Goleniewski, who also claimed to be the Tsarevich Alexei Nikolaevich murdered with his family by Bolsheviks at Ekaterinburg in 1918). At the centre of the ring was a man calling himself Gordon Lonsdale who turned out to be Konon Trofimovich Molody, a Soviet intelligence officer and illegal immigrant, one of the first 'sleeper' spies who operated in the UK under an assumed identity and without the support of the Soviet embassy. The other members of the ring were American-born Morris and Lona Cohen (exposed during the trial as veteran KGB agents Peter and Helen Kroger) and Harry Houghton and Ethel Gee, who worked at the Admiralty Underwater Weapons Establishment at Portland in Dorset where they had access to sensitive intelligence relating to the UK's first nuclear submarine, HMS *Dreadnought*. The case caused a sensation when it came to court at the Old Bailey in March, largely because the Cohens were revealed as KGB agents with past histories but there was also disquiet about the way Houghton, a known drunk and philanderer, had been allowed access to sensitive papers relating to top-secret sonar systems. Basically, Lonsdale ran the ring, Houghton and Gee acquired the papers, which were taken to the Cohens' bungalow in Ruislip where they were photographed or microdotted and the photos sent to the Soviet Union. When Special Branch raided the house, they found it to be a treasure trove of sophisticated spying equipment, including a radio transmitter, false passports, large amounts of money and a selection of gadgets such as a torch battery hollowed out to make a hiding place, a lipstick with a hollow base and flasks with secret compartments. All five spies received long sentences but Lonsdale and the Cohens (Krogers) were later exchanged for convicted British spies in the Soviet Union. By then the damage had been done, not least to the Royal Navy's fledgling nuclear fleet at Faslane. In 1967 the first-generation Soviet nuclear submarines began to enter retirement and they were replaced by the improved Victor and Charlie classes, which were equipped with sonar systems which bore a striking similarity to those used by the Royal Navy. As Prime Minister Harold Macmillan saw the case at the time, the Portland spy ring had been 'a dangerous conspiracy to obtain important information of a highly secret character regarding modern submarine methods', while Christopher Andrew, the historian of MI6, claims that Lonsdale and his gang 'marked a turning point in Cold War espionage in Britain'.[13]

The exposure also reinforced the notion that while spying and treachery was a sordid business it could also be infused with a certain glamour judging by the equipment discovered in the Ruislip bungalow, which could easily have come out of a James Bond novel. Both sides saw it as imperative to maintain a technological lead over the other and expended huge resources in making sure that they were not left behind in the race to gain intelligence; this led to a demand for equipment which was reliable and, above all, could be easily concealed. In addition to miniaturised cameras, similarly sized recorders were also widely used for a variety of purposes, such as covertly recording a conversation, tapping telephone lines, bugging a room and collecting incriminating evidence from a suspect. One of the most widely used by Western agencies was the West German-made Protona Minfon, with a microphone disguised as a wristwatch, while the CIA's favourite was the Swiss-made Nagra SN precision miniature tape recorder, which was so successful that it was cloned in Ukraine and entered service with the KGB as the Yachta. As happens so often in the development of resources for intelligence-gathering, the equipment also had military uses and much of the knowledge and techniques filtered down for use in the field, especially in the no man's land which sprang up with the division of Germany into West and East. At any one time during the confrontation the Warsaw Pact would have 20 frontline Soviet divisions and 6 frontline East German divisions plus supporting air power and they constantly carried out large-scale manoeuvres to practise for their war role in the event of any attack on, or by, the West. For that reason, NATO needed regular and up-to-date intelligence assessments of the opposition's capabilities, as well as advance warning of any hostile preparations.

That requirement meant that senior alliance commanders relied on the existence of three military missions, American, British and French, which were established shortly after the end of the Second World War under protocols between the chiefs of staff of the American, British, French and Soviet forces in Germany, known as the Huebner-Malinin, Robertson-Malinin and Noiret-Malinin Agreements. The most prominent and effective of these missions was the British Commanders-in-Chief Mission to the Soviet Forces in Germany, better known by its acronym BRIXMIS, which operated behind the Iron Curtain in East Germany between 1946 and 1990. Ostensibly an overt operation designed to 'maintain Liaison between the Staff of the two Commanders-in-Chief and their Military Governments in the Zones' and to improve relations between the two sides, it was also used to gather military intelligence through reconnaissance and surveillance and the occasional unofficial 'borrowing' of military equipment or, as one Scottish staff officer put it, 'their job was official spying'.[14] Although those who served in BRIXMIS liked to compare their work to the 'great game' – the nineteenth-century confrontation between British and Russian intelligence agents in Central Asia – and to imbue their activities with a Boy Scout appeal, operating in East Germany was not without its risks, one operative saying that it was 'as close to active service as one could get without shooting' but the rewards could be substantial. During the 1960s Major J. C. Cormack, an Edinburgh-born Royal Engineer officer who had served in Korea, made a significant breakthrough when he managed to get photographic evidence that the Soviets had developed an operational Scud-B tactical battlefield missile. Until that breakthrough NATO intelligence had believed that the missiles on display in the annual May Day parade in Moscow were dummies but Cormack's patience and courage in an East German operational area allowed him to photograph the readiness drill that confirmed that the Scud-B was fully operational. The success was compounded by Cormack's later identification of the Soviet introduction of the new Halle D-30 122 mm artillery piece which was later used in tracked self-propelled versions and was eventually deployed in over 60 Soviet-allied armies. In both cases Cormack used his ingenuity to find a hiding place for his vehicle where he and his driver could lie up to observe and photograph the Soviet military activity.[15] On each tour there were no more than 31 operatives or 'pass holders' – 10 officers and 21 NCOs – and over the course of its history several Scots served in senior positions with BRIXMIS, including Major (later Lieutenant-Colonel) Willie Macnair of the Queen's Own Highlanders and his predecessor as Operations Officer Major Charles Ritchie of The Royal Scots, later Brigadier and later still Secretary of the New Club in Edinburgh.[16] BRIXMIS was always a small and compact organisation, never numbering more than 80, commanded by a Brigadier with an RAF Group Captain as his deputy; the ratio of personnel was 60 per cent Army and 40 per cent RAF, although in the early days there was also a small Royal Navy or Royal Marines presence.[17] MI6 was also involved. The organisation's opposite number was the equally effective Soviet mission known as SOXMIS, which worked in tandem with the East German security services, Ministerium für Staatssicherheit, commonly known as the Stasi. It was under the command of the Commander-in-Chief Soviet Forces at Zossen-Wünsdorf south of Berlin and the administration was controlled by the Chief of the Soviet External Relations Branch (SERB), a three-star general.

As part of the post-war agreements each mission had mutually agreed rights to cross the border at will and to travel anywhere with restrictions on where they could and could not go. In fact, clearly specified areas were out of bounds. Known as Permanently Restricted Areas (PRAs) these were strictly adhered to but there were anomalies in the system which could be exploited, such as the existence of Temporary Restricted Areas (TRAs), which could be imposed by the Soviets at short notice and could be evaded using ignorance as an excuse. Despite these limitations, which affected at least 40 per cent of the East German land mass, there was no shortage of targets and BRIXMIS raised touring to a fine art, regularly sending out their teams – usually an officer, NCO and driver – in specially adapted vehicles on operations which could last several days. During that time they were on their own, largely out of radio contact and of necessity self-sufficient. They would also push the limits of the agreement by driving close to PRAs, photographing military installations, and taking careful notes of any troop movements. Discovering the provenance and capabilities of new Soviet military equipment was a priority and perhaps the greatest coup occurred on 6 April 1966 when a Soviet Yak-28P ('Firebar') all-weather interceptor aircraft crash-landed in the Havelsee, the lake straddling the British and Soviet sectors in Berlin. Britain and America knew that the aircraft had a top-secret onboard radar system and the crash gave them the opportunity to inspect it provided that the Soviets could be kept at bay. Under cover of retrieving the aircrew's bodies BRIXMIS retrieved the necessary parts and sent them back to the Royal Aircraft Establishment Farnborough for inspection before returning them to the Havelsee. Despite Soviet edginess over the delay the radar was inspected and found to be a revolutionary new model known as 'Skipspin', which, unlike the contemporary Western systems, could look up and down as well as straight ahead. The retrieval operation was controlled by Brigadier David Wilson, an Argyll and Sutherland Highlander who had served as a company commander in Korea, and it needed all his patience and good humour to convince his opposite number, Lieutenant-General Vladimir Bulanov, who was becoming increasingly suspicious about the delays in returning the bodies of the crew members, Captain Boris Kapustin and Lieutenant Yuri Yanov. Within the space of 48 hours the bodies had been returned to the Soviets and the wreckage was replaced at the crash site, although the look on Bulanov's face told the BRIXMIS officers that he knew had been tricked.[18]

Later, in the early 1980s, a BRIXMIS team returned to Potsdam with the calibre of a new Soviet 30 mm gun equipping the recently introduced BMP-2 armoured fighting vehicle; this had been obtained by the simple expedient of pushing an apple into the barrel thereby getting a precise impression, all the more praiseworthy as this was achieved while a Soviet equipment train transporting the vehicle stopped under a road bridge on the Magdeburg to Zerbst railway line. BRIXMIS operatives also used sophisticated tools including up-to-date thermal imaging equipment, image intensifiers and night-sight goggles which had been developed for intelligence and counter-intelligence operations, but the most important piece of kit was the touring car which BRIXMIS used for operations in East Germany. In the first instance Opel Admiral saloon cars were purchased but these gave way to the more modern and more reliable Opel Senator, but as Major (later Major-General) Peter Williams of the Coldstream Guards explained in his monograph about service in BRIXMIS in the 1980s, these were no ordinary vehicles.

Every Senator was fitted with Ferguson four-wheel drive, a modification that was very unusual and expensive at that time, and had strengthened suspension and half a tonne of armoured plating under its belly to protect its engine. Its fuel tank capacity was increased to 180 litres and all the internal surfaces (such as the dashboard, seats and ceiling) were blacked out with matt material to aid photography by minimising reflection.

Extra lights were fitted in order to enable all tour vehicles, including the Senators, to impersonate a motorcycle or a small East German Trabant car and curtains were fitted inside the back and rear side windows to help the Tour Officer in taking photographs unobserved by onlookers. The resulting Senator was a relatively inconspicuous, long range, very fast saloon car with good cross-country qualities and the ability to carry three men and all their camping and operating kit in all weathers and in some comfort too.[19]

Equipped with four-wheel drive transmission with a good turn of speed and the ability to transform the configuration of rear lights to disguise its identity, the Opel Senator proved to be no match for the opposition and the crews of many pursuing Stasi vehicles frequently found that they were on a wild goose chase. Although 'tourers' (as teams were known) did their utmost to maintain the security of their missions, both sides were obliged to display a special diplomatic licence plate, in the case of BRIXMIS this was coloured yellow, with a distinctive number. Extreme violence was rare – BRIXMIS crews were unarmed – but confrontations could become heated if touring cars were boxed in by the opposition 'narks', as Stasi personnel were described. If detained, there were standing orders that the matter had to be referred to the local Soviet Komendant (usually a lieutenant-colonel) because, as Williams explained, 'he alone could speak with the authority of the Chief of Staff in Zossen' [Headquarters Soviet Forces in Germany]. All too often the Soviet Komendant had an ill-disguised contempt for his Stasi colleagues and the meetings frequently ended with the appearance of vodka and whisky toasts and later hangovers. Indeed, socialising with the opposition was an integral part of 'keeping the peace' and all four sides entertained each other at important national days such the Queen's Birthday (UK), Bastille Day (France), Fourth of July (USA) and May Day (Soviet Union).

On that level the work of the military missions could be reasonably relaxed but when the need arose BRIXMIS operatives were prepared to get 'down and dirty' and on occasions there was nothing glamorous about their task. This applied particularly to Operation Tamarisk (later

Tomahawk), which for obvious reasons was not given any publicity during the Cold War. It was launched in December 1979 and lasted for ten years, and was prompted by the knowledge that shortages of lavatory paper had forced Soviet military personnel to use discarded office papers which if flushed away could have clogged the waste system. Instead, contaminated papers were placed in bins outside the lavatories and wash rooms of official buildings, including barracks and hospitals. Others were left in field latrines during exercises and manoeuvres and once located and excavated these sources provided a rich if unexpected source of intelligence information as many of the papers were manuals, including orders of battle, or restricted files related to military matters which should have remained secret. To BRIXMIS teams fell the unpleasant task of retrieving these documents and sending them for further analysis. There were persistent rumours that NATO instituted measures to disrupt the supply of lavatory paper in East Germany to make sure that the practice could continue unabated, but this has never been proved, perhaps because it was clear that from an early stage Soviet forces lacked adequate supplies of lavatory paper and often used private letters for that purpose. 'Shit-digging' or 'tamarisking' might not have been the most heroic of exploits carried out by NATO forces but as one historian of that period put it: 'The untidy habits of the Soviet Army consistently proved to be one of the most startling sources of material . . . notebooks and schedules of newly arrived material with sources and serial numbers for the latest equipment.'[20] When BRIXMIS teams reported finding amputated limbs in bins outside military hospitals, especially those with shrapnel or gunshot wounds, they too were purloined for analysis along with soiled dressings to enable Western medical experts to investigate the efficacy of certain types of weapons.

Perhaps the most audacious discovery from Tamarisk operations came in 1981 near a Soviet Army barracks at Neustrelitz in East Germany, when a BRIXMIS team managed to appropriate a personal logbook from 'under the noses of sleeping [Soviet] sentries'. Written in Russian, the logbook included technical drawings relating to Soviet tanks and equipment and according to a British Military Intelligence Officer who subsequently debriefed the team that discovered it, 'it was (at the time) the most important thing we have had from any source for ten years'. The logbook contained top-secret information detailing the composition of the armour and the strengths and weaknesses of the new Soviet T-64A main battle tank. It also contained the same type of information regarding the even newer and more mysterious T-80B main battle tank, which was found to be powered by a gas turbine engine and protected by modern reactive armour with significantly greater levels of titanium and vanadium. This detailed information from the Neustrelitz logbook led to a crash programme to develop new and more powerful ammunition for the British Chieftain main battle tank and resulted in the production of the British L23 120 mm Armour Piercing Fin-Stabilised Discarding Sabot (APFSDS) ammunition which included a newly designed, longer dart-like armour penetrator which came into service two years later and provided more penetrative energy at the point of impact in order to overcome the new Soviet reactive armour. [21]

Not all intelligence was hidden or restricted or came from seren-dipitous finds of the kind unearthed at Neustrelitz. Far from it. Throughout the Cold War Soviet cartographers compiled a library of maps of the whole world which gives a reasonably accurate picture of the main cities and conurbations and is noticeable for its production values. Printed on high-quality paper with clear print, the accent was on excellence and attention to detail: buildings were colour-coded by their function, brown for residential, black for industrial, green for military and purple for civil administration. These were produced through access to information which was easily available – Ordnance Survey (or national equivalent), tourist guides, school atlases and other brochures – as well as aerial photography and satellite imaging. Unlike earlier maps produced by the Nazis during the Second World War they were not thought to have any specific military value for invading forces, but they still provide an interesting snapshot of the country as it was in the late twentieth century and could have been valuable for command and control purposes, once a country had come under Soviet administration, and in that guise a series of detailed maps was produced for Scotland.[22] Inevitably perhaps, those created in the 1970s during a period of rapid change include several discrepancies. The 1983 map of Glasgow and Paisley, for example, shows the existence of St Enoch's Railway Station and the surrounding tenements even though they had been demolished in 1966 and the map for Dunfermline contains no reference to the nearby Rosyth naval base. As one British cartographer who worked on editing the maps after the Cold War put it, they were things of beauty which were remarkable for what the Soviets were able to do with little checkable information – 'Knowledge is power. You collect this information because one day it might be useful.' In that sense the Soviet mapping project represented the acme of intelligence gathering.[23]

The espionage war was also waged beneath the waves and it was conducted by attack submarines from both sides. For the submariners of the US Navy and the Royal Navy it was an opportunity to take their boats 'up north', namely into the waters of the Barents Sea and specifically to test the sea area around Murmansk, the headquarters of the Soviet Northern Fleet and the submarine dockyard at Polyarny. The first patrol into this strategically sensitive region was undertaken in August 1949 by two American submarines equipped with snorkels to allow them to remain submerged longer and although it nearly ended in disaster when one of the boats, USS *Cochino*, caught fire and sank it brought back the important intelligence that the Soviets had exploded their first atomic bomb. It also proved that the Barents Sea was ripe for exploration from an intelligence point of view and the Royal Navy made its first incursion three years later with HMS *Artful* from the Third Submarine Squadron, then based at Rothesay on the Isle of Bute. However, the experience also taught the Navy that these old 'A' and 'T' class boats were well-nigh obsolete and ill-equipped to undertake long-distance intelligence-gathering missions. Although they had been improved with up-to-date radio equipment and sensors they had no water distillation equipment and lacked the capacity to vent their diesel fumes. To add to the physical difficulties, the submarines also had to evade detection by the Soviets and in the 1950s and 1960s there were several unconfirmed or immediately denied instances of American or British submarines being attacked by depth charge. The introduction of the Porpoise class diesel-electric submarines in 1957 improved matters as they could operate for prolonged periods and not only possessed silent running capability but, with an enhanced air purification system, they were also more comfortable for the crews. They were followed by the Oberon class with greater stealth characteristics but the breakthrough in northern intelligence-gathering operations came in the 1970s with the advent of fast nuclear-powered attack submarines equipped with 'a new generation of sensors including thermal-imaging devices and TV cameras'.[24] Freed from the necessity of having to surface they could remain submerged almost indefinitely; fortunately there were also improved physical conditions for the crews.

At the same time and with the same purpose in mind, Soviet submarines conducted similar operations in Scottish waters, where they attempted to track British and American Polaris submarines before they 'disappeared' on their regular patrols. With that in mind, SSBNs departing from Holy Loch or Faslane were accompanied by a variety of attack submarines, surface warships and maritime patrol aircraft in a process known as 'delousing', designed to discourage the Soviets from getting too close. The most successful RAF ASW aircraft was the Hawker Siddeley Nimrod, the 'mighty hunter', which was the first jet-powered maritime patrol aircraft in the world when it came into service as the MR1 in 1969 and was succeeded by the improved MR2 ten years later. Based on the airframe of the civilian Comet 4C jet airliner, it provided the RAF with a capable aircraft that served not just in the anti-submarine warfare (ASW) role but also in the Anti Surface Unit Role (ASUR) and in the Search and Rescue role (SAR). It succeeded the piston-engine Avro Shackleton, whose design harked back to the Second World War bomber the Handley Page Halifax and in another nod to that conflict the Nimrod's main weapon in the ASW role was the Sonobuoy, which was developed by British scientists and introduced into service in 1942 as a small and expendable sonar system to detect submarines and other underwater activity. Inexpensive to manufacture and relatively simple to operate, it was dropped into the sea in a canister with a small parachute to slow the descent, and on contact with the surface deployed a radio transmitter while hydrophone sensors searched for acoustic information below the waves.[25] Most of the Nimrod fleet operated from RAF Kinloss, where they also provided cover for the Navy's Polaris-equipped boats leaving for patrol.

The hunters were also the hunted and in a reversal of role, while it was the duty of SSBN commanders to make sure that their boats remained undetected during their patrols and to do everything possible to evade Soviet boats, the commanders of attack submarines operated on an entirely different principle, knowing that it was their duty to make contact. Again, that was in direct contrast to the tactics of the Second World War, when submarines were used primarily against enemy shipping and there was only one recorded instance of a submerged submarine sinking another submerged submarine – on 9 February 1945 off the Norwegian coast HMS *Venturer* attacked and sank *U-864* while it was attempting to transport essential war materials to Japan. Now, during the Cold War, mainly in northern waters and in the expanses of the Atlantic and the Pacific, submarine against submarine was to become the norm, a war in the shadowy depths in which 'there were no battles, no victories, no defeats, only casualties'.[26]

The quote is from the fictional Soviet submarine captain Marko Ramius in Tom Clancy's novel *The Hunt for Red October* (1984), which managed to capture the ever-changing nuances of the secret undersea confrontation from both sides, but the truth was real enough. Inevitably the policy required strong nerves and there were several near-misses and unreported collisions but it is known that four US submarines were lost due to accidents or operational reasons while the Soviet Navy lost six boats. Details about such incidents are still sparse but the best available figure is that British and American nuclear submarines were involved in 20 collisions with Soviet vessels. Two of the most serious collisions involved the British attack submarines HMS *Warspite* and HMS *Sceptre* and both occurred in the Barents Sea as they were tailing a Soviet missile boat.[27] In October 1968 *Warspite* was making her first patrol in northern waters when she encountered a Soviet Echo-II class guided missile submarine which made physical contact, damaging *Warspite*'s hull and fin. Although badly damaged, the British submarine was able to limp towards the Shetland Islands for temporary repairs before proceeding to Barrow-in-Furness for a more thorough overhaul and rebuild. The second incident occurred in the summer of 1981 while the Swiftsure class submarine HMS *Sceptre* was tailing a Soviet Delta-III class submarine *K-211* in the Barents Sea and during the manoeuvres the British submarine suddenly started shaking, with a huge noise which to the crew sounded 'like a scrawling' along the length of the hull and suggested a collision with the opposing submarine. The tables were now turned, and *Sceptre* was pursued into the North Sea where it eventually surfaced, and the damage was revealed to be a lengthy tear caused by *K-211*'s screws along the hull and fin which had also lost the bridge area during the collision. Having made its way back to Plymouth for repairs the crew were sworn to secrecy and as with the *Warspite* incident the damage was blamed on the boat hitting an iceberg; the truth was only revealed after the end of the Cold War.[28]

Perhaps the most daring and the most profitable incursion into Soviet waters was Operation Ivy Bells which was mounted by the US Navy, the CIA and the National Security Agency (NSA) in the Sea of Okhotsk during the summer of 1972. Its intention was quite simple – to tap into an undersea communication cable which connected the major Soviet

Pacific Fleet naval base at Petropavlovsk on the Kamchatka Peninsula to the Soviet Pacific Fleet's mainland headquarters at Vladivostok – but the execution was fraught with difficulty. Not only was the line hidden in deep waters close to the east coast of the Soviet Union, but its very existence had to be discovered before any operation could proceed. In common with many audacious plans, Ivy Bells was born of a simple idea. It was the brainchild of Captain James Bradley, director of undersea warfare for the Office of Naval Intelligence, who looked back to childhood days boating on the Mississippi River and remembered seeing signs warning river users where utility cables were sited. If the Americans used such notices, he reasoned, then so might the Soviets. Bradley was right, but finding the evidence proved to be a difficult and dangerous business because the Soviets had placed a formidable array of listening devices in the Sea of Okhotsk, a huge area covering over 600,000 square miles bounded by the Siberian coastline and the Kuril Islands, but this was balanced by a certain complacency on the opposition side based on a supposition that the line was untraceable and that the Americans did not possess the ability to find it.

But the US Navy did have such a means in the shape of USS *Halibut*, a long-range nuclear-powered submarine built in the late 1950s to carry the Regulus missile, the short-lived immediate predecessor of Polaris which had to be fired while the submarine was on the surface. Instead of scrapping the obsolete boat the Navy adapted it for the different role of deep sea search and recovery using remote-controlled search vehicles and her first mission came in the summer of 1968 when she was involved in the search for *K-129*, a Soviet Golf-II class submarine which had sunk in the Pacific. The mission's success led to further modifications, including adapting the large internal missile hangar as accommodation for the boat's powerful Univac 1124 computer – it acquired the nickname 'Bat Cave' – while towards the stern what appeared to be a miniature submarine or deep submarine rescue vehicle was bolted to the deck and doubled as a pressure chamber for saturation divers. It was in that guise as a Search and Rescue submarine that *Halibut* entered the Sea of Okhotsk and began scanning the Siberian shoreline. Sure enough, notices were found warning local fishermen about the existence of a cable which was soon located by the diving team, allowing them to feed in a complicated wiretap. When the first results arrived, they yielded a 'virtual cacophony' but as the mission proceeded it became possible to differentiate the voices which were being transmitted unencrypted, so sure were the Soviet naval authorities that the line was secure. The operation continued for a decade and was only ended in 1980 when Ronald Pelton, an analyst employed by the National Security Agency, contacted the Soviets through their Washington embassy and divulged the secret of Operation Ivy Bells in return for a payment of $35,000 to pay off his debts. This came as a blow to the CIA and NSA but in that period Bradley's hunch had paid dividends by giving the USA unprecedented access to telephonic conversations which the Soviets had believed to be completely secure.[29]

Due to the digitisation of modern communications Operation Ivy Bells could probably never be repeated and much of its detail has not been released but it typifies the lengths to which both sides were prepared to go during the underwater intelligence and counter-intelligence operations conducted during the Cold War. One reason why that was possible was the global presence of the system known as SOSUS – Sound Surveillance System – a network of undersea hydrophone arrays which was begun in the 1950s as Project Caesar and which could detect submarines up to 1,000 miles away. Each submarine had a unique acoustic signature which allowed it to be identified by computer, hence the emphasis placed on the need for 'silent running', especially for the missile-carrying SSBNs. The main locations of SOSUS hydrophone arrays were anchored to the ocean floor in the Atlantic and the Pacific but the heaviest concentration was in the waters surrounding the GIUK gap used by American and British submarines throughout the Cold War. One of the main listening posts for these transmissions was the US Navy facility at Edzell covering the east Atlantic, and its importance was increased in the 1970s with the coming into service of US Naval Ocean Surveillance System (NOSS) or 'White Cloud' which gave real-time intelligence about submarine movements from a height of 600 miles above the earth.

Until satellite reconnaissance technology came of age in the 1960s and 1970s with the advent of the Corona and Hexagon systems which orbited 100 miles above the planet, the main aerial incursions over Soviet territory were made by specially adapted American and British aircraft such as the North American RB-45C Tornado and the English Electric PR7 Canberra, both of which could fly at altitudes and speeds unattainable by Soviet air defence fighters in the 1950s. Initially only the Tornado was ready for service – it was the reconnaissance version of the B-45, the first American jet-powered bomber – but for political reasons during the Korean War, Washington was not prepared to order American aircrews to fly on missions over the Soviet Union. At the same time the UK was keen to reinforce the special relationship with the USA and thus was born a unique Cold War transatlantic relationship. Operating out of RAF Sculthorpe in Lincolnshire under US Air Force command, the American Tornados flew 'special duties' flights deep into Soviet territory using RAF air crews and flying with RAF roundels but without serial numbers. They also used Prestwick and Kinloss for training purposes and were frequent visitors at both bases. These 'ferret' operations, as they were known, lasted over 12 hours and took the spy planes up to 1,600 miles into Soviet territory, often as far as the Ural Mountains, the aim being to identify targets in the eastern Soviet Union and to test the readiness and capacities of Soviet air defences. First of all, a dummy run was done in the air corridor to Berlin with the aircraft flying at maximum height and maximum speed, the aim being to gauge the Soviet reaction. There was none and, thus reassured, Prime Minister Churchill gave the go-ahead for the night-time operation to proceed in July 1951. Three Tornado aircraft were used with one in reserve and all were refuelled over Denmark or Germany before heading east into the darkness of the Soviet land mass. Later, the operational commander Squadron Leader Johnny Crampton, a Second World War bomber pilot, remembered the 'black hole' of the landscape below as they flew across East Germany toward the Soviet Union, with only isolated lights here and there to give any hint of human habitation. While heading towards Kiev on a deep southern route Crampton's aircraft came under attack from ground fire signifying that he was being tracked by radar but having taken the required photographs he increased power and headed home towards the West, 1,000 miles away. Short of fuel, he managed to land at a NATO base in West Germany before returning to Sculthorpe where he was relieved to see that the other two aircraft from the northerly route had already landed. Only later did he discover that Soviet night fighters had been scrambled in a fruitless attempt to hunt him down. The operation was kept secret at the time and details only began to emerge 40 years later, in 1994, after the Cold War had ended. Crampton retired from the RAF in 1957 and always refused to talk about the part he had played in these clandestine spying missions which had brought back much-needed intelligence about potential targets and Soviet radar profiling.[30] None of the aircraft used in this joint venture, known as Operation Jiu-Jitsu, was lost. It was not the only casualty. In such a high-risk operational environment there were bound to be accidents and deadly engagements in which lives were lost. By the 1980s the best estimates reckoned that the US Air Force had lost 27 aircraft on operational service, with the deaths of around 140 service personnel, while 60 other aircraft were attacked and damaged. In the worst incident, on 2 September 1958, 17 American National Security Agency officers were killed when their Lockheed C-130 aircraft was shot down by four Soviet MiG-17 interceptors over Armenia.[31] At the time the Soviet authorities refused either to acknowledge the incident or to return the bodies.

The success of the Jiu-Jitsu missions encouraged the RAF to develop their own expertise using the recently introduced Canberra jet-powered bomber, which spawned its own reconnaissance versions the PR-3 and PR-7 with a ceiling of 50,000 feet and a range of 3,500 miles. In August 1953 there is evidence to suggest that in the course of Operation Robin one such Canberra made a daring incursion into Soviet airspace to photograph a suspected missile testing site at Kasputin Yar in Astrakhan north of the Caspian Sea and east of Volgograd. Although only partially successful as the aircraft was hit by ground fire at the point the site was being photographed and the results were blurred due to the air frame being shaken, it proved that long-range high-altitude incursion flights were possible. To date, though, the UK authorities have never admitted that such a flight took place and no papers have been released into the public domain to settle the matter one way or the other. The other consequence of the Jiu-Jitsu and Robin operations was the willingness of the US Air Force and the CIA to use RAF air crews on clandestine U-2 flights not just over the Soviet Union but over the Middle East, where the UK had substantial strategic interests. Following the Gary Powers incident in 1960 the practice ceased and there is no evidence that RAF personnel flew missions on the U-2's successor, the powerful SR-71 'Blackbird', although the aircraft is known to have used RAF Mildenhall as an operating base until the end of the Cold War. In theory, the CIA retained a four-man RAF crew at the US Air Force Edwards base in California until 1974 but the reality was that after 1960 'RAF pilots never again conducted an Agency overflight'.[32]

During this same period the Soviets were far from inactive in intelligence-gathering on land, in the sea and in the air. Soviet attack submarines were frequent visitors off the west coast of Scotland, especially in the approaches to the Clyde where they attempted to tail

American and British SSBNs when they left on patrol. In November 1974 a Soviet attack submarine collided with the USS *James Madison* as it was leaving the Holy Loch on a Polaris patrol. The incident was so serious that it merited a 'secret eyes only' cable from the US National Security Adviser to Secretary of State Henry Kissinger and the papers were not revealed until 43 years later, even though a speculative report appeared in the *Washington Post* on 3 January 1975.[33] It was not the first such incident in Scottish waters. Two years earlier a Soviet Victor class submarine had been sighted in the Clyde approaches in the sea area 60 miles north-west of Donegal and the inner Hebridean island of Colonsay and had been kept under 24-hour surveillance for six days by an RAF Nimrod maritime patrol aircraft from Kinloss. Eventually it was chased away by the intervention of the attack submarine HMS *Conqueror*. Like the earlier incident, it was not revealed until after the end of the Cold War but already things were beginning to change. *Conqueror* had been able to deal with the Victor but within ten years the Soviets were beginning to gain parity with the West's submarines in terms of performance, particularly silent running. Firm evidence came in December 1986 when the attack submarine HMS *Splendid* had a close encounter in the Barents Sea with a huge Soviet SSBN which became entangled in *Splendid*'s towed sonar array. This was one of the new Typhoon class, a monster which was bigger than anything operated by the US Navy or the Royal Navy, being 516 feet long and powered by two nuclear generators, allowing it to travel at 25 knots; she was armed with 20 ballistic missiles, each with ten MIRV (multiple independently targetable re-entry vehicle) warheads. Confusingly, the Soviet name for this new class was Akula (shark), which was also the name given by NATO to a new attack submarine introduced in 1984 which was capable of 35 knots and found to be almost silent in operation. To the Soviets it was the Shchuka, meaning 'pike', and it caused consternation in the West because NATO had thought it would be another ten years before the Soviets could develop such sophisticated technology.[34] Even the US Senate Armed Services Committee was forced to admit that the Akula was 'the best submarine in the world today'.

By their very nature the submarine confrontations under the northern ice provided the most dramatic stories of the hidden intelligence war, but for the Soviets the best secrets came from elderly rust-bucket fishing boats known as AGIs – Auxiliaries, General Intelligence. From the 1960s onwards one of these instantly recognisable vessels was on permanent station between Ireland and the Mull of Kintyre, its job being to monitor British and American submarine movements from the Clyde and to pass on the information to waiting Soviet attack submarines off the west coast of Ireland. In 1969 the 'A' class submarine HMS *Andrew* went to have a closer look at this strange vessel which was festooned with antennae for SIGINT and ELINT activities but carried no fishing gear. The first officer was Lieutenant Eric Thompson, who later went on to have a distinguished career in nuclear submarines and to become commander of the Faslane submarine base: 'As we rounded the Mull of Kintyre on the surface, I sighted it sitting in its usual position, drifting on the tide. It would sit there for months on end and I wondered what on earth its crew did to pass the time. Probably they were revelling in the joys of British or Irish television, which must have been vastly more entertaining than the propaganda-riddled, State-controlled, Soviet equivalent. Our plan was to ascertain its exact location, head out to sea, dive, circle back and do a covert under-run. When it saw us, it got underway and headed towards us.'[35]

But the AGI trawler was not quite nimble enough. While the Soviet skipper played fifties pop music from his wheelhouse – much to Thompson's astonishment, as the music came from his parents' generation – HMS *Andrew* raced ahead over the horizon and submerged before returning to inspect the AGI below the waterline, where they found a sonar and torpedo tube. Formally, that made her a warship, but the main merit of these vessels was their intelligence-gathering capacity to record the comings and goings of NATO submarines, to observe practice firings of modern weapons and record the acoustic or electromagnetic signature of the sonar, search radar, fire-control radar, guidance and command electronics of each weapons system. Whatever else they were, the crews of the AGI trawlers were professional sailors with good ship-handling skills and it was often said that the scruffy bearded skipper seen on board the vessel invariably on station off Malin Head had probably just done a tour of duty as a destroyer captain in the Baltic.

These 'tattletales' as American sailors called AGIs also had a high nuisance value and were an unwanted presence across the globe during western naval exercises and replenishment operations, with AGIs cutting across Western ships without warning or manoeuvring dangerously close to surfaced submarines. In 1972 the US Navy revealed that there had been 79 near misses with Soviet naval surface vessels and that

32 of these had been AGIs but the authors conceded that many similar incidents had probably not been reported.[36] Under the rules of engagement, Western warships could not retaliate in any way and the commanders of escorting destroyers or frigates had to content themselves with 'shouldering' them, or, as Commander John Murphy USN put it, using the same kind of nuisance tactics: 'Bump and bruise them. Foul their propellers with steel wire or even melt the tubes in their electronic gear with high power electromagnetic radiations. They could get in the way of our operations, but they were going to pay for it.'[37] The frequency and prevalence of such actions suggests a high level of seamanship on both sides but clearly such a state of anarchy could not continue on the high seas. At the end of the 1960s, at Washington's instigation, bilateral talks began to introduce new protocols governing ships at sea and this resulted in the successful Incidents at Sea Agreement which was signed in May 1972 and put a stop to excessively aggressive behaviour by both sides when operating in close proximity. Specifically, 'there would be no gun pointing, low-flyovers with bomb bays open, or illuminations with firecontrol radars'.[38] This curtailed the confrontations, which were getting out of control, and it made life more difficult for the crews of the Soviet AGIs but ironically the agreement was a victory of sorts for Admiral Gorshkov, the instigator of the Soviet Union's deep sea maritime policy. From being a Cinderella service in the 1950s the Soviet Navy had become as influential in policy-making as the US Navy, the most powerful navy in the world.

Small wonder, then that the AGIs were included in the Soviet Navy's order of battle where they operated as *tral'shchiki* or trawlers but there was also another group of fishing boats which operated in a freelance capacity supplying titbits to Soviet intelligence on an ad hoc basis. Many came from East Germany and Poland and were a familiar summertime sight off the Scottish coast throughout the Cold War. Over the years the trawlers and the accompanying factory ships were nicknamed 'klondykers' and their presence was generally welcomed due to the trade they generated in Scottish coastal towns. In 1984 East German klondykers caused something of a sensation when they were invited ashore in Ullapool to play a game of football against local fishermen which was grandiosely described as Scotland versus the Soviet Union.[39] Eastern bloc spying by fishing boat was not a one-way process: during the same period British fishermen operating in northern seas were provided by the Ministry of Defence with silhouettes of Soviet warships and invited to log and where possible photograph their sightings just as, no doubt, the klondykers had been doing off the coast of Scotland. In March 1998 Armed Forces Minister Dr John Reid made public a paper describing the contribution of British trawlers to intelligence gathering off the North Cape and in the Barents Sea during the Cold War in which he praised 'a long tradition of support by the fishing fleet to the Royal Navy, where they would go about their business of fishing, and volunteer such information they thought right to report'.[40]

10

Trident and Thatcher

BY THE BEGINNING of the 1980s the presence of the nuclear deterrent on the Clyde was no longer the focus of aggravation that it had been two decades earlier. The local communities in the Strathclyde region had become accustomed to seeing the black hulls of the British and American submarines as they made their way to and from the open sea and while most people probably preferred not to dwell overlong on their cargos of weapons of mass destruction they had become familiar with Polaris and Poseidon as contributors to the West's security. It is also fair to claim that this sense of uneasy acceptance was assisted by the fact that there had been no notable safety incidents involving the nuclear-powered submarines and their lethal missiles. Neither, quite obviously, had there been any nuclear war which would have placed the west coast of Scotland in the front line. With the passing of time initial fears about safety had been assuaged by the absence of any major nuclear accidents and this was linked to a perception that the presence of the bases at Holy Loch and Faslane had contributed to the local economy. This implied consent did not mean that the population had suddenly fallen in love with Polaris, but it was a factor in normalising the nuclear presence in the west of Scotland. The other driver was the détente which permeated the superpower relationship in the early 1970s when Richard Nixon became the first US president to visit Moscow (and later Beijing) to discuss improved relations, most notably the moves aimed at controlling nuclear weapons as recommended by the Strategic Arms Limitation Talks (SALT) which yielded the Antiballistic Missile Treaty along with an interim agreement setting caps on the number of intercontinental ballistic missiles each side could develop. Although the thaw did not last, largely due to the Soviet invasion of Afghanistan in 1979 and Moscow's hostile attitudes to political dissidents, it did produce an awareness of the need to limit the manufacture and development of nuclear weapons.

It also prompted questions over the next generation of nuclear weapons and their delivery systems and how these could be replaced so that they could be kept within the terms of the new arms limitation agreements. In 1977 the Soviet Union reacted to the new strategic situation by installing solid-fuel SS-20 intermediate-range ballistic missiles (IRBMs), which they argued were not new weapons but replacements for the obsolete liquid-fuelled SS-4 and SS-5 missiles which had been in service for over two decades and were nearing the end of their useful service. As such they were permitted under SALT but in fact the new missiles, code-named Sabre, were game-changers in the Cold War arms race. Not only were they powered by solid fuel, making them safer (for their crews) and more reliable, but they were mobile, being transported and fired from large-wheeled portable launchers to avoid detection. They were also reputed to be more accurate but their main benefit was their ability to allow the Soviet Union to wage a limited war in which tactical targets such as airfields, military bases and cities could be hit, thereby confining future nuclear conflict to Europe. This capacity could have altered the balance of power in Moscow's favour, for as the authors of a recent Cold War history asked: 'If Europe alone were hit by nuclear missiles, would the United States intervene and risk the destruction of its own cities?'[1] As the SS-20s were not included in the SALT talks nervous European leaders worried that the answer might be negative.

Washington's response was the introduction of its own new generation of IRBMs, the Pershing II and the Ground Launched Cruise Missile (GLCM), officially designated BGM-109G Gryphon, which were introduced specifically to counter the Soviet initiative and were offered to Washington's European allies in 1979. West Germany and the UK took the lead in agreeing to the new missiles being sited in their countries in 1983 and the eventual deployment saw 108 Pershing II missiles being based in West Germany while GLCMs were sited across Western Europe: in the UK (160), West Germany (96), Italy (112) and 48 each to the Netherlands and Belgium. NATO had hoped that the relatively modest total of under 600 missiles would not create tensions or be unpopular with the local populations, but the deployments prompted widespread demonstrations. The Soviets, too, were alarmed because with their first-strike capability the new cruise missiles were regarded as an aggressive and dangerous escalation of the Cold War arms race and not as a valid response to the development of their own

SS-20 missiles. The demonstrations were especially virulent across West Germany and in England where a women's peace camp was quickly established at one of the main bases at RAF Greenham Common in Berkshire, 55 miles to the west of London and home to the USAF 501st Tactical Missile Wing. At one stage in the negotiations the Americans hoped that the UK would agree to accept cruise missiles as a replacement for the aging Polaris system but although these were considered, the GLCM was thought to be too vulnerable to attack while the submarine-launched system had already proved to possess the stealth requirements needed in a credible deterrent. Another factor was the widespread popular opposition to the siting of cruise missiles in England, which prompted renewed support for CND, whereas the submarine base at Faslane was regarded as a permanent fixture and while on patrol the Polaris-armed submarines were at least out of sight and out of mind.

At the time thought was being given to the continuing efficacy of the UK's nuclear deterrent and it was becoming clear that it would have to be enhanced and upgraded in the face of Soviet advances in missile technology, especially as this related to anti-ballistic missile (ABM) defences around Moscow. With only three warheads, Polaris was in danger of becoming irrelevant as one submarine carried an arsenal of 16 missiles, too few to offer an overwhelming response if fired against a well-defended Soviet target. In theory, a single Soviet anti-ballistic missile could destroy a Polaris missile during the re-entry stage, thus negating it as a tangible threat in the minds of Soviet commanders. This was less of a problem for the US with its larger submarine fleet but for the Royal Navy it caused considerable heart-searching and various solutions were investigated, including building additional submarine delivery systems to make good the deficit or purchasing the recently upgraded American Poseidon C-3 missile, which carried 14 independently targeted warheads giving it genuine multiple independently targetable re-entry vehicle (MIRV) capability but in a time of economic stringency both possibilities were discarded as being too expensive and therefore unpopular.

The result was the development of Chevaline, a top-secret weapons system whose existence was kept under wraps for over ten years until it was finally revealed in 1980 by Defence Secretary Francis Pym after Margaret Thatcher had become Conservative prime minister.[2] Part of this development, which cost £1 billion, was carried out at the Royal

Naval Torpedo Factory (RNTF) Greenock, so in addition to being a top-secret project for so long, Chevaline was also astonishingly expensive, the two facts obviously being related. Four different governments maintained the secrecy over this project – thrice under Labour administrations led by Wilson (1964–70 and 1974–6) and James Callaghan (1976–9) and once under the Heath-led Conservatives (1970–4). It was also enormously complicated to operate and this led to overruns in its development, with the result that it did not come into service until the early 1980s as timescales slipped and costs escalated. Basically, Chevaline was a Polaris A-3 missile with an enhanced warhead equipped with decoys which gave the weapon a better chance of surviving Soviet anti-ballistic missiles and therefore of breaching the defences around Moscow – the so-called 'Moscow criterion' which underpinned NATO's nuclear strategy during the Cold War. The system was described as consisting of 'two manoeuvring clusters of real warheads and decoys' which would overwhelm the defences by offering so many false targets that the actual warheads would be indistinguishable from the decoys. Or, as the official designation put it at the time, Chevaline was 'essentially a small space vehicle. It is fitted with manoeuvring jets, space reference units, electronic units/computer, and power and fuel supply systems, etc. that enable it, once separated from the missile, to deploy and position itself in sub-orbit, and releases both countermeasures and warheads in a pre-programmed sequence.'[3] While this did not give Chevaline true MIRV capability it was a solution to the problem posed by the Moscow criterion even though the Navy thought it over-complicated and would have preferred to purchase the new American Poseidon missile.

Such sophistication also came at a prohibitive cost, both financial and political.[4] In 1982, just a few months before Chevaline was finally deployed, the Public Accounts Committee issued a report which heavily criticised the Ministry of Defence's management of the whole programme, and the way it had been hidden from any form of parliamentary scrutiny since the instigation of feasibility and project definition. The report concluded that 'the failure to inform Parliament or this Committee until 1980 that a major programme on this scale was being undertaken, or that its cost was turning out to be so far in excess of that originally expected, is quite unacceptable. Full accountability to Parliament in future is imperative.'[5] With that rebuke the Chevaline programme was one of the most controversial aspects of post-war

British defence policy and became renowned as the most expensive publicly funded project to be undertaken without parliamentary supervision.[6]

There is little doubt, though, that the development of Chevaline allowed the UK to retain its independent nuclear deterrent at a time when the financial situation was suggesting that it would be unwise to do so. Although the missile made use of previous American research it was a British development and while there were setbacks during its manufacture it came into frontline service in 1982.[7] In that sense the secretive development of Chevaline was a declaration in favour of the UK maintaining an independent nuclear deterrent. Not only did it provide much-needed work for the nuclear weapons staff at the Atomic Weapons Research Establishment at Aldermaston but it gave notice that the UK was determined to stick to the Moscow criterion as a central part of its strategy of deterrence. In other words, the ability to attack Moscow successfully and decisively had to be retained, whatever the cost, or as the campaigning journalist Duncan Campbell explained the position: 'The raison d'être of the British nuclear deterrent has always been that, despite the normal commitment of British Polaris missiles and bombers to NATO, they can be used independently "where Her Majesty's Government may decide that supreme national interests are at stake".'[8] This commitment was to govern British nuclear policy into the twenty-first century and was to have a major say in the later decision to purchase the ultimate Cold War weapon, Trident, the successor to Polaris, Poseidon and Chevaline.

The development of Chevaline also underscored the importance of the 1958 US–UK Mutual Defence Agreement which formed the basis for cooperation between the US and the UK for the development of nuclear weapons. Known officially as the Mutual Agreement for Co-operation on the Uses of Atomic Energy for Mutual Defence Purposes, this concordat is the cornerstone of the British nuclear weapons programme, enabling exchanges of technical information and allowing the UK to draw on US warhead designs. An amendment to the Agreement was signed a year later, allowing purchases and exchanges of fissile and thermonuclear material and permitting the UK to use the US nuclear test site in Nevada. All this was conducted in conditions of great secrecy, leaving CND to complain during the equally secretive Trident programme in the 1980s: 'The British parliamentary system allows little scrutiny of money spent on the British nuclear weapons programme. Furthermore, there is little opportunity to question the justification of any such expenditure and no realistically achievable way to change or abandon any such expenditure.'[9]

The political background during that period was also significant. Against the odds Margaret Thatcher had been elected leader of the Conservative Party in February 1975, becoming the first female leader of a British political party and slowly starting a revolution in Westminster politics. Inexperienced and considered 'shrill' by her opponents, she owed her election largely to the Conservatives' dislike of her predecessor Edward Heath, but she soon became noticed in the rest of the world. Much to her pleasure a Soviet military newspaper in Moscow christened her the 'Iron Lady', while in the USA she made an early friendship with Ronald Reagan, the governor of California and a Republican presidential hopeful. Both were to have an impact on her attitude to the UK's future nuclear policy and the country's relationship with the Soviet Union, which she and Reagan castigated as 'evil'. When she took over control of the Conservative Party the country was in dire straits, with the ruling Labour government under Prime Minister James Callaghan seemingly unable to deal with the militant industrial action that was paralysing the economy and causing rampant inflation and rising unemployment. In the autumn of 1978 Callaghan, who had succeeded Harold Wilson two years earlier, passed up an opportunity to call a general election and this was followed by a worsening of the economic and political situation, a period known as the 'winter of discontent' which saw the country in free fall. A succession of destructive strikes by workers in the private and public sectors, demanding inflationary wage claims, meant that for several weeks refuse was not collected, graves were not dug, ambulances did not operate, and petrol stations remained closed due to lack of fuel supplies. Predictably, perhaps, Callaghan was unflustered by the chaos – one of his nicknames was 'Sunny Jim' – and although he tried to ride out the storm the spirit of the age was against him. In January 1979, on returning from a summit in Guadeloupe involving the USA, UK, West Germany and France he told a reporter from *The Sun* newspaper who asked him about the wisdom of leaving the UK at such a precarious time: 'I don't think that other people in the world would share your view that there is mounting chaos'. In the feverish atmosphere of the day this was translated into the damaging tabloid headline, 'Crisis? What Crisis?'[10]

Callaghan never recovered from the faux pas and his fate was sealed the following month by the failure of a devolution referendum held on 1 March 1979 in Scotland to address growing demands for home rule and the creation of a separate Scottish legislature. (A similar referendum was held in Wales.) At the end of March Thatcher forced a vote of no confidence which she won by a single vote and in the ensuing election she secured an overall majority of 43, becoming the UK's first female prime minister and ending Callaghan's political career. Paradoxically, the election came as the UK's nuclear deterrent policy was about to be revised and at a time when the future of the Polaris missile and its successor had to be decided. During the election campaign Labour's manifesto insisted that there had to be 'a full and informed debate' on the subject before any decision was taken but even so it still believed that non-renewal was 'the best course for Britain'. This created the impression that Labour was creating the conditions for a debate on the subject but as happens so often in manifesto pledges, appearances were deceptive. In 1977 a small group of Labour ministers including Defence Secretary Fred Mulley and senior civil servants had formed the Nuclear Planning Group and met in secret to discuss the future of Polaris, and its deliberations were assisted by the drafting of a study which came to be known as the Duff Mason Report and which provided the criteria for selection.[11] The authors were Sir Anthony Duff, an experienced and respected diplomat with links to MI5, and Sir Timothy Mason, Chief Scientific Adviser to the Ministry of Defence; their findings have been described as 'a key document in British military history', one which laid the foundations for the purchase of the US Trident missile system.[12] Produced in three parts covering the arguments for and against renewing the UK nuclear deterrent, the criteria governing target selection and the type of weapons which would be required to implement such a policy, the Duff Mason Report recommended conclusively that 'the only viable option for Britain to maintain a credible nuclear deterrent, a necessity for diplomatic leverage and the maintenance of prestige, was to once again seek an agreement with the US'.[13] It was a persuasive argument: Polaris was becoming obsolete, the Chevaline replacement had been time-consuming and expensive and that led the authors of the Duff Mason Report to conclude that surrendering the UK's nuclear deterrent would be a mistake at this critical moment in the country's history and one that had to be avoided. Not only would the country be denying itself the use of powerful strategic weapons, but it would also be giving up influence on the international stage because possession of the deterrent 'gives us access to and the possibility of influencing American thinking on defence and arms control policy and has enabled us to play a leading role in international arms control and non-proliferation negotiations'. The authors also recommended that any future weapon would have to destroy Moscow's improved ABM defences and the associated reinforced underground bunkers, both of which were beyond the capacity of Polaris and Chevaline.

Fortunately for their recommendations a window of opportunity was about to open. Callaghan was due to attend the aforementioned superpower summit in Guadeloupe and would have the opportunity of raising the question of American support with the new president, Jimmy Carter, who had been elected in 1976. Although Carter was determined to pursue a foreign policy with a high moral tone the latter part of his presidency was dominated by worsening relations with the Soviet Union and this encouraged him to take a more robust stance in negotiations over the second stage of the SALT agreement, which was beginning to stall. The USA had already begun work on the development of their own successor missile to Poseidon which would have a longer range, enhanced accuracy and greater destructive capacity. Known as Trident C-4 or Trident I, the new missiles also required larger submarines, which were being developed as the Ohio class. Earlier in his presidency it had seemed unlikely that Carter would favour selling Trident to the UK, due largely to concerns over the deteriorating domestic economic and political situation and fears that the country was becoming too Europe-orientated following its membership of the EEC in 1973. However, the worsening relationship with Moscow tipped the balance and during the Guadeloupe summit Carter told Callaghan that he would be in favour of continuing cooperation with London and that the UK could have Trident as 'in his view, it was better that there should be a shared responsibility in Europe, rather than that America should go it alone'.[14] Thus it was that the prime minister returned from the summit carrying not only the seeds of his own destruction in his unguarded comment to a newspaper reporter but also the promise of receiving the next generation of submarine-launched ballistic missiles which would keep the UK a nuclear power. Breaking with tradition and his own personal inclinations Callaghan passed on this information to Thatcher after she won the election and succeeded him as prime minister.

She took the hint, and on 10 July 1979, within the first two months of her premiership, she was in touch with Carter to confirm the details of his offer and to instigate the negotiations which she hoped would be based on the beneficial Polaris agreement of 1963. Carter did not go back on his word but it was not all plain sailing as the deal had to overcome scepticism in Washington where there was concern that Trident was being given away for nothing and in London where there was support for Callaghan's earlier promise to phase out the nuclear deterrent and not renew Polaris. Both problems had to be addressed before the deal could progress, as did the equally vexed issue of any sale to the UK being contrary to the spirit of the disarmament talks with the Soviet Union. During the horse-trading (for that was what it seemed to be) the fears of both sides were addressed and settled. Concerns in Washington that the Trident sale was too generous were allayed by a British agreement to provide close airfield defence for US bases in the UK through the development of the Rapier missile system and by an agreement to extend the US lease on the Diego Garcia base in the Indian Ocean even though Thatcher had never intended to revoke the licence. It also helped that the UK had displayed a cooperative attitude towards the deployment of cruise missiles in England. All these deals seemed to offer the opportunity of recouping the additional development costs of Trident and were accepted in Washington, where it was generally accepted that British possession of Trident strengthened rather than weakened the NATO alliance by providing a 'second centre' option at a time when the relationship with the Soviet Union was becoming increasingly tense.

There was one other factor: secrecy. Perhaps chastened by earlier scandals such the Cambridge spies and the Portland spy ring or perhaps because they understood the public's anxiety about the development of nuclear weapons, by the 1970s successive British governments had developed a culture of silence at the highest level, allowing them to pursue nuclear policies which might otherwise not have been tolerated. As one historian of this period put it, 'the historical divisiveness of the disarmament issue and the UK government's need to prove its dependability to the US concealed British nuclear decision-making in a shroud of secrecy that even outstripped that of their counterparts across the Atlantic'.[15] How else could four successive governments have kept the Chevaline project hidden from public view? The official furtiveness also allowed Callaghan to pursue a Polaris replacement with Carter while at the same time paying lip service to the notion that it might not be necessary to renew the nuclear deterrent – not an easy task when two leading members of his party, Michael Foot and Tony Benn, were prominent nuclear disarmers.

In December 1979 Thatcher visited Washington amongst other matters to agree the deployment of US cruise missiles and to take forward the question of acquiring the Trident C-4 missile, it being understood by both sides that 'both issues were interconnected in that a co-operative British attitude on the former would help negotiations on the latter'.[16] It helped matters that the visit coincided with the Soviet invasion of Afghanistan and their preparations to deploy SS-20 missiles in eastern Europe as both policies seemed to test Western willingness to modernise their own weapons systems. On that score Carter was anxious not to antagonise either France or West Germany, the former because they were traditionally touchy about the UK's relationship with the USA and the latter because West Germans were already protesting about the American deployment of Cruise and Pershing in their country. In keeping with the British intention to keep all nuclear policy secure most of the negotiations were conducted from Thatcher's side by a senior civil servant – someone whose comings and goings in Washington would attract no press scrutiny and would be inconspicuous in a way that a minister could never be – and the letters of exchange were not signed until July 1980.[17] This was Robert Wade-Gery, Cabinet Deputy Secretary and a distinguished diplomat who had served in the British Embassy in Moscow in the late 1970s. Also considered during this process were two further options – refurbishing the existing Polaris boats and missiles or scrapping the Polaris system altogether and changing to specially adapted submarine-launched cruise missiles – but both were rejected as the strategic submarines were due to be replaced anyway and the cruise missile only offered the option of a single nuclear warhead whereas Trident had eight and brought with it full MIRV capability and operational commonality with the US Navy.

Within a year the political situation had changed in Washington when Carter (whom Thatcher did not trust, thinking him weak and irresolute) was replaced as president by Ronald Reagan (whom Thatcher liked, admiring his free market philosophy and his sturdy opposition to the Soviet Union). There was certainly chemistry between them and there is good reason to suppose that Reagan was grateful to her for her earlier interest at a time when he was being ignored by the liberal political establishment. Whatever the reasons for the mutual attraction, she cemented her place in his affections by being the first head of government to visit him in Washington in February 1981. By then, too, another change of heart was in the offing. During the Carter discussions it had become clear that the Americans were developing a more powerful version of Trident, to be known as the D-5 or Trident II, capable of carrying up to 14 warheads with full MIRV capability, but this would not be ready to come into service until later in the 1980s. Reagan's arrival in the White House changed all that. Within a few months of taking office he took the decision to modernise US strategic forces against a perceived Soviet threat and amongst the enhancements was an accelerated development of Trident D-5 missile and the Ohio class submarines which carried them. On 1 October 1981 he wrote to Thatcher explaining that 'this comprehensive program . . . will demonstrate our resolve to restore the strategic balance and to maintain flexible, responsive and survivable retaliatory forces'.[18] The announcement came as a relief to Thatcher as it confirmed what she had already been told by Caspar Weinberger, the US Defense Secretary, on 24 August, namely that he had been authorised by Reagan 'to advise you, now, in advance of the public announcement, that we will use the D-5 missile in our Trident boats and will make that missile available to you should you desire to buy it'.[19]

Thatcher did indeed want the D-5 missile, as not only was it a more efficient weapon compared to the C-4, it had a longer life expectancy and could offer savings, but only if spending on the earlier version was stopped sooner than later. A confidential note of 24 August 1981 from the Cabinet Secretary, Robert Armstrong, to the prime minister warned that the UK was already spending money on production of the C-4 and that it was in British interests to 'cancel orders and stop unnecessary payments'. An added complication was the need to 're-motor' the Polaris missiles from 1986 onwards at a cost of 'several millions', but together with the new Chevaline warheads this enhancement would extend the life of the missiles into the 1990s, when they would be replaced by Trident. Even so, it is obvious from the briefing papers prepared for Thatcher during the negotiation process that the government was nervous about the costs and went out of its way to reinforce the benefits provided by the missile and the value-for-money which would accrue from the purchase of the system:

In broad terms . . . we assess the likely order of capital cost for a four-boat force, at today's prices, at four-and-a-half to five billion pounds, spread over some fifteen years. Rather over half of this would be likely to fall in the 1980s. The total would cover submarines, missiles, warheads and support equipment and facilities, including new construction required at the Coulport armament depot, the Faslane operating base and elsewhere.

Of the total initial cost over seventy per cent will spent with British establishments and industry, the biggest elements being in shipbuilding, construction and warhead procurement . . .

. . . We spent much higher proportions in the 1950s on the build-up of the V-bomber force. Even after spending on the Trident force, the Government is planning to spend more on conventional forces than it does now.[20]

On that basis, the government pursued the purchase of D-5 Trident over the winter of 1981–2 and the agreement was signed in January. At the same time, an initial order was placed for three larger submarines, to be known as the Vanguard class, increased two years later to four. As had happened with the Polaris boats, the Royal Navy would have preferred five submarines but this was quickly dropped as it was felt that technological advances had obviated the need for a 'spare'. However, both the Navy and the government believed that speed was of the essence and wanted to push ahead with the first order so that if Labour were to win the 1983 election the project would be too far advanced to cancel. On the matter of finance, the government's briefing document for the project made clear that the Trident programme had financial repercussions that went far beyond the cost of the vessels themselves and the enlargement of the submarine base at Faslane and that this could only benefit the wider UK economy. At Barrow-in-Furness, where the boats were to be built by Vickers, the Devonshire Dock Hall – the largest indoor shipyard in Europe – was built so that the submarines could be constructed in a secure environment and away from prying eyes. At Aldermaston, new facilities were required to produce the Trident warheads but there were some savings when the government took advantage of an American offer for the missiles to be processed at King's Bay in the state of Georgia. Whereas the Polaris missiles had to be removed from submarines for routine maintenance and a change of warhead, the design of Trident made that unnecessary: repairs could be done, and the warheads changed, without offloading the missiles. On the infrequent occasions when a missile had to be removed for other work or storage the US Navy proposed that the operation could be carried out at its main submarine base on the eastern Atlantic seaboard. So sensitive was this proposal – jobs in Scotland might have been at risk – that before Thatcher visited Scotland in September 1981 the Ministry of Defence prepared a briefing document for the Scottish Office explaining that there would be no adverse knock-on effects or job losses as far as Scotland was concerned.[21]

And so it transpired. Costing £1.9 billion (at 1994 prices), the rebuilding at Faslane and Coulport was the biggest single procurement project undertaken by the UK government and was second in cost only to the construction of the Channel Tunnel, which opened in 1994. Known as the Trident Works Programme, it embraced a massive covered ship-lift capable of hoisting a 16,000-ton submarine out of the water for repair or servicing, a power station with the capacity to generate enough electricity for 25,000 people, a small town's worth of accommodation blocks, offices, a hospital, mess rooms and canteens all surrounded by high security. And then there were the advanced facilities at Coulport which, far from being downgraded, were enhanced to allow the warheads to be loaded onto the missiles after their long journey from Aldermaston. At the heart of this heavily guarded site was the Trident Storage Area, which included 16 large underground bunkers with air-locked doors each able to store a single Trident missile. As the fuel in each missile had explosive power equivalent to 70 tonnes of TNT the bunkers were segregated and, according to the Royal Navy, could withstand the remote possibility of an earthquake. There were also stores for the nuclear warheads which were joined up to their missiles in the Nuclear Process Building before being transported to the Explosives Handling Jetty, a specially constructed covered floating dock, one of the world's largest floating concrete structures, in which the missiles were loaded vertically into the submarine by overhead crane. The Rosyth Dockyard was also a beneficiary of the purchase of Trident – in May 1986 the government announced an infrastructure improvement programme costing £220 million which included the addition of up to 1,100 new jobs, a substantial investment at a time when Scottish unemployment stood at 14.9 per cent, with Fife being particularly affected by the economic downturn.[22] As it turned out, most of these jobs failed to materialise due to the decision to close down the naval dockyard in April 1996, but Thatcher's government was relentless in promoting the message that Trident was a good deal for the British economy, not least in Scotland.[23]

As had become obvious during the procurement process, the D-5 Trident came with a hefty price tag and the revelation of its acquisition reignited support for the CND. After years of being a side-issue, nuclear disarmament returned to the political agenda in 1980 when the pacifist socialist Michael Foot – according to the *Daily Mirror*'s assessment 'a good man fallen among politicians' – replaced Callaghan and the Labour Party adopted the policy of unilateral disarmament for Britain's nuclear weapons, for long a key demand of CND. All this happened at a time when Thatcher's administration was in trouble on the domestic front, with galloping inflation, rising unemployment and social unrest spreading across the main English conurbations. She was also facing opposition from within her own party and according to national opinion polls, by the late summer of 1981 she was the most unpopular prime minister of recent times, so much so that it seemed unlikely that she could win the next general election. Then came the Falklands War, which transformed her fortunes and in 1983 and 1987 she easily won two general elections to become Britain's longest-serving peacetime leader and thereby cemented her own form of rigorous economic and political ideology, quickly christened 'Thatcherism'. It helped her cause that Labour was in disarray under Michael Foot and that the political balance had been upset by the emergence of the Social Democratic Party (SDP) launched on 16 March 1981 by the 'Gang of Four' defectors from the Labour Party (Roy Jenkins, David Owen, Bill Rodgers and Shirley Williams) and which looked as if it might achieve its aim of taking over the middle ground, its high point being Jenkins' by-election victory at Glasgow Hillhead in March 1982. However, the SDP won only six seats in the 1983 election and lost further ground four years later. But despite Thatcher's commanding lead in the Commons her administration continued to have problems on the domestic front, one of the most serious being the demonstrations by women protestors following the arrival of cruise missiles at RAF Greenham Common towards the end of 1983. By then she had appointed Michael Heseltine Defence Secretary and one of his first acts had been to declare war on the CND by establishing Defence Secretariat 19 (DS19) to combat anti-nuclear propaganda. A department within the Ministry of Defence that worked closely with MI5, its principal task was to promote the government's case on nuclear deterrence, to challenge the arguments put forward by the nuclear disarmament movement and to suggest that CND's main aim was the advancement of Communism with the support of the Soviet Union. When the official documents from 1981 were released under the 30-year rule CND was quick to draw attention to that aspect of DS19's campaign: 'One of its brochures featured a CND symbol blending into a hammer and sickle, with CND spelled out as "communists, neutralists and defeatists".'[24]

Initially the main focus was on the women's peace camp which had been established at RAF Greenham Common following the decision to deploy cruise missiles there and at other sites in England, notably RAF Molesworth in Cambridgeshire (USAF 303rd Tactical Missile Wing), and this was followed by the creation of a similar peace camp at Faslane as the Scottish CND used the decision to purchase Trident to revive interest in its activities and to protest against the imminent arrival of Cruise. In short order, the Faslane peace camp became a permanent fixture and it was supported by other anti-nuclear groups including Trident Ploughshares, Parents for Survival and the Ecology Party (later the Green Party). They too came under surveillance: in a Special Branch report of 25 October 1983 following a mass CND demonstration in London, at that stage the largest protest ever to be mounted in the city, there appeared a listing of 'every single CND group from Scotland in attendance including Blairgowrie CND and Aberdeen University CND'.[25] From that point onwards and well into the twenty-first century the peace camp at Faslane operated as a focus of protest for those opposed to the presence of the submarine base and also to the transportation on public roads of the nuclear warheads from Aldermaston and nearby Burghfield to their final destination at Coulport. These convoys of some 20 heavy trucks and assorted protection vehicles travelled north and returned south up to eight times a year – a round trip of 900 miles – and when carrying warheads they carried both nuclear materials and high explosives –'a dangerous combination', as the protestors noted.[26] As was the case with the submarine base, there were fortunately no untoward accidents but there were a worrying number of safety incidents such as minor crashes with other vehicles, breakdowns and delays due to inclement weather and traffic congestion. On one occasion, a convoy got lost en route and on another the vehicles were held up for an hour by a pack of dogs running 'loose on the carriageway'.[27] Given their cargos, the convoys were also subjected to protests and even though they were supposed to be secret they were often photographed and their presence recorded. While it was most unlikely that a severe road accident could trigger the nuclear warheads aboard the convoys, there were other hazards, as campaigning journalist Rob Edwards pointed out: 'A fire or, worse, the detonation of some of the conventional high explosives packed around the cores of nuclear bombs, could breach the containers and lift large clouds of contaminants into the air. This could result in the spread of radioactive plutonium, uranium and tritium from the warhead. Depending on which way the wind was blowing, many thousands of people could risk being contaminated.'[28]

As Edwards also explained, the danger was exacerbated by the convoy routes, which took the vehicles through heavily populated areas such as Glasgow, where the M8 motorway was used in the first or final stages depending on the direction of travel. The motorway runs east–west through the centre of the city and forms a direct link to the lower Clyde and the approaches to Coulport. Within a 10-kilometre radius there were 776,370 local residents, 265 schools, 59 railway stations and 19 hospitals which would have been affected by any accident involving the convoys. Evidence from Scottish CND claimed that 'A convoy crash at the junction between the M74 and the M8 or on the M8 near Govan would cause major disruption. Several major hospitals and many schools would be contaminated, and restrictions could be imposed on agricultural production in some areas.'[29] Even though by then the Cold War had come to an end, the Trident convoys continued into the twenty-first century and the risks remained. By then too, what was then the world's worst nuclear accident had occurred at Chernobyl in Ukraine, where a reactor exploded on 25 April 1986, causing uncontrolled radioactive release into the environment and leading to serious social and economic disruption across the western Soviet Union. Disastrous though the incident was at the time, with several workers killed in the immediate blast, the nuclear fallout created a multitude of long-term health problems including radiation sickness, cataracts and increased incidence of leukaemia and thyroid cancers which international medical experts believed would continue for 'many more years'.[30] It was not unreasonable to suppose that a similar accident in Scotland involving the release of radioactive materials would have produced a similarly dire outcome.

There is little doubt that the government took very seriously the opposition posed by CND and the various peace camps. Heseltine's initiative in establishing DS19 was continued by his successor George Younger, who had served in the Argylls during the Korean War and had previously been Secretary of State for Scotland between 1979 and 1986. He became Defence Secretary after Heseltine suddenly and unexpectedly resigned in January over a government refusal to back his proposal for a European consortium to take over the ailing helicopter manufacturer Westland. On taking office Younger reinforced his predecessor's robust approach towards handling CND, arguing that the nuclear deterrent had 'secured peace for us ever since the last war . . . don't let us throw it away'. Younger was also keen to reinforce the idea that Trident was good for Scotland by creating jobs and he fully supported the policy of building four submarines instead of three.[31] Even when there were technical glitches during the first test-firing of a D-5 missile on 21 March 1989 Younger remained unruffled by the public failure which took place off the coast of Florida with the missile 'spinning in a cartwheel pattern' after breaking the surface of the sea in the first phase of the launch.[32] He continued to support the new weapon and argued that the test had been a success as it revealed problems ahead of being introduced into service – a second failure in August merely confirmed his views.

By that time the political consensus of Thatcher's third term in office was beginning to unravel and change was in the air. Younger had already decided to leave the government to pursue a business career with the Royal Bank of Scotland, latterly as chairman of the board, a post that had been kept open for him for some five years, but it was not the end of his role in frontline politics. With disaffection about Thatcher's leadership growing within the Conservative Party a challenge was made by a so-called 'stalking horse' candidate, the hitherto little-known backbench MP for Clwyd North-West, Sir Anthony Meyer, and during the election Younger acted as her campaign manager. However, it was not the end of the matter. As expected, Meyer was soundly beaten but by the following year Thatcher's position was becoming increasingly embattled and she was losing the support of backbench MPs, not least because of her increasingly antagonistic attitude towards the emerging European Union. The end-game came in November when, having bided his time since his earlier resignation, Michael Heseltine challenged Thatcher for the leadership of the Conservatives and once again the prime minister turned to Younger to manage her campaign. By then he was deeply embroiled in his work for the bank and was never more than a figurehead, but it mattered not because Thatcher had become a deeply unpopular and divisive figure who had lost the support of her party, many of whose members had come to believe that she was an electoral liability. On 20 November, the first ballot showed that she won 204 votes to Heseltine's 152 (with 16 abstentions), but this was 4 votes short of the margin required and although she was determined to continue the fight to remain in power the harsh reality was she no longer commanded sufficient support. Two days later she resigned and was replaced by John Major, at that time serving as Chancellor of the Exchequer.

During the latter part of her premiership Thatcher had become something of a hate figure in Scotland. One reason was the collapse of the Conservative vote in the 1980s, with the party seeing its representation fall from 21 to 10 seats in 1987 and its share of the vote dropping to 24 per cent. With the Labour vote increasing to 42.4 per cent and the SNP vote rising to 14 per cent, this allowed opponents to argue that Scotland had voted for left-of-centre parties while being ruled by a right-wing party dominated by English MPs with little interest in Scottish politics. Another reason was that Thatcher was personally unpopular – 'widely loathed, even by some traditional Tories', was the view of the journalist and commentator Andrew Marr.[33] But the overarching reason was the appearance of the community charge, or 'poll tax' as it was characterised by those opposed to the policy which was introduced in 1989, a year earlier than in England and Wales. For many Scots, according to the historian Richard Finlay, 'it was claimed that this was the real evidence that Thatcher really did not care about Scotland and regarded it as a guinea pig for her most extreme policies'.[34] It mattered not that the policy was supposed to address the need to reform the equally contentious local rates structure or that the new system was deemed to be fairer: the poll tax quickly became a useful shorthand for imposed Thatcherite policies and it led not only to a long-lasting outcry in Scotland but also to a sustained campaign of non-payment which was later matched in England and Wales. All this added to an existing dislike of the Conservatives which had been reflected in the 1987 election and would be repeated in 1992, so much so that after his retirement from politics George Younger remarked ruefully that 'the Archangel Gabriel would have been rejected if he was thought to be a Tory'.[35]

All this was happening against a heightened sense of change across Europe, especially in the countries of the Warsaw Pact, each with their own Communist Party but still satellites of the Soviet Union, which provided the ideological glue holding the edifice together. In the early days, in the period after the Second World War, the Stalinist system promoted by Moscow insisted that it could be maintained by coercive cooperation and if necessary, in extremis, by using force, but by the 1980s change was in the air and the Communist empire in eastern Europe was beginning to fragment. Part of the problem was that the Soviet economy could no longer sustain the huge military infrastructure which had been perceived by the West as the Kremlin's greatest asset and which would be used if the Cold War ever became hot. One of the first to notice this change was Ronald Reagan, who said of the Soviet Union when he came to power that it possessed a 'political structure that no longer responds to its economic base, a society where productive forces are hampered by political ones' and that it was doomed to come second best to his own country.[36] Another part of the problem was that reform was afoot and the variegated entity that was the Warsaw Pact was moving inexorably towards change, albeit with the various components moving at different speeds. A quarter of a century earlier Hungary and Czechoslovakia had resisted Moscow rule only to be subjugated by the mailed fist, but a new awakening was now on the horizon; the Baltic States were also restless and keen to end their enforced annexation; within a decade Yugoslavia would have broken up; only East Germany seemed to be demanding resistance to change. But the biggest harbinger was in Poland, where the emergence of the Solidarity trade union under Lech Wałęsa in 1980 presaged the fall of Communist rule first in Poland itself and then across Eastern Europe. Suddenly all the old certainties were being abandoned; even the Soviet Union was in a state of flux with its moderate new leader Mikhail Gorbachev promoting the policies of Glasnost (openness) and Perestroika (economic restructuring). All this was happening at such a bewildering speed that participants in the process such as Anatoly Dobrynin, Soviet Ambassador to Washington, claimed that Gorbachev and his colleagues 'never foresaw that the whole of eastern Europe would fly out of the Soviet orbit within months or that the Warsaw Pact would crumble so soon'.[37] Suddenly, at long last, it seemed that the Cold War could be consigned to history.

11

The Walls Came Tumbling Down

THAT THE COLD WAR started coming to an end was due in no small measure to the emergence of two very different leaders in Washington and Moscow – Ronald Reagan and Mikhail Gorbachev. It would be stretching the truth to claim that they alone were responsible for ending the Cold War but they were certainly significant parts of an ever-changing jigsaw that started falling into place in the 1980s. Both came from disparate political backgrounds, one being a Republican conservative who was sworn in for a second term in office as US president in 1985, the other a Communist who had been voted General Secretary of the Communist Party of the Soviet Union that same year, but during the course of four summit meetings between 1985 and 1988 both came to a subtle understanding that they had arrived concurrently at a point in history which could end the long years of Cold War confrontation. On the face of it neither leader had anything in common other than a personal determination to make their talks successful and a desire to prevent any move which might lead to the outbreak of a nuclear war. More than any other factor, that was the driving force propelling their talks in the mid-1980s. During his first term as president, Reagan had anathematised the Soviet Union as the 'evil empire' and authorised increases in US defence spending, including the controversial development of the Strategic Defense Initiative (SDI or 'Star Wars') which envisaged the creation of an advanced anti-missile system utilising space-based defences to destroy incoming ballistic missiles thereby obviating the principle of instant retaliation. It seems that Reagan was genuinely alarmed by the prospect of mutually assured destruction, describing it as a 'suicide pact', and believed that the global defensive shield provided by SDI would make nuclear war impossible.

Gorbachev, too, was impelled by missionary zeal. While his background was that of a typical Soviet apparatchik who had risen through the Party ranks, he had also gained a reputation as a moderniser and reformer and was quickly marked for greater things. In 1978 he was summoned to Moscow to join the Politburo, the country's executive council, and while his arrival was initially ignored in the West it soon became clear that he was a rising star who was determined to introduce change. One of the first leaders to recognise his potential was Margaret Thatcher, who invited him to London in December 1984 – he arrived accompanied by his wife Raisa, itself an unusual occurrence for a Soviet leader – and the British prime minister promptly told the press, 'I'm cautiously optimistic. I like Mr Gorbachev, we can do business together.'[1] The visit also included a trip to Edinburgh where he was due to be entertained at a banquet in the Great Hall of Edinburgh Castle, which contains an ancient feature known as the 'Laird's Lug' (ear), a ventilation hole above the fireplace which had been used in the distant past as a covert listening device.[2] So alarmed were the accompanying Soviet security officers that they demanded it be bricked up ahead of the dinner, but the precaution was unnecessary as Gorbachev had to return to Moscow following the death of the Soviet Defence Minister Dmitri Ustinov, a Stalinist hardliner. Even so, the visit provided his host George Younger, at that time still Scottish Secretary, with a useful insight into his guest's current thinking. When he asked Gorbachev what he would tell the press about his unexpected return to Moscow the initial response was the traditional Soviet reaction of silence but, pressed by Younger, he relented, saying 'I shall tell the truth. I shall tell that Ustinov has died.' Later Younger would claim that 'he had given the future Soviet leader his first lesson in democracy'.[3]

The message was duly passed on to Washington and within a few months Gorbachev had succeeded the ailing Konstantin Chernenko as Party Secretary, thereby ending the Kremlin's gerontocracy – his predecessors were Leonid Brezhnev and Yuri Andropov, both elderly and in poor health – and encouraging Reagan to think about responding in a positive fashion. Not only did Vice-President George Bush and Secretary of State George Schultz attend Chernenko's funeral but Reagan announced that it was 'high time' that he met the new leader and the first steps were taken to negotiate a series of summit conferences. The White House approach did not imply American weakness; on the contrary, Reagan believed that he could gain leverage over the Soviet Union by getting to know Gorbachev and by applying pressure on a number of fronts, including the demonstration of growing US military superiority. It helped that the Soviet Union's existing leadership had become sclerotic and that within the country there were growing calls for a change of direction and an acceleration of economic and social reforms. Perversely, Gorbachev's rise to power had come about at a time when East–West relations had deteriorated in the previous year, leading to a belief on both sides that each was preparing a first strike which would lead to all-out nuclear war. Certainly, the portents were not encouraging. By the middle of the decade it had become apparent that Soviet forces had become bogged down in Afghanistan, where the USA had been lending covert support to the mujahideen opposed to the occupation and using them as proxies in the wider struggle against the 'forces of evil', notably by supplying Stinger surface-to-air missiles to bring down Soviet aircraft. As casualties began rising the Afghan war became unpopular at home, putting pressure on Moscow to withdraw its forces and extricate itself from a seemingly unwinnable conflict. The Soviet economy was also in trouble, largely as a result of unrealistically high defence expenditure. The reformist movement in Poland instigated by Solidarity was also destabilising Moscow's control of its Warsaw Pact allies. To add to the Soviet woes, NATO had begun deploying Pershing and cruise missiles in Europe, persuading the Kremlin to believe that conflict was inevitable and would be caused by an American first strike, or, as Andropov told East German Foreign Minister Erich Mielke in July 1981, 'the US is preparing for war, but it is not willing to start a war. They are not building factories and palaces in order to destroy them. They are striving for military superiority in order to "check" us and then declare "checkmate" against us without starting a war.'[4]

In that tense atmosphere uncontrolled disagreements or misunderstandings were always going to be inflammatory, especially in Moscow where the Soviet intelligence services consistently warned the Kremlin that an attack by the West was imminent. The first flashpoint came on the night of 31 August 1983, when a Soviet air force Su-15 fighter shot down a Korean Airlines Boeing 747 airliner, Flight KAL 007, over the Kamchatka Peninsula in the Russian far east, killing 269 passengers and crew while it was on a regular flight from New York to Seoul and had strayed into Soviet airspace. At the time the Soviets alleged that the South Korean airliner was on a spying mission over Soviet territory and although this was later changed to claims that it was a genuine accident caused by nervous local commanders, the shooting-down of KAL 007 pushed the relationship between the two sides into a new low. Worse followed three months later when NATO mounted a regular ten-day military exercise in West Germany codenamed 'Able Archer 83', which was designed to practise command and staff procedures, with emphasis on the transition from conventional to nuclear weapons. This was an annual occurrence and one which the Soviets would have been expecting, but in the heightened atmosphere of November 1983 it caused panic in Moscow because Soviet military planners thought that NATO might launch a first-strike attack under the cover of a military exercise; as a result defence forces were placed on special alert in Hungary and East Germany. Nuclear weapons were loaded onto aircraft and SSBNs went to prearranged positions below the Arctic ice cap.

Arguments still rage about how close to Armageddon the world came during Able Archer 83.[5] There continue to be doubts about whether Moscow was on a hair trigger and was prepared to retaliate or the Soviet leadership made use of the incident as part of a wider campaign to forestall the deployment of Pershing missiles, but one thing cannot be denied. Thanks to the presence in London of the KGB double agent Colonel Oleg Gordievsky, who was local head of the KGB (*rezident*) but had been recruited by MI6 a dozen years earlier, the West had been given a unique insight into the Kremlin's thinking at one of the most dangerous periods in the Cold War. At this point in history when the Soviet leader, the paranoid Yuri Andropov, was convinced that Able Archer was a cover for a pre-emptive NATO nuclear strike, Gordievsky was able to convince his Western masters otherwise by explaining the distrustful atmosphere in the Kremlin, and that advice was accepted.[6] The stand-off came to an end when the exercise concluded on 11 November but the incident, unheralded and unnoticed by the wider public, had a profound effect on Reagan, who had a horror of doing anything which might cause a nuclear war. In the aftermath, as tempers cooled, he announced his intention to initiate a fresh dialogue with Moscow, thus beginning an unstoppable period of rapprochement. According to the official historian of MI5 it had been 'the most dangerous moment since the Cuban missile crisis of 1962', and that it did not spark a third world war had everything to do with the confidence which was the placed in Gordievsky, who eventually defected from the Soviet Union in 1985 to take up residence in the UK. From those unpromising beginnings came the summit meetings which led to something approaching peace.

The optimistic mood was helped by the involvement of several widely travelled and influential private individuals, including Lord Ritchie Calder, who amongst many other responsibilities served as president of the Scotland–USSR Friendship Society between 1967 and his death in 1982. A lifelong socialist and peace activist who was born in Forfar and trained as a journalist in Dundee, Peter Ritchie Calder also held a chair in International Relations at Edinburgh University and had been one of the founders of CND. In October 1980, at a time when relations with the Soviet Union were tense due to the US boycott of the Moscow Olympic Games in response to the invasion of Afghanistan, Ritchie Calder led a Society delegation to the Soviet Union and perceived the need to maintain dialogue on the subject of 'Survival in a Nuclear Age'. His discussions produced mixed messages from his hosts and he feared that he had been rebuffed, but out of this initiative came the 'Edinburgh Conversations', a series of annual discussions held on alternate years in Edinburgh and Moscow which provided a channel of communication at a time when others were frozen and promoted confidence-building on both sides. It worked because the Conversations had the backing of Edinburgh University, thereby giving the initiative academic respectability, and because of the presence of the polymathic historian and analyst Professor John Erickson, who had excellent contacts at the highest level on both sides and enjoyed a long-established and credible relationship with the Soviet leadership.

One of the intellectual giants of Cold War scholarship, Erickson was the Director of the Centre for Defence Studies in Edinburgh University and a fluent Russian speaker who had built up an unrivalled knowledge of the Soviet armed forces during the Second World War, having been granted unique access to Soviet archives and to the evidence of retired commanders. After graduating in history from St John's College, Cambridge University, he taught at St Anthony's College, Oxford, and at the universities of St Andrews, Manchester and Indiana before transferring to teach defence studies at Edinburgh University in 1967. He also enjoyed the confidence of the Soviets' British and American counterparts and was much in demand for advice and insights in the upper echelons of the NATO command structure. As a historian, his monument is the two-volume history of the Second World War, *The Road to Stalingrad* (1975) and *The Road to Berlin* (1982), which his student and fellow military historian Christopher Bellamy described as 'unsurpassed in any language, drawing on German and Soviet sources, and turning volumes of minute detail into epic prose'.[7] That reputation counted for much when the Edinburgh Conversations were initiated, and it was clear from the outset that Erickson would be a central figure in helping to make the ensuing sessions realistic and credible. The first Conversation took place in Edinburgh between 5 and 7 October 1981, where the British delegation consisted of Erickson, Ritchie Calder, General Sir Hugh Beach, formerly Commandant of the Army Staff College in Camberley and Dr John Burnett, the Principal of Edinburgh University, who chaired the meeting, while the Soviet delegation was led by Professor Vitaly Kobysh of the Department of International Information of the Communist Party and included the editor of the newspaper *Pravda* and two army generals. So successful was the opening Conversation that a second set was held in Moscow the following year from 25 September to 2 October and during this session the Soviets asked for an American delegate to be added; this arrived in the person of Colonel Lynn Hansen USAF, a former student of Erickson's who was also an expert on arms control and was later nominated US ambassador to the Conventional Armed Forces in Europe (CFE) Joint Consultative Group arms reduction talks.[8]

Again, this was considered a success and was followed by a third set in Edinburgh from 17 to 22 September 1983 which were held a fortnight after the shooting down of KAL 007 and began in an atmosphere of mutual suspicion. As remembered by Malcolm Mackintosh, a fellow Soviet expert and working at the time as an Assistant Secretary to the Cabinet Office, 'the challenge was regarded by Erickson as an important one, and he used his authority and friendly relationships with all concerned to keep the delegations together – and talking'.[9] The Edinburgh Conversations continued annually until the seventh meeting, which began on 4 December 1988 and was influenced by the continuing thaw in the political and military relationships between the two sides. Although an eighth Conversation was planned for 1989 the British delegation argued that the international situation had improved to such an extent that state-to-state diplomatic relations had taken over the aims of the academic links and that therefore the Conversations should be ended. This was agreed in London, Washington and Moscow but as Mackintosh maintained in his appreciation of Erickson for the British Academy, 'there can be no doubt that they [the Edinburgh Conversations] contributed significantly to the retention of worthwhile contacts between East and West during a period of very tense diplomatic and military relationships'.[10] Erickson also became the epicentre of a group of Western experts such as Hansen and Mackintosh who were Russian-speaking historians or had direct experience of working with the Soviet armed forces and were therefore respected by their counterparts in Moscow. It was not always a smooth passage. Mackintosh, a Scot, first visited the Soviet Union in 1973 as part of a delegation led by Foreign Secretary Sir Alec Douglas-Home and was denounced by Soviet officials as 'a falsifier of history'. Later he was one of the experts who advised Mrs Thatcher to begin a dialogue with Gorbachev and later still, after the Cold War had ended, he received an apology from Moscow for the slur on his professionalism.

The decision to end the Edinburgh Conversations was timeous because by the end of 1988 it was clear that a sea change had taken place in the relationship between the Soviet Union and the rest of the world and this was marked by the two leaders' willingness to meet to 'escape the prison of mutual terror' as Reagan so graphically described Cold War confrontation. The first meeting began in Geneva on 19 November 1985 and it would be fair to say that it got off to a frosty start, with Reagan attacking the Soviets on their human rights record while Gorbachev was critical of the American policy of fomenting an arms race involving the use of space. Fortunately, both men seemed to get on well together at a personal level and were able to develop a rapport which allowed them to announce on the second day that in principle they would work towards reducing their countries' nuclear arsenals by half, with a joint communiqué agreeing that 'a nuclear war cannot be won and must never be fought'. Observers could not help noticing that despite their differences of opinion both men were relaxed in each other's company, so much so that it seemed likely that the dialogue would continue. It did not turn out quite like that though, as decades of suspicion meant that Gorbachev's offer to reduce Soviet nuclear weapons in Europe was regarded by Washington as little more than propaganda. Despite the tensions it was agreed that they would meet the following year and eventually a second summit was announced to take place in October 1986 in Reykjavik in Iceland, symbolically halfway between the two countries. During the discussions Reagan made the astonishing proposal to eliminate all US nuclear weapons within ten years but this was balanced by his equally dramatic refusal to yield ground on SDI. Although the Reykjavik summit ended with no agreement, Reagan insisted that its true significance was that 'we got as close as we did'. (To put this into context, in the following year, 1987, John Erickson visited Washington where he was informed that the Americans were keen to see the Edinburgh Conversations continue for the time being.)

There were other setbacks, especially for Reagan, whose administration was plunged into scandal at the end of 1986 by the revelation of an endlessly complicated arms deal known as the Iran-Contra Affair which involved the provision of weapons to right-wing Contra guerrillas in Nicaragua using Iran, a sworn US enemy, as cover. The exposure of this dubious and illegal plot caused huge embarrassment to Reagan, who famously quipped that it was 'going to make a great movie one day'. Although his credibility had been eroded by the scandal he remained in office and took advantage of a visit to Berlin in June 1987 as part of the celebrations for the city's 750th anniversary. Sensing that the Soviets were wilting under the pressure of their internal financial problems and the growing demands for arms reduction, Reagan sidestepped diplomatic advice and produced one of the great iconic speeches of the Cold War, standing at the Brandenburg Gate and laying down a direct challenge to his opposite number:

There is one sign the Soviets can make that would be unmistakable, that would advance dramatically the cause of freedom and peace.

General Secretary Gorbachev, if you seek peace, if you seek prosperity for the Soviet Union and Eastern Europe, if you seek liberalisation, come here to this gate.

Mr Gorbachev, open this gate!

Mr Gorbachev, tear down this wall![11]

There was some optimism that the words would bear fruit as throughout that year progress had been made on the arms reduction talks which had stalled in Reykjavik. First the West German government decided unilaterally to remove Pershing missiles from their territory; Gorbachev responded by uncoupling his long-standing dislike of SDI from his support for arms control. This concession paved the way for agreement on the Intermediate-Range Nuclear Forces (INF) Treaty, which eliminated all nuclear and conventional missiles, as well as their launchers, with ranges of up to 3,420 miles, a move which condemned to history the Soviet SS-20 missiles and their US Pershing and cruise counterparts, whose deployments had sparked the confrontation in the first place. Sea-launched missiles were excepted, which allowed the Scotland-based submarines to remain operational from the bases on the Clyde, but for the first time there would be intensive verification on both sides of the divide. To great fanfare the INF Treaty was signed in the White House on 8 December 1987 and more than any other measure it helped thaw the Cold War as it was the first arms-control treaty to require an actual reduction in nuclear arsenals rather than merely restricting their proliferation. All told, 2,692 missiles were destroyed under the INF terms.

It was not the end of the Cold War but it was the beginning of the end. After the INF Treaty was signed there could be no turning back and it was followed by the Strategic Arms Reduction Treaty (START 1) of 31 July 1991, which signalled the abolition of the Poseidon missile system. Although Gorbachev was beginning to face some internal resistance to his reforms the concept of Glasnost had taken hold and was beginning to spark changes in people's attitudes and ambitions. The pace of change also encouraged emergent nationalism in the Soviet satellites, especially in the Baltic states and the southern Islamic republics, where there was a growing desire to break free from Soviet control. Further west the two Germanys were also on the move towards reunification and the removal of the 40-year-old Iron Curtain. This process accelerated in the middle of August 1989 when the Hungarian government effectively opened its border with Austria thus allowing East German citizens to use their country as a transit point. A similar move was triggered in Czechoslovakia and was followed by mass demonstrations in East Germany itself. On 18 October President Erich Honecker resigned and his regime began to implode. Three weeks later, on 9 November, the border in Berlin was breached as people on both sides of the Berlin Wall began to pull it down and stream across to the other side. It was a historic occasion: the fall of the Berlin Wall, the most significant symbol of the Cold War, turned out to be the first step towards German reunification and this was formally concluded on 3 October 1990. In the aftermath of this astounding event other Eastern European countries began to slough off their dependence on the Soviet Union and to reject the Communist political philosophy which they had shared during the Cold War as members of the Warsaw Pact.

By then the US had a new president in George Bush, Reagan's deputy, and he brought in a new foreign policy team to review the relationship with Moscow, notably James Baker as Secretary of State who, after a shaky start, developed a good working relationship with his Soviet opposite number Eduard Shevardnadze, a young Georgian who had been made Foreign Minister in 1985 and was also a reformist. Bush and Baker were naturally cautious about the turn of events and were minded to adopt an attitude of safety-first and see what was happening in Europe before making further concessions. This was not to Gorbachev's liking – he complained frequently of Washington's tardiness in creating a new US–USSR partnership – but he too was under pressure both from reactionaries who deplored the rapid rate of reform and also from the growing unrest in the Warsaw Pact countries. This would previously have been met with force, as had happened during the insurrections in Hungary in 1956 and Czechoslovakia in 1968. Putting tanks on the streets of any Warsaw Pact country was not an option in 1989 and the faltering regimes soon realised that they were on their own and could not rely on intervention by Moscow: in Prague the government resigned en masse, the dissident playwright Václav Havel was released from prison and following free elections was made President of Czechoslovakia. To add to the sense of justice Alexander Dubček, who had led the Prague Spring revolution in 1968, was elected speaker of the new federal assembly. At the end of the year revolution broke out in Romania, bringing to an end four decades of Communist rule and leading to the trial and execution on Christmas Day of the hard-line Stalinist president, Nicolae Ceaușescu and his wife Elena. The violence in Bucharest, in which 1,104 people were killed, provided a precautionary warning of what could have happened elsewhere if other Communist governments had attempted to hang on to power as Ceaușescu had done.

Ceaușescu was the last Stalinist leader to be toppled and to the last he attempted to hold on by using force in the shape of his much-feared secret police, the Securitate. It was perhaps fitting that he met his end shortly after the last summit of the Cold War round of meetings which was held in the storm-tossed harbour of Valletta in Malta at the beginning of December where, according to one Soviet official, Bush and Gorbachev agreed to bury 'the Cold war at the bottom of the Mediterranean Sea'. That turned out not to be the case as there were still twists and turns to be faced across the divide, but it was a neat summation of the pace of change. As the century's last decade began, the Baltic states began declaring their independence from Soviet rule and they were followed by Hungary, which held free elections at the end of March 1990. These moves tested to the utmost Gorbachev's powers of leadership as there was still opposition from left and right about the pace of change – the former bemoaning the slow reform progress and the latter complaining that it was taking place at all. The reunification of Germany also caused difficulties, not least because of its continuing membership of NATO, but it helped that the new administration led by Chancellor Helmut Kohl agreed not to station nuclear weapons in former East Germany and promised to meet the cost of removing half a million Soviet troops from the country and resettling them in the Soviet Union. While this was happening the new world order was put to the test in the Middle East, where Kuwait was invaded by Iraq, a long-term Soviet ally, and this was opposed by the United Nations with the issue of Resolution 678, which gave the Iraqis until 15 January 1991 to remove their forces from the country or face expulsion from coalition forces under US command. Once upon a time this could have created a flashpoint, but Moscow joined the condemnation of the Iraqi invasion and when Baker travelled to Moscow to meet Shevardnadze Soviet support was readily forthcoming and the short, sharp and successful war could not have been fought without it.

Closer to the Soviet capital, as the constituent parts continued to demand independence, Gorbachev could find no support for his proposals for the creation of a new federation of sovereign republics. He was also facing the end of the line as backing ebbed away from him and in August 1991 the inevitable happened when a coup was mounted against him and he became a virtual prisoner in his holiday villa at Foros on the Black Sea. Help and deliverance came for him in the unlikely figure of Boris Yeltsin, who had emerged as the coming man following his earlier election as the leader of the Russian Federation which had come into being in June. Gorbachev was allowed to return to Moscow, but his political career was at an end. On 24 August he resigned as leader of the Soviet Communist Party, which now had no further authority and dissolved itself a week later. In place of the Soviet Union came the Commonwealth of Independent States (CIS), which was founded on 8 December 1991 by Russia, Belarus (Byelorussia) and Ukraine. Just over a fortnight later, on 25 December 1991, the Soviet Union passed into history. The Red Flag with its gold hammer and sickle was lowered for the last time and the Cold War was finally over. To ram home the point the US announced that funds would be made available to help former

Soviet republics dismantle their nuclear weapons, although within three months there was a reminder that little had changed in the UK when the first Trident submarine HMS *Vanguard* was rolled out at Barrow-in-Furness on 4 March 1992. By the time it came into service and arrived at its home port of Faslane the Soviet Union had been dead for two years: as one commentator put it, she and her sister boats had 'arrived too late for the party'.[12] The last to arrive, HMS *Vengeance,* came into operational service in November 1999, by which time the UK government had announced that Moscow, St Petersburg (Leningrad) and other former Soviet cities had been dropped as targets.

As happened in many parts of the world, the end of the Cold War changed Scotland in many told and untold ways. The most obvious transformation was the departure of the American submarines from the Holy Loch. Throughout the confrontation the sight of various submarine tenders and the huge *Los Alamos* dry dock plus the assorted small boats and the submarines themselves had provided incontrovertible evidence of the American presence in Scotland. When the Polaris boats and their crews had arrived in 1961 they sparked noisy protests and remained a focus for feelings ranging from outright dislike through resigned dismay to complete indifference but over the decades they had become accepted if not entirely loved. Their departure had been fondly anticipated by CND and by others on the political left but when the moment came it was accompanied by a sense of anticlimax balanced by fears that an uncertain future was in the offing. The mood was caught by the uncompromising headline on the front page of the *Dunoon Observer* the day after the decision was announced on 6 February 1991: 'Base Bombshell'. Over the years the newspaper had recorded the comings and goings at the 'base' (as it was always known locally) and the main points of interest (both high and low), and through its correspondence columns, intriguingly called the 'Safety Valve', it balanced the views of those who had welcomed the arrival of the American submarines as guarantors of peace during the Cold War and those who believed that they and their missiles were the work of the devil.[13] The announcement that they were leaving was hardly a surprise as the collapse of Communism in Eastern Europe and the Soviet Union had been well enough documented and understood. By then, too, it was clear that the newer Trident D-5 missiles with their longer range would take over from Poseidon under the terms of the START 1 Treaty and make Refit Site One redundant as the US Navy would no longer need a forward operating base on the other side of the Atlantic, but the news still caused a shock as not only did it seem to have arrived so precipitately but also because the base would close within 15 months.

Suddenly the local community had to come to terms with the fact that in just over a year's time some 4,000 'Yanks' would be gone, taking with them around 1,000 families as well as the naval infrastructure which had become as familiar a sight as the surrounding hills. All that would be left would be 342 leased houses which had been used by Navy personnel and their dependants, mainly in the lochside village of Sandbank. Also going would be their spending power in the Cowal peninsula as well as an estimated 240 jobs which were filled by local people. In short, a time of dislocation lay ahead as the US Navy made ready to abandon one of its larger overseas bases.

The departure was helped in that unlike similar American naval presences in Japan or the Middle East the Holy Loch base was formed almost entirely from seaborne assets and could be readily dismantled and transported back to the US without further ado. Some were easier to move than others. Whereas the submarines, the tender and the resident tugs USS *Apopka* and USS *Saugus* were able to leave under their own power, the huge USS *Los Alamos* dry dock had to be partially dismantled before being transported back to the US in February 1992 on board the *Wijsmuller Mighty Servant III*, a 27,000-ton specialist semi-submersible heavy lift ship which was also used to carry oil rigs.

The last tender at Refit Site One was the USS *Simon Lake*, which had arrived at Holy Loch in May 1987 to replace the USS *Hunley*. Launched in 1964, she had already served in Scotland between 1966 and 1970 and when she sailed down and out of the Firth of Clyde on 6 March 1992 under the command of Captain William J. Riffer she brought to an end 31 years of US naval activity in Scottish waters. Three months later, on 1 June, Submarine Squadron 14 under the command of Captain Ronald D. Gumbert was deactivated as the longest serving Polaris/Poseidon squadron, but not before the last two Poseidon submarines had left on their final operational patrols from Refit Site One before sailing back to Groton in the USA and retirement. These were the USS *Ulysses S. Grant* and the USS *Kamehameha*; on 9 November, the USS *Will Rogers* became the last Poseidon boat to leave the Holy Loch when she departed for New London in Connecticut after being serviced and prior to being deactivated and prepared for scrapping at the US Navy's Nuclear-Powered Ship and Submarine

Recycling Program at Bremerton, Washington State. A small group of American naval families gathered on the shore to wave her off and they were joined by CND demonstrators who 'whooped in delight' as the *Will Rogers* headed out of the loch. Symbolically, the submarine was followed briefly by a small inflatable boat 'manned by three CND protestors' – a telling reminder of the demonstrations that had greeted the arrival of the first tender, USS *Proteus*, all those years ago.[14] Amongst those demonstrating was Keith Bovey, president of the Scottish Campaign for Nuclear Disarmament, who had taken part in the original demonstrations in 1961 and who now told reporters that he would 'welcome Americans back to Scotland as tourists'.[15]

That was a reasonable summary of the feelings at the time. While very few local people were sorry to see the US Navy go, the three decades of their presence left a footprint which could not be ignored. It could not have been otherwise as the sailors had forged links with the community which were both social and economic and long outlasted the 'American Years'. The web-based historians of 'Sub Ron 14' noted that while sailors were used to this kind of turnaround with thoughts turning to home, duty done and pride in achievement, the leaving of Submarine Refit One was different because it produced memories of 'friendships abbreviated and opportunities missed'. Bearing that sentiment in mind, a farewell ceremony was held on 21 February to mark the occasion and every American sailor was presented with a certificate marking their service in suitably self-mocking language: 'Having displayed special talents while residing in Scotland, you are hereby recognised for your attainments in such noble pursuits as left-side driving, pub crawling, digesting fish and chips, midgie fighting in summer and dodging horizontal raindrops on the pier'.[16]

With the departure of the US Navy the Holy Loch went back to what it had been before the Cold War – a picturesque west-coast sea loch ringed by high tree-clad hills – but that was just for the picture postcards. Inevitably, after three decades, there was a considerable amount of detritus lying around, especially in the Ardnadam Pier area where the US Navy had had several on-shore sites such as a library and clinic. In his 1970s study, Giarchi had noted local complaints about the debris left by the sailors on- and off-shore, including the rusting carcase of a car complete with US number plates.[17] Robertson's Yard at Sandbank, the famed builders of wooden racing yachts, was also affected by the mess but it had gone into liquidation in 1980, with the lower and upper

yards being sold for housing development in 1993 and 2003 respectively. All too quickly the naval pier at Ardnadam fell into disrepair. It
had been built in 1858 and had the distinction of once being the longest
pier for Clyde steamers during the heyday of the Victorian trips 'doon
the watter'. Just as bad as the waste on the shore was the lazy custom of
simply dumping rubbish overboard from the tender ship and the visiting submarines, with the result that in 1997 – long after the US Navy
had left – two reports commissioned by the Ministry of Defence found
that the Holy Loch was one of the filthiest stretches of coastal water in
the world: 'Almost a quarter of the floor of the loch, which is 4 kilometres long and a kilometre wide, is covered with rubbish. There are
several piles of debris up to six metres high around the sites in the
middle of the loch where the dry dock and depot ship were moored. An
MoD underwater video survey last year identified scores of different
items, including a huge boiler, girders, ladders, air ducts, oil drums,
washing machines and nine shipwrecks.'[18]

Worse, as journalist Rob Edwards revealed, much of the detritus was
toxic and its presence was blamed for the elevated levels of trace metal
organic pollutants found in the sea bed. This waste would be difficult to
clear up comprehensively and above all safely, and it was not until 1998
that an £11 million clean-up operation got underway, funded by the
Ministry of Defence; as a result some 2,700 tonnes of rubbish and debris
were removed by 2001.[19] During the work there was heated debate
locally about the rationale for the clean-up with concerns being expressed
that getting rid of the rubbish could make matters worse by removing
the silt and exposing possible radioactive material. However, under the
Host Nation Agreement, the UK government had a legal obligation to
clean up debris left by guest forces and as the press reported on the first
day of the operation the powerful electromagnetic crane on the salvage
barge *Molly McGill* 'yielded nothing more sinister than broken pipes,
cable, old hand tools and two unidentified, rusty gas cylinders, which
could hold oxygen, freon, or acetylene'.[20] Noise pollution had also been a
problem, from the constant but often comforting sound of the engines
of the liberty boats as they traversed the loch to the frequently annoying
thrumming of the engines from the tenders which reached a crescendo
in January 1976 when both *Canopus* and *Holland* were on station
simultaneously, prompting complaints from the Sandbank residents.[21]
Curiously, most people only became aware of the noise pollution once
the Americans had departed and it had disappeared.

Arguments also raged about the economic impact of the withdrawal, with fears about any decline caused by the absence of American spending power being balanced by a belief that the presence of the US Navy had held back the economy of the Cowal peninsula. Returning service personnel expecting to come across familiar landmarks amongst the local pubs, hotels and cafés found that many had closed down by the end of the decade but a year after the departure a local government official told a visiting American journalist from Connecticut, the home state for the US submarine fleet, that far from being devastated Dunoon was prospering as a result: 'Dunoon was caught in a time warp, it was a dependency economy. The businesses in the area did not have to be competitive. They did not have to provide a good service. The base closing will allow us to bring Dunoon up to date.'[22] The town also benefited from the sale of renovated properties previously owned or rented by US Navy families; when they came on the market they were considerably less expensive than others in the area and allowed incomers to regard Dunoon as a base for commuting by ferry and train via Gourock to work in Glasgow.

Five years later the second-largest American presence in Scotland closed on 30 September 1997 when the Stars and Stripes and a Royal Air Force ensign were lowered in the 'watery sunshine' at RAF Edzell, thus ending 37 years of service by the US Navy in Angus. Over 100 people attended the simple decommissioning service, which was presided over by the station's last commanding officer, Lieutenant-Commander Sharon Channis. The pipes played and the assembled audience sang together the haunting song of farewell, 'We're No Awa Tae Bide Awa'; then to everyone's pleasure a specially commissioned commemorative stone monument was unveiled to record the fact that 'This was the site of the United States of America Naval Security Group'. That was not all. As the commanding officer said in her closing remarks, 'the "family" of NSGA Edzell has contributed over half a million pounds sterling to local charities, given over 10,000 pints of blood to the Scottish blood bank, and married over 300 members, male and female, from the local communities'.[23] She also reinforced the fact that the base had been left in an ergonomically sound condition and she voiced the hope that friendships made over the years would be continued. As was the case with Holy Loch, the coming of the internet eased this process and veterans from both bases soon created websites and later used social media forums such as YouTube and Facebook to keep in touch with their former hosts. At the same time the American security and signals intelligence infrastructure across Scotland was also dismantled or reduced as the need to keep a frontline presence in the country diminished due to the lowering of the threat level as well as the advent of technological advances which allowed the automation of monitoring stations. In Caithness the US Navy closed its communications centres at Forss and West Murkle in 1992 and the northern microwave relay stations associated with Edzell were returned to British control the following year – Kinnaber, Clochandighter, Inverbervie and Craigowl Hill – as was the communications centre on Mormond Hill. In the latter case the site was turned over to BT for commercial use.

It was not just the American connection that was being revised. With the end of the Cold War the British government started looking for a 'peace dividend', in other words savings which could be made from the defence budget to reflect the changed strategic situation. There was nothing new in this kind of thinking as throughout British history wars have been followed by reductions in the size of armed forces and the axing of military personnel. The end of the Cold War was no different. Shorn of the need to defend Western Europe from the Soviet threat there was no longer any reason to station large and expensive land and air forces in Germany. In 1994, the garrison was reduced in size and BAOR's name was changed to British Forces Germany, with a further announcement that the permanent deployment would end in 2020. At the same time the diminution of the Soviet naval threat called for a reconfiguration of NATO's maritime assets, especially anti-submarine warfare destroyers and frigates. The case for revised thinking was put by the new Defence Secretary Tom King in the House of Commons on 25 July 1991 following a NATO summit in London: 'Europe has entered a new, promising era,' he said. 'This alliance must and will adapt.'[24] Having promised a wide-ranging debate on the subject, King, who had succeeded Younger in the post, let it be known that the review would be known as 'Options for Change'. It soon became clear that this innocuous title was a euphemism for deep cuts, especially in personnel, at the expense of preserving equipment and that the bulk of these would be visited upon the Army, which would be reduced from 155,000 to 116,000 soldiers; the infantry would lose 17 of its 55 battalions through a process of amalgamation. Hopes that the worst could be avoided by the successful Gulf War at the beginning of 1991 were dashed when several of the regiments involved in the operation were earmarked for amalgamation to enable the size of the infantry and cavalry to be reduced. Because of this process many famous names were slated for removal from the *Army List* but although historical longevity is no reason to resist the march of time the imposition of the Options for Change review caused considerable public disquiet and dismay, especially in Scotland, where regimental attachments ran deep. When it was announced in July 1991 that two sets of Scottish regiments would be ordered to amalgamate – The Royal Scots with The King's Own Scottish Borderers and Queen's Own Highlanders with The Gordon Highlanders – immediate steps were taken to protest the decision and have it reversed. A well-organised and high-profile campaign, Keep Our Scottish Battalions, was initiated under the chairmanship of Lieutenant-General Sir John Macmillan, a Gordon Highlander and a former GOC Scotland, and partly as a result of the campaign and partly because of the need to retain personnel at a time of unrest in the Balkans the amalgamation of the two Lowland regiments was cancelled on 3 February 1993, together with the proposed amalgamation of The Cheshire Regiment with The Staffordshire Regiment in England. However, the second Scottish amalgamation was ordered to proceed, even though it was only 34 years since the earlier amalgamation of The Seaforth Highlanders and Cameron Highlanders to form Queen's Own Highlanders. Later still, in 2006, there was further change when the surviving Scottish infantry regiments were amalgamated as the multi-battalion Royal Regiment of Scotland which combined five (later four) Regular Army battalions and two Territorial (later Army Reserve) battalions.

It was not just in the Army that reform was the order of the day during the reconfiguration of the armed forces following the end of the Cold War. In Scotland the most dramatic changes were in the Royal Navy and the RAF, where the senior Scottish naval and air force commanders lost their NATO roles and the joint maritime headquarters at Pitreavie Castle in Fife was closed down and put on sale. In February 1996 its Cold War command bunker was sealed after 55 years of continuous service. The castle was converted into domestic accommodation and the surrounding land became a business park, and all that can be seen of the bunker which would have become the centre of UK operations if Northwood had been destroyed in a war with the Soviet Union is a grass-covered mound. At the same time the Flag Officer Scotland and Northern Ireland (FOSNI) moved his flag to the naval base at

Faslane and his remit was extended temporarily to include northern England as far as the Dee–Humber line. In his new role he was responsible for the following installations and facilities in Scotland: HM Naval Base Faslane, including the Royal Naval Armament Depot at Coulport, Superintendent Ships at Rosyth, NATO Fuel Depots at Campbeltown, Loch Striven and Loch Ewe, the Oil Fuel Depot Garelochhead, HMS *Caledonia* at Rosyth (responsible for support of naval personnel) and the Navy Buildings at Greenock. The Air Officer Scotland and Northern Ireland (AOSNI) also moved, in his case to RAF Leuchars, which remained an air force base until April 2015 when it was transferred to Army control as the home of the Royal Scots Dragoon Guards heavy tank regiment previously based in Germany. In its new guise it was known as Leuchars Station, although the old runways were retained in a reserve role. Another air base disappeared in October 2010, when RAF Kinloss became surplus to requirements following the cancellation of the Nimrod MRA4 maritime patrol aircraft and was handed over to the Army two years later, becoming the home of 39 Engineer Regiment (Air Support), Royal Engineers. This left Lossiemouth as Scotland's only fast-jet base and it took over from Leuchars the responsibility for the Quick Reaction Alert flight for guarding the UK's northern skies. By then low-flying had decreased – from 11,608 hours in 1995 to 7,866 in 2001.

And what of the Soviet Union which had provided the opposition for almost half a century and had helped to fuel the nightmare of nuclear annihilation? At the end of the Cold War it disappeared from history and people had to relearn the habit of referring to Russia. In most cases this involved little more than some linguistic tinkering as throughout the Cold War there was a tendency to refer to the Soviet Union as Russia in much the same way as the UK was often called England, but inevitably perhaps there were exceptions at the formal level. The much-respected Great Britain–USSR Society experienced internal constitutional difficulties in re-emerging as The Britain–Russia Centre and The British East–West Centre, abbreviated to BEWC, but this was as much to do with personalities and funding by the Foreign and Commonwealth Office (FCO) as it was to do with recent history. Confusingly, a non-FCO-funded GB–Russia Society continued as a private membership social and debating society which is proud of the fact that 'it adheres to the ethos of our predecessor organisations'. In that way there was a continuum in the cultural relationships which had been constructed during the Cold War and could have evaporated in its aftermath. However, that was a problem for the West to resolve. As the Soviet Union fell apart and with it its once-feared armed forces were now cut adrift, bereft of political control, there was a period of massive readjustment which had no equal in the NATO countries. For a start there was a pressing need to ensure that former Soviet weaponry did not fall into the wrong hands and this stricture applied especially to the nuclear variety. In 1991 it was estimated that the global stockpile amounted to 52,000 nuclear warheads, 97 per cent of which were in the possession of the USA and the Soviet Union, which possessed the lion's share of some 28,000, mainly as warheads for ICBMs. These were shared with Ukraine (5,000), Belarus (1,200) and Kazakhstan (80), all of whom agreed to begin a process of disarmament which was completed by 1996, with many warheads being returned to Russia.[25] Even so, by the beginning of 2016, 15 years after the end of the conflict, Russia still had an estimated 8,500 nuclear warheads, 1,800 of which were operationally deployed.[26]

This did not mean that nuclear weapons were also passing into history. Russia was still engaged with the USA in bilateral talks about reducing arms further – a new START agreement was in the offing – large numbers of delivery systems were obsolescent and due for replacement with more modern designs and there was a feeling that once the Cold War was over, there was no conceivable need for nuclear weapons in the modern world. Reducing the size of the armed forces also caused problems simply because they were such monolithic organisations whose primary purpose was waging war. With the reunification of Germany, the Soviet Army lost its largest extra-territorial garrison. In 1991 Soviet troops occupied 777 barracks at 276 locations and numbered about 338,000 soldiers in 24 divisions, distributed among five land armies consisting of approximately 4,200 tanks, 8,200 armoured vehicles, 3,600 artillery pieces, 106,000 motor vehicles and an air army of 690 aircraft, 680 helicopters and 180 missile systems. To this can be added 47 airfields and 116 exercise areas, most of which were situated in Brandenburg.[27] All these assets had to be returned to Russia in a massive operation which did not end until the summer of 1994. There were few tears shed. Unlike the NATO forces in what had been West Germany Soviet troops had continued to be discouraged from making contact with the local communities and relationships between the sexes could lead to the soldier being returned home. The last bastion to be closed was the so-called 'secret city' of Zossen-Wünsdorf, which was vacated in August 1994 and was basically left to rot until it was taken over for housing development in the twenty-first century, some buildings being used to house Somalian refugees. (Paradoxically, given its previous status, as Wünsdorf-Waldstadt it became a 'book town' in 1998, similar in purpose to Hay-on-Wye in Wales or Wigtown in Scotland.) Situated 25 miles south of Berlin it maintained the headquarters of the Soviet forces and was a home from home for the 55,000 soldiers based there who had access to their own shops, clinics and leisure facilities including a theatre and Olympic-sized swimming pool. Every Thursday night a train left for Moscow from Zossen-Wünsdorf, a journey of over 36 hours, and the whole area was effectively cut off from German life even though it had been a military base since the reign of Kaiser Wilhelm II and by one of history's ironies, soldiers from the garrison had taken part in Hitler's invasion of the Soviet Union in 1941, which was planned and controlled from the deep underground bunkers within the perimeter.[28] So ephemeral did the Soviet presence turn out to be that modern references to the location concentrate on the Nazi period while the Soviet occupation attracts only fleeting comments.

The costs of this massive evacuation were borne more or less entirely by the reunified German government and were thought to have amounted to over £10 billion in grants and loans, mainly to rehouse and retrain Soviet soldiers who would be leaving the armed forces and attempting to rebuild their lives as civilians. It was a formidable operation which lasted three years, with 120 trains being used each day; nothing usable was left behind – doors, windows, pipes, plumbing fixtures, electric cables and rain gutters – it was all removed. At the nearby Soviet air force base at Neuruppin, troops even dismantled the concrete-panelled runway and packed it for transport home. Yet despite all the attention to detail and the Soviet determination to leave nothing behind – 'not even used cartridge cases' – the withdrawal was not universally popular, not least because the German-funded building programme ran behind schedule and many military families were left homeless and forced to live temporarily in tented accommodation. There was also a growing tendency for some Soviet soldiers to believe that they were being treated as the losers in the Cold War and that Germans failed to acknowledge their own guilt in invading the Russian homeland in 1941. This was not helped by Germans looking at the

Americans, British and French who were leaving Berlin at the same time and comparing the experience badly with the departing Soviets. The quandary was summed up by a leader in the centre-left newspaper *Der Tagesspiegel*, which tended to reflect government thinking at the time: 'Our former enemies from the West helped us give birth to a stable German democracy, a military alliance and great friendship. Soviet units, on the other hand, remained what they were from the beginning: occupiers and great obstacles to a free, united and democratic Germany. It is not yet time to forget the difference.'[29]

The speedy Soviet withdrawal helped to assuage hurt feelings on both sides, but it took longer for the returning Soviet soldiery to get over the belief that they had been sold down the river. For them, as for their civilian counterparts, an uncertain future lay ahead. Initially, the signs were promising as Boris Yeltsin continued his inexorable rise to power and promised that further change was on the way. As Russia's first elected president he introduced sweeping reforms, casting off the old Communist hegemony and bringing in a raft of free market policies which he described as 'shock therapy' and which astonished and enraged Russians in equal measure. As a result, Yeltsin's name is indelibly linked with Russia's faltering experience in trying to create democracy in a country which had known centuries of authoritarianism, but the feelings of optimism could not last. By 1992 the Russian economy was in free fall with inflation running at 2,000 per cent, savings were wiped out and although many Russians came to regard the Yeltsin reforms as a period of hope and euphoria it soon became clear that he was ill-equipped to deal with the business of ruling Russia; only steady political and financial support from the West staved off disaster. Like many politicians schooled in the Soviet system he proved to be his own worst enemy. In October 1993, in a bizarre episode for an emerging democracy, he ordered tanks to assault the seat of the Russian parliament in the climax of an 18-month struggle with elected deputies. Finally, just over a year later, he ordered Russian troops, most of them conscripts, to try to put down a rebellion in Chechnya which rapidly turned into an insurgency war and has remained a heated issue ever since. By the end of his first decade in power it was obvious that matters could not continue. Yeltsin's health was worsening and his predilection for excessive alcohol consumption was turning him into an international embarrassment. The end came on 31 December 1999 when he unexpectedly resigned in favour of his prime minister, Vladimir Putin, a former KGB officer who served as acting president of the Russian Federation before being elected president on 26 March 2000. It was the beginning of a new chapter: by then the Cold War had ended and with the dawn of a new century it seemed to be the start of what the world hoped would be a new age.

Epilogue

A New Cold War?

THROUGHOUT THE COLD War it was acknowledged (though not always accepted) that Scotland was on the front line and the presence of so much nuclear hardware and the associated command, control and communications infrastructure meant that the country was a prime target for Soviet aggression or retaliation. It could not have been otherwise but in the so-called 'new world order' that followed hard upon the end of the Cold War and was epitomised by the terrorist attacks on the USA in New York and Washington on 11 September 2001, a new kind of asymmetric war was ushered in and Scotland came to understand that far from being redundant the country was still part of the defence structure of the United Kingdom and, beyond that, NATO. It also posed a puzzle: although the Cold War had ended, Scotland still retained weapons of mass destruction in the shape of the Trident submarines at Faslane and their nuclear warheads at Coulport. The high walls, barbed wire and chain-link fencing kept the curious at bay, the bland institutional buildings were suitably anonymous and forbidding, but the naval presence was not so amorphous that it failed to excite emotions. For a few, pride in naval power could have been part of the equation, but for most people, the overweening feeling was a mixture of suspicion, fear and dislike. Small wonder that the area remained a magnet for demonstrations orchestrated by Scottish CND, some of them violent.

In separate protests in 2001 and 2002 Scottish church leaders united with trade unionists and politicians to demand the closure of the base and the scrapping of the Trident weapons system which, according to the Ministry of Defence, costs the taxpayer £1.5 billion a year at 2006 prices.[1] The demonstrations attracted high-profile publicity, as did the earlier trial in 2000 of three female protestors (Angela Zelter, Bodil Roder and Ellen Moxley) who had boarded a Trident support vessel in

Loch Goil and damaged computer equipment by throwing the items overboard. Charged in October 1999 in Greenock Sheriff Court they escaped sentence because the sheriff-substitute Margaret Gimblett deemed nuclear weapons to be illegal under international law and that the women had been acting lawfully to prevent a further crime. Under those circumstances she directed the jury to return a verdict of not guilty.[2] Although the decision was not upheld in the High Court in Edinburgh before the Lord Advocate Lord Hardie, the unease conjured up by the Clyde Submarine Base and its occupants remained a constant factor in Scottish political life into the twenty-first century, with regular demonstrations both outside the Faslane base and against the convoys carrying nuclear warheads between the UK government's Atomic Weapons Establishment in Berkshire and the Royal Naval Armaments Depot at Coulport on Loch Long. The Scottish CND's peace camp at Faslane that had been established in 1982 had become a permanent fixture and a focus for attempts to breach security at the base: the UK government's decision to replace Trident with a new and more powerful weapons system at a cost of £41 billion in November 2015 only exacerbated the protests.[3]

The decision seemed to demonstrate that Cold War-style confrontation was far from over and that following a brief period of respite it was a matter of business as usual. At the beginning of the new century Vladimir Putin had become President of Russia and won a second term four years later. Russia's electoral laws did not allow him to stand for a third term but after a return to the premiership in May 2012 he was elected president again in succession to Dmitry Medvedev, followed by a fourth term in May 2018. During that eighteen-year period his foreign policy changed from a willingness to develop a partnership with the West towards a new and worrying alienation which seemed to be a return to Cold War standards of conduct. During his 2012 election campaign Putin set out his new foreign policy theories in a series of speeches in which he announced that in place of his earlier ideas about integration with the West he was now intent on 'preserving Russia's distinct identity in a highly competitive global environment'. According to analyst Dr Dmitri Trenin, who served in the Soviet Army in East Germany in the 1980s, in that new 'Russian World' the country's 'independence and sovereignty would be elevated to supreme national values'.[4] Russia's relationship with the USA, NATO and the European Union began to deteriorate but this was balanced by a new closeness to

China; once more Russia was embroiled in the Middle East by propping up the regime of President Bashar al-Assad in Syria and lending support to the Iranian regime, both against Washington's wishes. Closer to home Russia's relationship with Ukraine disintegrated, leaving both countries in a state of constant confrontation which was worsened by Russia's annexation of the Crimean peninsula in March 2014. By the end of that year the two countries were in a state of open conflict as the government of Ukraine used its armed forces to counter Russian-backed militias in the Donbass region of eastern Ukraine who were supporting the self-styled separatist Donetsk and Lugansk People's Republics. These forces included Russian military personnel fighting without any insignia but using Russian Army military equipment and weapons.

This outburst of violence persuaded many in the West that Putin was returning Russia to a Cold War style of confrontation and that a new and aggressive foreign policy was in the offing. However, the Russian president countered by claiming that he was merely defending countries within Russia's sphere of interest from what seemed to Moscow to be aggressive NATO moves to include former Soviet states within the Alliance as part of its policy of 'enlargement'. Instituted in 1995 the process continued an 'open door' commitment which allowed European countries to apply for membership and by March 1999 three new members had joined the Alliance, bringing the total to 19 – Czech Republic, Hungary and Poland. At the NATO summit held in Prague in November 2002 the following countries joined the Alliance as part of the Membership Action Plan – Bulgaria, Estonia, Latvia, Lithuania, Romania, Slovakia and Slovenia – and that same year President Leonid Kuchma announced Ukraine's goal of eventual NATO membership. The hope was repeated more recently by his successors Arseniy Yatsenyuk and Petro Poroshenko, who both claimed that Ukrainian membership of the Alliance was essential to deter Russian aggression. During this period of enlargement NATO also launched its Partnership for Peace programme, which included former members of the Soviet Union and Yugoslavia as well as EU members such as Austria, Finland, Ireland and Sweden which did not aspire to full membership but subscribed to the partnership's strategic aims.

While these innovations were imaginative and pragmatic in that they were aimed at cementing peace in Europe and the wider world in the post-Cold War age, they were not met with universal acclaim in

Russia which looked on helplessly as former Warsaw Pact allies threw in their lot with NATO. This applied especially to 14 neighbouring countries which formed the 'near abroad', a historic term to describe countries along Russia's borders in the Baltic states, eastern Europe, central Asia and Transcaucasia. To put that into strategic perspective, for Russian warships operating from St Petersburg any voyage into the Atlantic meant passing the coastline of five former allies which had joined NATO – Estonia, Latvia, Lithuania, Poland and former East Germany. These were vital holdings for the defence of Russia and the policy can be compared to the American Monroe Doctrine of 1823 which sought to prevent further European colonial incursions into Latin America, thereby turning the western hemisphere into a predominantly US sphere of influence. As the conservative politician and commentator Pat Buchanan asked his fellow Americans, 'If we awoke to find Mexico, Canada, Cuba, and most of South America in a military alliance against us, welcoming Russian bases and troops, would we regard that as "the hand of partnership"?'[5]

Seen from that perspective it is possible to understand Putin's alarm at NATO's steady intrusion into territory which had once formed part of the Soviet Union and the need for him to revise Russian foreign policy to counter the threat. What is less easy to understand is his methodology, which seems to hark back to the confrontational days of the Soviet Union. On becoming president for his fourth term Putin outlined his thinking in a lengthy article, published in the state-owned *Rossiyskaya Gazeta* newspaper in which he outlined plans for military reform and rearmament that would see the Russian government spend 23 trillion roubles (some £264 billion) over a ten-year period. Tellingly, the main expenditure was on offensive equipment and included over 400 modern ground and sea-based ICBMs, 8 strategic missile submarines, 20 attack submarines, over 50 surface ships (mainly frigates) some 100 military-purpose spacecraft, 600 modern aircraft, including fifth-generation fighters, more than 1,000 helicopters, 28 regimental sets of S-400 surface-to-air missile systems, 38 divisional sets of Vityaz air defence systems, 10 brigade sets of Iskander-M short-range tactical missile systems, more than 2,300 main battle tanks, 2,000 self-propelled artillery systems and guns, and more than 17,000 military vehicles.[6]

In addition to re-equipping Russian forces with the kind of weaponry that would have been deployed during the Cold War, Russia also reverted to the tactics used during that same period. Twenty years after the end of the Cold War Russian reconnaissance aircraft appeared once more over the North Sea and North Atlantic, testing NATO air defences and forcing RAF QRA flights to intercept them. Russian aircraft were also intercepted close to Dutch, Danish, Swedish, Latvian and Estonian airspace and even further afield in Canadian and US airspace, taking part in activities reminiscent of the Cold War, when NATO air forces routinely intercepted Soviet planes flying close to their territories. Although not as numerous as in the last century these flights caused concern as there was no valid strategic reason for them other than a desire to remind the West of Russia's capabilities at a time when NATO was relaxing its defensive posture in Europe. The second decade of the twenty-first century also saw a renewal of submarine activity on NATO's northern flank. Reflecting the fact that little of Russian naval expenditure had been spent on surface ships other than on ASW frigates and corvettes the Russian Navy had expanded its submarine fleet by replacing the Typhoon class with the improved Borei SSBN and introducing the Yasen class multi-purpose attack submarine. Just as had happened during the Cold War, Russian submarines became regular visitors to Scottish waters and they were able to go about their business relatively unimpaired due to the shortage of aerial reconnaissance in the country's defences. This was due to the cancellation in 2011 of the RAF's Nimrod MRA4 maritime patrol and attack aircraft and the subsequent closure of its main base at RAF Kinloss, a decision which left a large hole in the country's northern defences and could not be filled by the proposed use of C-130 Hercules aircraft or Merlin helicopters, both of which lacked range and the capacity to loiter over the target area. The problem was finally addressed in 2015 when the British government announced that the RAF would acquire eight American-built Boeing Poseidon P-8 maritime patrol aircraft and that they would be based at RAF Lossiemouth to fill the gap, a decision which acknowledged the threat posed by Russian submarine incursions as well as the problem of a lack of aerial reconnaissance support for the Royal Navy's Trident fleet.[7] Although this about-turn was welcomed, it was balanced by the fact that the Boeing's engines were 'very thirsty', giving the aircraft a shorter range and time on station than the cancelled Nimrod. There were also doubts about the American aircraft's ability to operate British-built sonobuoys and Sting Ray acoustic homing torpedoes, the main UK weapons in airborne ASW warfare.[8]

Confrontational harassment was not one-sided in the post-Cold War period. NATO aircraft and warships regularly tested Russian defences and in 2016 the Alliance responded to Russia's annexation of Crimea and the confrontation with Ukraine by deploying forces including four multinational battle groups to Estonia, Latvia, Lithuania and Poland. These were described as an 'enhanced forward presence' which sent 'a clear message that an attack on one Ally would be met by troops from across the Alliance' in line with Article 5 of the North Atlantic Treaty and it seemed to mark a return to the Cold War politics of hostile deterrence.[9] Predictably, the Russians described the deployments as provocative and dangerous while pouring scorn on the size and capabilities of the forces in the event of an outbreak of hostilities. A year later, in September 2017, to underline their determination to resist further NATO encroachment the Russians launched a massive military exercise along their western borders which was designed to replicate an attack mounted by three fictional adversaries – Veishnoriya, a Western-backed aggressor along with its two allies, Lubeniya and Vesbasriya – which were intent on driving a wedge between Russia and Belarus. Codenamed 'Zapad' (West), the Russian war games sparked huge interest within NATO. Not only were they the largest since the end of the Cold War but there were fears in Ukraine that Zapad-2017 was a smokescreen for further Russian military action against the country and a prelude to outright invasion. That turned out not to be the case – Russia had neither the desire nor the capability to open hostilities with NATO – but as one Western military observer commented at the time, Russia was simply making its presence felt: 'When Moscow clears its throat, the region will hear it.'[10] NATO responded a year later by mounting Trident Juncture 2018, its largest live exercise since the end of the Cold War, which involved 55,000 troops from 31 countries. In an intriguing echo of NATO's Operation Mainbrace held in 1952 it simulated an invasion of Norway following the triggering of an Article Five mutual security guarantee commitment from Alliance member states.[11]

By then the East–West relationship had been complicated further by the election of Donald J. Trump as President of America in 2016 following a campaign promising to put 'America First'. The choice of this maverick businessman and television personality took everyone by surprise because not only did he have very little political experience, but he polarised political opinion – rarely in modern times has a presidency so divided the American people. Trump's foreign policy was as volatile as the man himself. He began his presidency by threatening to reduce US expenditure on NATO and by offering the hand of friendship to President Putin, yet by 2018 he had agreed to supply the Patriot anti-missile defence system to Poland and was threatening to withdraw the USA from the 1987 Intermediate-Range Nuclear Forces Treaty (INF) which had led to the end of the Cold War. Both were perceived as moves against Russia and the matter was complicated further by allegations that Putin had authorised Russian interference in the US presidential election. It is too soon in the Trump presidency to assess his willingness to provoke a new confrontation between the West and Russia but with two single-minded and powerful leaders in control in Washington and Moscow, both accustomed to getting their way in their personal and political lives, nothing can be ruled out.

Fortunately, a re-run of the Cold War seems unlikely as the circumstances surrounding the first confrontation have disappeared. While the USA remains a dominant world power its main rival is not Russia but China, which has emerged as a far more important player in world politics and economics than it ever was 30 years ago. The harsh reality is that despite Putin's blustering and his noisy ambition to remain a global influence, shorn of the Soviet Union Russia is a relatively minor economic power without the financial or industrial muscle to engage in a lengthy confrontation. Other things have also changed. Unlike the Soviet Union at the height of its influence, Russia cannot claim leadership of an international ideological movement and despite its involvement in Assad's Syria, itself a hangover from the Cold War, Putin has been unable to turn that country into a new point of proxy confrontation with the West. That leaves the nuclear threat, but with any future conflict unlikely to be determined by weapons of mass destruction the emphasis has turned to other means such as espionage and cyber-warfare, with incidents taking place in a grey world where actions are hard to discern and can also be conducted by individuals or groups claiming to be agents of the state. In such an arena denial usually trumps attribution.

Put simply, as Professor Sir Lawrence Freedman reminds us, the first Cold War took place before the advent of the internet while a second Cold War would be fashioned by it, thereby providing opportunities for new forms of aggression such as cyber-attacks on critical communications infrastructures as well as on government, banking and media networks. This offensive/defensive type of operation does not kill hundreds of thousands of people indiscriminately but causes widespread social and political chaos, becoming 'more analogous to irregular warfare than strategic bombing, another way to harass and subvert, to confuse and annoy'.[12] In fact, Russia had already shown its hand in 2007 by bombarding Estonia's defences with a massive cyber-attack, followed by a similar assault on Georgia a year later which paralysed both countries, if only temporarily. Since then there has been a succession of cyber-attacks in which Russia's security services copied tactics used by cyber-criminals as they blurred 'the line between state and non-state activities in cyberspace'.[13] In much the same way, espionage and counter-espionage still had roles to play by imitating criminal activities and in the world of spying Russia followed on from earlier Soviet tactics by initiating a concentrated and sustained intelligence confrontation against the UK. This type of operation reached a nadir in the summer of 2018, when the identities of two Russian military intelligence agents were revealed after they used Novichok nerve agent to attempt to murder Sergei Skripal, a former colleague and double agent, in the English cathedral city of Salisbury. As a result, the UK retaliated by expelling 23 suspected Russian intelligence officers while sources within MI5 claimed that Russia had up to 200 intelligence officers in the country, more than five times as many as during the Cold War.[14]

Revelations of that kind gave a clue to the way in which any future confrontation would be conducted – a war in the shadows in which sabotage and espionage were the main weapons and any attacks by either side would be instantly refuted. In any conventional war with Russia or indeed with any country to the east, Scotland would find itself again on the front line thanks to its geographical position and the presence of Trident-armed submarines at Faslane on the Clyde, but however alarming that prospect might appear, it is balanced by the implausibility that a future conflict would be a second Cold War. For a start, the strategic imperatives created by the international system have changed utterly. The Soviet Union has collapsed, as has the Warsaw Pact (with greater alacrity), the Communist system no longer holds sway, the East–West bipolar rivalry has been condemned to history and a new generation of political leaders has replaced the Cold War warriors. In that environment Scotland's role has also changed and its future relationship with the political unions provided by the UK and the EU are still a matter of conjecture. There was a flurry of excitement in

2015 when the Russian news agency Sputnik and the broadcaster RT opened an office in Edinburgh, leading to accusations that the Kremlin had established a media Trojan Horse in Scotland, but as time passed they came to be regarded as little different in editorial approach from their American counterpart, the government-funded Voice of America, or the Rupert Murdoch-backed Fox News.

The ever-changing geo-political balance has also affected Scotland, which ended the immediate post-Cold War period in a state of flux which was not dissimilar to what had been happening to Europe in the 1990s. This applied in particular to the increasingly vociferous demand for home rule or even complete independence from the UK, which was spurred on by cross-party support for a referendum on the subject following Labour's landslide victory in 1997 under the reformist prime minister, Tony Blair. Two years later Scotland voted overwhelmingly for a devolved administration, with 74.3 per cent of those who voted supporting the creation of a Scottish parliament while 63.5 per cent agreed that it should have tax-raising powers.[15] By then the Cold War was almost a decade in the past but it had influenced, however tangentially, what was happening in Scotland. Just as the constituent parts of the old Soviet Union had started questioning the validity of the centralism of Moscow rule so too did the many supporters of the cross-party Claim of Right conclude in March 1989 that 'the United Kingdom has been an anomaly from its inception and is a glaring anomaly now. It is unrealistic to argue that the improvement of government must be prevented if it cannot be fitted within some preconceived symmetry. New anomalies that force people to think are far more likely to be constructive than impossible ambitions to eliminate anomaly.'[16] Although the document had no legal significance, its demand for the creation of a devolved parliament or assembly carried considerable constitutional weight by stressing that the people of Scotland were sovereign and had the right to determine the form of government best suited to their needs.

Shortly after the beginning of the new century Scotland underwent further political change with the election of SNP governments in 2011 and 2016, and there was a landmark referendum on independence in September 2014 in which the country voted to reject independence by a margin of 55.3 per cent (against independence) to 44.7 per cent (in favour of it). Further shocks were on their way: in a separate referendum held in June 2016 the United Kingdom voted to leave the European

Union, although Scotland (as well as most notably Northern Ireland and London) bucked the trend by voting to stay within the EU. Coupled with the continuing agitation for political and constitutional change, this brought into question the solidity of the UK union. It also raised the spectre that Scotland could still follow the trend that had begun in eastern Europe with the collapse of the Soviet Union and the disappearance of Communist hegemony by demanding independence, although this was balanced by the residual strength and influence of those who did not want to break up the United Kingdom. Whereas the glue holding together the Warsaw Pact had proved to be highly friable when put under pressure, the 300-year-old British union appeared to be standing the test of time. At least for the time being.

Notes

PROLOGUE: SAXA VORD

1. The use of the verb is borrowed from George Bruce's poem 'For Voyagers', *Collected Poems*, Edinburgh, 1971, 20.
2. 'A History of RAF Saxa Vord', http://ahistoryofrafsaxavord.blogspot.co.uk/.
3. Spaven, *Fortress Scotland*, 56–7.
4. NA DEFE 11/646 'Probable nuclear targets in the United Kingdom: Assumptions for planning', 2 May 1972.
5. Trevor Royle, 'Scotland and Defence', Linklater and Denniston, *Anatomy of Scotland*, 73.
6. 'Local Interest in Buying Saxa Vord', *Shetland Times*, 29 October 2008.
7. 'Shetland radar base "nearing completion"', *BBC News*, 26 January 2018.

I. LAST SHOTS, FIRST SHOTS

1. Mass Observation, *The Journey Home*, Advertising Service Guild, London, 1944, 84.
2. Nigel Nicolson, *Monty: The Field Marshal 1944–1976*, London, 1986, 633–721
3. Royle, *Best Years of Their Lives*, 48.
4. Ibid, 31.
5. Nicholas Mansergh, editor-in-chief, *Constitutional Relations Between Britain and India: The Transfer of Power 1942–47*, vol. xii, London, 1983, 771.
6. Royle, *Last Days of the Raj*, 217.
7. Ibid, 219.
8. Philip Ziegler, *Mountbatten*, London, 1985, 334.
9. Ibid, 330–3.
10. General Sir William Jackson and Group Captain T. P. Gleve, eds, *The Mediterranean and Middle East*, vol. VI, *Victory in the Mediterranean*, Part III: 'November 1944 to May 1945, Trieste and Austrian Crises'. London, 1988, 337.
11. Ibid, 336.
12. Ibid, 346.
13. NA WO 170/1355, War Diary, 3rd Battalion Welsh Guards, 19 May 1945.
14. Per Anders Rudling 'They Defended Ukraine': The 14 Waffen-Grenadier-Division der SS (Galizische Nr. 1) Revisited', *The Journal of Slavic Military Studies*, 25:3, 2012, 329–68.

15. R. J. Aldrich, *The Hidden Hand: Britain, America and Cold War Secret Intelligence*, New York, 2002, 142–4.
16. Ben Shephard, *The Long Way Home: The Aftermath of the Second World War*, London, 2010, 220–4.
17. Douglas MacLeod, *Morningside Mata Haris: How MI6 Deceived Scotland's Great and Good*, Edinburgh, 2005, 128–40.
18. Ben Macintyre, *A Spy Among Friends: Kim Philby and the Great Betrayal*, London, 2014, 134–6.
19. Shephard, *Long Way Home*, 224.
20. Ze'ev Jabotinsky, *Writings: On the Road to Statehood*, Jerusalem, 1959, 251–20.
21. Corelli Barnett, *Britain and Her Army 1509–1970*, London, 1970, 481.
22. JIC (48) 9 (0), 'Russian Interests, Intentions and Capabilities', 23 July 1948.
23. NA FO 800/453, War Office to Attlee, 7 July 1948.
24. Clarke, *Hope and Glory*, 235.
25. T. G. Carpenter, 'NATO's Search for Relevance', S. V. Papacosma, S. Kay and R. Rubin, eds, *NATO After Fifty Years*, Wilmington, 2001, 25–41.
26. Royle, *Best Years of Their Lives*, 147.
27. Eric Grove and Geoffrey Till, 'Anglo-American Maritime Strategy in the Era of Massive Retaliation, 1945–1960', John B. Hattendorf and Robert S. Jordan, eds, *Maritime Strategy and the Balance of Power: Britain and America in the Twentieth Century*, New York, 1989, 278.
28. 'Navies Meet the Test in Operation Mainbrace', *New York Times*, 28 September 1952.
29. Grove and Geoffrey, 'Anglo-American Maritime Strategy', 287.
30. 'NATO Exercises: Mainbrace', *Flight Magazine*, 26 September 1952, 404–6.
31. NA PREM 11/48 Operation Mainbrace; David Clark, *The UFO Files: The Inside Story of Real-Life Sightings*, National Archives, Kew, 2009.
32. Dean C. Allard, 'Strategic Views of the US Navy and NATO on the Northern Flank, 1917–1991', *Northern Mariner*, xi, no. 1 (January 2001), 15.

2. WHEN COLD WAR BECAME HOT WAR

1. Ina Zweiniger-Bargielowska, 'Bread Rationing in Britain, July 1946–July 1948', *Twentieth Century British History*, vol. 4, no. 1, 1993, 57–85.
2. Robert Schuman, Strasbourg Speech, 16 May 1949.
3. Jean Monnet, *Memoirs*, London, 1978, 98.
4. Linklater, *Our Men in Korea*, 32.
5. Anthony Farrar-Hockley. 'The Far Side of the World', Julian Thompson, ed., *The Imperial War Museum Book of Modern Warfare*, London, 2002, 102.
6. P. J. R. Mileham, *Fighting Highlanders: The History of the Argyll and Sutherland Highlanders*, London, 1993, 149.
7. Colin Mitchell, *Having been a Soldier*, London, 1969, 80.
8. Hastings, *Korean War*, 161–3.
9. Royle, *Best Years of Their Lives*, 184.
10. *The Red Hackle*, June 1952.
11. Royle, *Best Years of Their Lives*, 1977.
12. Obituary, *The Times*, 22 June 2018.
13. *The Borderers Chronicle*, December 1951.
14. Anthony Farrar-Hockley, 'The Far Side of the World', in Julian Thompson, ed., *The Imperial War Museum Book of Modern Warfare*, London, 2002, 122.

15. 'British plea to North Korea over fate of 82 soldiers', *Daily Telegraph*, 2 February 2001.
16. Hastings, *Korean War*, 350.
17. NA ADM 1/27482, Marine Andrew Condron: return from China; SNLR1953–1962.
18. *The Thistle*, November 1954.
19. This is not strictly accurate, as during that year service personnel on loan to the Sultan of Dhofar were engaged in a little-known armed struggle in Dhofar.
20. *The Times*, 6 July 1950.
21. James Cameron, *Point of Departure*, London, 1986, 74–5.

3. THE YANKS ARE COMING

1. Martin Gilbert, *Churchill: A Life*, London 1991, 879.
2. John Saville, 'The Price of Alliance: American Bases in Britain', *The Socialist Register*, 1987, 32–60.
3. Hennessy, *Never Again*, 356.
4. Jonathon Colman, 'The 1950 Ambassador's Agreement on USAF bases in the UK and British fears of US atomic unilateralism', *Journal of Strategic Studies*, 30, London, 2007, 285–308.
5. 'A Bewildered Elvis Pays a Flying Visit', *Daily Mail*, 3 March 1960.
6. Alastair Campbell, 'Junior Military Command during the Cold War', Jamieson, *Scotland and the Cold War*, 90.
7. NA CAB 158/11, Part 2 JIC (50) 111, 'Likelihood of Total War with the Soviet Union up to the end of 1954', 15 February 1951.
8. Hansard, HL Deb 03 May 1960, vol. 223 cc223–89.
9. Graham Boiling, *Secret Students on Parade: Cold War Memories of JSSL Crail*, London, 2005, *passim*.
10. Geoffrey Elliott and Harold Shukman, *Secret Classrooms: An Untold Story of the Cold War*, London, 2003, *passim*.
11. Royle, *Best Years*, 132.
12. Leslie Woodhead, 'I was a teen spy', *London Evening Standard*, 24 November 2003.
13. A. J. Wohlstetter, F. S. Hoffman, R. J. Lutz and H. S. Rowen, 'Selection and Use of Strategic Air Bases,' RAND, R-266, 2 April 1954.
14. 'Vulcan test reactor closes down', *Press and Journal*, 25 July 2015.
15. Dan Van der Vat, *Stealth at Sea: The History of the Submarine*, London, 1994, 320.
16. Quoted in Norman Polmar and Captain Dominic A. Paolucci, USN (Ret.), 'Sea-based Strategic Weapons for the 1980s and Beyond', *US Naval Institute Proceedings*, May 1978, 107.
17. Jackson, *Strike Force*, 38.
18. Hansard, HC Deb 01 April 1957, vol. 568, cc37–170.
19. Robert S. Norris, *The Cuban Missile Crisis: A Nuclear Order of Battle October/November 1962*, Woodrow Wilson Center, Washington, October 2012, 22.
20. Stephen Twigge and Len Scott, 'The Other Missiles of October: The Thor IRBMs and the Cuban Missile Crisis', *Electronic Journal of International History*, Article 3 (2000). https://sas-space.sas.ac.uk/3387/.
21. VADM Charles H. Griffiths, 'Role of Polaris Submarines in the Cuban Missile Crisis,' U.S. Naval Academy Alumni Association and Foundation, https://www.usna.com/SSLPage.aspx?pid+2861.
22. Ibid.
23. Lavery, *Shield of Empire*, 424–53.

24. Dean C. Allard, 'Strategic Views of the US Navy and NATO on the Northern Flank, 1917–1991', *The Northern Mariner*, vol. xi, January 2001, 16.
25. Proceedings of the US Naval Institute, vol. 107/3/937, March 1981.
26. NA ADM 205/222 Macmillan to Kennedy, June 1960.
27. Jackson and Bramall, *The Chiefs*, 344.
28. David Andress, *Cultural Dementia: How the West Has Lost its History and Risks Losing Everything Else*, London, 2018, 19.
29. Ibid, 345.
30. G.M. Dillon, *Dependence and Deterrence: Success and Civility in the Anglo-American Special Nuclear Relationship, 1962–1982*, Aldershot, 1983, 35.
31. Chalmers and Walker, *Uncharted Waters*, 17–25.
32. 'Last flight of the Vulcan bomber', *The Guardian*, 30 November 2015.

4. FRONTLINE SCOTLAND

1. Trevor Royle, 'Scotland and Defence', Linklater and Denniston, eds, *Anatomy of Scotland*, 72.
2. Spaven, *Fortress Scotland*, 41.
3. Inquiry into the Scottish Fishing Industry, Royal Society of Edinburgh, March 2004, 15–16.
4. Spaven, *Fortress Scotland*, 42.
5. 'Pentagon admits sub in net was American', *The Herald*, 19 February 1987.
6. *Report of the Chief Inspector of Marine Accidents into the collision between the Fishing Vessel ANTARES and HMS TRENCHANT with the loss of four lives on 22 November 1990*, London HMSO, 1992.
7. NA DEFE 11/646 Probable nuclear targets in the United Kingdom: Assumptions for planning, 2 May 1972.
8. 'Wrangle disrupted Faslane plans', *The Herald*, 1 January 2002.
9. NA ADM 1/28887, Faslane Submarine Base: design and equipment of support services, 1963–1968.
10. Chief Polaris Executive, *Polaris and the Royal Navy*, London, 1966, 1.
11. Hansard HC Deb 26 October 1966, vol. 734, c184W.
12. Hansard, HC Deb 24 April 1967, vol. 745, c203W.
13. Lavery, *Shield of Empire*, 445.
14. 'Polaris: Taking the Black Pig to Sea', BBC documentary, written and produced by Jonathan Crane, 1985.
15. Hennessy, *Secret State*, 190–2.
16. 'Secrets of the UK's True-Life Hunter Killers', *Warships International Fleet Review*, 15 November 2013.
17. Thompson, *On Her Majesty's Nuclear Service*, Chapter 1.
18. Toby Elliott, quoted in Ring, *We Come Unseen*, Chapter 10.
19. 'Polaris: Taking the Black Pig to Sea', BBC documentary written and produced by Jonathan Crane, 1985.
20. Karl Haynes, 'Decline and Devolution: The Sources of Strategic Military Retrenchment', *International Studies Quarterly*, vol. 59, issue 3, September 2015, 490–502.
21. Robert Fleming, 'A Jungle Too Far: Britain and the Vietnam War', Lecture, National Army Museum, London, 6 December 2012.
22. Marc Tiley, 'Britain, Vietnam and the Special Relationship', *History Today*, vol. 63, issue 12, 12 December 2013.

23. Slaven, *Fortress Scotland*, 105–10.

24. 'CTR 3 Flanagan travels globe via radio', *Tartan Log*, 17 July 1971.

25. Spaven, *Fortress Scotland*, 71–5.

26. Dennis Barker, *Guarding the Skies: An Unofficial Portrait of the Royal Air Force*, London, 1989, 17.

27. Ibid, 17–21.

28. 'The RAF base where Britain's flying aces are on perpetual scramble alert to defend the UK', *Daily Mail*, 5 December 2010.

29. Trevor Royle, 'Scotland and Defence', Linklater and Denniston, *Anatomy of Scotland*, 70.

30. Hansard, HC Deb 20 November 1957, vol. 578, cc361–4.

31. MOD Missile Test Range Uists, Economic Impact Assessment, Sneddon Economics, Inverness, 19 August 2009.

32. Rob Edwards, 'Risk from radiation leaks at military base', *Sunday Herald*, 4 April 2004.

33. Andro Linklater, *Compton Mackenzie: A Life,* London, 1987, 317.

34. Jennifer Cole, Royal United Services Institute, review of Matthew Grant, *After the Bomb: Civil Defence and Nuclear War in Britain, 1945–68*, Institute of Historical Research, review no. 898, April 2010.

35. NA CAB 21/5808, Parliamentary question asked in the House of Commons by William Hamilton MP about the TV film *The War Game*, 2 December 1965.

36. British Library, *Learning: Dreamers and Dissenters, Spies for Peace*, http://www. bl.uk/learning/histcitizen/21cc/counterculture/civildisobedience/spiesforpeace/ spiesforpeace.html.

37. *Protect and Survive*, Prepared for the Home Office by the Central Office of Information, London, 1980.

38. NA CAB, Civil Defence Committee (48), 10, 7 July 1948.

39. NA CAB 134/942, Home Defence Committee Working Party, 'Estimates of House Damage, Note by Home Office', May 1953.

40. NA DEFE 11/646 Probable nuclear targets in the United Kingdom: Assumptions for planning, 2 May 1972, B-3.

41. Ibid, B-3.

42. NA CAB 134/82, Civil Defence Committee (48) 10, 7 July 1948.

5. DING DONG DOLLAR: OPPOSING ARMAGEDDON

1. CND Resolution 1958, quoted in Sue Donnelly, 'CND: The Making of a Peace Movement', *History Today*, vol. 58, issue 4, April 2008.

2. Lavery, *Shield of Empire*, 430.

3. Bruce Kent, 'Half a Century of CND', *New Statesman*, 11 February 2008.

4. Ray Monk, 'Russell, Bertrand Arthur William, third Earl Russell (1872–1970)', *Oxford Dictionary of National Biography*, Oxford, 2004.

5. 'Artists wage war on war', anonymous report of anti-Polaris Count Down exhibition in McLellan Galleries, Glasgow, *Daily Herald*, 23 January 1961.

6. 'Holy Loch's Unholy Row', *Life Magazine*, 17 March 1961, 44–5.

7. 'The spies in CND's midst', *The Guardian*, 22 September 1999.

8. *Glasgow Herald*, 15 May 1961.

9. *The Times*, 22 May 1961.

10. Gordon McCulloch, 'a.k.a. Thurso Berwick: Doon Amang the Eskimos', *The Bottle Imp*, Association for Scottish Literary Studies, issue 9, May 2011.

11. 'Evil faces of Glasgow's gangsters revealed', *The Scotsman*, 19 July 2004.
12. Des Geraghty, *Luke Kelly: A Memoir*, Cork, 1994, 47.
13. Bobby Campbell, 'Songs with Teeth', *International Socialism*, no. 10, Autumn 1962, 15–20.
14. Folkways Records, *Ding Dong Dollar Anti-Polaris and Scottish republican songs*, 1962 Folkway Records FD 5444, together with demonstration and songsheet notes.
15. McVicar, *Eskimo Republic*, 102.
16. Ron Ferguson, *George MacLeod, Founder of the Iona Community*, Glasgow, 1990, 24.
17. 'Cartoonist Bob tells of 55-year struggle to rid us of nuclear weapons', *Islington Tribune*, 26 February 2016.
18. 'Scottish CND: Remembering the Early Days', *Then and Now: Fifty Years of Struggle for a Better World*, Nuclear Free Scotland, May 2008.
19. Tom A. Cullen ' Story of the Invisible Americans', *Park City Daily News*, Kentucky, 20 November 1962.
20. Harvie, *Scotland and Nationalism*, 203–6.
21. Ferguson, *George MacLeod,* 291.
22. Helen Steven, *Roger: An Extraordinary Peace Campaigner*, Glasgow, 1990, 43.
23. Ibid, 58.
24. 'General Assembly About-turn on Disarmament', *West Highland Free Press*, 28 May 1982.
25. Alastair Ramage, 'The Role of the Churches in the Peace movement', Jamieson, ed., *Scotland and the Cold War*, 35.
26. NA AIR 8/2400, 'Medium Bomber Force: Size and Composition'; 'Defence Board, The V-Bomber Force and the Powered Bomb. Memorandum by the Secretary of State for Air', DB (58) 10, 29 October 1958.
27. Willie Thompson, 'Scottish Communists in the Cold War', Jamieson, ed., *Scotland and the Cold War*, 40–1.
28. Geoff Andrews, *Endgames and New Times: The Final Years of British Communism*, London, 2004, 30.
29. Toby Fenwick, 'The Future of Political Opposition to Trident', Andrew Futter, ed., *The United Kingdom and the Future of Nuclear Weapons*, London, 2016, 196.
30. Lindsay, *Thank You for Having Me*, 126.
31. George Bruce, *Festival in the North*, London, 1975, 47.
32. *Manchester Guardian*, 13 September 1947.
33. Colm Brogan, 'Dishonour at Edinburgh', *Catholic Herald*, 24 August 1962.
34. 'Our Origins', *Scotland–USSR Society: Forty Years Working for Friendship, A Brief Account*, Glasgow, 1985, 2.
35. Ibid, 3.
36. Bold, *MacDiarmid*, 410.
37. Hugh MacDiarmid, *A Drunk Man looks at the Thistle*, Edinburgh, 1926, ii, 141–4. The words are also inscribed on the poet's headstone in Langholm.
38. Hugh MacDiarmid, 'Why I Rejoined', *Daily Worker*, 28 March 1957, 2.
39. Hugh MacDiarmid, *The Complete Poems*, vol. ii, London, 1978, 1412.
40. Yevgeny Yevtushenko, 'The Art of Poetry No. 7', *The Paris Review*, Spring–Summer 1965, no. 34.
41. 'The Burns Connection', *Scotland–USSR Society: Forty Years Working for Friendship, A Brief Account*, Glasgow 1985, 8.
42. R. D. S. Jack, 'Robert Burns as Dramatic Poet', in Patrick Scott and Kenneth

Simpson, *Robert Burns & Friends: Essays by W. Ormiston Roy Fellows Presented to G. Ross Roy*, Columbia, University of South Carolina Libraries, 2012, 41.

43. 'Tourism Passport to Peace', *Scotland–USSR Society: Forty Years Working for Friendship, A Brief Account*, Glasgow 1985, 9.
44. Roberts, *Speak Clearly into the Chandelier*, 53.
45. Personal knowledge.
46. Roberts, *Speak Clearly into the Chandelier*, xi.
47. Interview by Valerie Bierman, *Books for Keeps*, issue 60, January 1990.
48. Sheila Douglas, 'Scots wha Haena', in Paul Henderson Scott, ed., *The Saltoun Papers: Reflections on Andrew Fletcher*, Edinburgh, 2003, 134.
49. Henderson, *Poems and Songs*, 143.
50. Lena Jeger, 'Among us taking a century's notes', *The Guardian*, 13 January 1999.
51. Linklater, *The Dark of Summer*, 247.
52. Ibid, 250.
53. Eric Linklater, *Fanfare for a Tin Hat*, London 1970, 326.
54. Buchan, *Dolphins at Cochin*, jacket blurb.
55. Ibid, 'The Low Road', 48–9.
56. Muir, 'The Horses', *Collected Poems*, 246–57.
57. Ibid, 'After a Hypothetical War', 265.
58. Peter Butter, *Edwin Muir: Man and Poet*, Edinburgh, 1966, 272.
59. Finlay, *Modern Scotland*, 292–4.

6. THE PAST IS A FOREIGN COUNTRY: FAMILIES ON THE FRONT LINE

1. James Blaker, *United States Overseas Basing*, New York, 1990, 32.
2. Clarence A. Robinson, 'Anti-Ship Missiles Studied to Block Sea Chokepoints', *Aviation Week and Space Technology*, vol. 118, no. 9, 28 February 1983, 24–6.
3. *Chicago Tribune*, 4 March 1961.
4. Simon Duke, *US Defence Bases in the United Kingdom*, London, 1987, Chapter Six.
5. William McIlvanney, 'Growing Up in the West', in Karl Miller, ed., *Memoirs of a Modern Scotland*, London, 1970, 168.
6. 'Town Fears for its Future After US Sub Base Closes', *Chicago Tribune*, 8 February 1991.
7. Timothy Stone, 'Analysing the Regional Aspect of Defence Spending: A Survey', *Aberdeen Studies in Defence Economics*, no. 3, Aberdeen: Centre for Defence Studies, 1973.
8. *Sunday Standard*, 29 August 1982.
9. Messersmith, *American Years*, 28.
10. Ibid, 34.
11. 'Town Fears for its Future after US Sub Base Closes', *Chicago Tribune*, 8 February 1991.
12. Giarchi, *Between McAlpine and Polaris*, 194.
13. *Glasgow Herald*, 19 October 1963.
14. *Dunoon Observer*, 29 June 1963.
15. Ibid, 14 April 1962.
16. Giarchi, *Between McAlpine and Polaris*, 192.
17. *Scottish Daily Express*, 30 November 1965.
18. *Daily Telegraph*, 16 October 1973.

19. *The Guardian*, 21 June 1997.
20. Duncan Campbell, 'Getting High on Poseidon', *New Statesman*, 1981.
21. 'Drug Use by US Army Enlisted Men in Vietnam, A Follow-up on Their Return Home', *American Journal of Epidemiology*, 99, issue 4, 1974, 235–49.
22. 'House Unit Cites Rise in GI Drug Use', *New York Times,* 25 May 1971.
23. 'United States Congress Senate Committee on Armed Services: Subcommittee on Drug Abuse in the Military', US Government Printing Office, Washington DC, 1971.
24. Robins, L. N., Helzer, J. E., and Davis, D. H. (1975), 'Narcotic use in Southeast Asia and Afterward: An Interview Study of 898 Vietnam Returnees', *Archives of General Psychiatry*, 32 (8), 955–61.
25. Hansard HC Deb 11 April 1984, vol. 58 c221W.
26. Ronald Spector, *At War, At Sea: Sailors and Naval Warfare in the Twentieth Century*, London, 2001, 331–41.
27. 'Sailors Learn Sub Standards', *Los Angeles Times*, 9 December 1990.
28. Mike H. Rindskopf, *Steel Boats, Iron Men: History of the U.S. Submarine Force*, Nashville, 1994, 49.
29. The story was revealed by Duncan Campbell in the *New Statesman*, 27 November 1981.
30. Joshua Handler and William M. Arkin, *Neptune Papers*, vol. III, Naval Nuclear Accidents at Sea, Greenpeace International, 1990.
31. Hansard HC Deb 26 November 1981, vol. 13 c462W.
32. NA DEFE 19/218, Radioactive contamination in the Holy Loch, Argyllshire by US Navy submarine, 5 February 1965–11 May 1966.
33. *Daily Telegraph*, 4 March 1961.
34. Giarchi, *Between McAlpine and Polaris*, 117.
35. Messersmith, *American Years*, 73.
36. House of Commons, *Official Report*, vol. 668, 5 December 1962, cols 1463–8, London, HMSO, 1962.
37. A. P. Dobson, 'Operation Lemachus: the Holy Loch US Nuclear Base and the dangers of Local Radiation Pollution', in Luís Nuno Rodrigues and Sergiy Glebov, eds, *Military Bases: Historical Perspectives, Contemporary Challenges*, NATO Science of Peace and Security Series, Amsterdam, 2009, 29.
38. Messersmith, *American Years*, 44.
39. Bob Fritsch, 'Saturday Night at the Central', *Cryptolog*, US Naval Cryptologic Veterans Association, vol. 19, no. 4, August 1998.
40. 'Dan's Love Letter to Edzell Sparks Cold War Memories', *The Courier*, 2 November 2015.
41. Jay R. Browne, 'Mixing with the Scots', *Cryptolog*, US Naval Cryptologic Veterans Association, vol. 19, no. 4, August 1998.
42. Finlay, *Modern Scotland*, 333.
43. NRS Annual Reports of the Registrar-General for Scotland, Edinburgh HMSO 1961 and 1963.
44. Giarchi, *Between McAlpine and Polaris*, 211.

7. THE WATCH ON THE RHINE: SCOTS IN GERMANY AND ON OTHER FRONTS

1. Antony Beevor, *Inside the British Army*, London, 1981, 163.
2. *Instructions for British Servicemen in Germany (The British Soldier's Pocket Book)*, Foreign Office, November 1944.

3. Beevor, *Inside the British Army*, 168.
4. *Tiger and Sphinx*, February 1948.
5. Christopher Sinclair-Stevenson, *The Life of a Regiment, The Gordon Highlanders 1945–1970*, vol. iv, London, 1974, 21–36.
6. NLS Acc 5540, Kennaway Papers, Kennaway to his mother, undated, probably March 1948.
7. Michael Yardley, 'What shall we do with the drunken soldier?', *New Statesman*, October 1981.
8. *The Thistle*, 1969.
9. Robert H. Paterson, *Pontius Pilate's Bodyguard: A History of the First or The Royal Regiment of Foot The Royal Scots (The Royal Regiment)*, vol. ii, 1919–2000, Edinburgh, 2000, 378–9.
10. Tony Parker, *Soldier, Soldier*, London, 1985, 123.
11. Alan Mallinson, *The Making of the British Army*, London, 2009, 442–3.
12. Quoted in Victoria Schofield, *The Black Watch: Fighting in the Front Line 1899–2006*, London, 2018, 526.
13. Personal knowledge.
14. Laszlo Borhi, 'Containment, Rollback, Liberation or Inaction? The United States and Hungary in the 1950s', *Journal of Cold War Studies*, Cambridge, MA, 1999, 1 (3), 67–108.
15. Yardley and Sewell, *New Model Army*, 81.
16. Christoph Bluth, 'The Warsaw Pact and Military Security in Central Europe during the Cold War', *Journal of Slavic Military Studies*, vol. 17, issue 2, 2004, 229–331.
17. Alastair Campbell, 'Junior Military Command during the Cold War', in Jamieson, ed., *Scotland and the Cold War*, 105.
18. NATO, Overall Strategic Concept for the Defence of the North Atlantic Treaty Organization Area MC 14/3 (Final), 16 January 1968, 345.
19. J. H. Michaels, 'Revisiting General Sir John Hackett's "The Third World War"', *British Journal for Military History*, 3(1), 88–104.
20. Hackett, *Third World War*, 98–9.
21. Duncan Campbell, 'Secret Laws for Wartime Britain', *New Statesman*, 6 September 1985.
22. John Lindsay, ed., *Brits Speak Out: British Soldiers' Experience of the Northern Ireland Conflict*, Londonderry, 1998.
23. Paterson, *Pontius Pilate's Bodyguard*, 387–8.
24. *The Thistle*, 1970.
25. The Belfast Agreement, Northern Ireland Office, 10 April 1998.
26. Andrew Sanders and Ian S. Wood, *Times of Troubles: Britain's War in Northern Ireland*, Edinburgh, 2012, Chapter 2.
27. James Taylor, quoted in Ring, *We Come Unseen*, Chapter 11.
28. Bonzo, Hector, *1093 Tripulantes del Crucero ARA General Belgrano*, Editorial Sudamericana, 1992, 402.
29. Toby Elliott, quoted in Ring, *We Come Unseen*, Chapter 11.
30. Pearce, *The Shield and the Sabre*, 170–1.
31. Ibid, 167.
32. Rear Admiral J. R. Hill, 'The Realities of Medium Power, 1946 to the Present', in J. R. Hill, ed., *The Oxford History of the Royal Navy*, Oxford, 1995, 393.
33. Interviewed, BBC Storyville, *Cod Wars*, 28 May 2001.

8. PLOUGHSHARES INTO SWORDS: PROFITING FROM THE COLD WAR

1. Johnston, *Ships for a Nation*, 236.
2. David Newlands, 'The Regional Economies of Scotland', Devine, Lee and Peden, *Transformation of Scotland*, 237.
3. 'Hope for Submarine Plan', *Greenock Telegraph*, 30 May 2014.
4. Hugh Murphy 'Scotts of Greenock and Naval Procurement 1960–1977', *The Mariner's Mirror*, 87:2, 2001, 196–211.
5. Johnston, *Ships for a Nation*, 258.
6. Hugh Murphy 'Scotts of Greenock and Naval Procurement 1960–1977', *The Mariner's Mirror*, 87:2, 2001, 209.
7. Finlay, *Modern Scotland*, 325–6.
8. Keith Aitken, 'The Economy', Linklater and Denniston, *Anatomy of Scotland*, 261.
9. Robert Crawford, 'The Electronics Industry in Scotland', *Quarterly Economic Commentary*, 9 (4), 1984, 79.
10. David Newlands, 'The Regional Economies of Scotland', Devine, Lee and Peden, *Transformation of Scotland*, 176.
11. Scottish Office, *Scotland: An Economic Profile*, Edinburgh, 1988.
12. Robert Crawford, 'The Electronics Industry in Scotland', *Quarterly Economic Commentary*, 1984, 9 (4), 78.
13. Wilson, *Ferranti*, ii, 270.
14. Hansard HC Deb 18 March 1991, vol. 188 c136.
15. Hamilton-Paterson, *Empire of the Clouds*, 99.
16. Eric Grove, *Vanguard to Trident*, London, 1987, 24.
17. Hamilton-Paterson, *Empire of the Clouds*, 184–5.
18. Wilson, *Ferranti*, ii, 38.
19. Obituary, Sebastian de Ferranti, *Daily Telegraph*, 26 October 2015.
20. Keith Aitken, 'The Economy', in Linklater and Denniston, *Anatomy of Scotland*, 251–2.
21. NA ADM 202/870, Comacchio Company, Royal Marines, 1 January 1982–31 December 1982.
22. Keith Aitken, 'The Economy', in Linklater and Denniston, *Anatomy of Scotland*, 245.
23. Hansard, HC Deb 22 November 1948, vol. 458 cc839–41, Jet Engines (Foreign Sales).
24. Eric Brown, *Wings on my Sleeve*, London, 2007, 184.
25. 'US overtakes Soviets in Arms Sales to Third World', *Christian Science Monitor*, 19 April 1983.
26. Alvin Z. Rubinstein, *Red Star on the Nile*, Princeton, 1977, 29.
27. Interview, *The Times*, 4 July 1976.
28. 'Israeli Aircraft Losses, by Date, by Battlefront, and by Aircraft Type, 16–24 October 1973, and Loss Rates as a Percentage of Total Sorties', Central Intelligence Agency (CIA), *Intelligence Report: The 1973 Arab–Israeli War. Overview and Analysis of the Conflict*, Washington DC, September 1975, approved for release, 4 September 2012, table 2, 34.
29. Ibid, 16.
30. Ibid.

9. WAR IN THE SHADOWS

1. Christopher Andrew and Oleg Gordievsky, *KGB: The Inside Story*, London, 1992, 247.
2. Miranda Carter, *Anthony Blunt: His Lives*, London 2001, 189.
3. Yuri Modin, *My Five Cambridge Friends*, London, 1994, 107.
4. Peter Wright, *Spycatcher*, London, 1987, 281.
5. Obituary, *New York Times*, 10 October 1995.
6. Dwight Garner, review of *A Legacy of Spies* by John Le Carré, *New York Times*, 28 August 2017.
7. Richard Sakwa, *Putin: Russia's Choice*, London, 2003, 6.
8. Roberts, *Speak Clearly into the Chandelier*, 169.
9. David Holloway, *Stalin and the Bomb: The Soviet Union and Atomic Energy, 1939–1956*, New Haven, 1994, 86.
10. Oleg A. Bukharin, 'The Cold War Atomic Intelligence Game, 1945–70, From the Russian Perspective', Central Intelligence Agency (CIA), Washington DC, April 2007.
11. Annual Report, KGB, Moscow, 1967.
12. Philip Knightley, *The Second Oldest Profession, London: The Spy as Bureaucrat, Patriot, Fantasist and Whore*, London, 1987, 319.
13. Alistair Horne, *Macmillan, 1957–1986*, vol. 2 of the Official Biography, London, 1988, 98–102; National Archives Podcast Series, Christopher Andrews, Security Service File Release, 28 November 2017.
14. Alastair Campbell, 'Junior Military Command during the Cold War', in Jamieson, *Scotland and the Cold War*, 98.
15. Obituary of Lieutenant-Colonel John Napier Cormack, *The Times*, 5 May 2018.
16. 'Brigadier medalled with Russki who beat him up', *The Scotsman*, 6 October 2006; my conversations with both men (William Macnair and Charles Ritchie) over the years have informed my knowledge about the activities of BRIXMIS during the Cold War.
17. Major-General Peter Williams, *BRIXMIS in the 1980s: The Cold War's Great Game, Memories of Liaising with the Soviet Army in East Germany*, Parallel History Project on Cooperative Security, Center for Security Studies at ETH Zurich and the National Security Archive at the George Washington University, 1999–2007, 7.
18. 'Britain's secret jet crash Cold War coup', *Daily Telegraph*, 26 December 2003.
19. Major-General Peter Williams, *BRIXMIS in the 1980s: The Cold War's Great Game, Memories of Liaising with the Soviet Army in East Germany*, Parallel History Project on Cooperative Security, Center for Security Studies at ETH Zurich and the National Security Archive at the George Washington University, 1999–2007, 26.
20. Richard Aldrich, *The Hidden Hand: Britain, America and Cold War Secret Intelligence*, London, 2001, 414.
21. Tony Geraghty, *BRIXMIS: The Untold Exploits of Britain's Most Daring Cold War Spy Mission*, London, 1996, 218–35.
22. Christopher Fleet and Carolyn Anderson, *Scotland: Defending the Nation, Mapping the Military Landscape*, Edinburgh, 2018.
23. John Davis and Alexander J. Kent, *The Red Atlas: How the Soviet Union Secretly Mapped the World*, London and Chicago, 2017.

24. Ring, *We Come Unseen*, Chapter 4.
25. Clive Radley, *Sonobuoy History from a UK Perspective: RAE Farnborough's Role in Airborne Anti-Submarine Warfare*, Camberley, 2016, 6–7.
26. Tom Clancy, *The Hunt for Red October*, London, 1984, 198.
27. Both incidents are described in Iain Ballantyne, *Hunter Killers: The Dramatic Untold Story of the Royal Navy's Most Secret Service*, London, 2014.
28. 'Soviets depth-charged Navy submarines during Cold War chases', *Daily Telegraph*, 16 June 2003.
29. The operation is described in Sherry Sontag and Christopher Drew, with Annette Lawrence Drew, *Blind Men's Bluff: The Untold Story of American Submarine Espionage*, New York, 1998.
30. Obituaries, Squadron Leader John Crampton, *The Times*, 14 July 2010; *Daily Telegraph*, 1 August 2010.
31. Duncan Campbell, 'Spy in the Sky', *New Statesman*, 9 September 1983, 8–9.
32. 'The Final Overflights of the Soviet Union 1959–1960', CIA Archives, NOFORN, approved for release, 25 June 2013.
33. 'Scottish cold war nuclear submarine collision kept secret for 43 years', *The Guardian*, 25 January 2017.
34. Colin Norman, 'Quiet Soviet Subs Prompt Concern', *Science*, 31 March 1989, 243.
35. Thompson, *On Her Majesty's Nuclear Service*, 98.
36. David F. Winkler, 'The Evolution and Significance of the 1972 Incidents at Sea Agreement', *The Journal of Strategic Studies*, April 2005, vol. 28, no. 2, 361–77: 362.
37. Commander John Murphy USN, 'Cold War Warriors: Spy Ships – Theirs and Ours', *Emmitsburg Journal*, n.d.
38. David F. Winkler, 'The Evolution and Significance of the 1972 Incidents at Sea Agreement', *Journal of Strategic Studies*, April 2005, vol. 28, no. 2, 361–77: 369.
39. 'Ullapool's controversial Cold War football games recalled', *BBC Scotland News*, 22 May 2015.
40. Hansard 1803–2005, 16 March 1998, written answers, Commons, Defence.

10. TRIDENT AND THATCHER

1. Isaacs and Downing, *Cold War*, 316.
2. John Baylis and Kristan Stoddart, 'Britain and the Chevaline Project: The Hidden Nuclear Programme 1967–1982', *Journal of Strategic Studies* 4, 2003, 131–3.
3. IWM MUN 4773, *Penetration Aids Carrier, Polaris Chevaline: British & American missile*.
4. NA PREM 19/191 E4 Sect 2.3.
5. Hansard HC 269, V, 15, 20 'Ministry of Defence Chevaline Improvement to the Polaris Missile System', Ninth Report from the Committee of Public Accounts, Session 1981–2.
6. 'The History of the UK Strategic Deterrent: The Chevaline Programme', *Proceedings of the Royal Aeronautical Society*, London, 28 October 2008.
7. NA PREM 19/14 'Future of UK strategic nuclear deterrent; Chevaline-related Polaris flight trials; Polaris successor' Part 1, 4 May 1979–4 December 1979.
8. Duncan Campbell, 'Too Few Bombs to go Round', *New Statesman*, 29 November 1985, 12.
9. CND Special Report, 'The Next Chevaline scandal?', London, 5 June 2007.

10. 'Crisis? What Crisis?', *The Sun*, 11 January 1979.
11. NA PREM 19/275 Duff Mason Report on factors relating to the further consideration of the future of the UK nuclear deterrent, 1–31 December 1978.
12. Ian Jack, 'Trident: The British Question', *The Guardian*, 11 February 2016.
13. Anthony Eames, 'The Trident Sales Agreement and Cold War Diplomacy', *Journal of Military History*, 81, January 2017, 169.
14. James Callaghan, *Time and Chance*, London, 2006, 555.
15. Anthony Eames, 'The Trident Sales Agreement and Cold War Diplomacy', *Journal of Military History*, 81, January 2017, 168.
16. Jackson and Bramall, *The Chiefs*, 390.
17. NA PREM 19/417, f232, Sir Robert Wade-Gery, 'Anglo-American Negotiations on Polaris Replacement', 13 June 1980.
18. Ibid, f78, Reagan to Thatcher, 1 October 1981.
19. Ibid, f64, Weinberger to Thatcher, 24 August 1981.
20. Ibid, f33, 'Britain's Strategic Nuclear Force: The Choice of a System to succeed Polaris', 9 June 1980.
21. Ibid, f68a MoD to Scottish Office, 'Prime Minister's Visit to Scotland – Trident Depot', 2 September 1981.
22. *The Herald*, 2 May 1986.
23. Harvie, *No Gods and Precious Few Heroes*, 169.
24. Kate Hudson, 'Thatcher's Dirty Tricks and CND', Campaign for Nuclear Disarmament, London, 31 December 2011.
25. Special Branch Files Project, 'CND Files, 1980–', http://specialbranchfiles.uk/.
26. David Mackenzie and Jane Tallents, 'Unready Scotland: A report by Nukewatch UK into nuclear weapons transport and community safety in Scotland', *Nukewatch UK*, June 2017.
27. Rob Edwards, 'Nukes of Hazard: The Nuclear Bomb Convoys on Our Roads', *International Campaign to Abolish Nuclear Weapons*, London, 2016, 18.
28. Ibid, 20.
29. Ibid, 30.
30. World Health Organisation, 'Chernobyl at 25th Anniversary', New York 23 April 2011.
31. Torrance, *George Younger*, 238.
32. 'Trident Missile Explodes in Test; Failure is 2d of 3 Sea Launchings', *New York Times*, 15 August 1989.
33. Marr, *Battle for Scotland*, 170.
34. Finlay, *Modern Scotland*, 362.
35. George Younger, *Scotland on Sunday*, 17 October 1993.
36. President Ronald Reagan, address to British Parliament, 8 June 1982.
37. Anatoly Dobrynin, *In Confidence: Moscow's Ambassador to Six Cold War Presidents*, New York, 1995, 632.

11. THE WALLS CAME TUMBLING DOWN

1. Interview, *BBC News*, 17 December 1984.
2. 'Castle gives up swastika secret', *The Scotsman*, 9 August 2008.
3. Torrance, *George Younger*, 203–4.
4. Quoted in Gordon Barrass, 'Able Archer 83: What Were the Soviets Thinking?' *Survival: Global Politics and Strategy*, vol. 58, no. 6, 21 November 2016, 10.

5. Benjamin B. Fischer, *A Cold War Conundrum: The 1983 Soviet War Scare*, Washington DC, March 2007; Nate Jones, ed., *Able Archer 83: The Secret History of the NATO Exercise That Almost Triggered Nuclear War*, New York, 2016; Nate Jones, ed., *The Able Archer 83 Sourcebook: The definitive online collection of over 1,000 pages of declassified documents on the 1983 War Scare*, Washington DC, 2017.

6. Ben Macintyre, *The Spy and the Traitor: The Greatest Espionage Story of the Cold War*, London, 2018.

7. Christopher Bellamy, Obituary of John Erickson, *The Guardian*, 12 February 2002.

8. NLS Acc. 13596, 'Edinburgh Conversations, 10, History of the Edinburgh Conversations 1980–1989', possibly by M. J. H. Westcott.

9. Malcolm Mackintosh, 'John Erickson 1929–2002', *Proceedings of the British Academy*, 124, London, 2004, 64.

10. Ibid, 67.

11. Peter Robinson, '"Tear Down This Wall": How Top Advisers Opposed Reagan's Challenge to Gorbachev—But Lost', *Prologue Magazine*, New York, Summer 2007, vol. 39, no. 2.

12. Ian Jack, 'Trident: The British Question', *The Guardian*, 11 February 2016.

13. Giarchi, *Between McAlpine and Polaris*, 62–6.

14. 'After 30 years the last US submarine sails out', *The Herald*, 11 November 1991.

15. 'Last US Sub leaving Scotland for Home', *New York Times*, 10 November 1991.

16. 'A Second Dunoon Landing: American sailors return to the Argyll town that will always be in their hearts', *Scottish Daily Record*, 3 May 2001.

17. Giarchi, *Between McAlpine and Polaris*, 122.

18. Rob Edwards 'Cold War Waste Fouls the Clyde', *New Scientist*, issue 2,072, 8 March 1997.

19. *Fortress Scotland*, Scottish CND, Glasgow, September 2004, 63.

20. 'Holy Loch clean-up operation under way', *The Herald*, 25 February 1998.

21. Giarchi, *Between McAlpine and Polaris*, 116.

22. 'Town Adjusting To US Pullout Discovers There Is Life After the Americans', *Hartford Courant*, 16 August 1993.

23. 'Flag lowered for the last time at Edzell base', *The Courier*, 1 October 1997.

24. Hansard, HC Deb 25 July 1991.

25. Graham Allison, *What Happened to the Soviet Superpower's Nuclear Arsenal? Clues for the Nuclear Security Summit*, Harvard Kennedy School Faculty Research Working Paper Series RWP12–038, John F. Kennedy School of Government, Harvard University, 2012.

26. Hans M. Kristensen and Robert S. Norris, 'Russian nuclear forces, 2016', *Bulletin of the Atomic Scientists*, vol. 72, no. 3, 2016, 125–34.

27. William E. Odom, *The Collapse of the Soviet Military*, London, 1998, 302.

28. Hans Georg Kampe, *The Underground Military Command Bunkers of Zossen, Germany: History of their Construction and Use by the Wehrmacht and Soviet Army 1937–1994*, Atgen, PA, 1996.

29. Quoted in 'Bitter Goodbye: Russians Leave Germany', *New York Times*, 4 March 1994.

EPILOGUE: A NEW COLD WAR?

1. House of Commons Defence Committee, *The Future of the UK's Strategic Nuclear Deterrent: the White Paper*, Ninth Report of Session 2006–07, vol. i, London, House of Commons, 27 February 2007.
2. *BBC Scotland News*, 'Sheriff dubs nuclear programme illegal', 21 October 1999.
3. HMSO, *National Security Strategy and Strategic Defence and Security Review 2015: A Secure and Prosperous United Kingdom*, London, 2015, 36.
4. Dmitri Trenin, *Russia's Breakouts from the Post-Cold War System: The Drivers of Putin's Course*, Moscow, December 2014, 9.
5. Patrick J. Buchanan, 'Who Started the Second Cold War?', *The American Conservative*, 3 May 2015.
6. Vladimir Putin, 'Being Strong Is a Guarantee of Russia's National Security', *Rossiyskaya Gazeta*, 20 February 2012.
7. 'Scrapping the RAF's £4bn Nimrod fleet "risks UK security",' open letter to *Daily Telegraph* by four former UK defence chiefs of staff, 26 January 2011.
8. Clive Radley, *Sonobuoy History from a UK Perspective: RAE Farnborough's Role in Airborne Anti-Submarine Warfare*, Camberley, 2016, 151.
9. NATO Communiqué, 'NATO battlegroups in Baltic nations and Poland fully operational', 28 August 2017.
10. 'The Ominous, Massive Military Exercises in Eastern Europe', *The Atlantic*, 18 September 2017.
11. Jack Watling, 'NATO's Trident Juncture 2018 Exercise: Political Theatre with a Purpose', *Journal of the Royal United Services Institute*, November 2018.
12. Freedman, *Future of War*, 238.
13. James Sullivan, 'Russian Cyber Operations: State-led Organised Crime', Commentary, Royal United Services Institute, 28 November 2018.
14. 'Number of Russian spies in UK has risen fivefold since Cold War', *The Times*, 21 October 2018.
15. Devine, *Scottish Nation*, 617.
16. Owen Dudley Edwards, ed., *A Claim of Right for Scotland*, Edinburgh, 1989, 53.

Select Bibliography

OFFICIAL PAPERS AND RECORDS

Glasgow Caledonian University
Scottish CND Archive (SCND)

Glasgow City Archives and Special Collections, Mitchell Library
Holds some SCND material

Imperial War Museum: Department of Sound Records (IWM)
The Sound Archive holds over 33,000 recordings relating to conflict since 1914

London School of Economics: Campaign for Nuclear Disarmament Archive (CND)
NRA 15920 CND: 1959–2006, Records, minutes and correspondence

National Archives, Kew (NA)
ADM 205 Admiralty: Office of the First Sea Lord, later First Sea Lord and Chief of the Naval Staff: Correspondence and Papers
DEFE 11 Ministry of Defence: Chiefs of Staff Committee: Registered Files
DEFE 13 Ministry of Defence: Private Office: Registered Files
FCO 7 Foreign Office and Foreign and Commonwealth Office: American and Latin American Departments: Registered Files
FO 371 Foreign Office: Political Departments: General Correspondence
PREM 19/47 The Future of the UK Deterrent
WO 281 War Office: British Commonwealth Division of United Nations Force: War Diaries, Korean War
WO 308 War Office: British and Commonwealth Forces: Historical Records and Reports, Korean War

National Archives of Scotland, Edinburgh (NAS)
HH 16 Criminal Case Files
HH 51 Civil Defence Files
HH 56 Scottish Emergency Committee Files
SC 51 Dunoon Sheriff Court Records
SEP 4 Regional Industrial Promotion and Development Files

National Library of Scotland (NLS)
Acc 5540, Kennaway Papers
Acc 13596 Edinburgh Conversations: Correspondence, memoranda and related papers, 1974–1997, concerning Professor John Erickson's involvement in the 'Edinburgh Conversations'

NEWSPAPERS AND JOURNALS

The Borderers Chronicle (KOSB regimental magazine)
Catalyst
Cencrastus
Courier & Advertiser (*Courier*)
The Covenanter (Cameronians regimental magazine)
Daily Telegraph
Dunfermline Press
Dunoon Observer and Argyllshire Standard
Greenock Telegraph
Guardian (*Manchester Guardian*)
Helensburgh Advertiser
The Herald (*Glasgow Herald*)
History Today
Journal of Cold War Studies
Journal of the Royal Highland Fusiliers
Lennox Herald
The Mariner's Mirror
Northern Mariner
Nuclear-Free Scotland
Peace News
Press and Journal
Quarterly Economic Commentary
The Queen's Own Highlander
Radical Scotland
The Red Hackle (Black Watch regimental magazine)
Scotland on Sunday
Scotsman
Scottish Daily Record
Scottish Historical Review
Scottish International Review
Scottish Labour History
Shetland Times
Stornoway Gazette
Sunday Herald
Sunday Standard
Tartan Log (Edzell base journal)
The Thin Red Line (Argyll & Sutherland Highlanders regimental magazine)
The Thistle (Royal Scots regimental magazine)
Tiger and Sphinx (Gordon Highlanders regimental magazine)
The Times
West Highland Free Press

PERSONAL ACCOUNTS, FICTION AND POETRY

Buchan, Tom, *Dolphins at Cochin*, London, 1969.

Crumey, Andrew, *Sputnik Caledonia*, London, 2008.

Dalyell, Tam, *The Importance of Being Awkward*, Edinburgh, 2011.

Gray, Alasdair, *Why Scots Should Rule Scotland 1997: A Carnaptious History of Britain from Roman Times Until Now*, Edinburgh, 1997.

Henderson, Hamish, *Collected Poems and Songs*, Edinburgh, 2000.

Hurd, Douglas and Osmond, Andrew, *Scotch on the Rocks*, London, 1971.

Imlach, Hamish and McVicar, Ewan, *Cod Liver Oil and the Orange Juice: Memoirs of a Fat Folksinger*, Edinburgh, 1992.

Kay, Jackie, *Red Dust Road: An Autobiographical Journey*, London, 2010.

Kennaway, James, *Tunes of Glory*, London, 1956.

Lindsay, Maurice, *Thank You for Having Me*, London, 1983.

Linklater, Eric, *The Dark of Summer*, London, 1956.

MacDiarmid, Hugh, *The Letters of Hugh MacDiarmid*, ed. Alan Bold, London, 1984.

Mackenzie, Compton, *On Moral Courage*, London, 1962.

Macpherson, Ian, *Wild Harbour*, London, 1936.

Miller, Karl, ed., *Memoirs of a Modern Scotland*, London, 1970.

Morgan, Edwin, *Crossing the Border, Essays on Scottish Literature*, Manchester, 1990.

Muir, Edwin, *Collected Poems*, London, 1963.

Robertson, James, *And the Land Lay Still*, London, 2010.

Thompson, Eric, *On Her Majesty's Nuclear Service*, Oxford, 2018.

Wolfe, William, *Scotland Lives*, Edinburgh, 1973.

SECONDARY SOURCES (SELECTED) – SCOTLAND

Bartie, Angela, *The Edinburgh Festivals: Culture and Society in Post-War Britain*, Edinburgh, 2013.

Bold, Alan, *MacDiarmid: A Critical Biography*, London, 1988.

Chalmers, Malcolm and Walker, W., *Uncharted Waters: The UK, Nuclear Weapons and the Scottish Question*, East Linton, 2001.

Devine, T. M., *The Scottish Nation 1700–2000*, London, 2001.

Devine, T. M. and Finlay, R. J., eds, *Scotland in the Twentieth Century*, Edinburgh, 1996.

Devine, T. M., Lee, C. H. and Peden, G. C., ed, *The Transformation of Scotland: The Economy Since 1700*, Edinburgh, 2005.

Devine, Tom and Logue, Paddy, *Being Scottish: Personal Reflections on Scottish Identity Today*, Edinburgh, 2002.

Ferguson, William, *Scotland: 1689 to the Present*, Edinburgh, 1968.

Finlay, Richard, *Modern Scotland 1914–2000*, London, 2004.

Giarchi, George Giacinto, *Between McAlpine and Polaris*, London, 1984.

Gosselin, Frank L., *Holy Loch: The Scottish American Connection*, Cleveland, 2016.

Hamilton-Paterson, James, *Empire of the Clouds: When Britain's Aircraft Ruled the World*, London, 2010.

Harvie, Christopher, *Scotland and Nationalism: Scottish Society and Politics 1707–1977*, London, 1977; *No Gods and Precious Few Heroes: Twentieth-Century Scotland*, Edinburgh, 1998.

Herdman, John, *Another Country: An Era in Scottish Politics and Letters*, Glendaruel, 2013.

Hutchison, I. G. C., *Scottish Politics in the Twentieth Century*, Basingstoke, 2001.

Jamieson, Brian P., ed., *Scotland and the Cold War*, Dunfermline, 2003.

Johnston, Ian, *Ships for a Nation: John Brown & Company Clydebank*, West Dunbartonshire Libraries & Museums, 2001.

Kellas, J. G., *Modern Scotland*, London, 1968.

Kemp, Arnold, *The Hollow Drum: Scotland Since the War*, Edinburgh, 1993.

Knox, W. W., *Industrial Nation: Work, Culture and Society in Scotland 1800 to the Present*, Edinburgh, 1999.

Lavery, Brian, *Shield of Empire: The Royal Navy and Scotland*, Edinburgh, 2007.

Linklater, Magnus and Denniston, Robin, eds, *Anatomy of Scotland: How Scotland Works*, Edinburgh, 1992.

McVicar, Ewan, *The Eskimo Republic: Scots Political Song in Action 1951 to 1999*, Linlithgow, 2010.

Marr, Andrew, *The Battle for Scotland*, London, 1992.

Messersmith, Andrene, *The American Years: Dunoon and the US Navy*, Glendaruel, 2003.

Munro, Ailie, *The Democratic Muse: Folk Music Revival in Scotland*, Aberdeen, 1996.

Nairn, Tom, *The Break-up of Britain*, London, 1981.

Neat, Timothy, *Hamish Henderson: A Biography*, 2 vols, Edinburgh, 2007–9.

Spaven, Malcolm, *Fortress Scotland: A Guide to the Military Presence*, London, 1983.

Torrance, David, *George Younger: A Life Well Led*, Edinburgh, 2008.

Underwood, Robert, ed., *The Future of Scotland*, London, 1977.

Webb, Keith, *The Growth of Scottish Nationalism*, Glasgow, 1978.

SECONDARY SOURCES (SELECTED) – COLD WAR

Barnett, Correlli, *The Lost Victory: British Dreams, British Realities 1945–1950*, London, 1995.

Bissell, Richard Jr., Jonathan E. Lewis and Frances T. Pudlo, *Reflections of a Cold Warrior: From Yalta to the Bay of Pigs*. New Haven, 1996.

Campbell, Duncan, *War Plan UK: The Truth about Civil Defence in Britain*, London, 1982; *The Unsinkable Aircraft Carrier: American Military Power in Britain*, London, 1984.

Clarke, Peter, *Hope and Glory: Britain 1900–1990*, London, 1996.

Crowley, Robert, ed., *The Cold War: A Military History*, New York, 2006.

Freedman, Lawrence, *The Future of War: A History*, London, 2017.

Gaddis, John Lewis, *Strategies of Containment: A Critical Appraisal of American National Security Policy during the Cold War*, Oxford, 1982; *The Cold War: A New History*, New York, 2005.

Hackett, Sir John, *The Third World War: The Untold Story*, revised edition, London, 1982.

Harper, John Lamberton, *The Cold War*, Oxford, 2011.

Hastings, Max, *The Korean War*, London, 1987.

Hennessy, Peter, *Never Again: Britain 1945–1951*, London, 1992; *The Secret State: Whitehall and the Cold War*, London, 2002.

Isaacs, Jeremy, and Downing, Taylor, *Cold War: For 45 Years the World Held Its Breath*, London, 1998.

Jackson, Bill and Bramall, Dwin, *The Chiefs: The Story of the United Kingdom Chiefs of Staff*, London, 1992.

Jackson, Robert, *Strike Force: The USAF in Britain Since 1948*, London, 1986.

Kennedy, Paul M., ed., *Grand Strategies in War and Peace*, New Haven, 1991.

Keylor, William R., *A World of Nations: The International Order Since 1945*, New York, 2008.

LaFeber, Walter, *America, Russia, and the Cold War, 1945–2006*, 10th edn, Boston, 2008.

Leffler, Melvyn, and Odd Arne Westad, eds., *The Cambridge History of the Cold War*, 3 vols, Cambridge, 2010–12.

Linklater, Eric, *Our Men in Korea*, London, 1952.

Pearce, Nigel, *The Shield and the Sabre: The Desert Rats in the Gulf 1990–1991*, London, 1992.

Ring, Jim, *We Come Unseen: The Untold Story of Britain's Cold War Submariners*, London, 2001.

Roberts, John C. Q., *Speak Clearly Into the Chandelier: Cultural Politics Between Britain and Russia 1973–2000*, London, 2000.

Rosie, George, *The British in Vietnam: How the Twenty-Five Year War Began*, London, 1970.

Royle, Trevor, *The Best Years of Their Lives: The National Service Experience 1945–1963*, London, 1986; *The Last Days of the Raj*, London, 1989.

Sandbrook, Dominic, *Never Had It So Good: A History of Britain from Suez to the Beatles*, London, 2005.

Westad, Odd Arne, ed., *Reviewing the Cold War: Approaches, Interpretations, Theory*, London, 2000; *The Global Cold War: Third World Interventions and the Making of Our Times*, Cambridge, 2007.

Yardley, Michael and Sewell, Dennis, *A New Model Army*, London, 1989.

Zubok, Vladislav M., *A Failed Empire: The Soviet Union in the Cold War from Stalin to Gorbachev*, Chapel Hill, 2007.

WEBSITES

http://bellacaledonia.org.uk
http://cnduk.org
http://www.scotsatwar.org
http://www.banthebomb.org/
http://ahistoryofrafsaxavord.blogspot.co.uk/
http://www.rememberingscotlandatwar.org.uk/
http://specialbranchfiles.uk/
http://www.tridentploughshares.org
http://thistlegroup.net/holyloch/history

Index